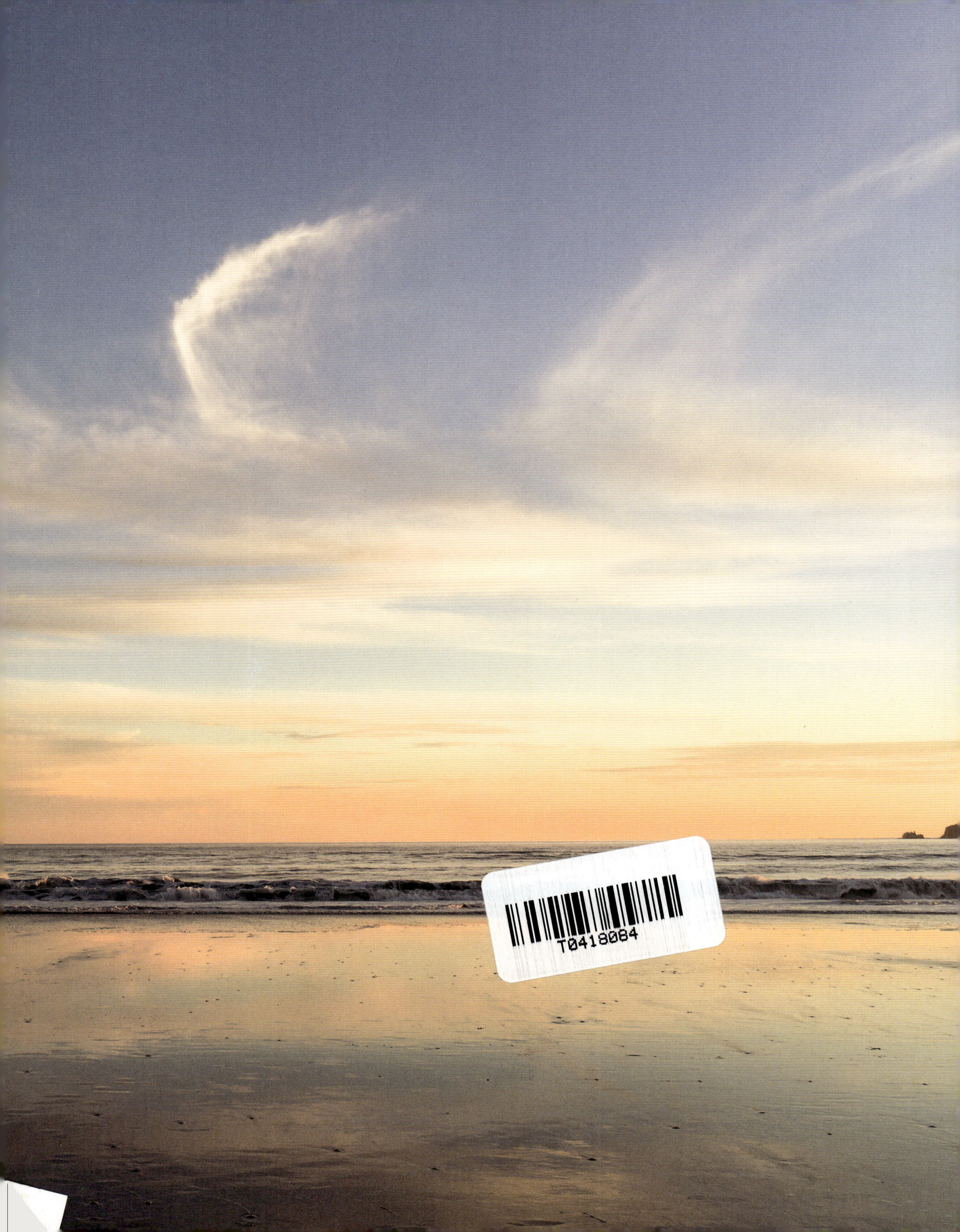

CALIFORNIA COASTAL

CALIFORNIA COASTAL

SEASIDE LIVING FROM SEA RANCH TO SAN DIEGO

HEATHER SANDY HEBERT
AND CHASE REYNOLDS EWALD

Gibbs Smith

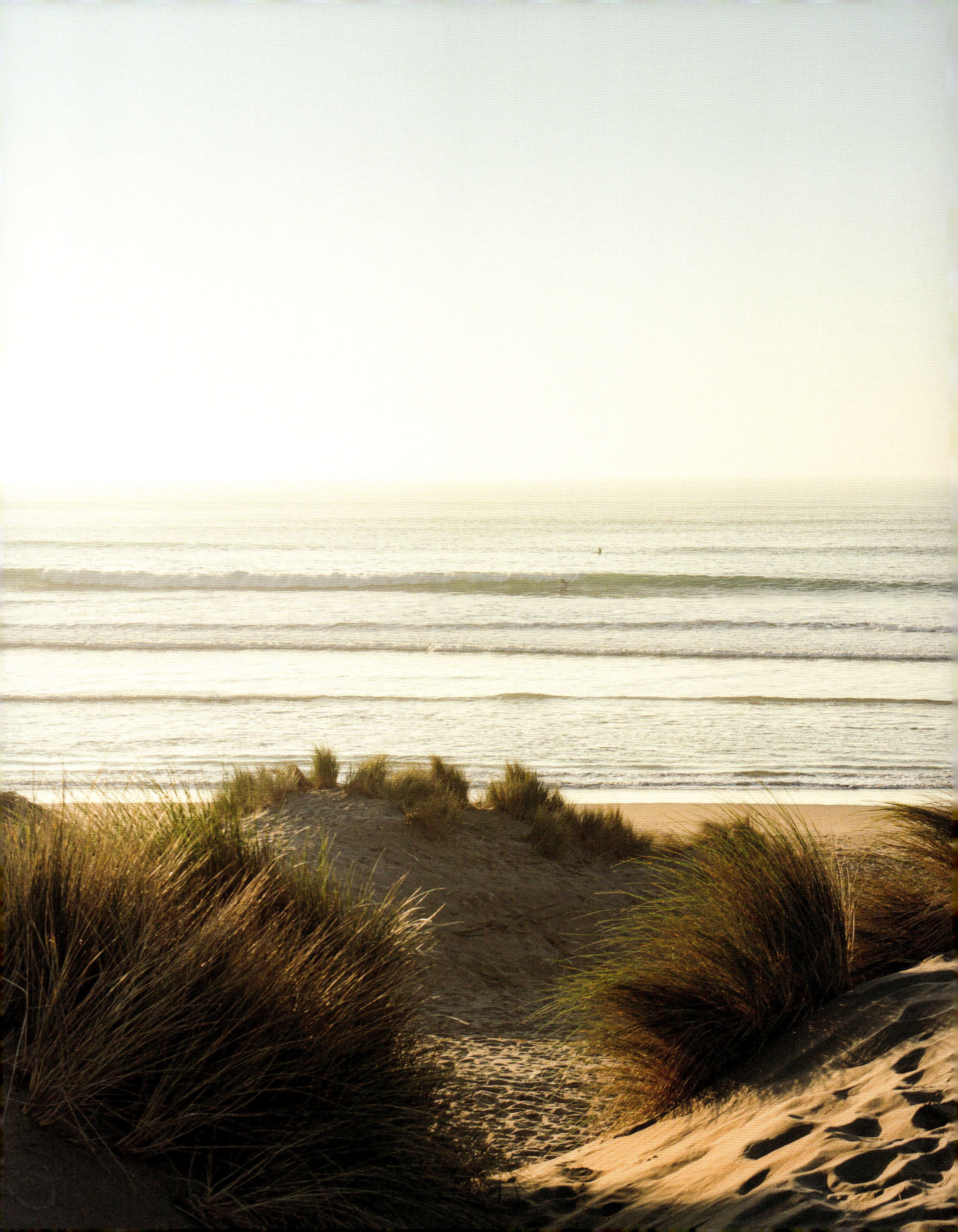

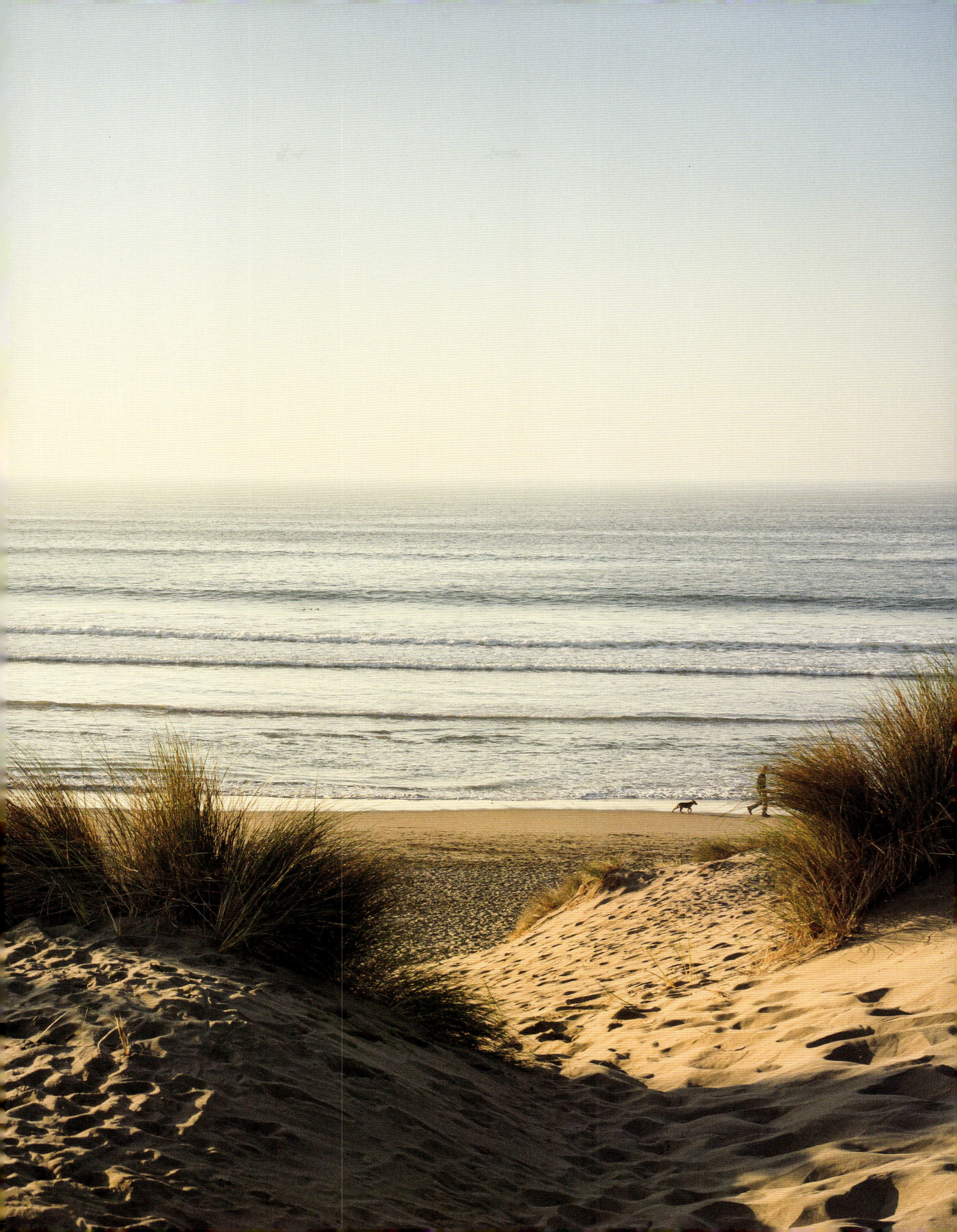

NORTHERN COAST

INTRODUCTION	9	INFORMED BY NATURE SEA RANCH	15
		THE COLOR OF SHADOWS SEA RANCH	31
		LAGOON LIVING STINSON BEACH	41
		ZEN AT THE BEACH STINSON BEACH	55
		EAST MEETS WEST SOUTHERN BAY AREA	69
		BOHEMIAN SURF HOUSE SANTA CRUZ	85

CENTRAL COAST

BIRD'S-EYE VIEW — 103
CARMEL

BEACH HOUSE + BOARDWALK HOUSE — 115
CARMEL

GROUNDED IN PLACE — 131
BIG SUR

PROSPECT + REFUGE — 143
BIG SUR

OFF-GRID GUESTHOUSE — 159
SANTA BARBARA COUNTY

SOUTHERN COAST

ATABEI — 175
PACIFIC PALISADES

COASTAL SERENITY — 191
MALIBU

BEACH, OCEAN, SKY — 203
HERMOSA BEACH

SEASIDE SANCTUARY — 215
LA JOLLA

BEACH RYOSHA — 227
DEL MAR

SUNSET CLIFFS — 241
SAN DIEGO

CREDITS — 252
ACKNOWLEDGMENTS — 254
AUTHORS — 255

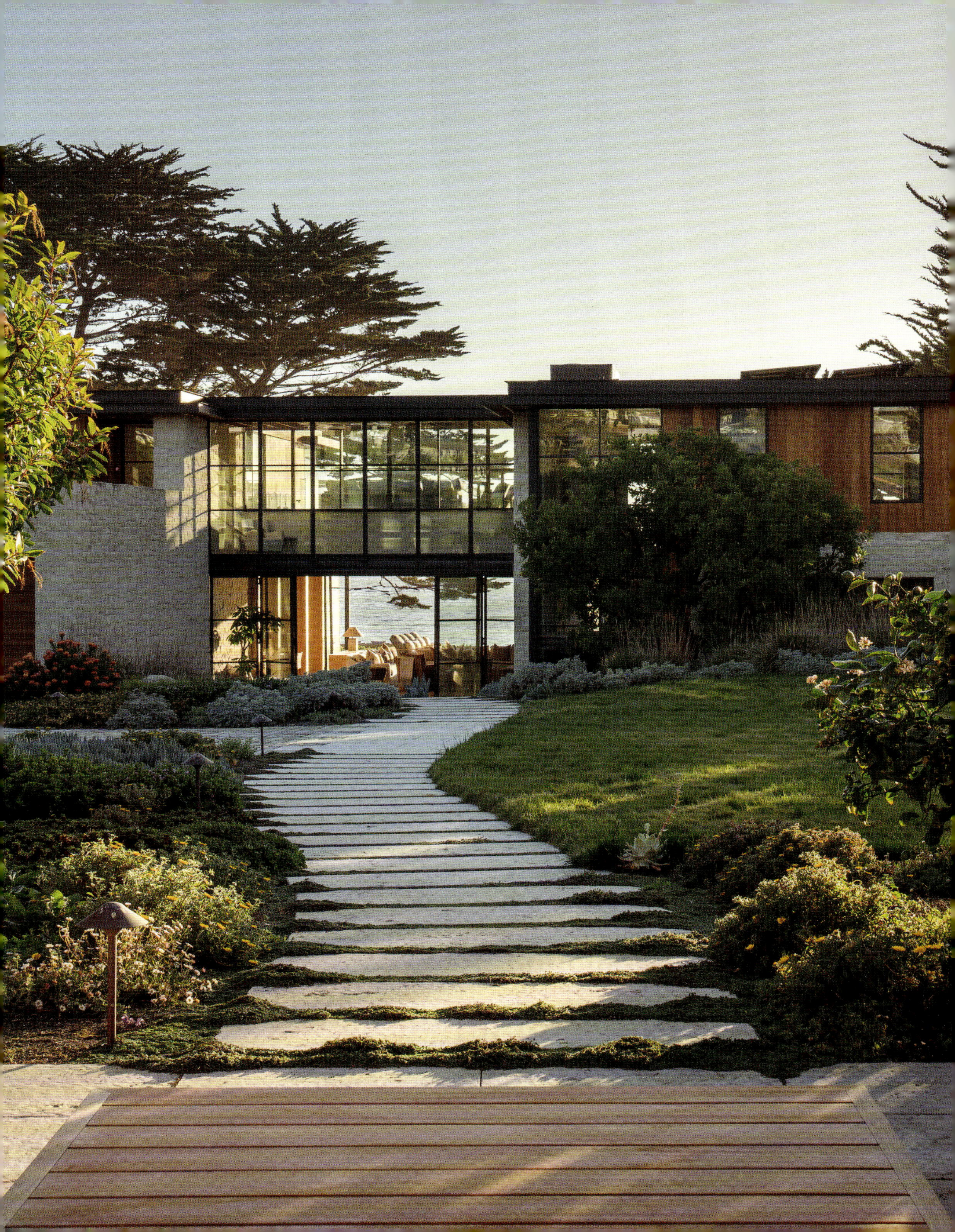

INTRODUCTION

California is made up of many coastlines, each distinct in contour, weather patterns, flora, and fauna. The 840-mile coast, which runs from the Oregon border to where the United States meets Mexico, consists of bluffs, cliffs, and, in the north, forests as well as low-lying beaches, dune landscapes, estuaries, and lagoons. With 360 miles of its beachfront open to the public, California ranks among the best states in the nation for sharing its coastline with its people.

The edge of the North American continent, where the world's largest ocean meets one of its longest coastlines, is formed in large part by the geological forces at play as two tectonic plates grind against one another. These plates cleave the state in two, with Big Sur southward on the Pacific Plate and the coastline to the north falling on the North American Plate. Known as the "elbow of California," Point Conception, near Santa Barbara, marks the point where the north-south coastline veers eastward and the transition from northern and southern marine ecosystems takes place.

While the image that comes to mind is one of sunny summer beaches, 70 percent of California's coast is made up of not beaches, but of cliffs and bluffs. This tendency—what Obi Kaufmann, the gifted chronicler of California, calls a "high-relief profile"—contributes to the unique nature of the California shore, in which geographic forces have created a land of coastal mountain ranges. Those mountains crash into the sea, shaped by the power of the Pacific Ocean. The state's unique topography results in large estuary systems teeming with marine life where freshwater and seawater meet. Breaks in the mountain ranges, along with deep bays that create a dance between sun and fog, define life here and help support the coast's immense biodiversity.

According to the Monterey Bay Aquarium, California's coastal waters are some of the most biologically productive on earth. The California Current provides feeding grounds for billions of fish, mammals, and birds and attracts migratory animals from all corners of the Pacific Ocean, including fish, sharks, sea turtles, and whales, which traverse the coast on their journey between their feeding grounds in Alaska and breeding grounds along the Baja Peninsula. From the tule elk grazing in Point Reyes to the sea lions barking in San Francisco Bay, from the sea otters floating amidst Santa Cruz surfers to the monarch butterflies clustering in Pacific Grove's Monterey cypress trees, the state's native species define and give life to the coastal experience.

This book is a love letter of sorts to the California coast, near which we both make our homes. In our search for exceptional coastal homes to include in our survey of life on these shores, we were mindful of the beauty and vulnerability of the coast. While development is inevitable, the homes we include in our book represent thoughtful, beautifully rendered interventions. From cabins in the iconic northern enclave of Sea Ranch and immersive structures set seamlessly into the Central Coast landscape to contemporary homes woven into the more urban fabric of the Southern Coast, each exhibits a respect for its unique and highly varied environment, an appropriate sense of scale, and a deep, abiding passion for the coast. It seemed logical to divide *California Coastal* into three distinct regions. The far north of the state—its least-developed region—feels like a "land out of time," with old-growth forests and mountains, mighty rivers, and large bays. The craggy coastline of Mendocino and Sonoma counties, north of San Francisco, are an interplay of bluffs, fertile tide pools, coastal meadows, and oak woodlands. Just to the south the coastline turns deeply inland to form San Francisco Bay, one of the most famous bays in the world and the largest in the state. The Central Coast, characterized by its iconic cliffs and jagged edges, is perhaps best known for Big Sur—one of the most magnificent and iconic stretches of coastline anywhere—where the mountains plunge thousands of feet into the sea. The state's Southern Coast's identity, while it is also home to sandy bluffs and volcanic rock formations, is most often defined by its broad beaches, many of them highly developed, as 60 percent of the state's population lives in California's southernmost lands.

Densely developed stretches of coastline are more vulnerable to the constant change that results from the interplay between land and sea, more at risk from seas that are expected to rise several feet over the next hundred years, and in greater need of protection and positive intervention than ever. Californians' commitment to protecting the coastline dates to 1972, when voter initiative established the California Coastal Commission, which was then made permanent by the California Coastal Act of 1976. Citizens agreed to "preserve, protect, and where possible, restore the resources of the coastal zone for the enjoyment of the current and succeeding generations." The 50th anniversary of this landmark protection, which occurs in 2026, will truly be a cause for celebration.

Coastal California is a living landscape, continually formed and reformed as land, sea, and weather patterns converge. The shoreline is ever-changing, vulnerable not only to nature's forces but to the human hand, which has dramatically reshaped the coastline. Recent decades have seen greater advocacy, stricter guidelines, and a hopeful push toward renewal of the most degraded coastal landscapes. The increasing thoughtfulness shown by those who design and build along the coast demonstrates their respect for not only the current landscape but in planning for the future, as the coast will need the space and flexibility to adapt and change over time.

The most compelling projects—those we chose to include in this book—worked in tandem with the goals of the California Coastal Act. The designers and owners of these homes displayed a shared reverence for the land, which we found reflected in their homes and work. In the words of architect Jess Field, they "listen to the land." The fundamental impacts of topography and weather are heightened where the land meets the sea. Attuned to the influences of sun, wind, water, and coastline, each architect in this book has created a home that provides protection from the elements, an immersive experience of the coastal environment, and a palpable sense of place.

—HEATHER SANDY HEBERT AND CHASE REYNOLDS EWALD

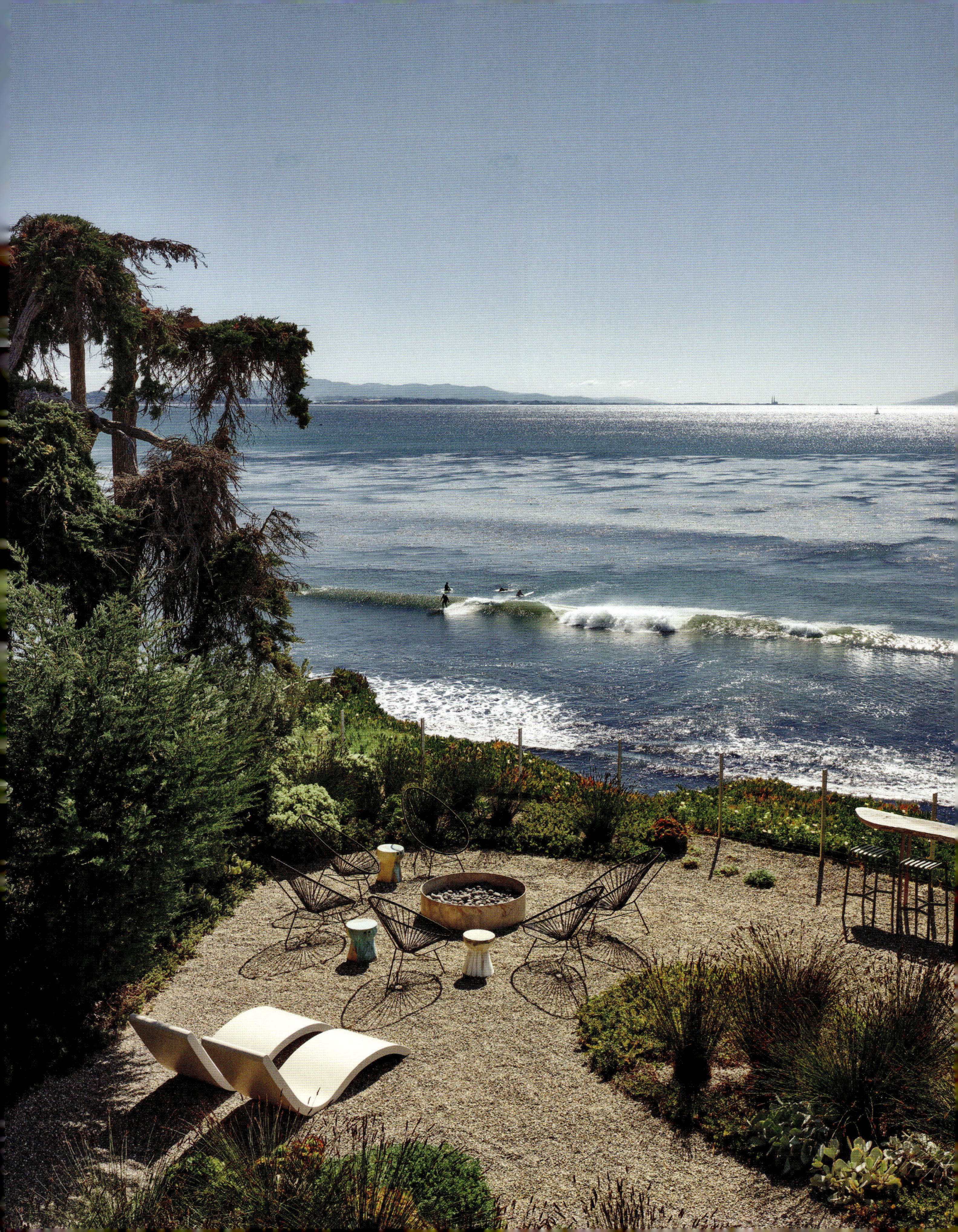

NORTHERN COAST

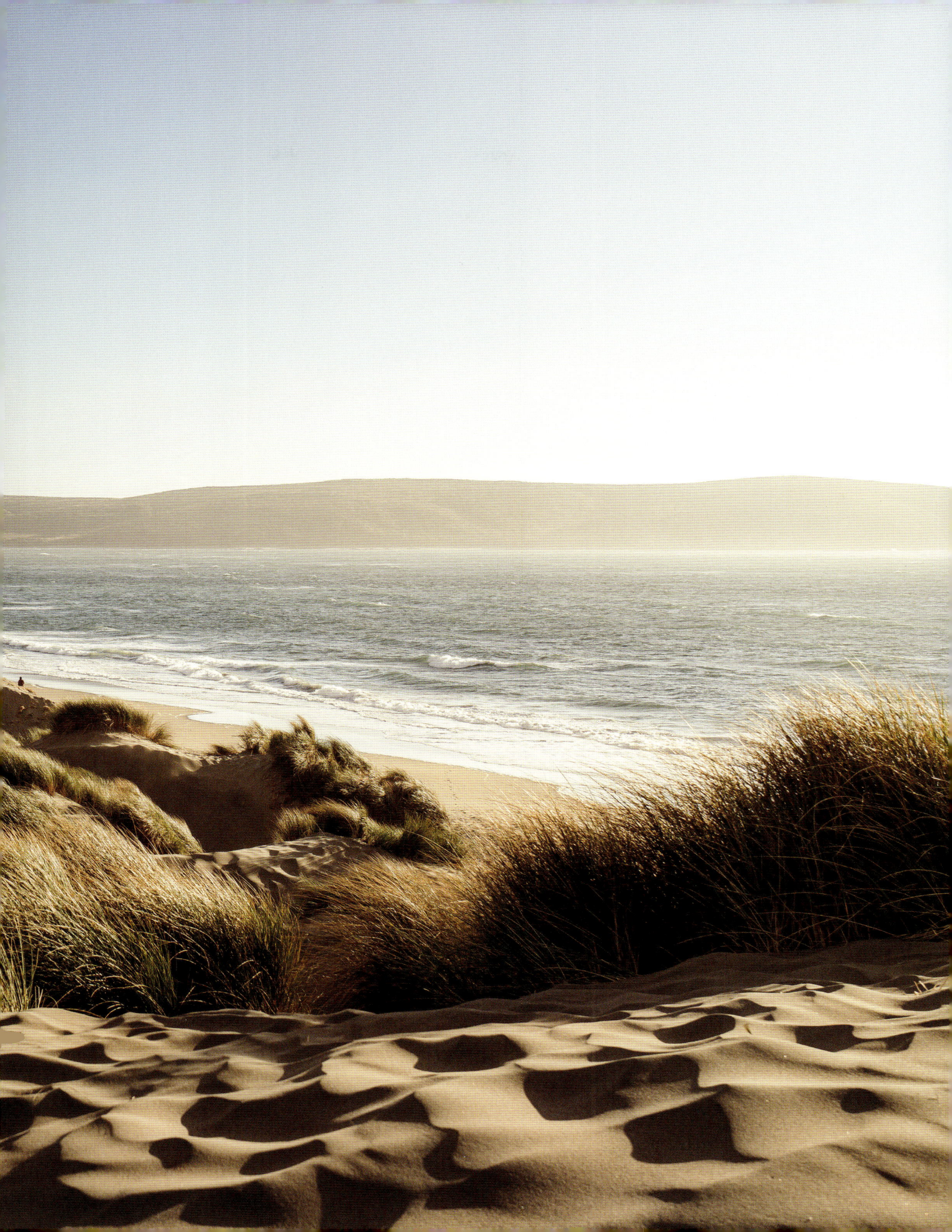

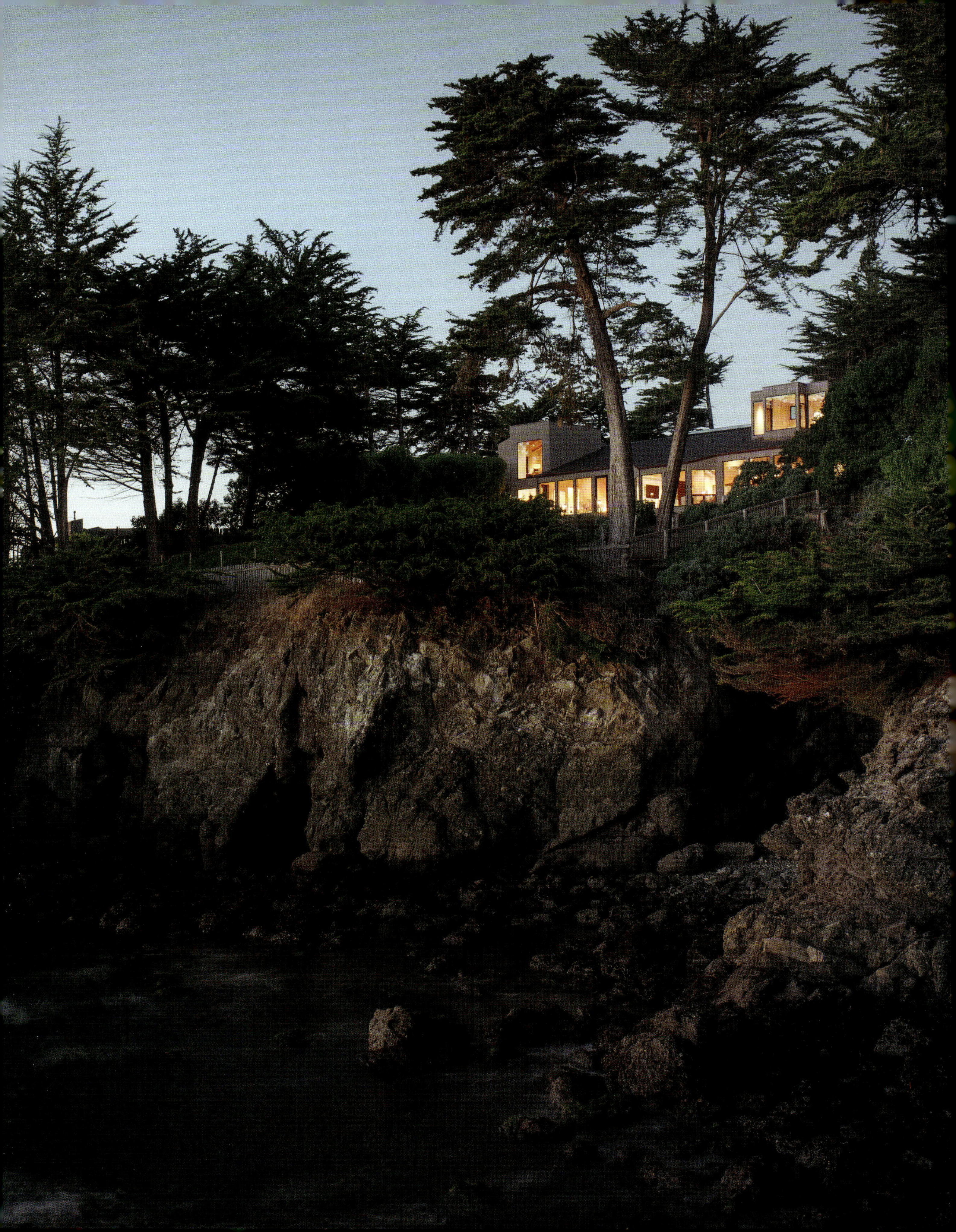

INFORMED BY NATURE

/ SEA RANCH /

Adapting and augmenting an iconic design in an unparalleled location is as much a daunting challenge as it is a singular opportunity. For Butler Armsden Architects, the chance to practice architecture at Sea Ranch created the perfect moment to explore and celebrate northern California's unique design ethos.

A planned community born of the mid-1960s back-to-the-land mindset, Sea Ranch stretches along ten spectacular miles of the rugged, windswept Sonoma Coast. The architects and creative thinkers behind it were clear in their intention: Sea Ranch would be a distinct community that grew directly from the land and immediate influences of ocean and the elements; any structures would be as understated and as harmonious in the landscape as possible. From the beginning, buildings were conceived as simple timber-frame houses of local Douglas fir and clad in redwood shingles or siding. A nod to the shapes of the region's agricultural buildings, they were meant to weather over time to a neutral gray, ultimately becoming one with the endless blue depths of the Pacific and a landscape of evergreen trees and open meadows dotted with sheep.

This project involved renovating and adding onto a 1974 home nestled among mature trees on a bluff overlooking the ocean. An additional structure would serve as garage and guesthouse. When architects from Butler Armsden and interior designer Matthew Leverone first saw the house, small windows yielded dark interiors, 1980s interventions felt out of sync, and skylights had been added in a way that detracted from the originals, which ran along the spine of the structure and served as its organizing principle. "We didn't want it to feel like a time capsule from 1974," explains architect Glenda Flaim, "but we all really wanted to be respectful of original ideas—both in the materials we were choosing and elements we were adding. We wanted to allow the context and the environment to speak."

The work was a combination of adding, subtracting, and rearranging. The house was taken down to the studs for a thorough refresh; the exterior siding and interior paneling, sourced from Evan Shively of Arborica, were replaced with natural fallen old-growth redwood and Douglas fir. On one end, the garage became a family room, while the existing turret-like second story, its striking geometry jutting out from the peak of the roof and side of the house, was turned into an office aerie for the wife. On the opposite end of the house, a cohesive addition created a new primary suite with immediate access to steps leading down to open pasture and the view. The terminus of the long, light-filled central corridor is marked by a modern spiral steel staircase that ascends to the husband's office—a kind of minimalist lookout housed in a rectangular tower that echoes the original architecture.

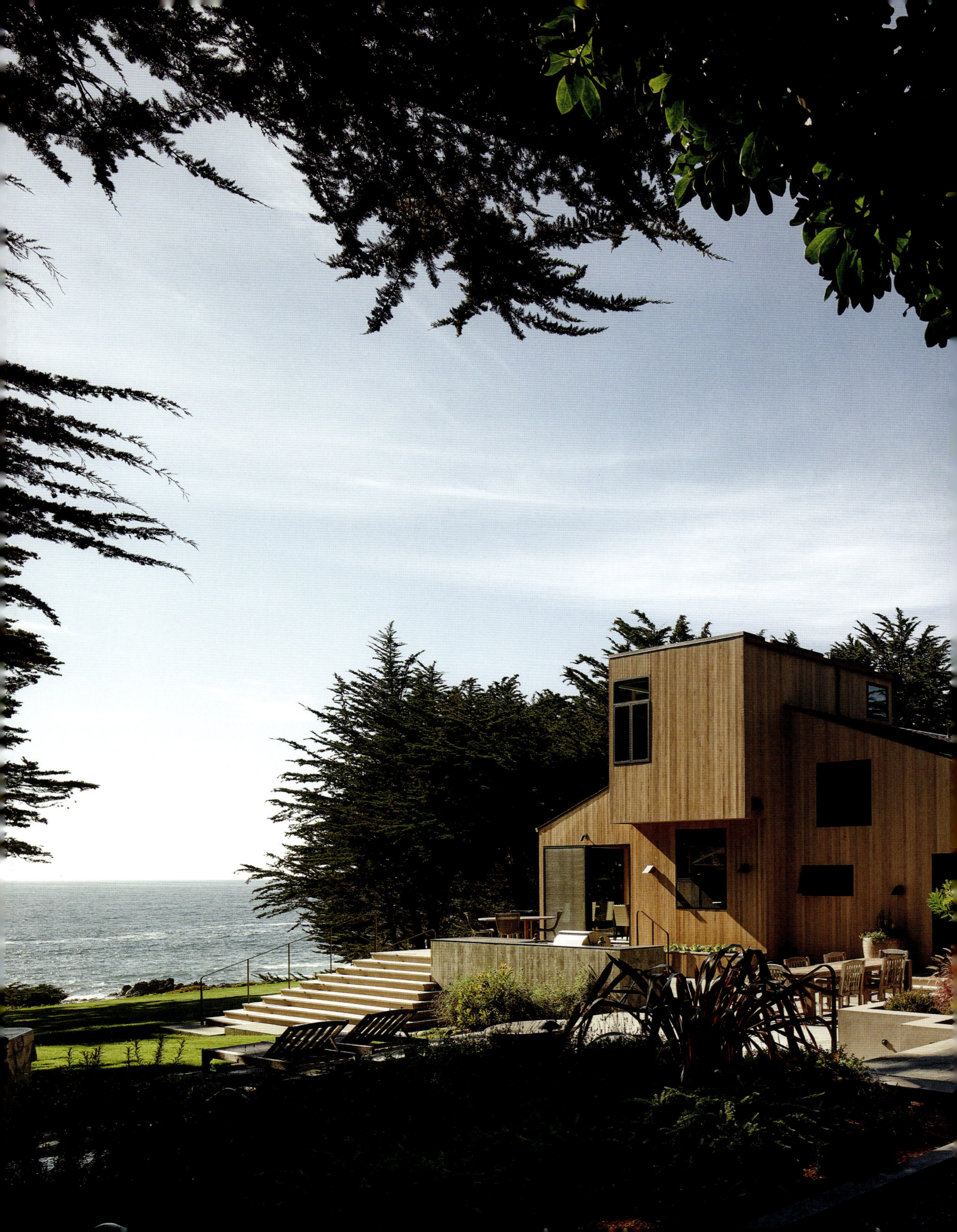

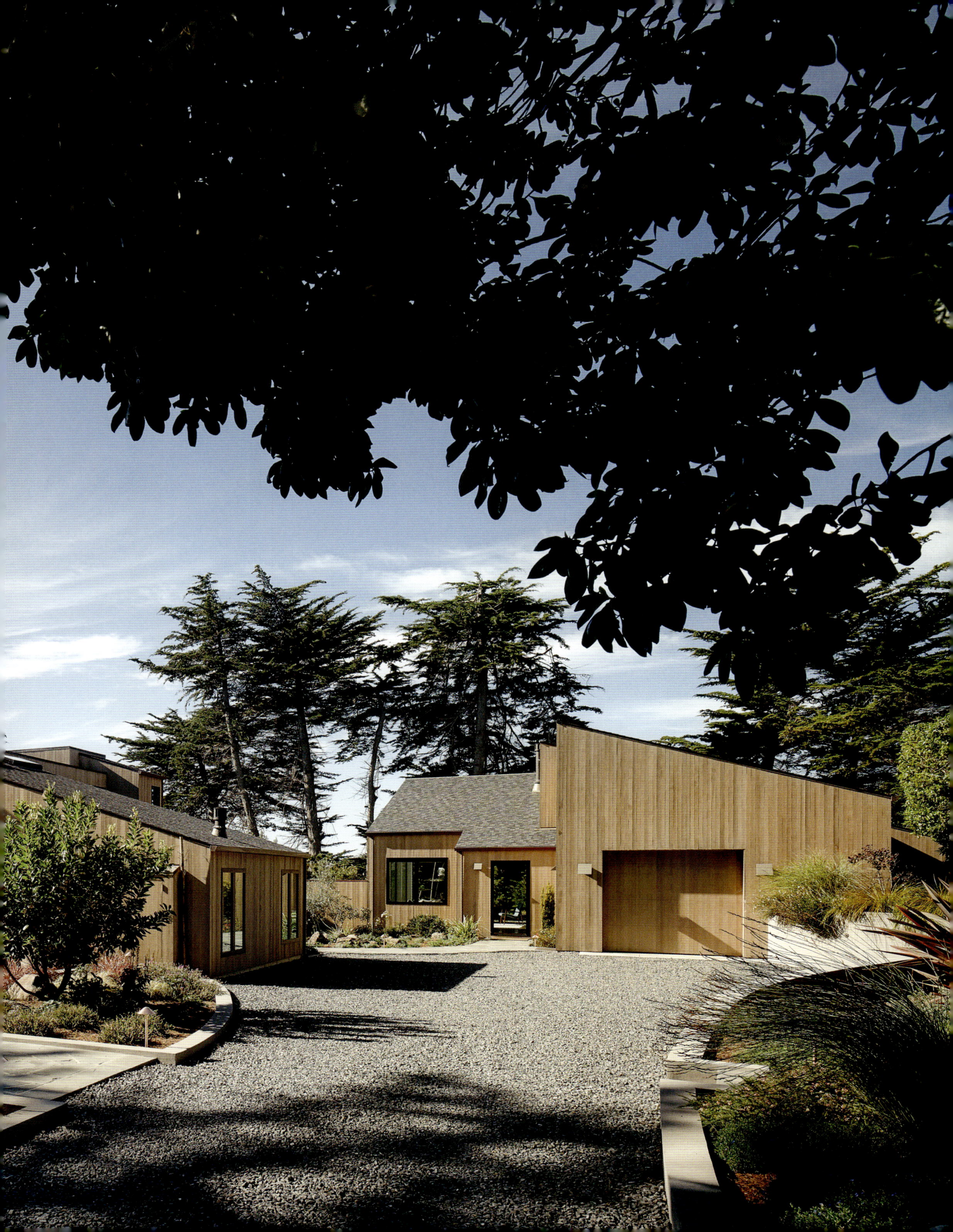

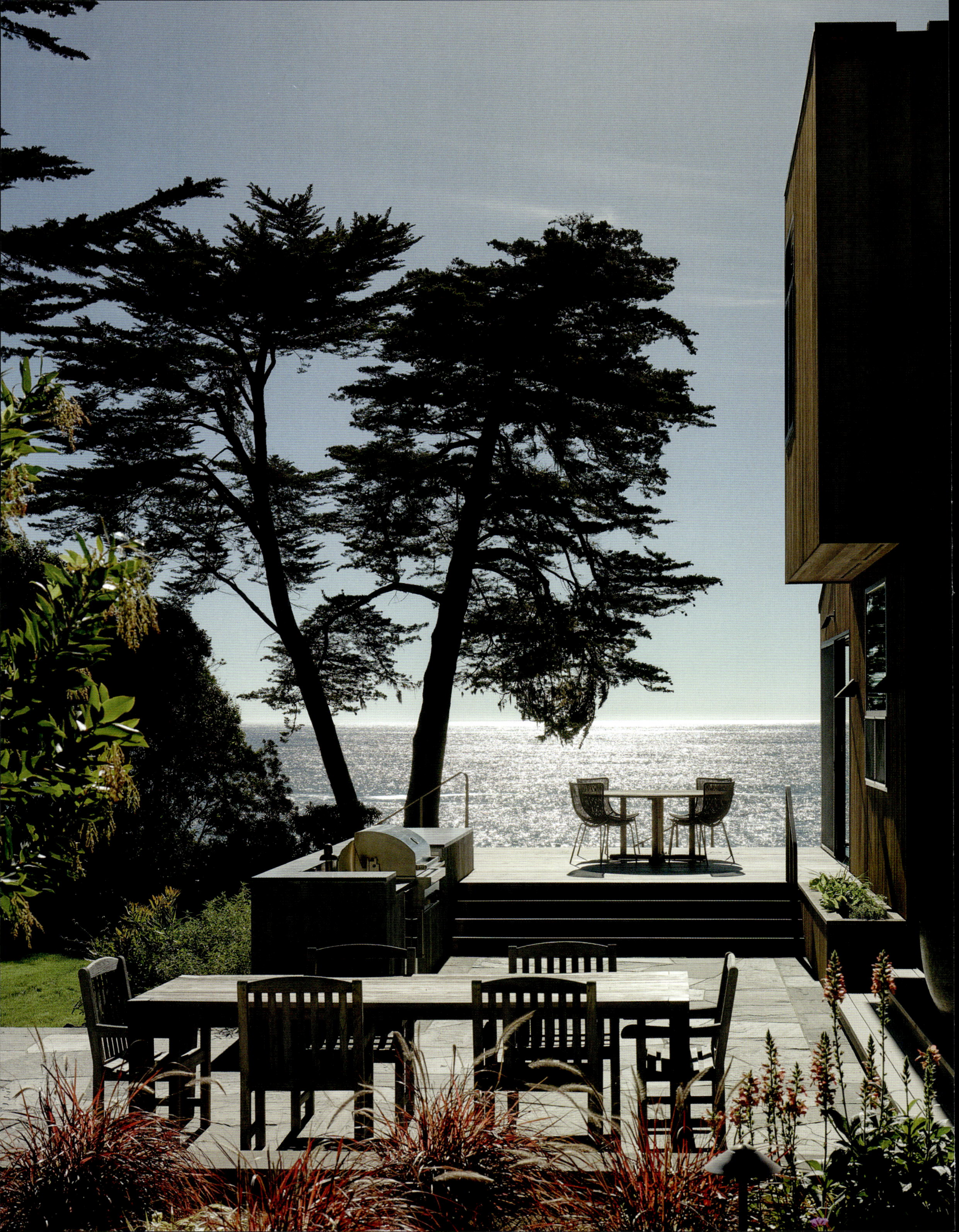

The goal for the interiors, says Leverone, "was to maximize the views. That was the most important thing." Stained fir cladding and plank oak floors stained a darkish gray to complement the paneling set the tone. Seating was maximized for guests to look out over the meadow as it slopes toward the ocean. The dark countertops of the custom Bulthaup kitchen were combined with a painted glass backsplash in shades of blue that speak to the sea. Living room lighting by David Weeks helps pull down the scale of the vaulted ceiling above custom-designed stone-and-steel coffee tables. Bathrooms were kept simple with linear light fixtures, long-lasting materials like Caesarstone, and floating cabinetry.

The new build, separated from the main house by a protected courtyard, contains a garage with two bedrooms, a bath, kitchenette, and living area. The intent was to engage in a coherent dialogue with the main house but, through differing roof angles and volumes, remain secondary to it. Unlike the existing structure, the guesthouse was built on a level grade, allowing for an enhanced indoor–outdoor experience and an intimate view into hedges and trees. Inside, white walls and extensive glazing with metal frames set up a black-and-white palette, in distinct contrast to the warm wood interiors of the main house.

A favorite activity at Sea Ranch is hiking the spectacular cliff path along the shore, available to all. Since fences are not allowed, privacy can be an issue for houses on the water. Due to the natural contours of the shoreline, this home is one of the few that lies between the path and the coast; it occupies its own hidden corner. One of the most sublime moments in the project takes advantage of this seclusion with a window seat in the wife's second-story office. Flanked by additional windows, it presents as a glass box that juts into space, with a view across the ocean to the horizon perfectly framed by tall coastal evergreens that provide protection from the constant winds. For architect Glenda Flaim, it speaks to the essence of California design. In her native Italy, she points out, "there's a strong sense of place, but it's a very different sense of place. There, it's the layers of history that inform the architecture. At Sea Ranch, nature informs how you build."

PRECEDING PAGE: Working with an existing design on the edge of a cliff at Sea Ranch, Butler Armsden Architects gave a 1974 home a thorough renovation and sympathetic addition as garage and guesthouse. Intentional, place-inspired design is mandatory in this iconic Sonoma County community.

OPPOSITE: Minimalism reigns on the outdoor deck, where it's all about the view. Both siding and deck are vertical grain cedar. The patio is bluestone, the barbecue cast-in-place concrete. A Restoration Hardware table offers a formal dining spot sheltered from the wind, while the round table and chairs from Janus et Cie provide a perfect vantage point for gazing out over the blue expanse.

RIGHT: Great attention was paid to furniture shape and how each piece would play against the other, says interior designer Matthew Leverone. "The two coffee tables in the great room were custom designed and made by us. They're very strong in style with the stone tops and blackened steel bases. They ground the room, which is large and has a high ceiling. The David Weeks Studio lighting fixture above also gives scale to the room." The sofa and swivel chairs are by A. Rudin, and the area rug was sourced from Woven Designs in San Francisco.

OVERLEAF LEFT: In the extensive remodel of the main home, interior siding was replaced with whitewashed vertical grain Douglas fir paneling, which beautifully frames the sculptural custom spiral staircase. The large painting is by David Simpson, the painting over the sofa by Ross Bleckner.

OVERLEAF RIGHT: The kitchen combines Bulthaup cabinets and dark Caesarstone countertops with a custom back-painted glass backsplash. Floors throughout are white rift oak stained a smoky tobacco tone.

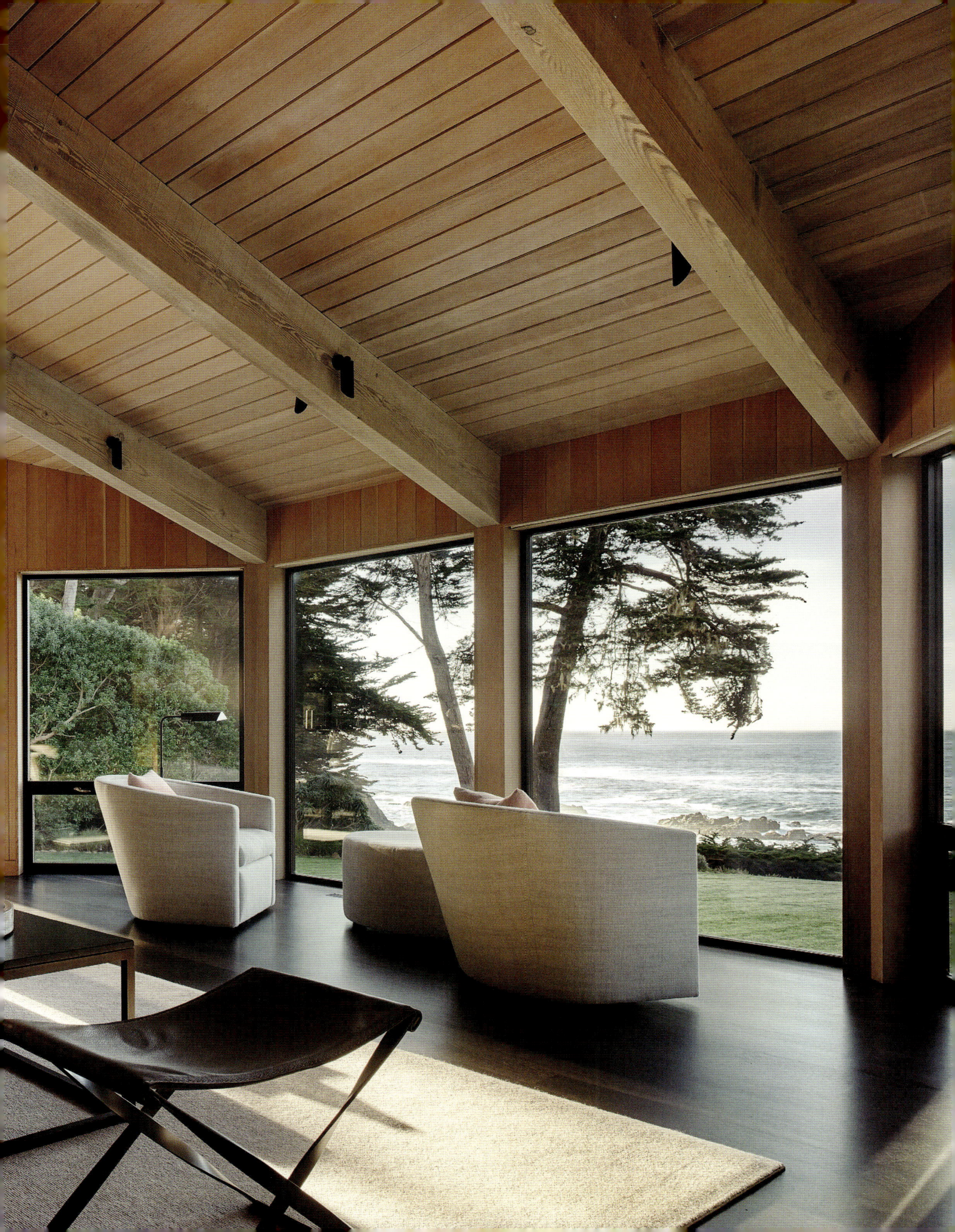

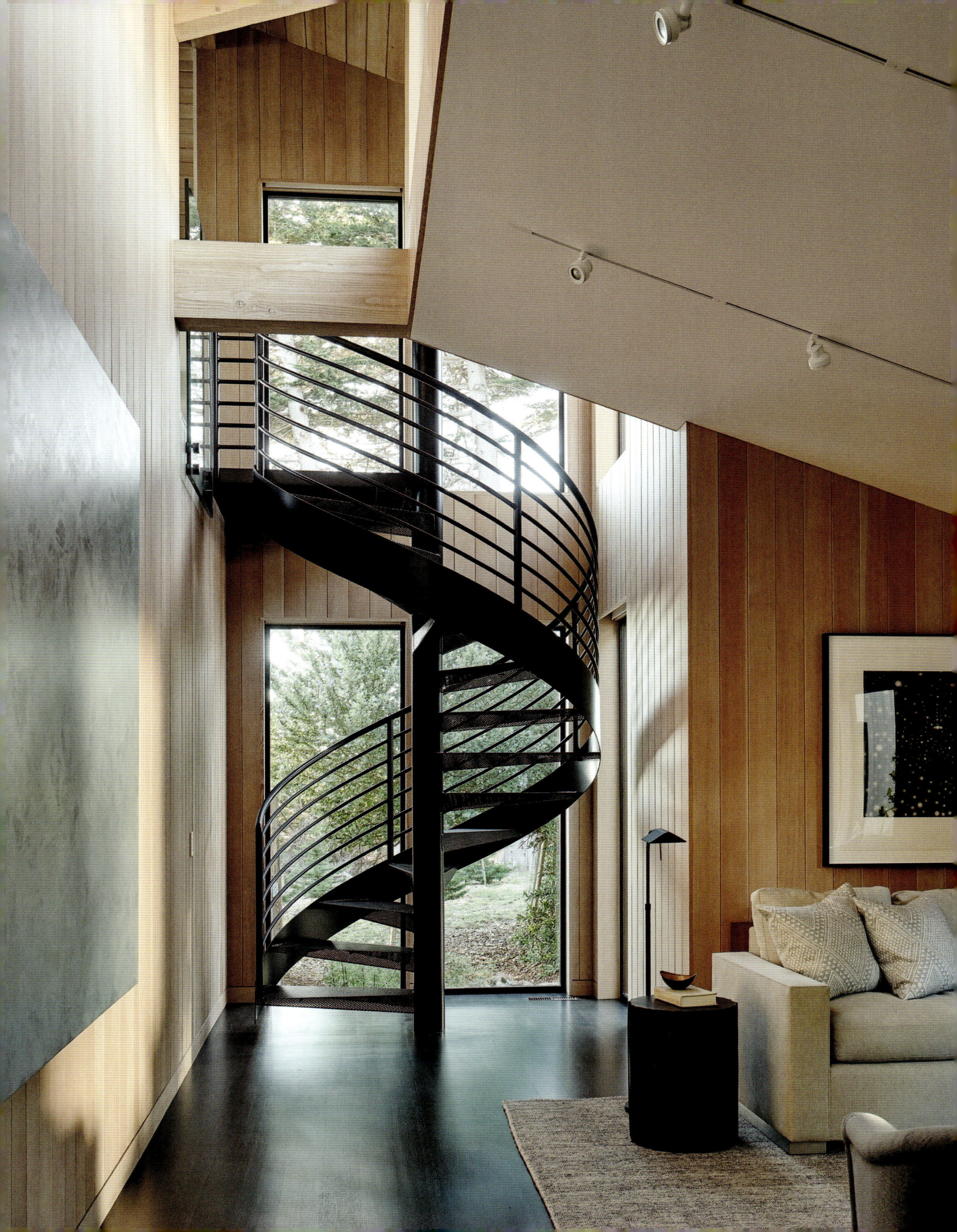

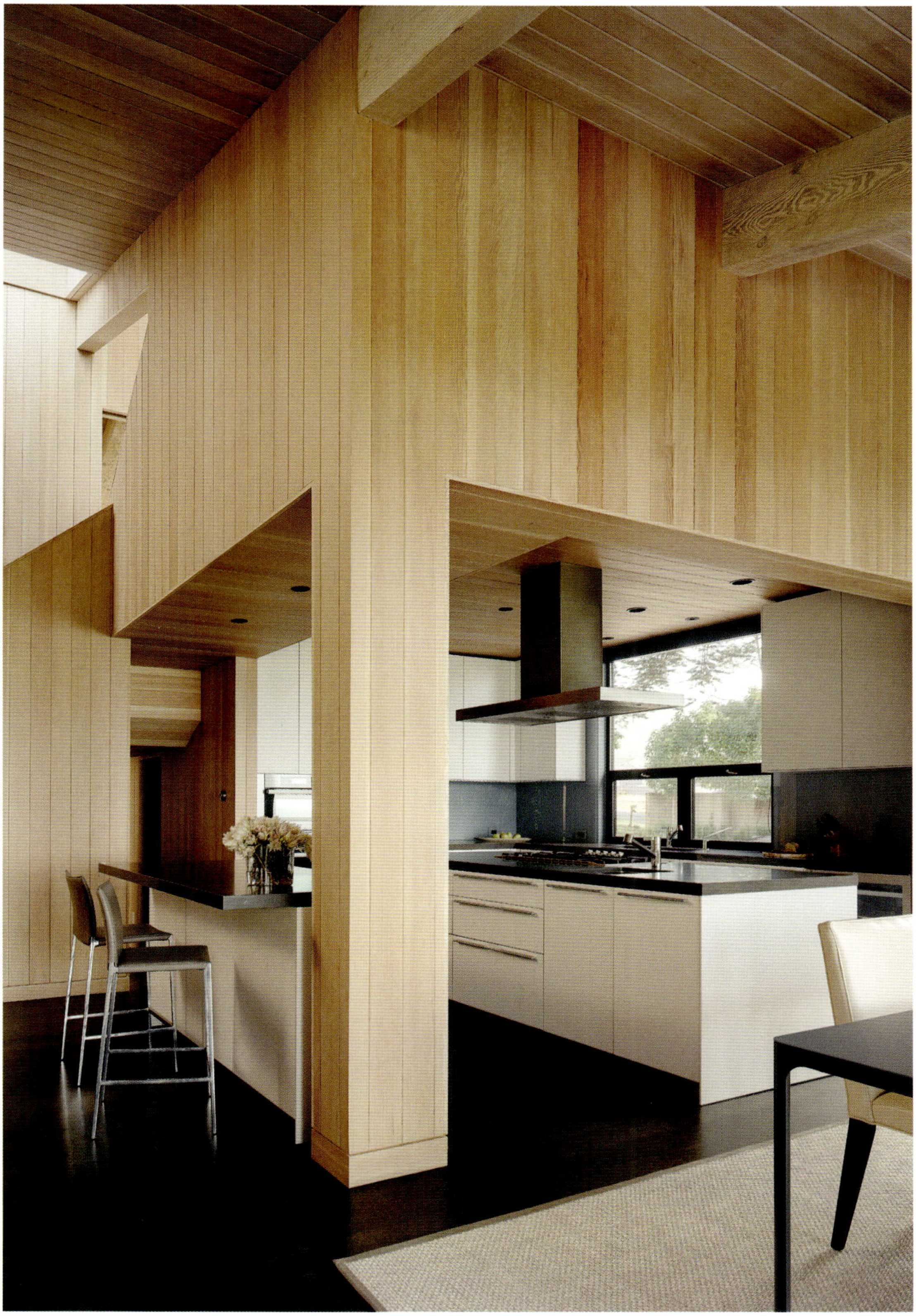

One of the most powerful moments in the house—the window seat located across from the wife's desk—is all about the view. The fabric, from Holly Hunt Great Plains Collection, is minimal and textural. The throw and pillows are from Homelosophy.

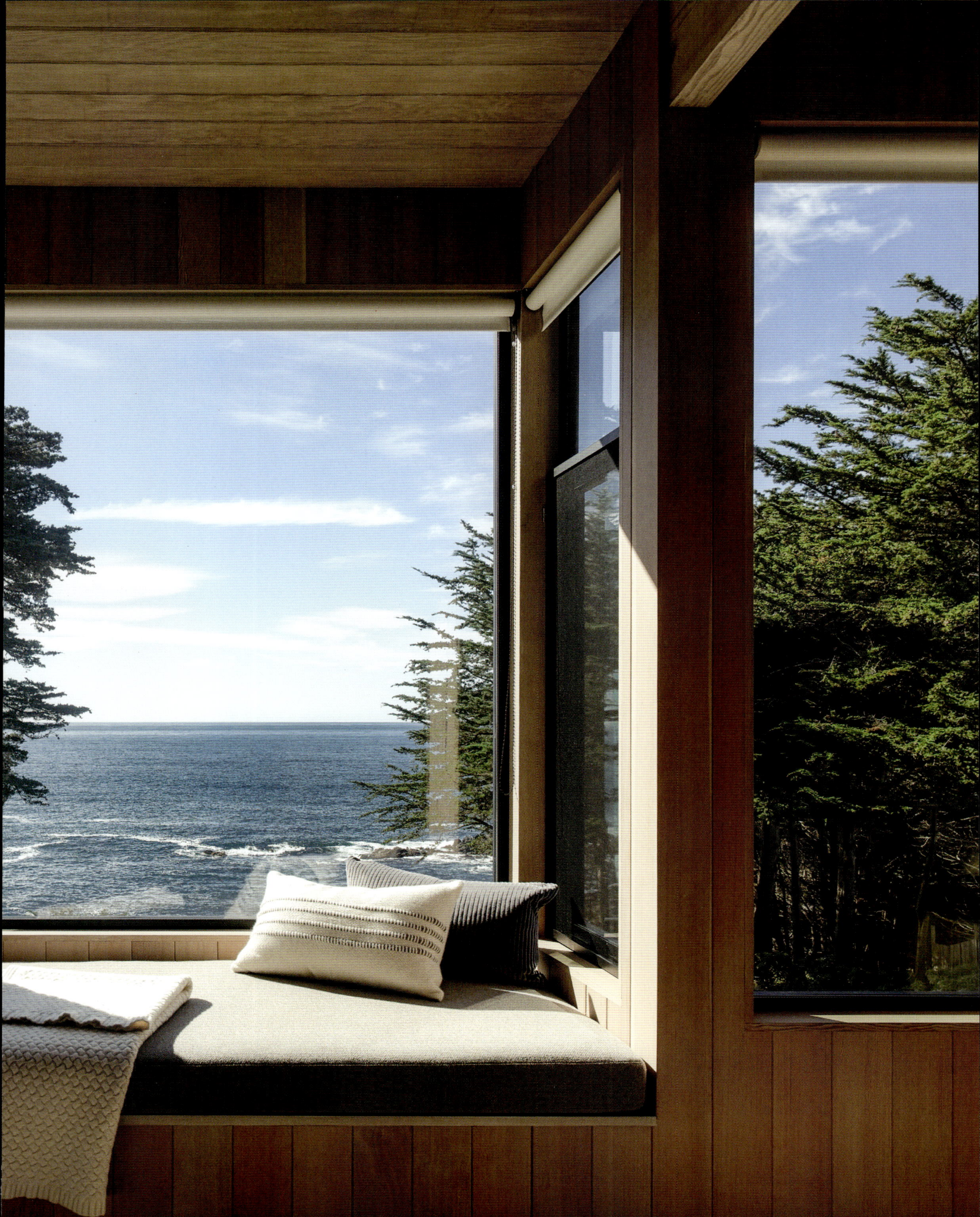

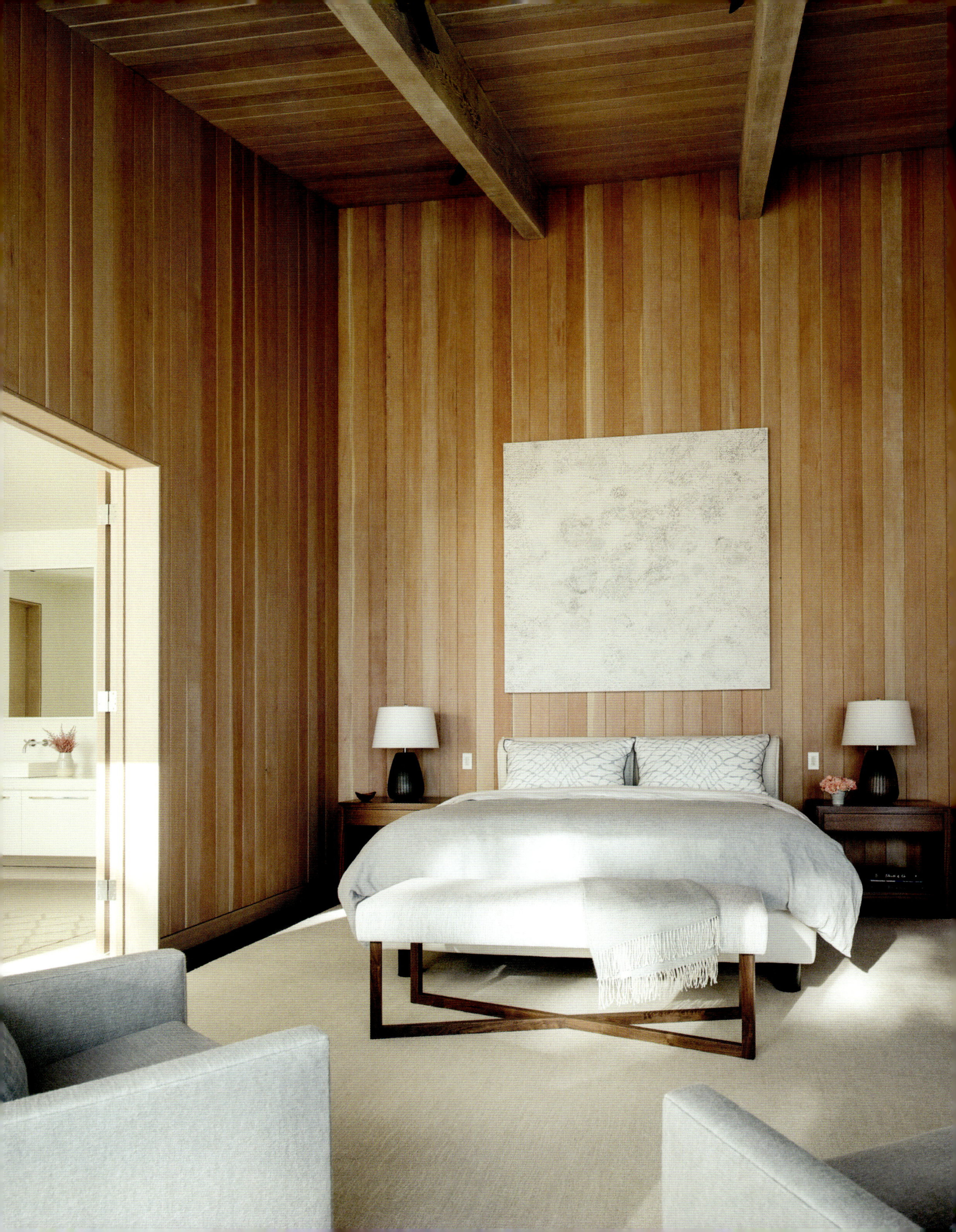

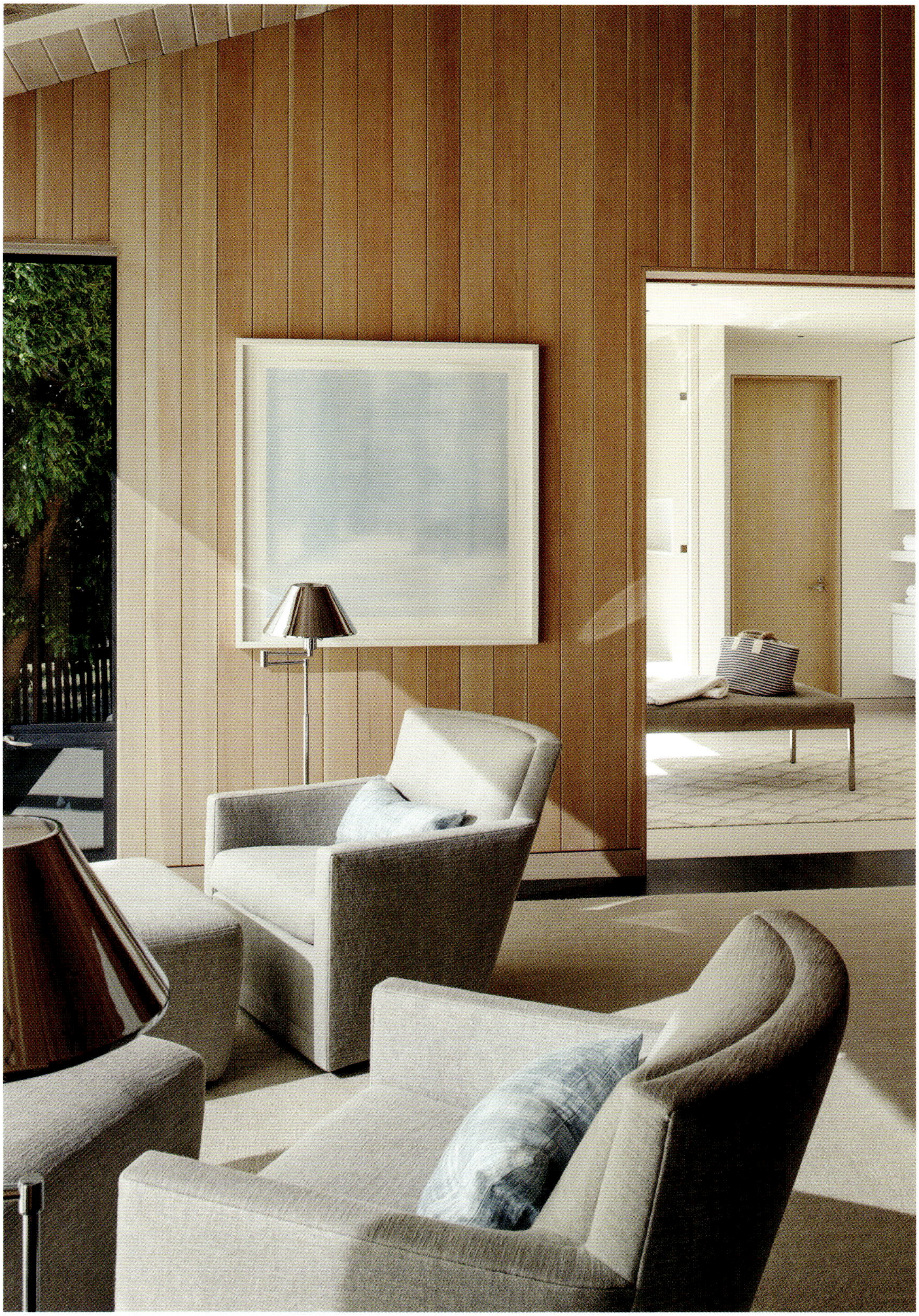

PRECEDING PAGE LEFT: The designer sought to achieve a harmonious cadence from one room to the next while deferring to the views for drama. The bed is Duxiana, the painting by Indira Morre. The walnut bedside tables are A. Rudin, topped with artisan glass lamps from Arteriors.

PRECEDING PAGE RIGHT: Swivel chairs—always a positive addition to a room with a view—are A. Rudin, upholstered in Romo Silver Birch textured linen. The chalk pastel is by Gale Antokal.

RIGHT: The primary bathroom vanity features Caesarstone, known for its durability and resistance to discoloring. The Ann Sacks porcelain floor and wall tile create a beautiful, serene backdrop for the Wet Style tub with a tub filler from Lacava. An upholstered bench with stainless steel legs provides a place to perch.

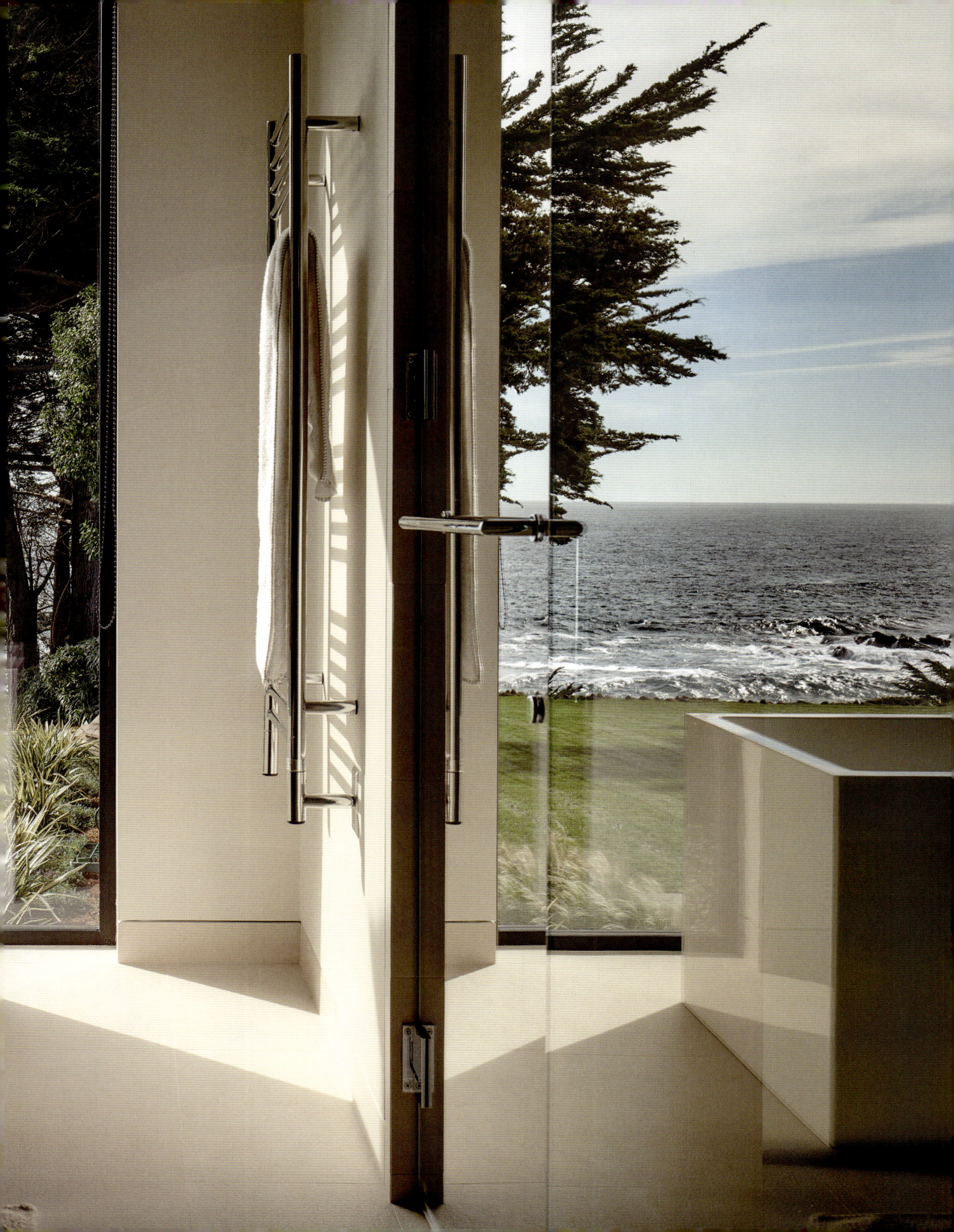

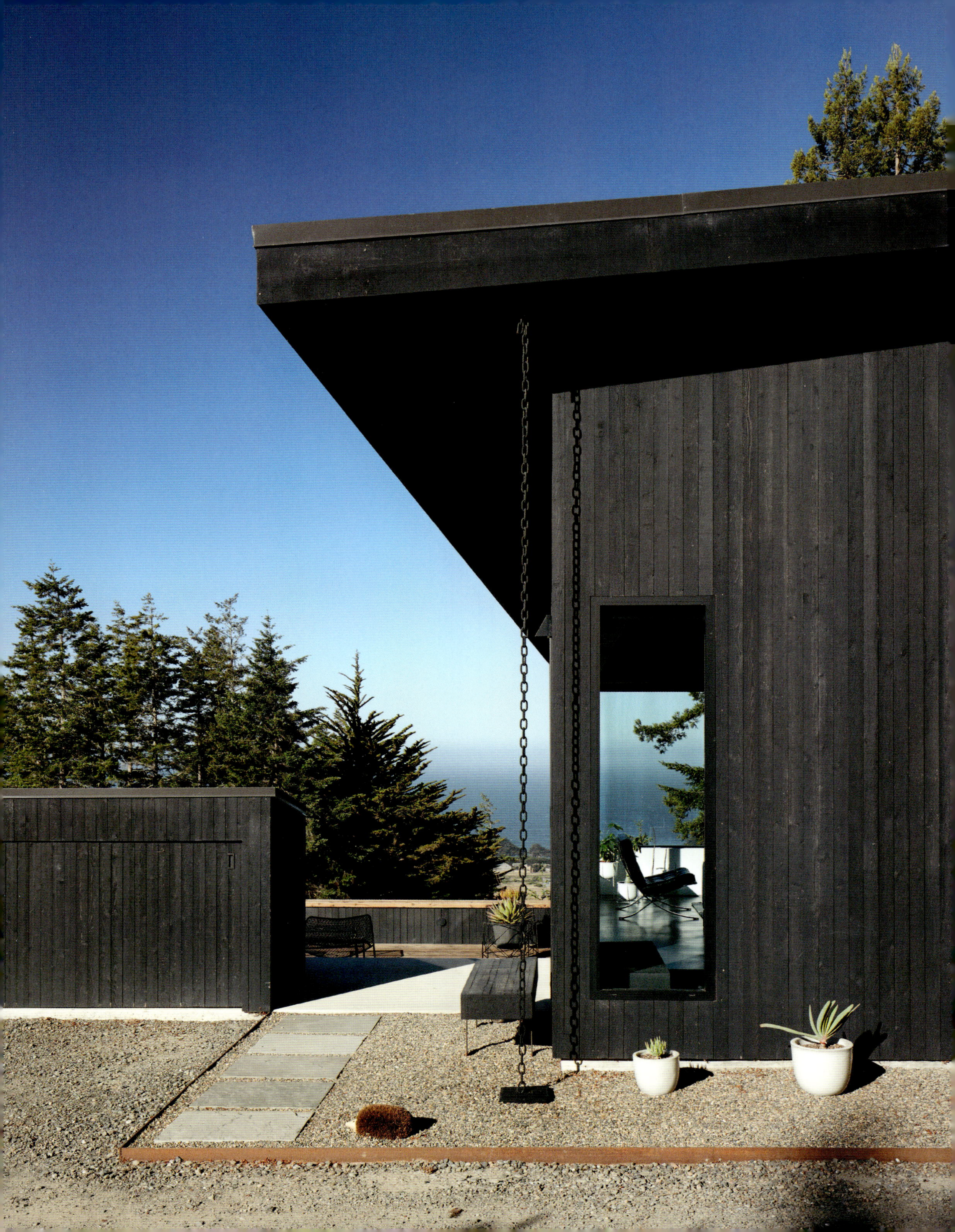

THE COLOR OF SHADOWS

/ SEA RANCH /

One can't practice architecture in the Bay Area without developing some curiosity about Sea Ranch, the iconic eco-conscious, architecture-driven community on the Sonoma Coast. After all, the original designers' firms are still active in the Bay Area architecture scene; many who had trained under them are as well. It was inevitable, then, that Geoff Campen, principal architect at Klopf Architecture, and his wife, architect-artist Diana Ruiz, would one day make the drive up the coast.

When Campen and Ruiz reached the ten-mile stretch of coastline marked by cliffs, rock outcrops, meadows, and forests and dotted with modest structures built of materials drawn from nature, they were profoundly impressed by both the dynamism of the landscape and the ethos of the architecture within it. What struck them most of all, though, was the overriding sensation of calm the place engendered. "The contrast to San Francisco was stark," Campen recalls. "We liked the consistency and direction of the architecture, the environmental setting, the ocean, the forest. And we liked the contrast of the two lifestyles. Everything slowed down for us here, and it made us appreciate the culture and energy of the city much more."

That contrast energized and informed their work and art, and it kept drawing them back. Initially looking for a home they might renovate, Campen and Ruiz stumbled across a property that is of the forest and the meadow yet still enjoys a relationship to the ocean. From this perch, backed by trees and facing the sea, they enjoy the best of both worlds.

The design review process is intensive at Sea Ranch, a community formed on the precept that architecture should be minimal, take simple forms, and defer to the landscape. "The philosophy is that the house should live harmoniously with the landscape around it," explains Campen. "They want the structure to respond to the geometries of the site and surrounding natural habitat as much as possible. The geometries of the house need to work with the slopes and the site. There are also no visible manicured plantings, as natural foliage and grasses come right up to the house, completing the idea of a shared landscape."

Campen and Ruiz designed their home in direct response to site. Tucked up against the tree line, its front opens to ocean views. With its siding stained dark, the home disappears into the tree line, while its form—high in the back, its rooflines sloping down toward the sea—is designed to minimize its visual impact along the forest edge. The windows also react to the site: in the rear, tall and vertical in relation to the trees, at the front wide and horizontal in dialogue with the meadow and ocean. Inside, the material palette is straightforward: white oak, white walls, concrete floors, and raw steel trim, with decorative tile in the kitchen and bathrooms. In places, the dark exterior siding is carried inside to the ceilings, creating an energizing contrast. The entire house is open plan, from the main living area, where the L-shaped kitchen wraps around the central form enclosing the bathroom, to the office-studio, which doubles as a guest room with a Murphy bed and curtains. A loft, open to the floor below, accommodates the bedroom.

For the architect pair, says Campen, the process was organic. "It was very much a back-and-forth coming up with the interior layout and spaces and the composition of the exterior. Given the slope and height of the roof, there was a particular composition that made sense from the outside and also created usable interior spaces. And with the idea that the back space would be an office 95 percent of the time and a guest room only when necessary, we were cognizant of trying to make every square foot of the house work for us."

At the outset of Sea Ranch's design-review process, architects create a diagram delineating factors specific to the site: the orientation of the house in relation to views, prevailing winds, sunrise and sunset in summer and winter, and the locations of streams, trees, and other houses. For Campen and Ruiz, the exercise drove home the point that any design in the community must harmonize with the site and its conditions. Those conditions are ever changing, from the intermittent creek on the far side of the trees to the sheep grazing the meadows to the turkeys roosting in the trees behind their home. Campen and Ruiz have relished having the opportunity to add their own signatures to the timeless yet evolving expression that is Sea Ranch. "As architects," Campen observes, "ultimately you like to have your fingerprints on the place you live."

PRECEDING PAGE: Sea Ranch is a community conceived by architects. More than half a century after its founding, it still exerts a strong pull over creative people. A home owned by Geoff Campen, principal at Klopf Architecture, and architect-artist Diana Ruiz embraces the view from the driveway through the house and front deck to the ocean. Dark-stained cedar siding helps the structure blend into the evergreens at its side and back. The front benches are repurposed from ridge beam cutoffs.

OPPOSITE: The house was designed to sit unobtrusively in the shadows of the trees that back it on the gently sloping site and blend into the native landscape that characterizes Sea Ranch.

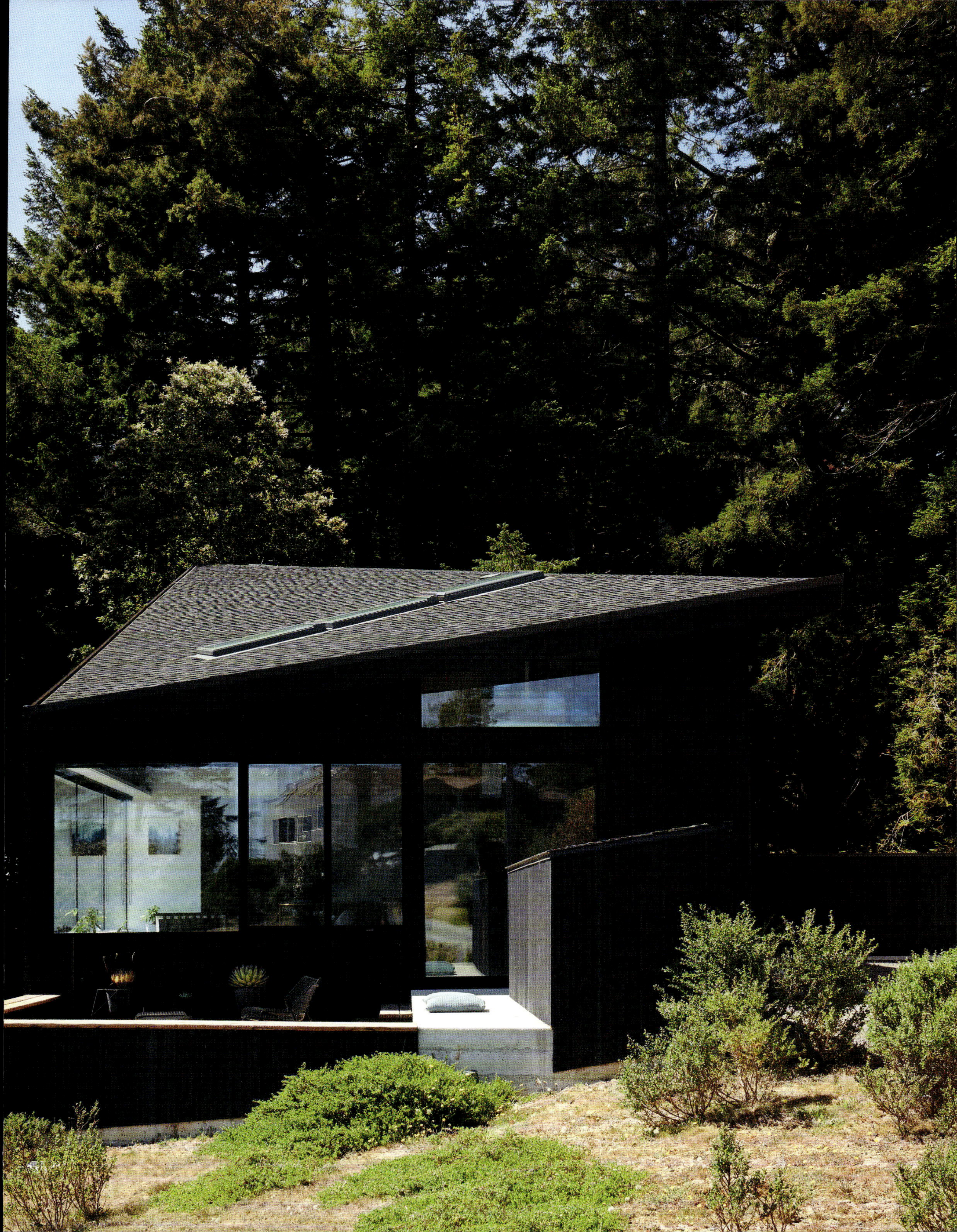

The dining and living area, oriented toward expansive views over the Pacific, are furnished with a Tenon table from Modernica, a Fairfax fixture from Avenue Lighting, a Blu Dot sofa and chairs. Barcelona chairs provide additional seating.

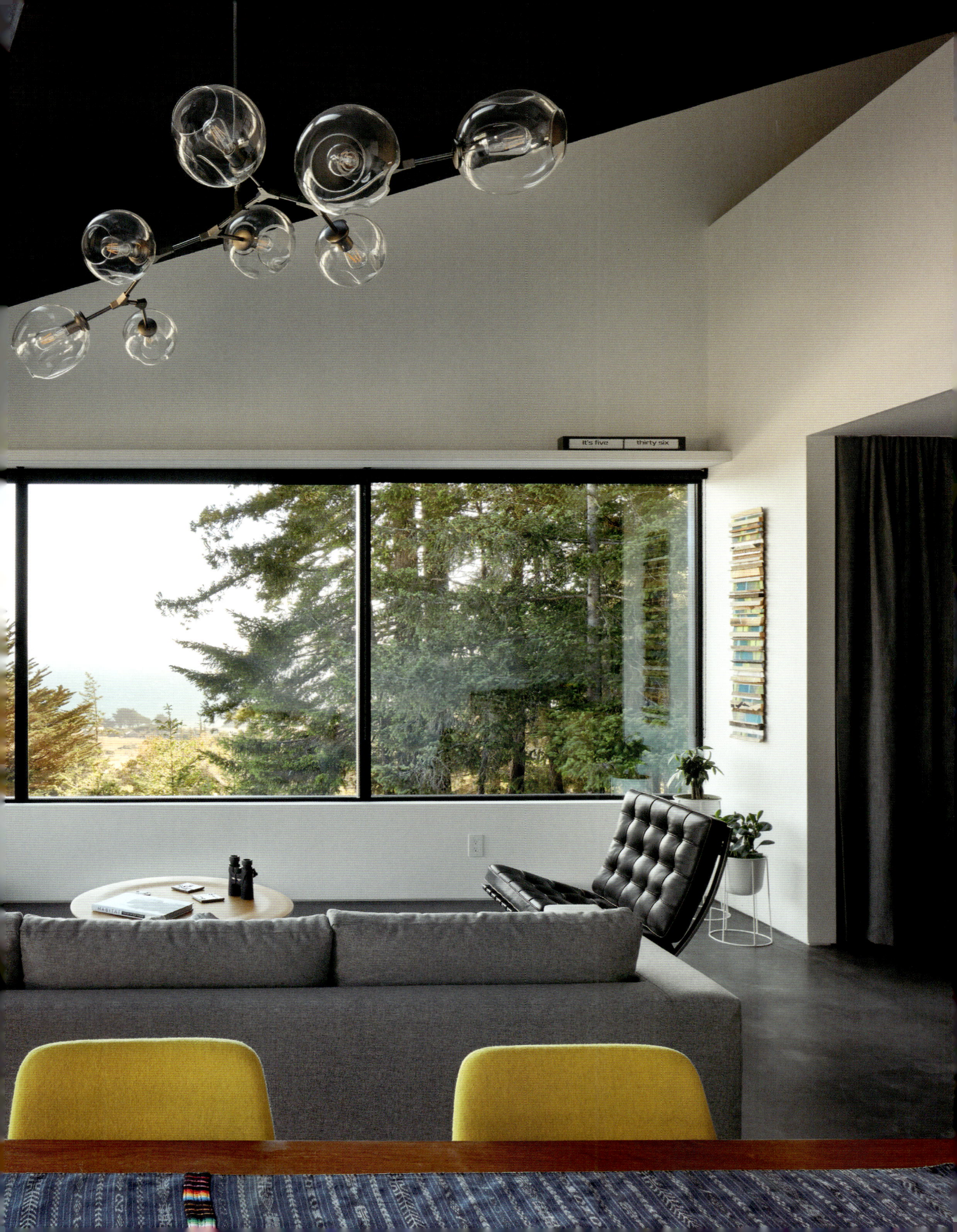
It's five
thirty six
HABITAT

ABOVE: The house is extraordinarily open, even to the upstairs bedroom, with the kitchen designed as an L-shape wrapping around the volume that contains the bathroom. The Heath tile backsplash has integrated artwork by Brendan Monroe. The kitchen cabinets from Ikea have custom white oak plywood inserts.

OPPOSITE: The natural sealed concrete floor extends into the art room, which serves as a second bedroom.

OVERLEAF: The open-loft primary bedroom, its ceilings stained dark to match the exterior siding, is tucked up into the forest. The rug is from Peace Industry, the square ottomans are from Blu Dot, the side chair and table are Eames.

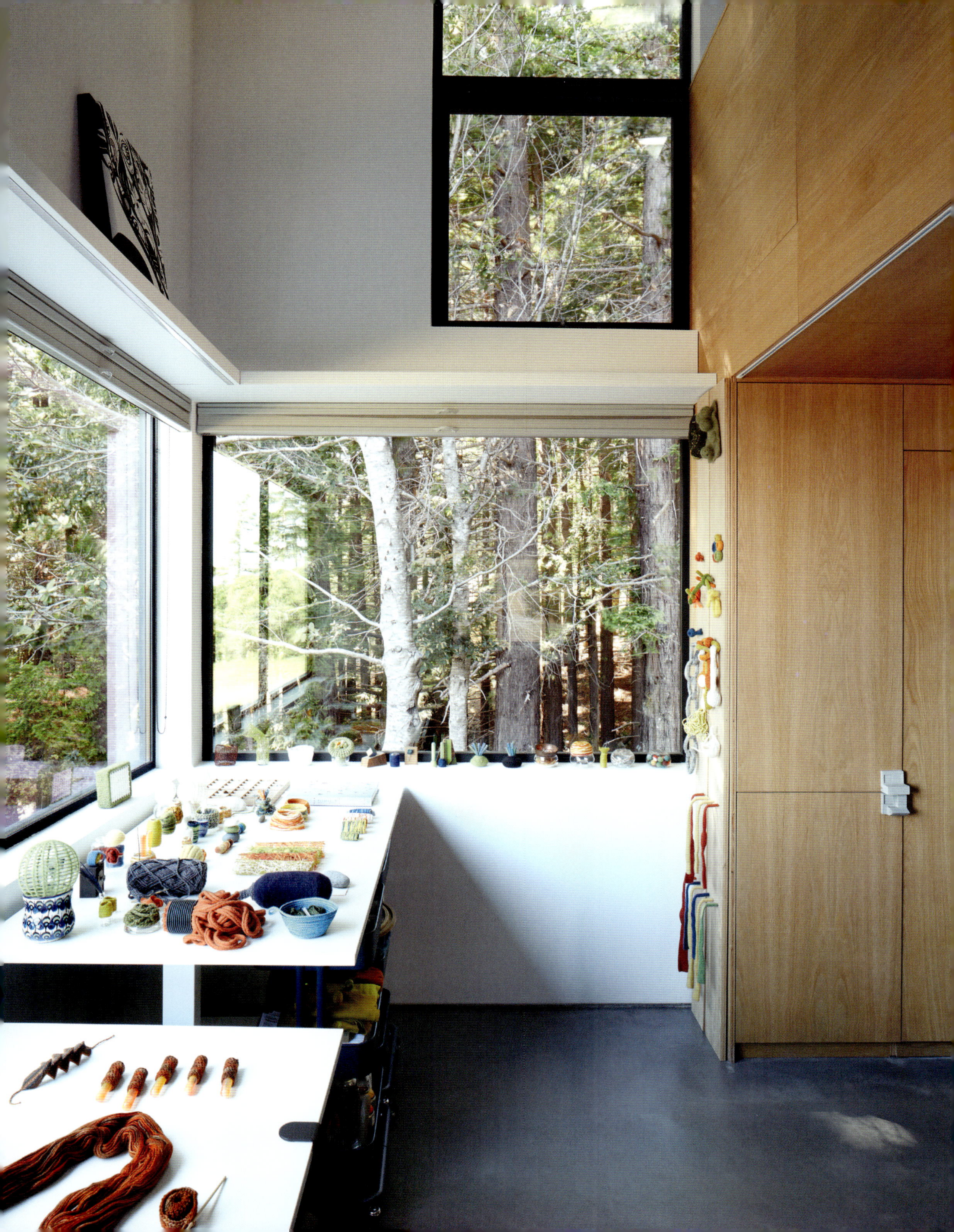

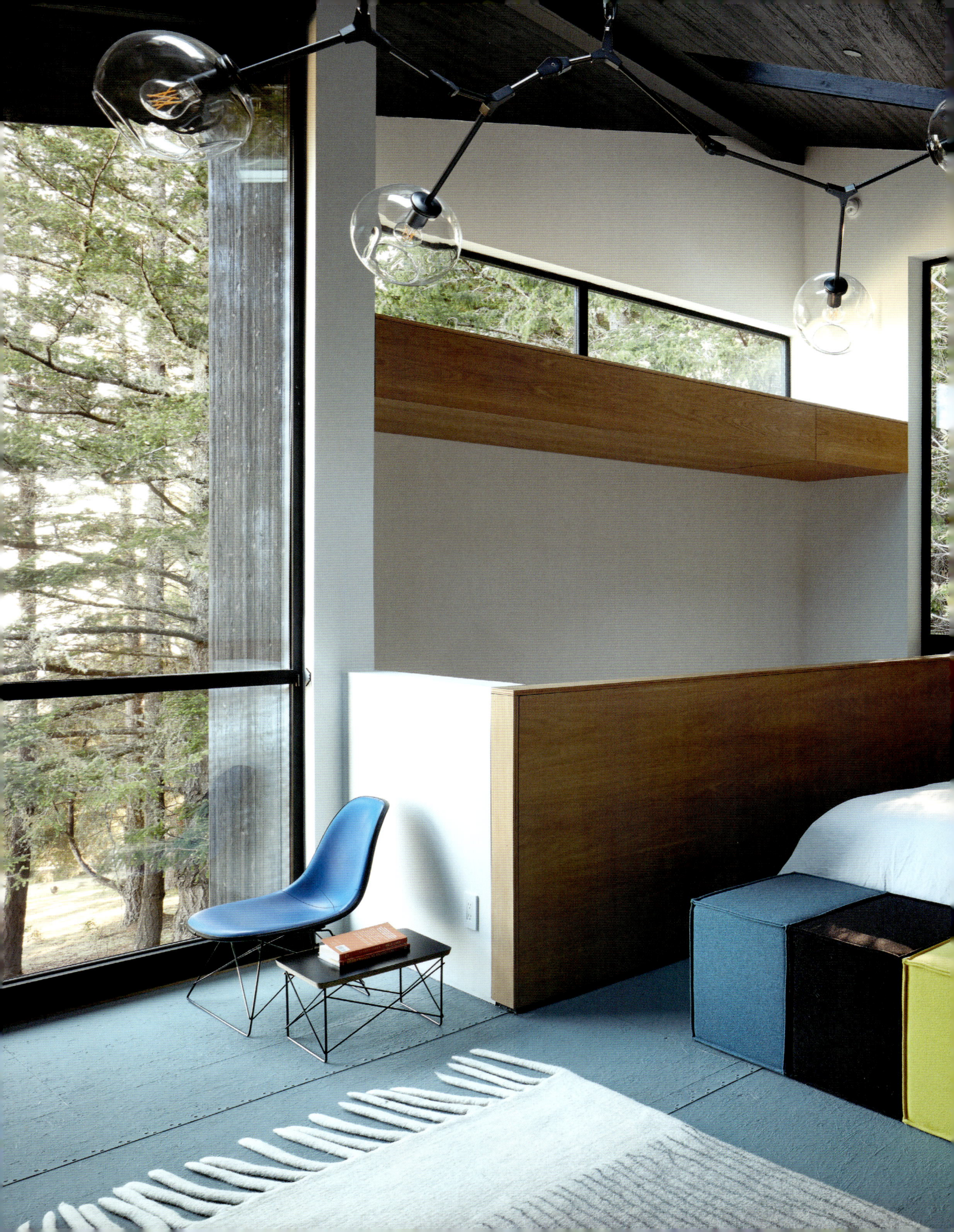

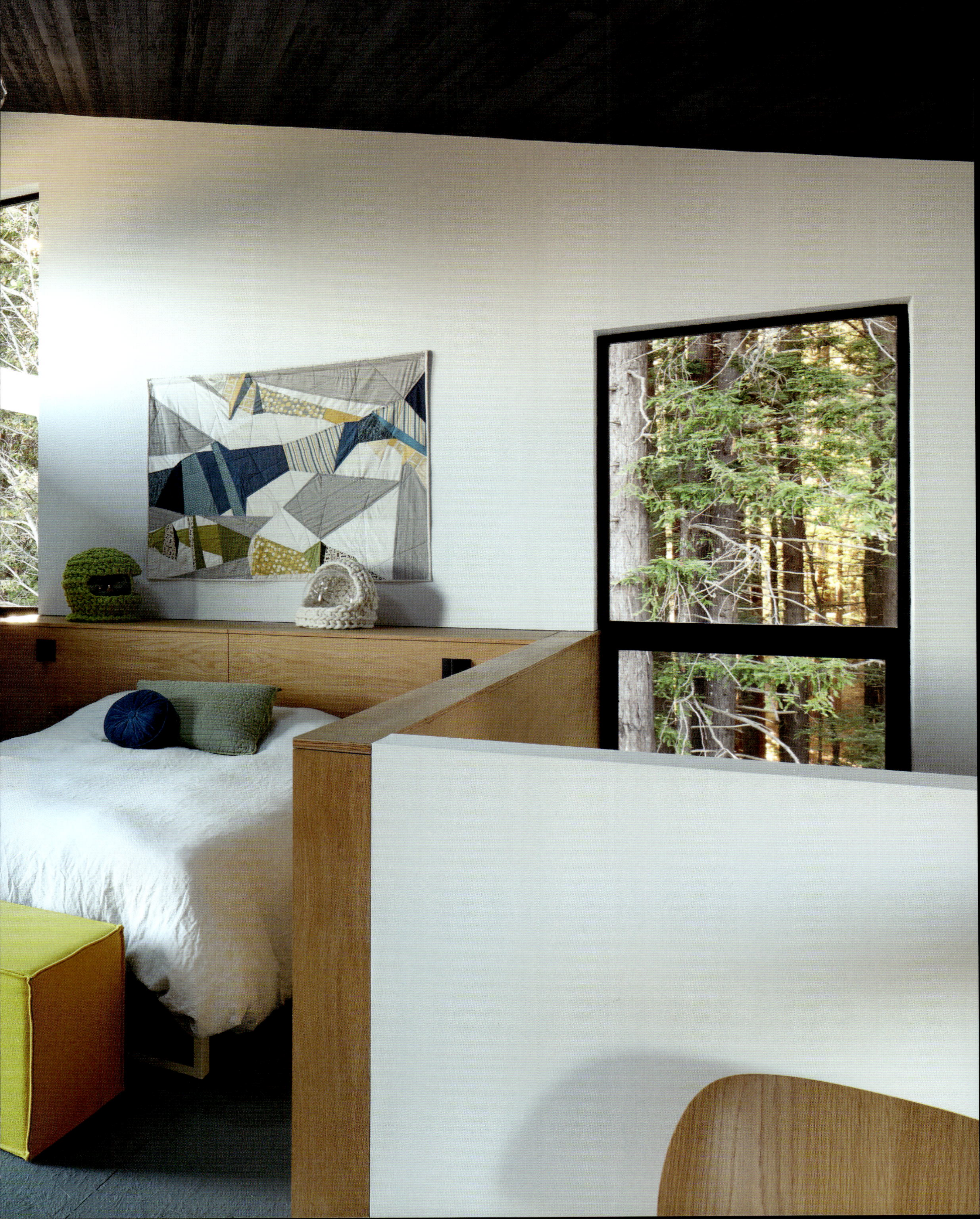

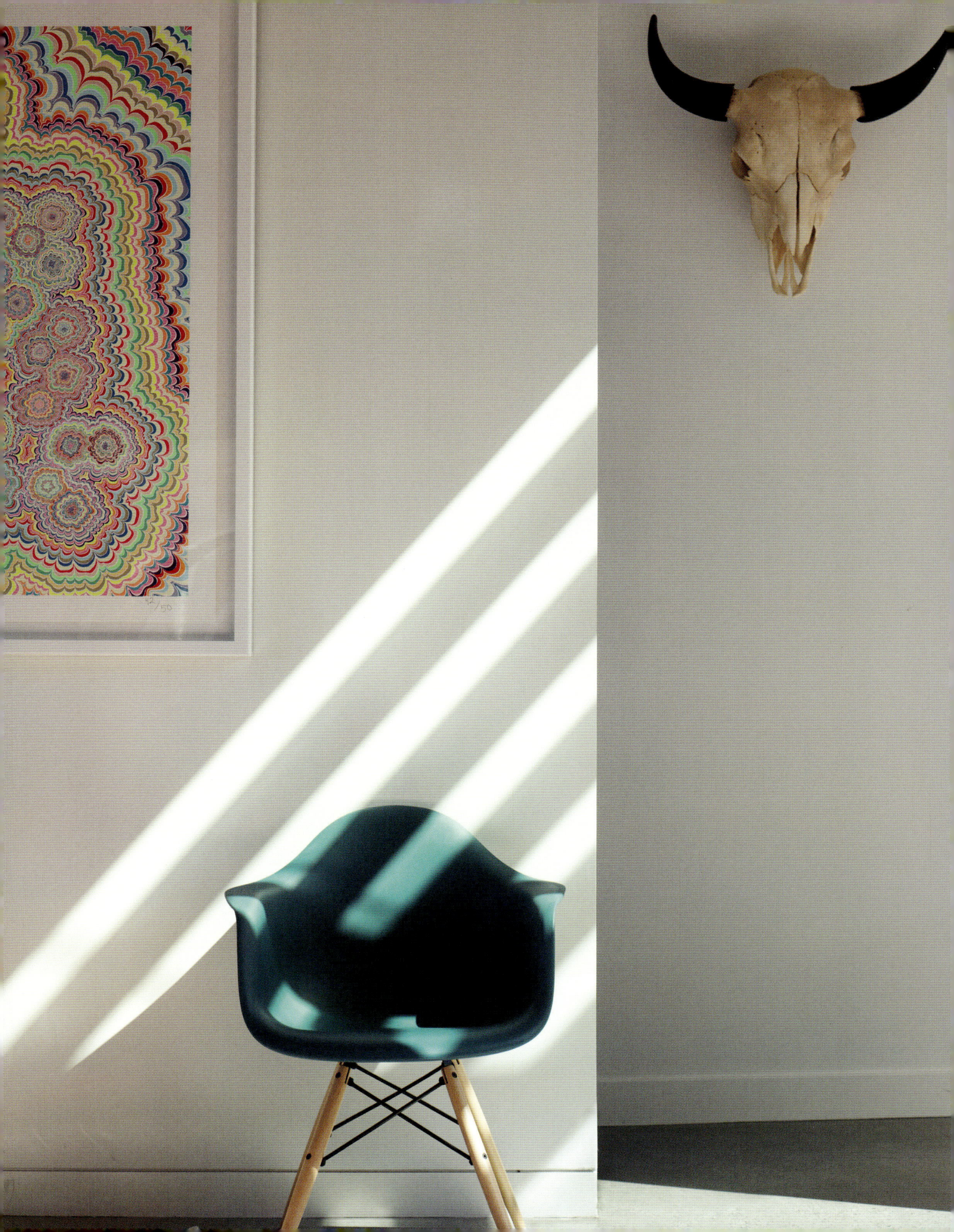

LAGOON LIVING

/ STINSON BEACH /

Set at the northern end of Stinson Beach, an hour's drive north of San Francisco, the private community of Seadrift sits on a narrow spit of sand that divides the Bolinas Lagoon from the adjacent bay. While many of the houses here front the Pacific, others have the ocean at their backs, with views of the lagoon and the mountains of Bolinas Ridge. However, it is very much a coastal existence, with the sound of the waves washing ashore along with pelicans and other seabirds riding in on the breeze.

Though the community is private, the beach is public, and the lifestyle retains its down-to-earth, back-to-the-beach vibe. The houses are unostentatious, for the most part, and steeped in the architecture and history of the area. An indoor–outdoor lifestyle, along with materials that can withstand some wear, are a given. At the same time, residents and designers alike have embraced contemporary design, which, when combined with a modest program and a deep awareness of the surroundings, results in homes that are very much of this place. A number of architects have come to represent this approach, designing numerous homes here as their reputations spread in this small enclave. Cass Calder Smith is one of them.

"I used to go to Fire Island as a kid, and that experience is in my brain when I work out here—the boardwalks, the sand, the freedom," says Smith.

Owners Dan and Caitlin Lockwood met Smith through a neighbor, who had been the architect's first client in Seadrift. A family of surfers, the Lockwoods had purchased a lot set just a half mile down the road from the prime surfing beach. They wanted a weekend getaway—a small, simple house with a less-is-more approach—where they could retreat with their kids and often their friends and turn them loose.

Rather than facing the Pacific Ocean to the west, the lot they found faces east toward the community's distinctive crescent-shaped lagoon. Only 60 feet wide, their small lot allowed for just 1,900 square feet of interior space. Like so many coastal properties, the home's defining facade faces the water, where the family is most likely to see their neighbors kayaking by. With no front fence and no formal entry, the street-facing facade functions primarily as a promenade to the water; visitors travel up the boardwalk, through the breezeway, and into the courtyard with the water in view all along the way, to arrive at the heart of the house.

On the exterior, a cohesive palette of horizontal cedar siding is stained gray to match the coast's signature fog. The garage, which functions as Dan's workshop, and a bunk room front the street. A cantilevered roof suspended above the breezeway adds sculptural interest, and a collection of six small windows turns the front facade into a work of art.

When asked about the home's transparency from the street, owner Dan Lockwood responds with a question of his own: "We moved here for the community—why would we want to build a wall out front?"

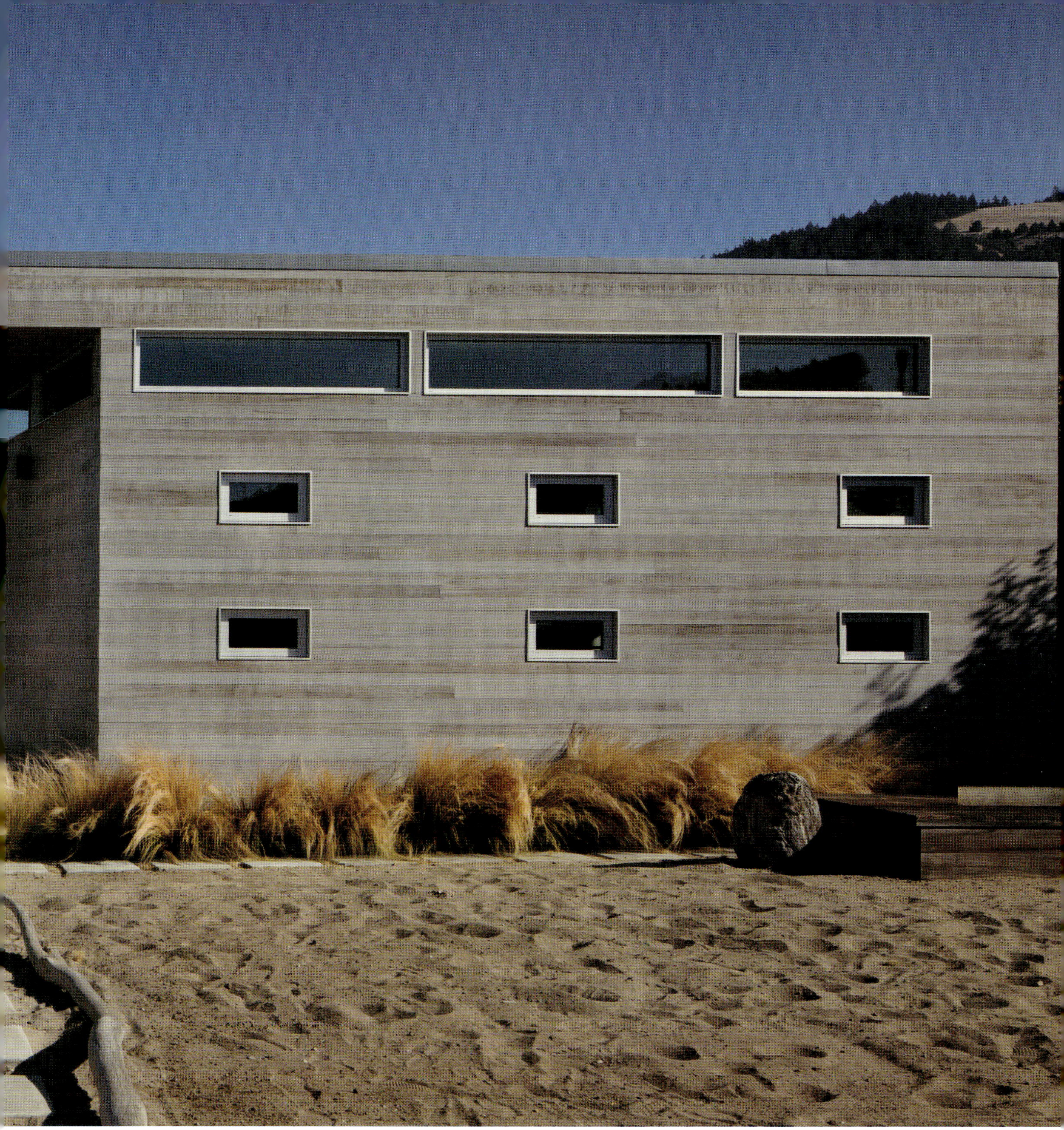

Dan and Caitlin were collaborative, design-oriented, and clear about what they liked and didn't like. "They knew exactly how they wanted to live in the house, and we helped make that life happen for them," says Smith. The house they created together is designed with its arms wide open, just like its owners, who have been known to host beer pong parties in the courtyard.

The great room is completely transparent, with kitchen, dining, and living spaces flowing one into the other. The living area, framed by glass on three sides, overlooks the lagoon and gives the sense of floating above the water. There is ample storage below for boats and gear, and surfboards are tucked away in a closet set unnoticeably into the siding along the side of the house.

The family wanted to pack a lot into a small footprint, so the compact design includes everything they need and nothing they don't. In a nod to nautical design, nearly everything is built in. The open kitchen is lined in sinker cypress, its waterfall island surrounded by generous clearance to accommodate a crowd. The bunk room sleeps six, and a "teen lair" just off the kitchen can be easily closed off with pocket doors. Honed concrete floors fitted with radiant heating are nearly bulletproof. The whole interior is light, bright, and filled with pops of color, forming a playful contrast to the neutral background of lagoon and hills.

On the lagoon-facing facade, the house turns its back to the prevailing winds, embracing the views of the lagoon in the foreground and Bolinas Ridge in the near distance. A tiered terrace steps down to the waterline, incorporating multiple seating arrangements, a firepit, and a hot tub placed just steps from the house.

As often happens on the best projects, Smith and his clients remain close friends and continue to work together as they tweak and tune. "These guys are fun," he says. "It is really a house designed for a party."

In the dining room, classic chairs in multiple hues set on a graphic black-and-white carpet pull up to a much-used custom dining table by Bay Area artist Evan Shively.

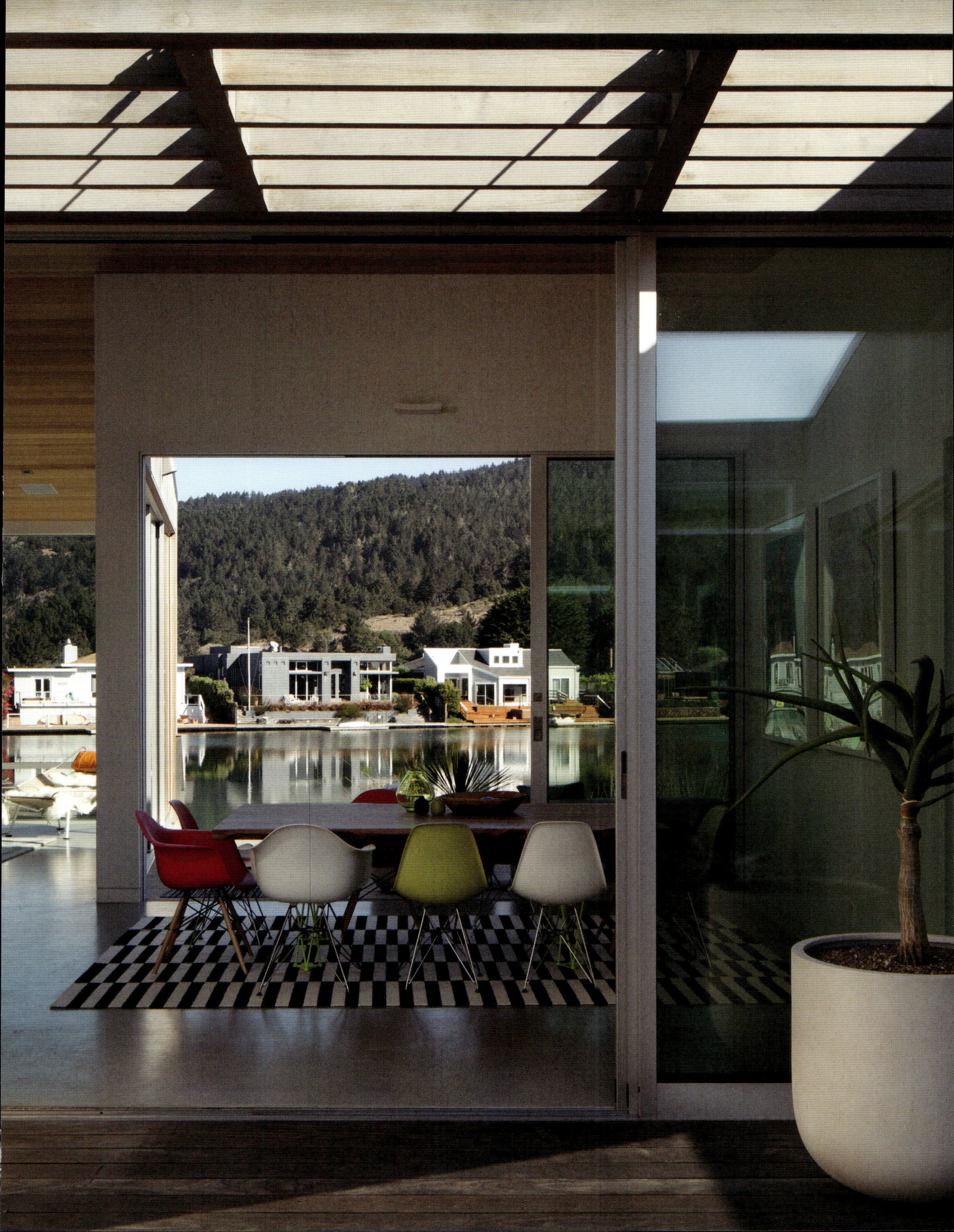

In the kitchen, the clean lines of the sinker cypress cabinets are adorned with minimal hardware. Under-cabinet windows pull in light from the side yard, and a 45-inch pathway around the generous central island is designed for a party.

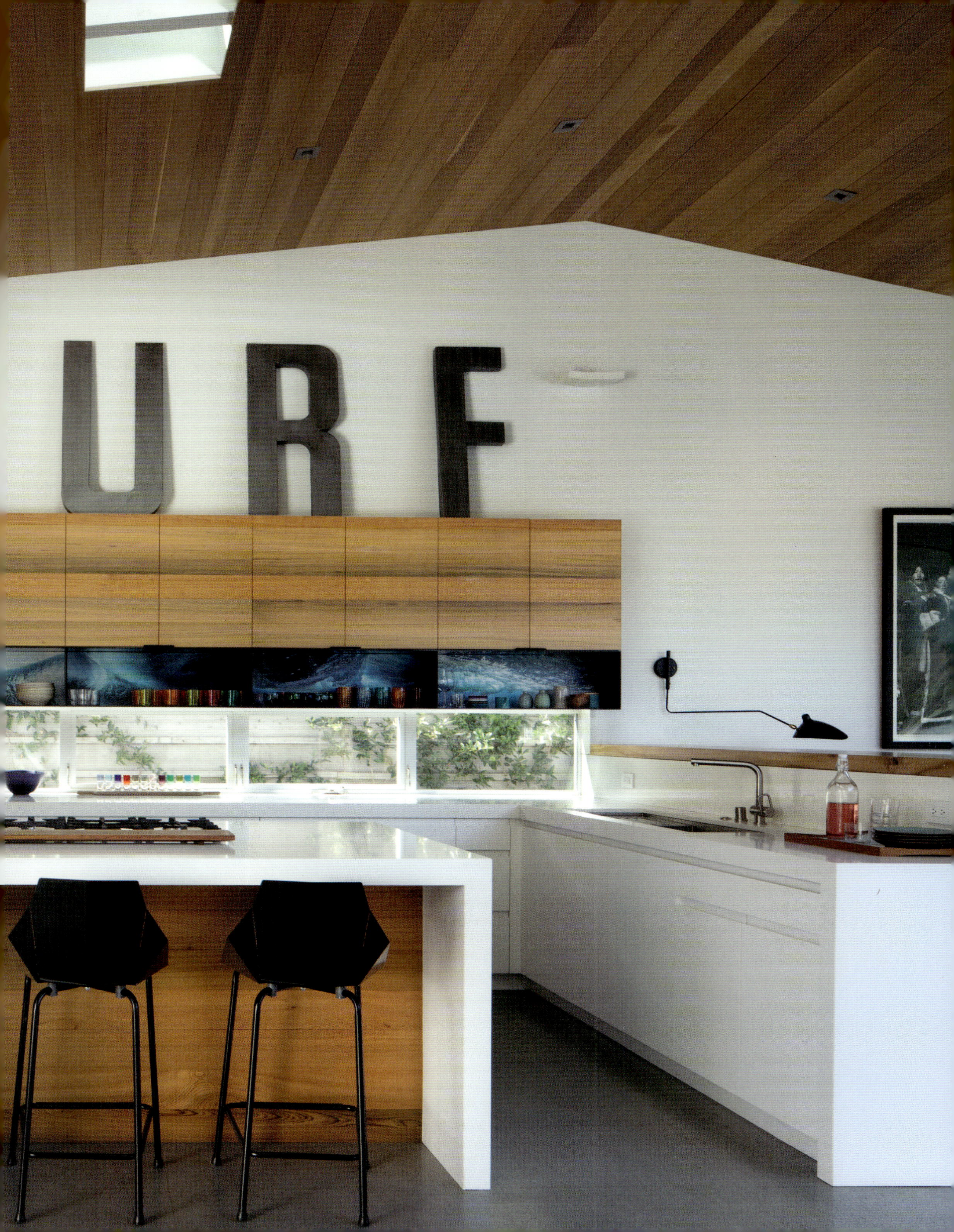
URF

ABOVE + OPPOSITE: The primary bedroom is simply furnished, with a free-standing headboard serving as a room divider and sink wall for the adjacent bath.

OVERLEAF: The small living room provides a perfect spot to watch the boaters and wildlife that enliven the lagoon. The hanging fireplace is by Fireorb.

PAGES 52-53: The lagoon-facing terraces are designed to fit together in a single, integrated space, expertly constructed by contractor Jim Allen.

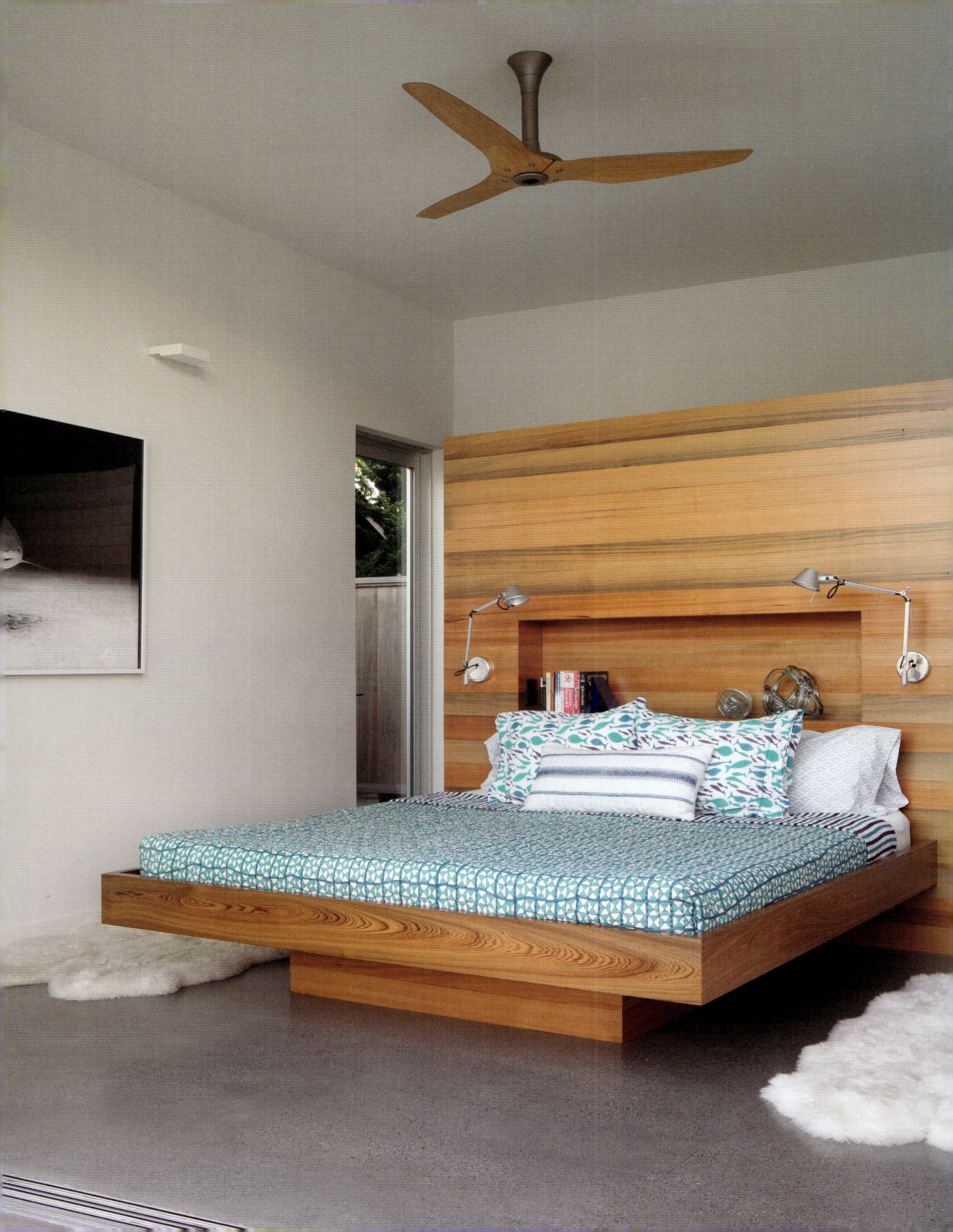

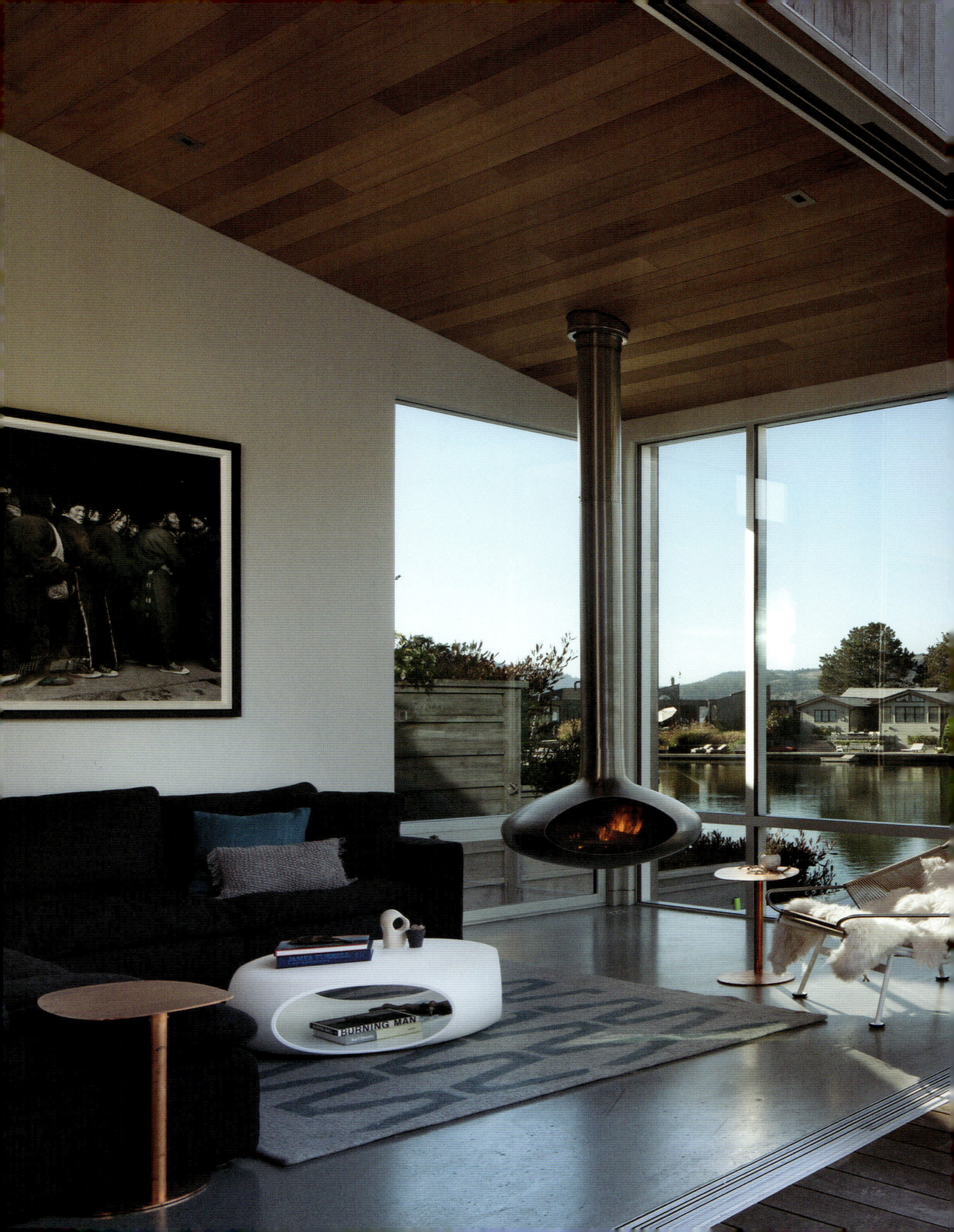
BURNING MAN

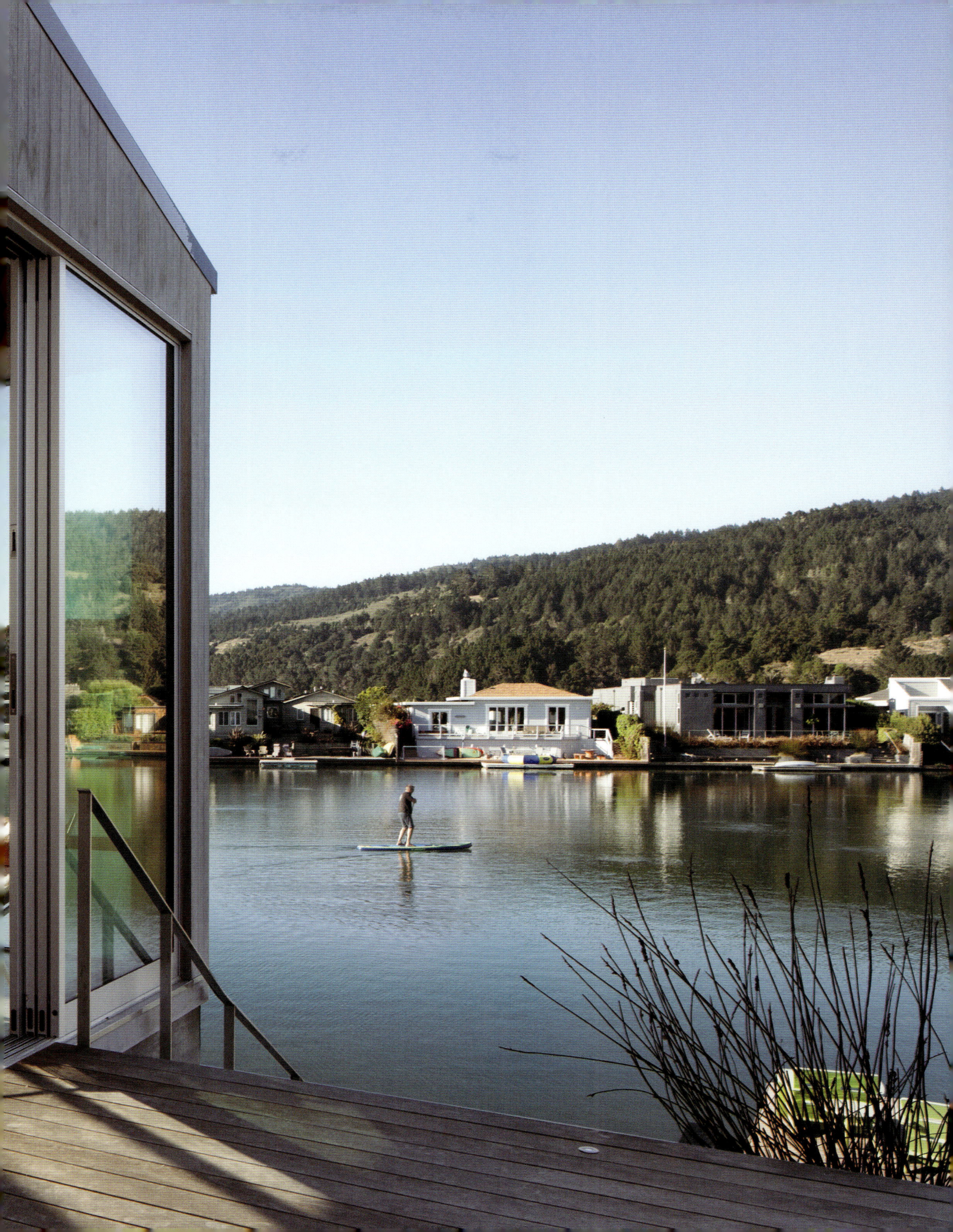

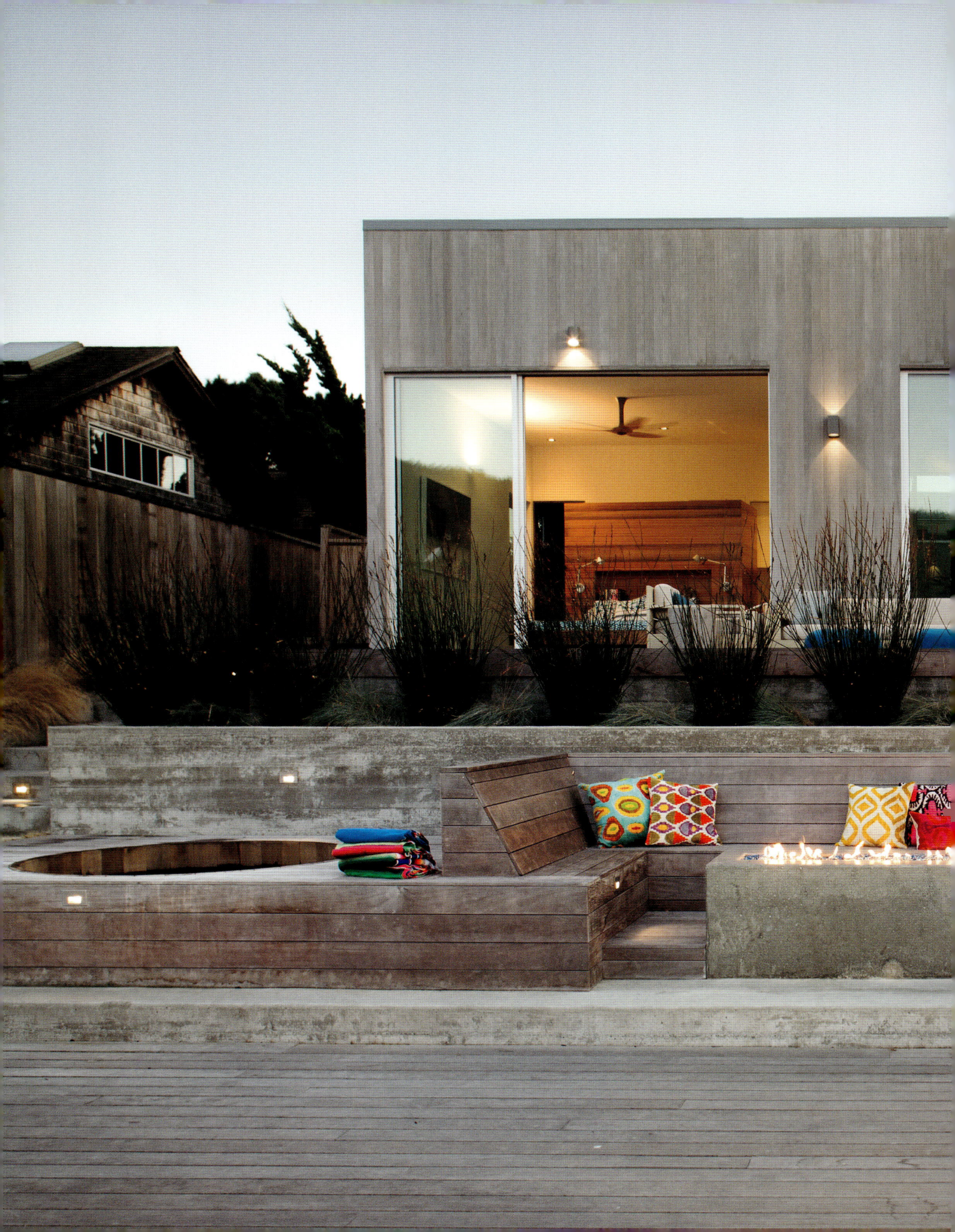

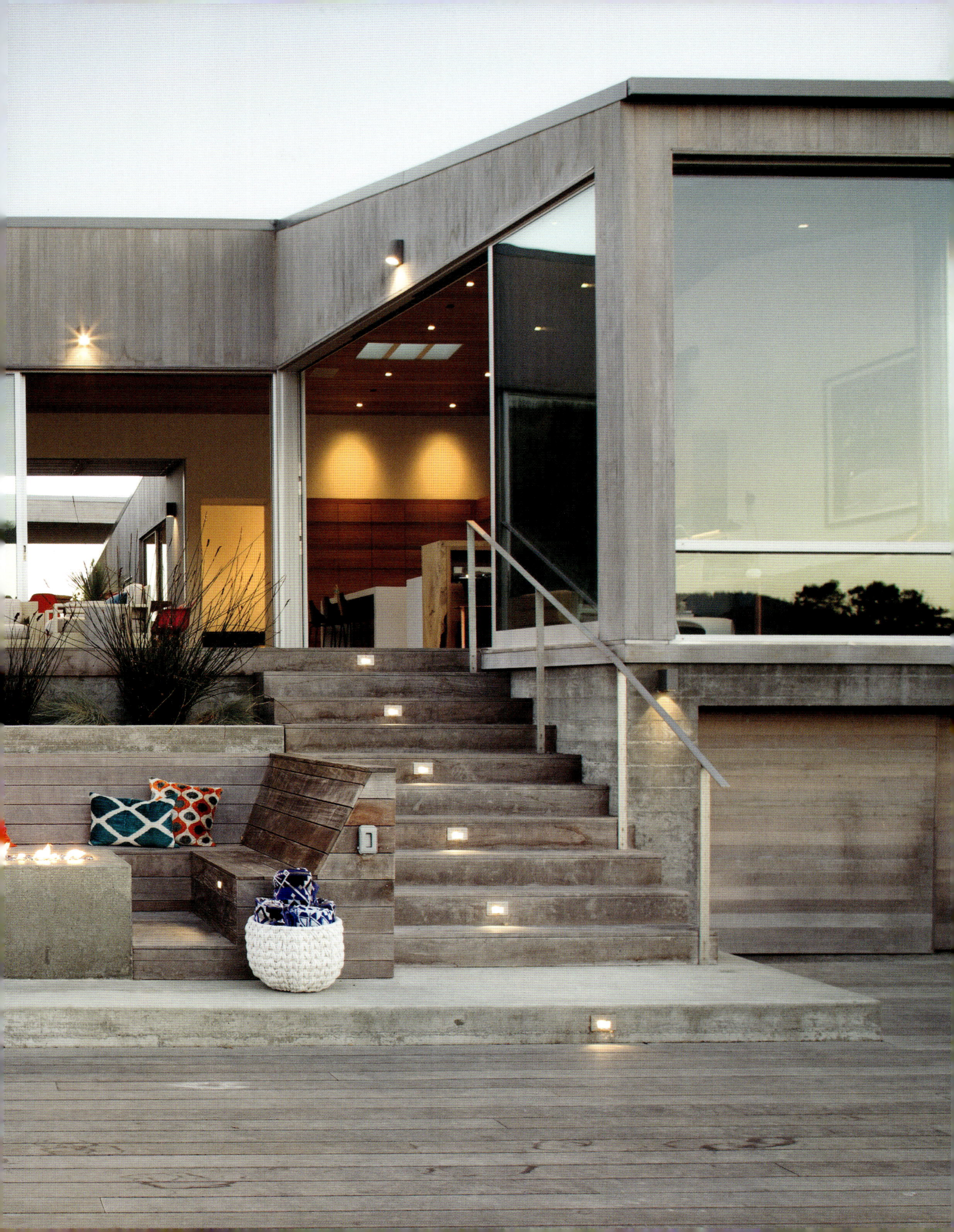

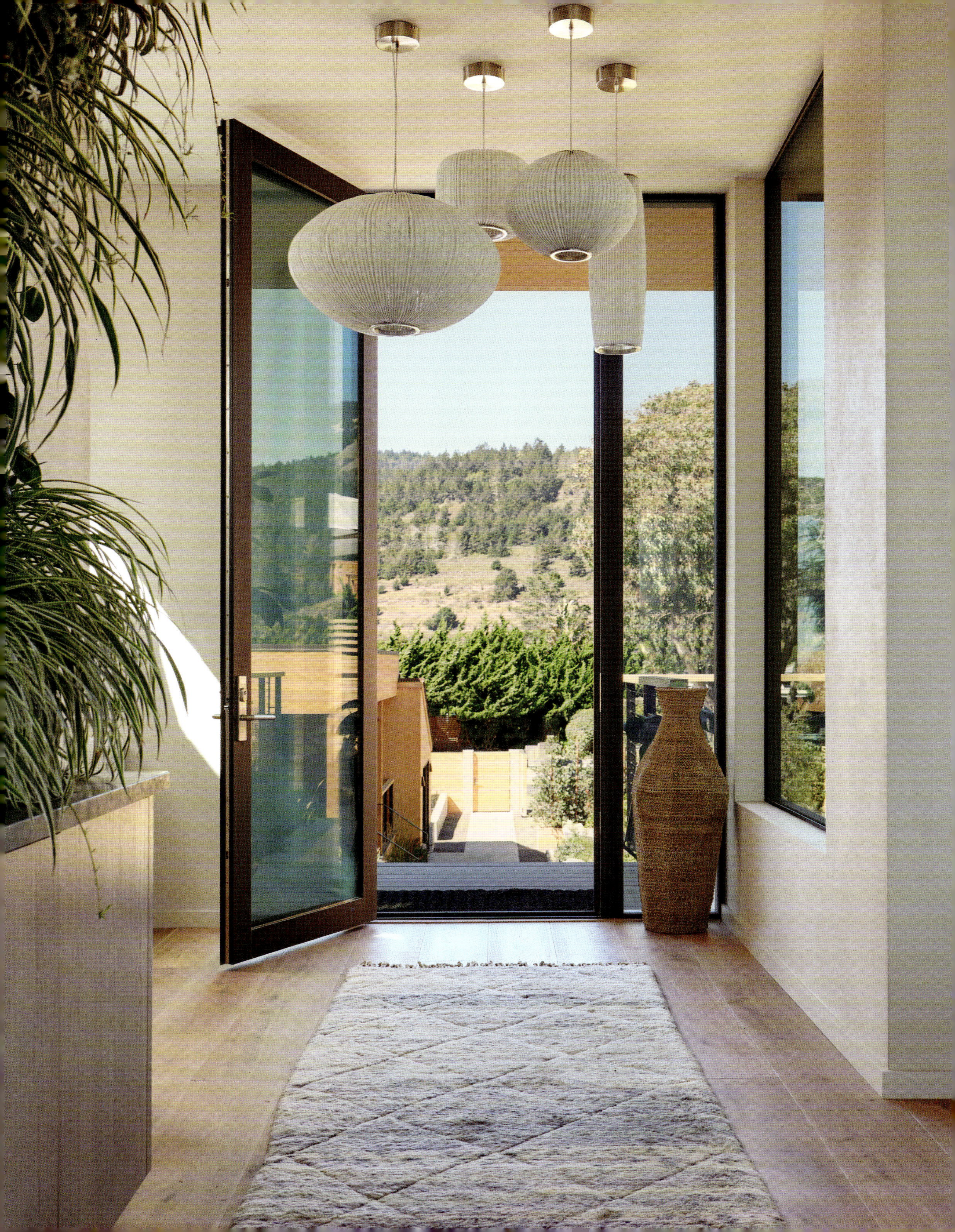

ZEN AT THE BEACH

/ STINSON BEACH /

This is a story of blessings. A story of a cohesive, collaborative team filled with joy; a project designed with a deep sense of intention; a place with connection to natural beauty; and a house wired for indoor–outdoor flow.

Interior and landscape designer Susan Skornicka met her client for this home nearly two decades ago at a yoga retreat in India. The two connected immediately, and over the years they have collaborated on a number of projects.

From their primary home not far away, the family had often ventured over the hill to nearby Stinson Beach, renting a series of houses over the years and forming a deep attachment to the coast. In 2014, the couple purchased an oceanfront bungalow—one of the original homes in this part of Stinson Beach. Though the original layout informed how they live in their present house, it had no sense of flow and little connection to the beauty of its surroundings. When it became clear that they would need to build anew, the couple turned to Susan, who assembled a local team with deep connections to this beachfront community: her daughters and design assistants Lily and Maia, architect Michael Mitchell, and contractor Peter Gubbins, who grew up in this coastal community and owns a surf shop in town with his wife. They embarked on a journey that included a three-year permitting process, working together with a sense of equanimity and shared purpose.

Tucked on a narrow strip of land between the beach and adjacent lagoon, the lot is long and narrow, graced with views in every direction that encompass Stinson Beach and the Pacific Ocean, Bolinas Ridge, and Mount Tamalpais State Park. To meet coastal regulations, the house is elevated, enhancing the views and creating a protected valley between the entry gate and the house, framed by a two-bedroom guesthouse on one side and a line of trees on the other.

"Part of the rhythm in the garden is the row of olive trees, which stand like sentinels watching over us," says the owner.

Along the journey from the entry gate to the front door, visitors feel their blood pressure drop, drawn through the garden toward the view of the beach visible through the glass-paned front door. Warm and inviting, the courtyard garden is a treat for the senses. Plantings were chosen to attract bees, butterflies, and hummingbirds; a seating area holds the owners' beloved Balinese Buddha from a local gallery; and a bird bath encourages birds to dip and splash.

Uniformly clad in Alaskan yellow cedar, which will mellow to a soft gray over time, the house and guesthouse frame the garden. Crossing the threshold elicits the distinct impression that this is a sanctuary—a sacred space. Windows and doors reach to the ceiling and usher in a luminous sense of

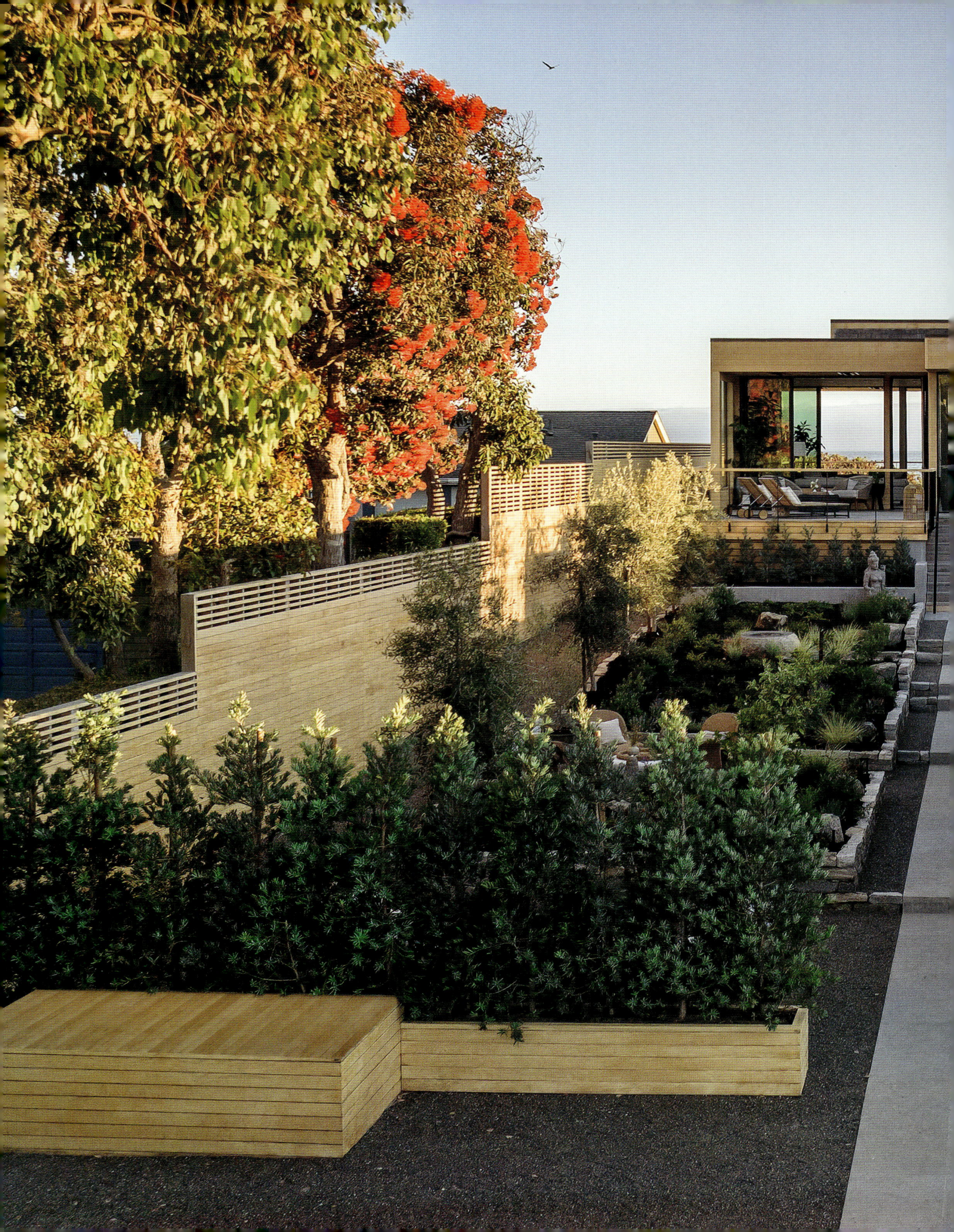

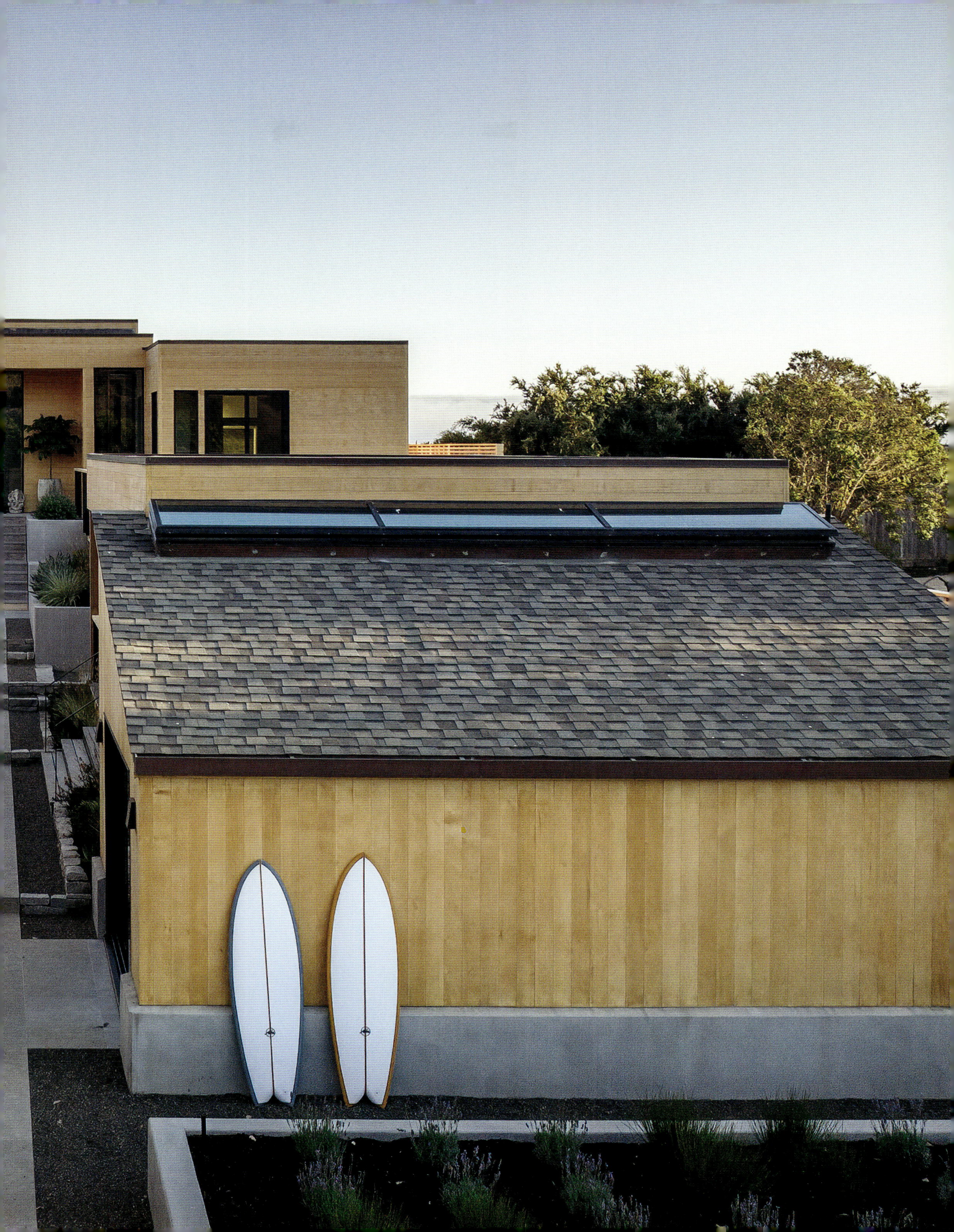

light, west-facing windows are filled to the brim with ocean views, and a living wall seems to purify the very air. Somehow, the house seems completely transparent and connected to its surroundings while enveloping its occupants like a cocoon.

Soft and inviting, the interior palette takes its cues from nature. Rift white oak paneling in every room forms a cohesive palette. Limestone and plaster reflect the tones of sand and stone, and hints of gray-blue reference the ocean. A single piece of teak (found at the Malibu Design Center) formed the kitchen island, dining room table, and fireplace mantel.

The light-filled central space is the heart of the house, with living, dining, and kitchen flowing together effortlessly. The living room is a cozy space built around the central fireplace and a sofa placed to capture the view. The kitchen is light, airy, and open to the ocean, a happy place for friends and family to gather while listening to the sound of the waves. The true hub of the house is the dining table, set against a wall of windows that quite literally opens to the deck and beach. Here is where people tend to gather, soaking up the full impact of the view.

As both a designer and a general contractor, Susan brings to each project an outlook that is equal parts practical and spiritual and, in the process, she forms a bond with clients that feels like family. She pulled in treasured collaborators to help with furnishings and artwork, working hand in hand with her friend Jane Walter to source most of the furnishings from Jane's Summer House design showroom in Mill Valley and with Seager Gray Gallery, also in Mill Valley, to place the work of local artists throughout the home. Nearly all the home's paneling and custom cabinetry was carefully crafted by Mitchel Berman Cabinetmakers.

In a key early decision, the team had decided to pull the house back twenty feet from the beachfront property line, allowing the house to be nestled lower on the site. Where the house could have been, a deck provides a viewing platform and forms a natural connection between house and beachfront. A wooden walkway carefully cuts through the naturally occurring ice plant, connecting the owners to the beach they love.

The owners' continuing sense of wonder is palpable. "It's such a thrill to live amongst it all—the tides, the birds, the plants, the stars. We feel gratitude and a sense of grace."

PRECEDING PAGE: Throughout the journey through the courtyard garden, nestled between the house and guesthouse, a sense of serenity reigns.

OPPOSITE: Situated between two decks and lightly enclosed by walls of windows, the living spaces are defined by the sounds, scents, and breezes that flow uninterrupted from the ocean through the house to the interior garden.

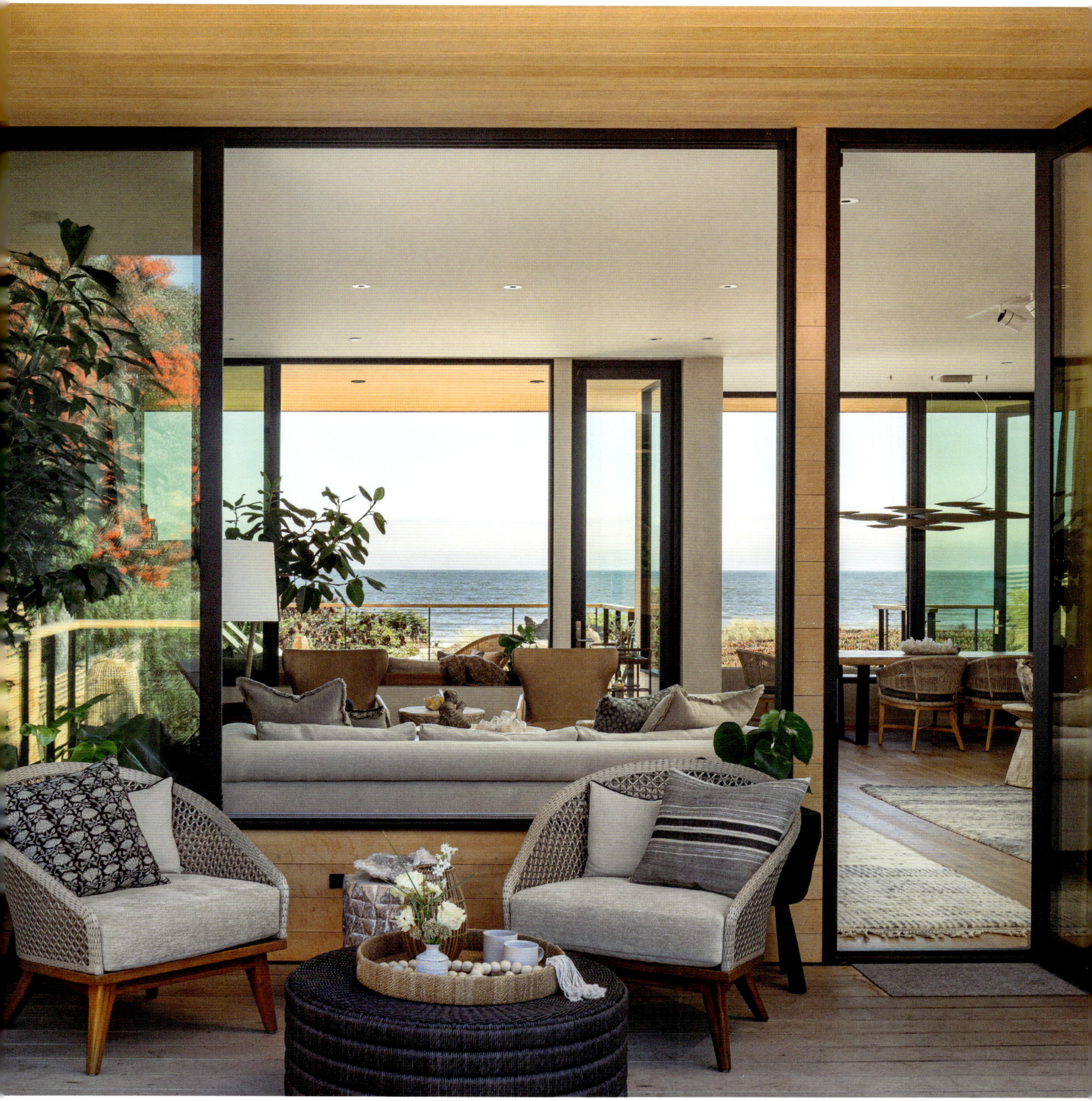

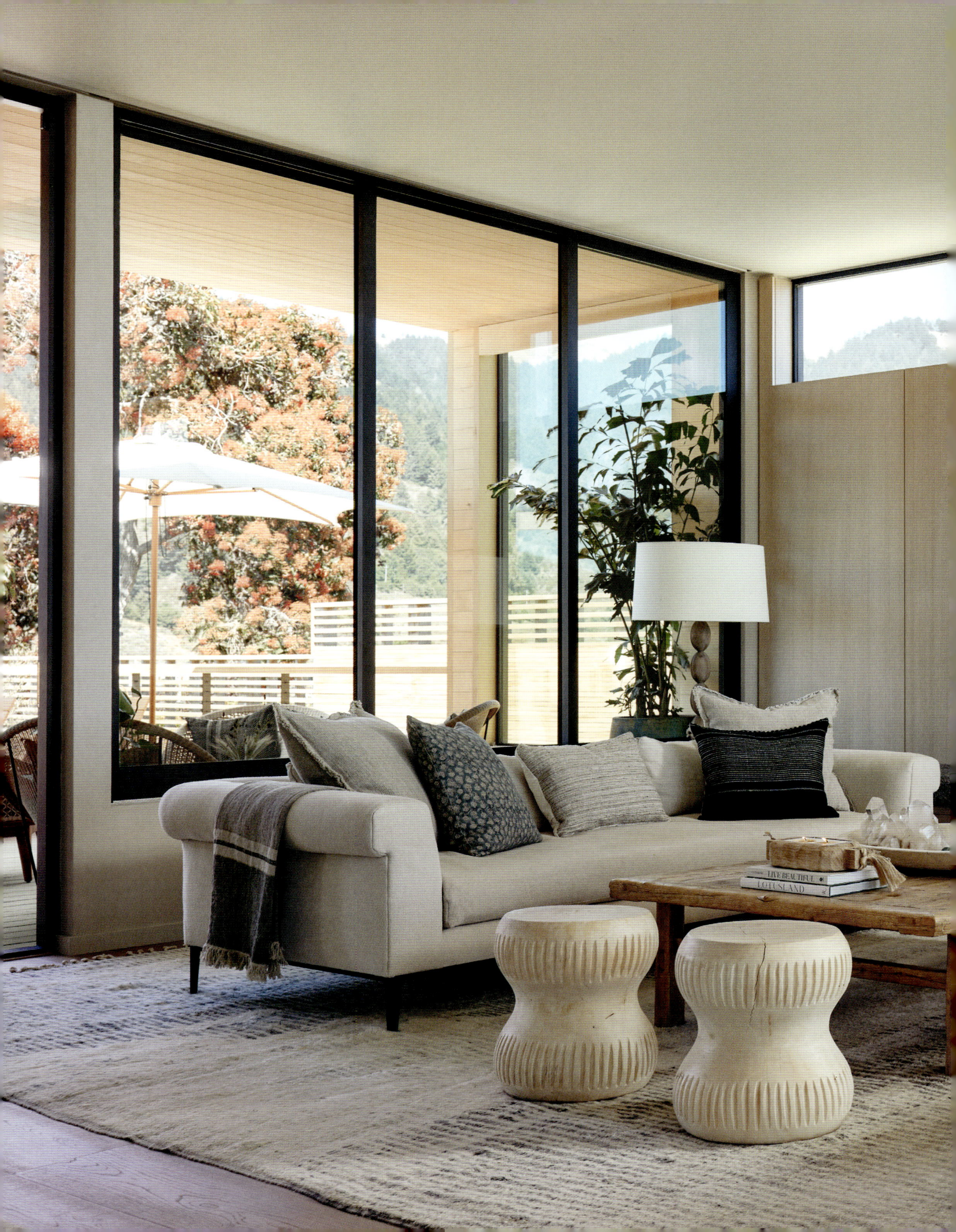
LIVE BEAUTIFUL
LOTUSLAND

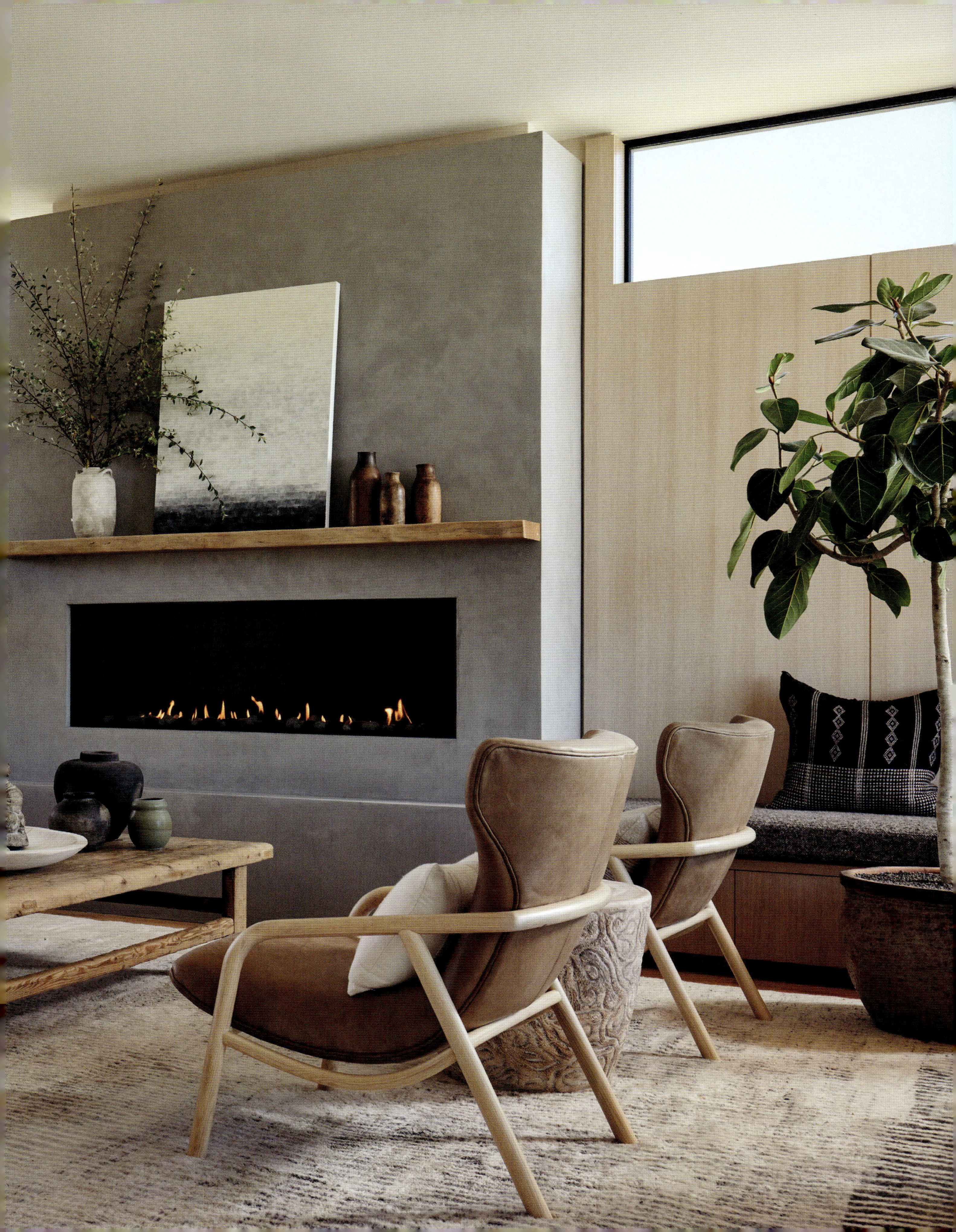

PRECEDING PAGE: The living room was designed around the sofa, set to capture the very best of the view and reinforce the sense of ease. Faced in EcoStucco, the fireplace is flanked by cozy window seats topped by high windows that add to the room's abundant natural light. Artwork by local artist Pegan Brooke site on the mantel. Furnishings and rugs were sourced through Summerhouse in Mill Valley.

ABOVE: White oak kitchen cabinets crafted by Mitchel Berman Cabinetmakers are topped with Fontainebleau limestone and accented with a teak dining counter. White Moroccan Zellige tiles from Ann Sacks reflect the sunlight, and round pendants from Uniqwa Collections are handwoven from banana fibers.

OPPOSITE: Many of the design elements—particularly the light fixtures chosen in collaboration with lighting designer Anna Kondolf—reference the sea in a way that is subtle and abstract. The pendant over the dining table is reminiscent of a school of fish, while fixtures in the entry loosely resemble sea urchins.

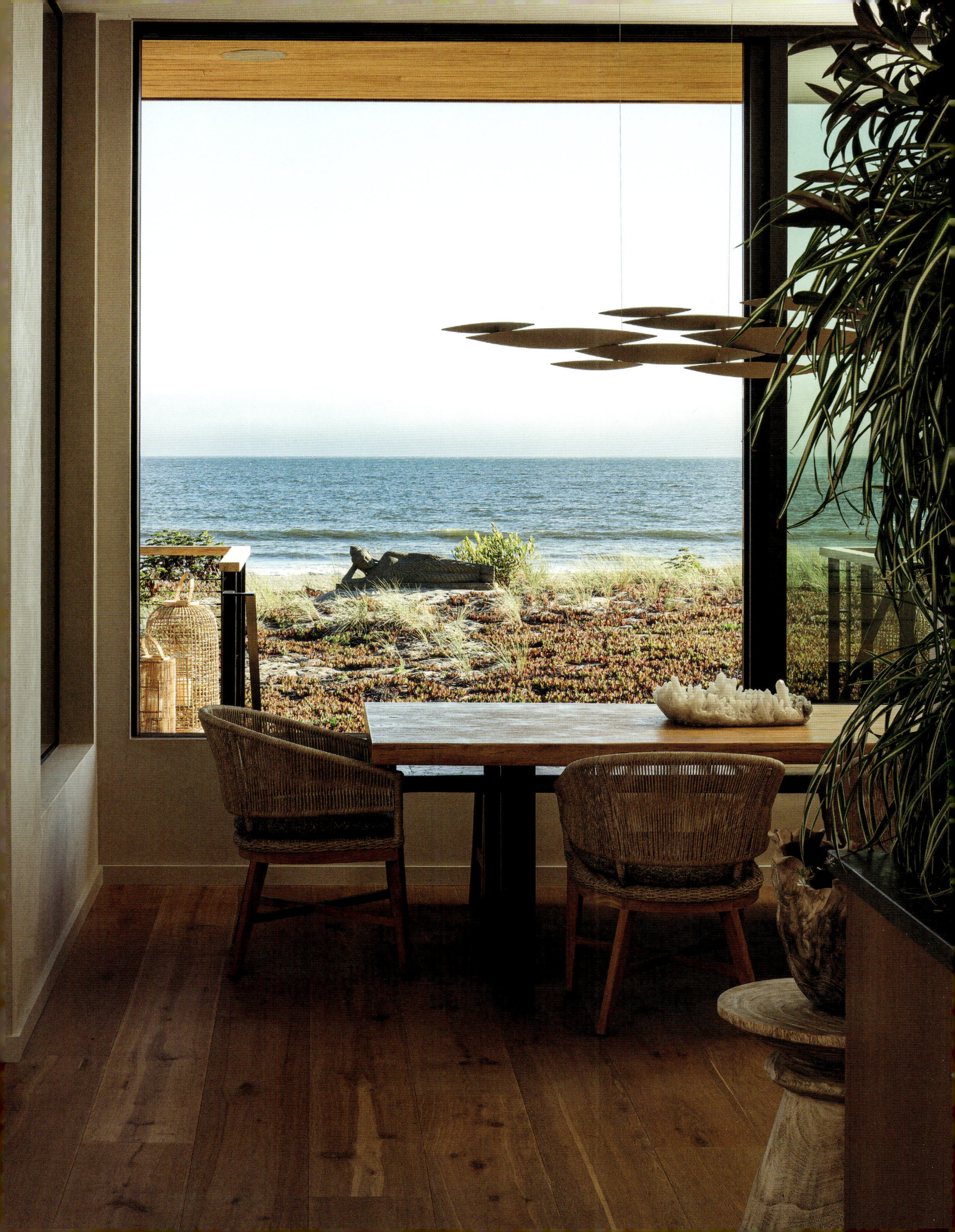

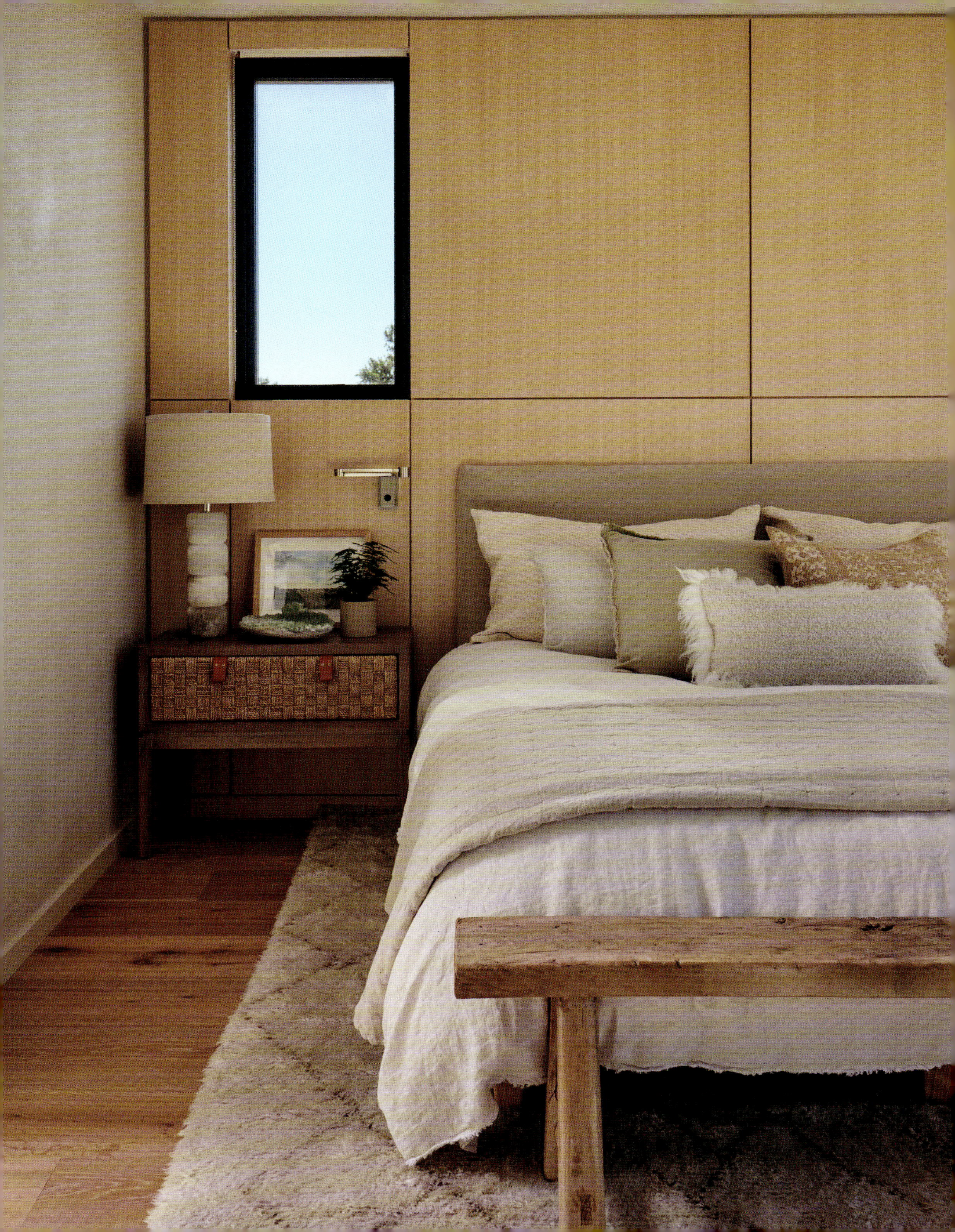

OPPOSITE: Custom panels of rift white oak line an accent wall in the primary bedroom.

ABOVE: A window seat beside the primary bedroom's fireplace is the perfect spot to curl up and relax. Fabric and the pillows are from SummerHouse. Artwork by Marin-based artist Plamen Tanev dresses the mantel.

OVERLEAF: "We became like a family," says the owner about the team that worked together to create her home at the beach. "We still get together and celebrate here."

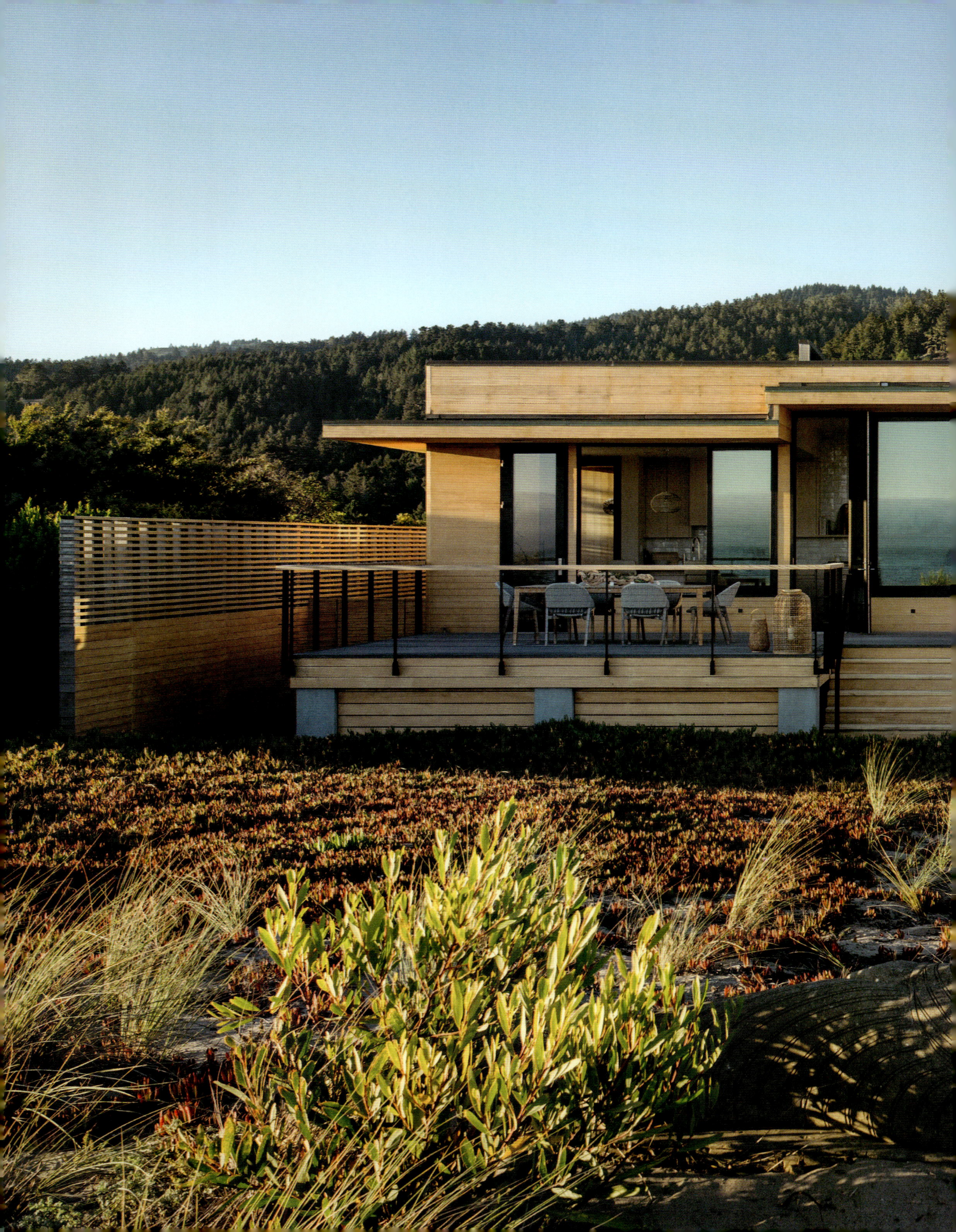

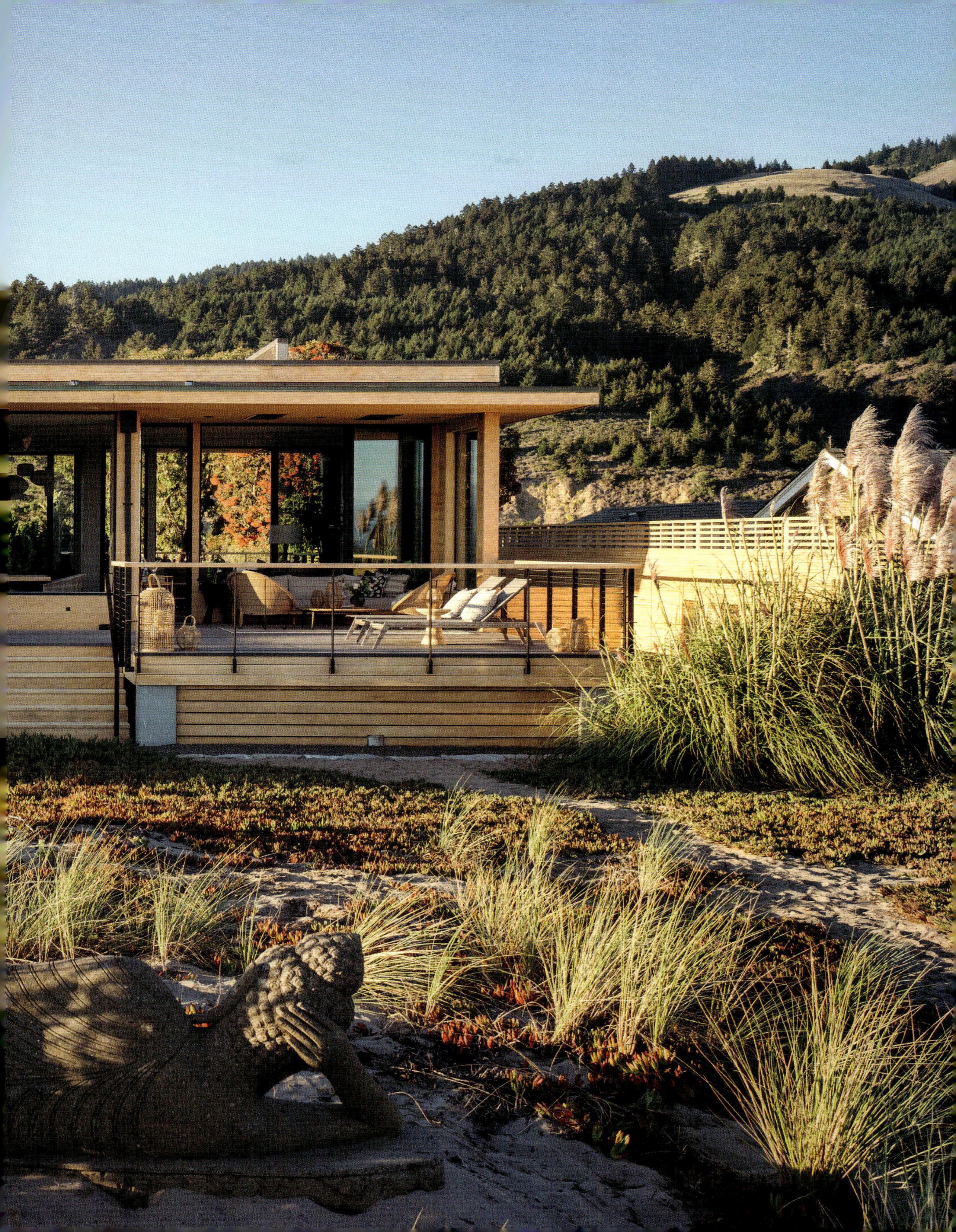

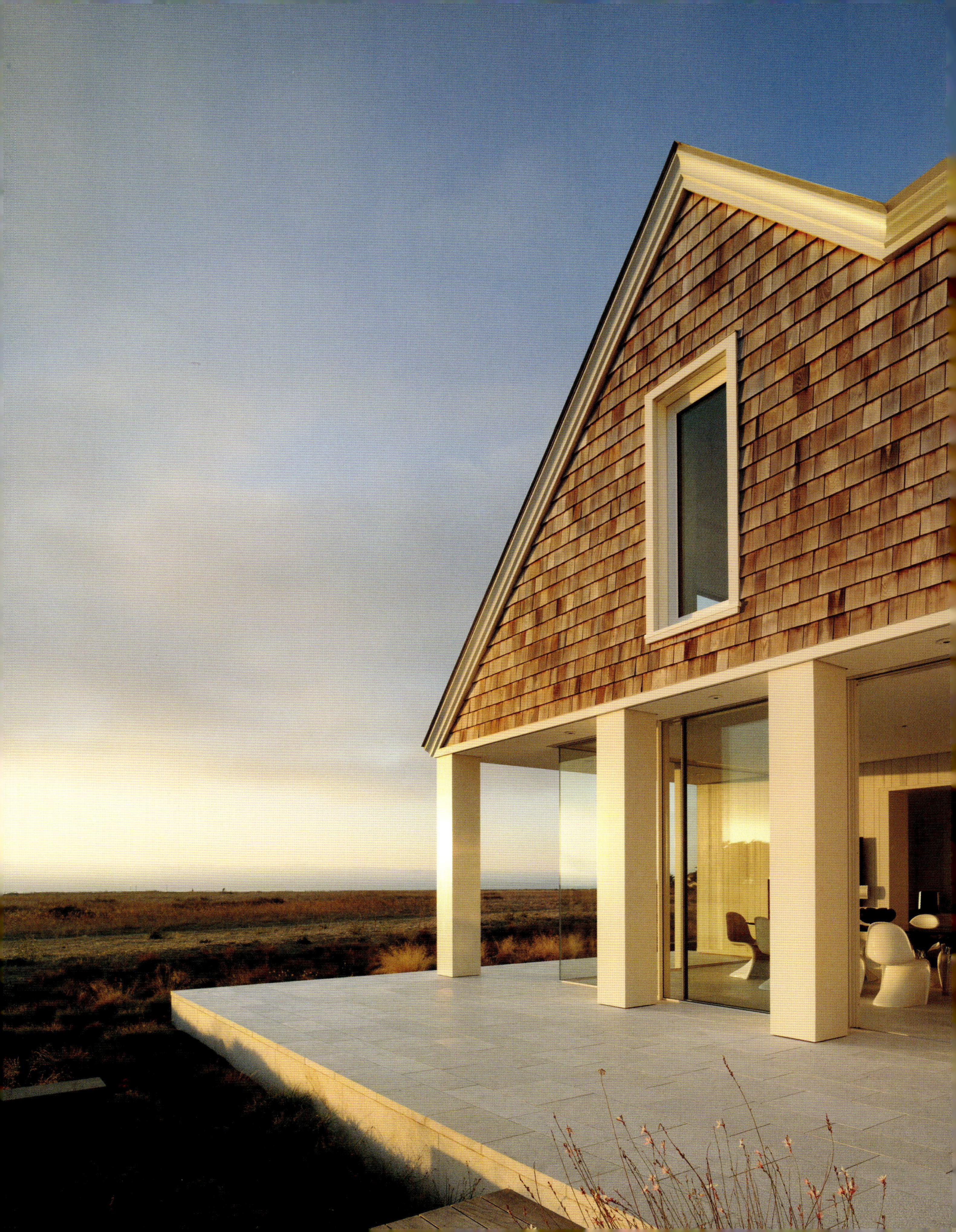

EAST MEETS WEST

/ SOUTHERN BAY AREA /

Equal parts East Coast traditional and West Coast cool, this unique coastal home is an expression of two very individual personalities and design perspectives seamlessly blended as one.

He is a modernist with a traditional spirit. She is a traditionalist who loves texture and craft. Both natives of Massachusetts, they came to California together and made it their home. She had always loved the thought of living near the ocean, so they settled on the coast south of San Francisco and raised their children there. With their sons now adults, they decided to pursue their dream of a cottage by the sea—a home they would envision purely for themselves—and ended up buying a house just down the road.

Though their design viewpoints differed, each had great respect for the vision and taste of the other. They tapped architects Walker Warner, well known for their deft approach to residential design, and interior designer Kristi Will to help them. "The challenge was threading the needle between two aesthetics that could have been at odds, but weren't, and making the house feel seamless and cohesive, weaving it together with a level of architectural integrity and intention," says Brooks Walker, partner in charge of the project.

For Will, who lives in the area and knows the land and light here well, it was the opportunity of a lifetime. "This project has been one of the most impactful of my career," she says. "I get to live with this beautiful house right in my own backyard."

Set back from the edge of the bluff, the house has a layered aspect as the view of the meadow gives way to the view of the ocean. The fog here is often a tangible presence, and the sense of light is glorious. The home's traditional gabled forms, reminiscent of the wife's beloved Cape Cod, are clad in hand-sawn sinker cypress shingles sourced from salvaged logs, which will gray out naturally over time.

Balancing the views with necessary privacy from the boardwalk that crosses the open space between the house and the water, the design team recessed the ocean-facing walls of glass behind rows of columns. Vertical fins on the living room windows provide further privacy and segment the view. The L-shaped plan wraps around a private garden framed and protected by the house. "The carefully considered architectural details are not capricious," says Walker. "Each is there for a reason."

Inside, the material palette contributes to the strong sense of indoor–outdoor connection. Floors are covered in white granite with a lightly flamed finish that crosses the thresholds to connect interior and exterior spaces. It closely resembles congealed sand, for a casual, coastal feel and easy

ABOVE + OPPOSITE: A stone backsplash in soothing tones has lines reminiscent of flowing water. The couple had loved this particular stone when they renovated their first home, but it was beyond their reach at the time. When they found a slab of the same stone twenty years later, it was nothing short of miraculous. The custom cabinetry is set high, with shelves that descend and recede to allow more wall space to showcase the stone.

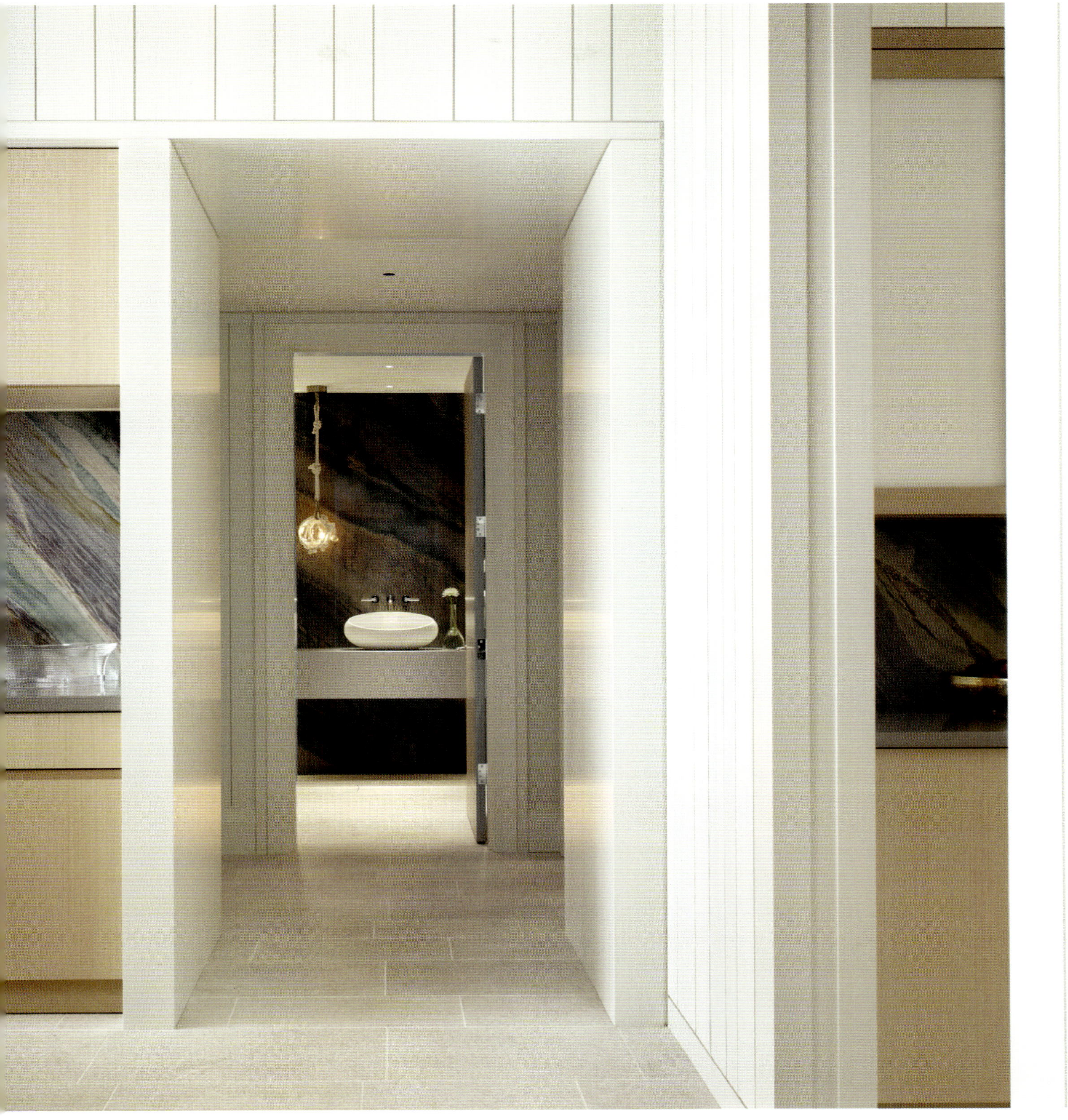

maintenance. Interior walls are covered in a trio of whites, all by Benjamin Moore: Paper White in most of the rooms, Super White in the baths, and Simply White where designer Kristi Will wanted to warm things up a bit.

Like the coastal fog that often surrounds the house, light is a defining feature. Clean and bright, the walls reflect the light differently at various times of day, forming a perfect foil for the ocean views outside the windows and the colorful artwork within. The team worked with art consultant Jackie Becker, who discovered many of the home's pivotal pieces, including the lightbox installation in the living room by Leo Villareal, well known in the Bay Area for his light installation on the San Francisco Bay Bridge. Throughout the house, consultant Anna Kondolf Lighting Design worked with a deft hand. Plaster cove ceilings are subtly impactful, forming a luminous cocoon around those inside.

The interiors lean toward a modern sense of minimalism, while curves, texture, and color keep things warm and inviting; statement pieces are given the opportunity to shine. "They didn't want anything they had seen before," Will says of her clients. "They wanted a home that felt truly unique to them as a couple." She recalls the husband saying at the outset, "I want to open the front door and have my breath taken away."

One of the couple's desires was to have a unique spot where they could host friends for whale watching. In what is probably the home's most dramatic architectural move, the architect, interior designer, lighting designer, and craftsmen worked closely together to design a spiral staircase topped with an operable skylight that leads to a rooftop widow's walk and an upper terrace complete with a firepit and heated benches. To avoid blocking the incoming light from the skylight, the team used low-iron, cast-glass stair treads that stop short of the wall and float. The glass treads, illuminated by LED lights embedded in the central column, are filled with bubbles, and the stairwell walls are coated with blue-gray paint that subtly lightens as it rises. Ascending the staircase is like floating up through the sea, and the moment is magical.

Like so much of the house design, the stairwell was an exercise in teamwork and ingenuity, which created an amazing space and brought the clients' vision to life.

Vertical fins on the living room windows segment the view and provide some privacy from the public boardwalk that crosses the open space between the house and the water. With no visible exterior hardware, the coffee table forms a lovely surprise, popping open to reveal games and a Shinola record player hidden within. A Flexform sofa complements a classic Eames chair from Knoll.

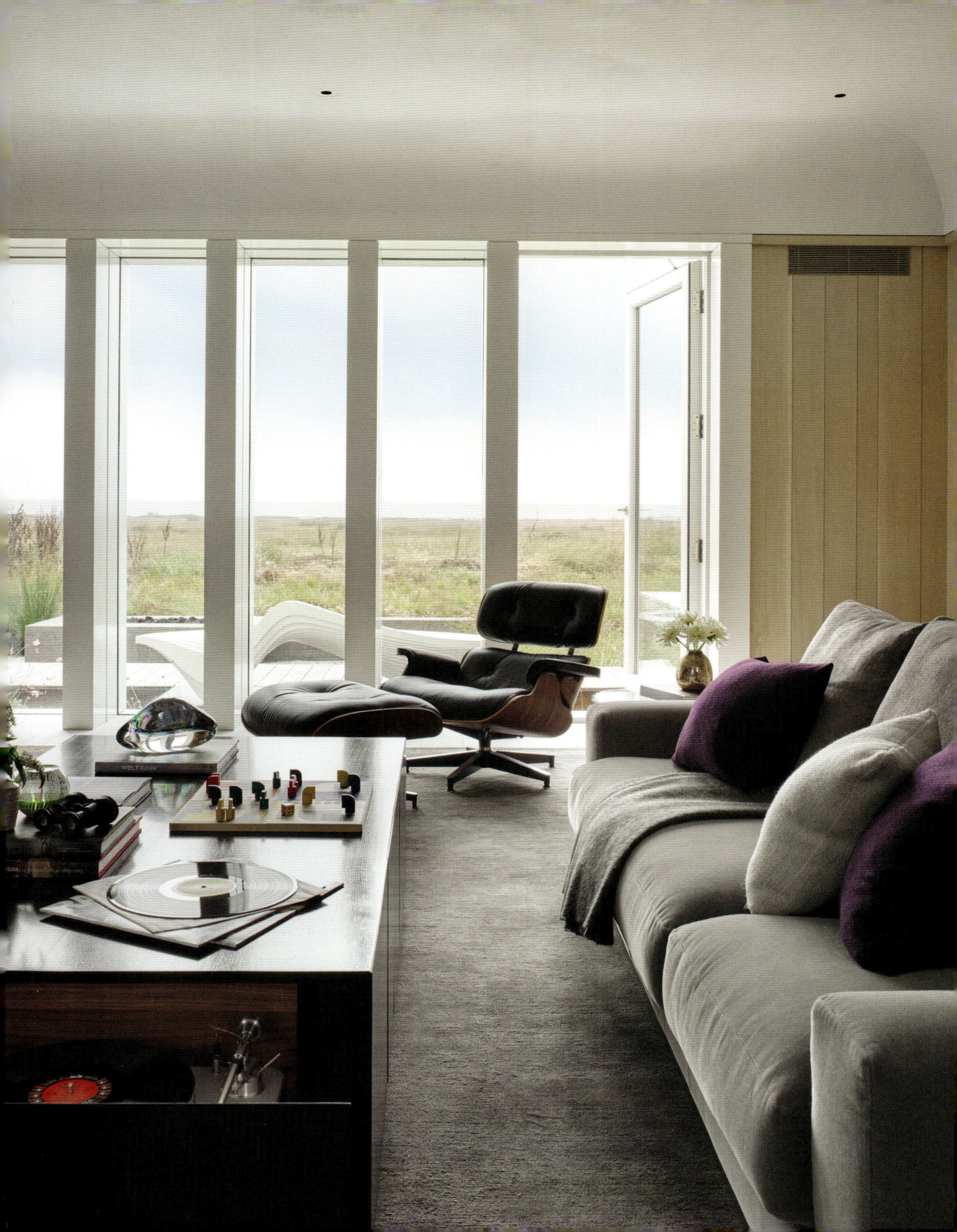

ABOVE: Looking for something that no one had seen before, Will came upon a glacial dining table designed by Zaha Hadid to give the impression of a melting glacier. Custom lighting highlights the hand-crafted, limited-production table.

OPPOSITE: The Rothko-inspired Leo Villareal artwork in the living room projects a never-ending array of colors.

OVERLEAF LEFT: Artwork by J. Prichard Design lines the walls of the light-filled stairwell, enhanced by an intricate Knotty Bubbles chandelier by Lindsey Adelman.

OVERLEAF RIGHT: A backlit slab of Azul is the defining element of the powder room. The Knotty Bubbles pendant fixture is by Lindsey Adelman.

PAGES 78-79: The house is set back from the bluff, creating layered views as the meadow gives way to the bluffs and ocean.

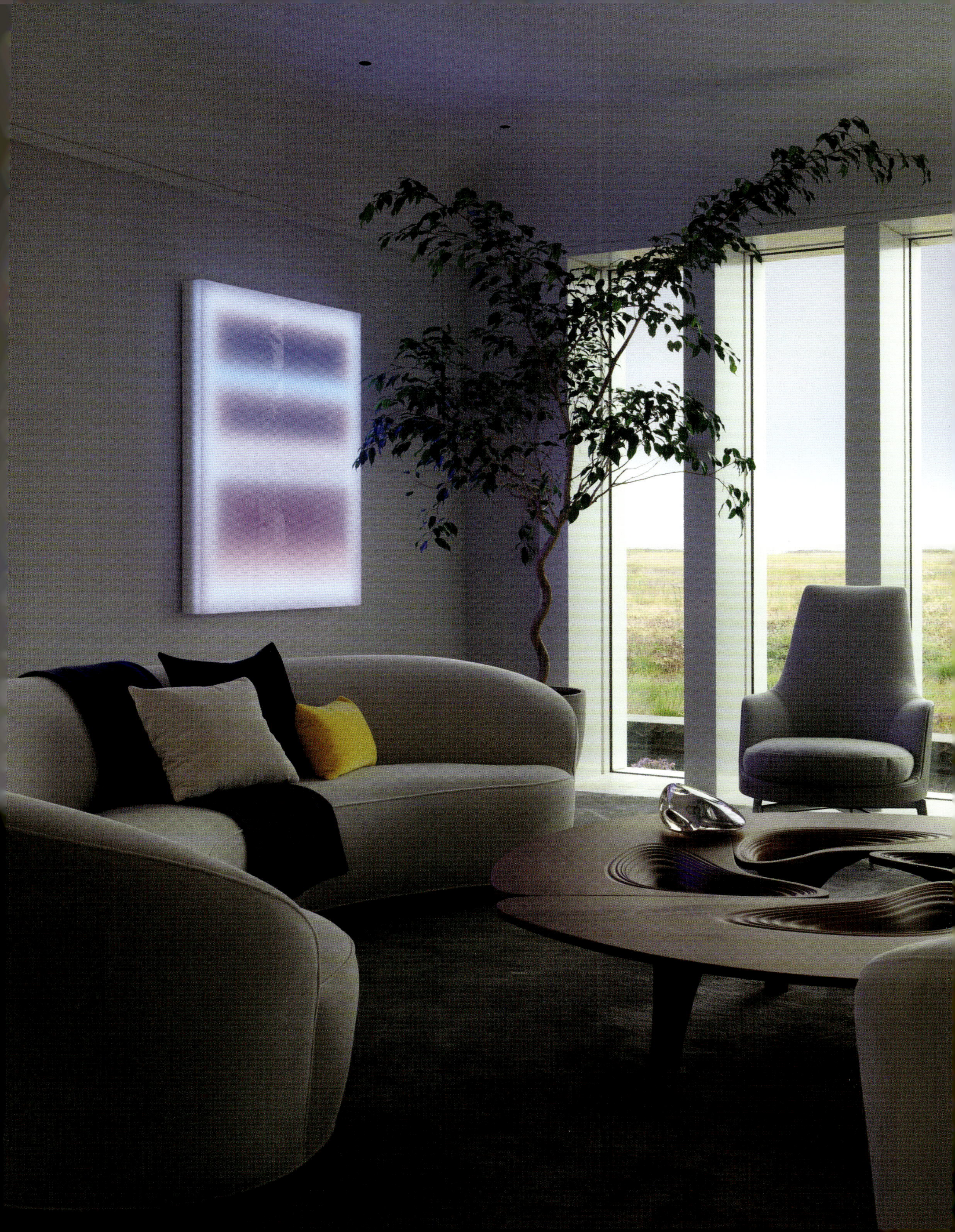

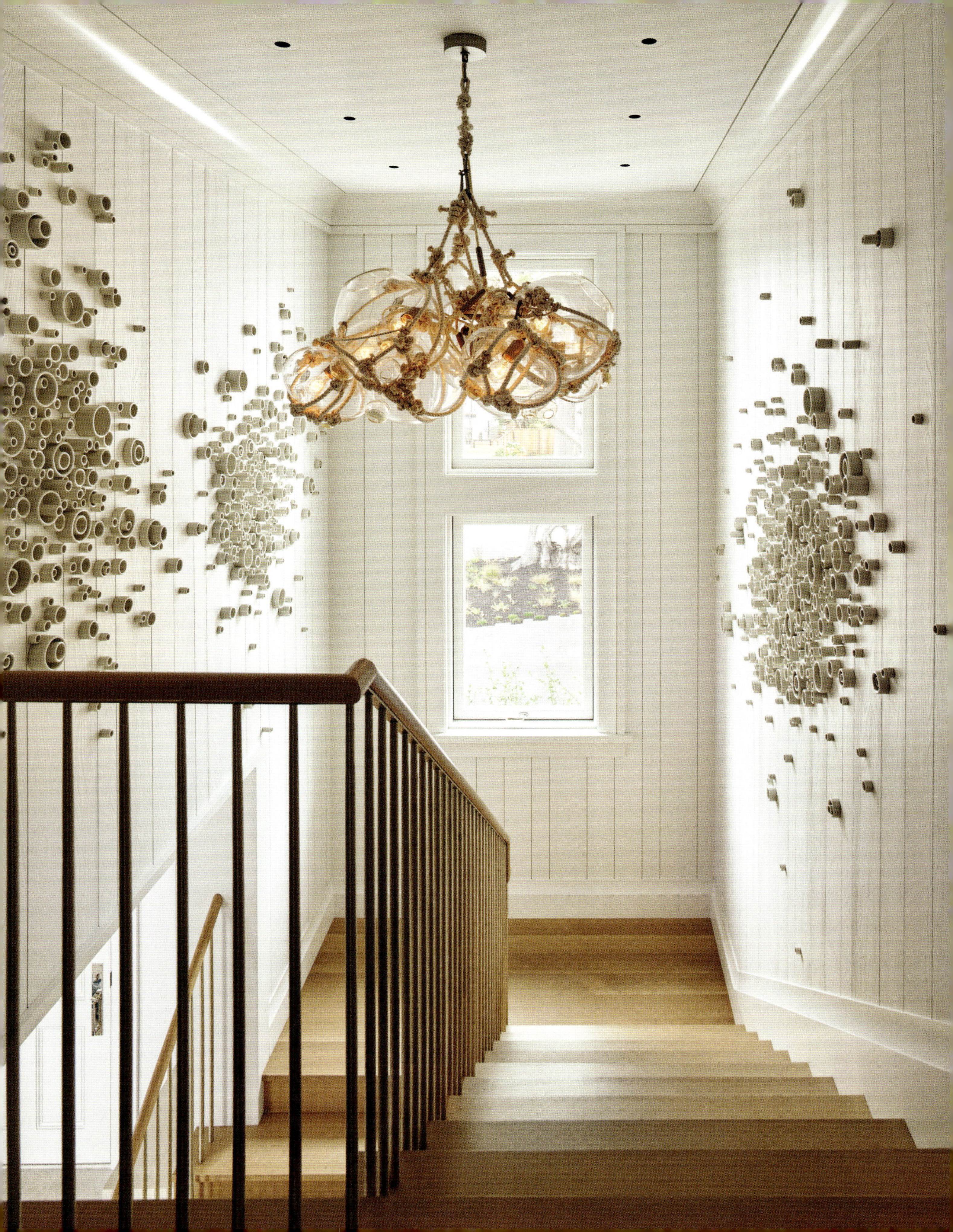

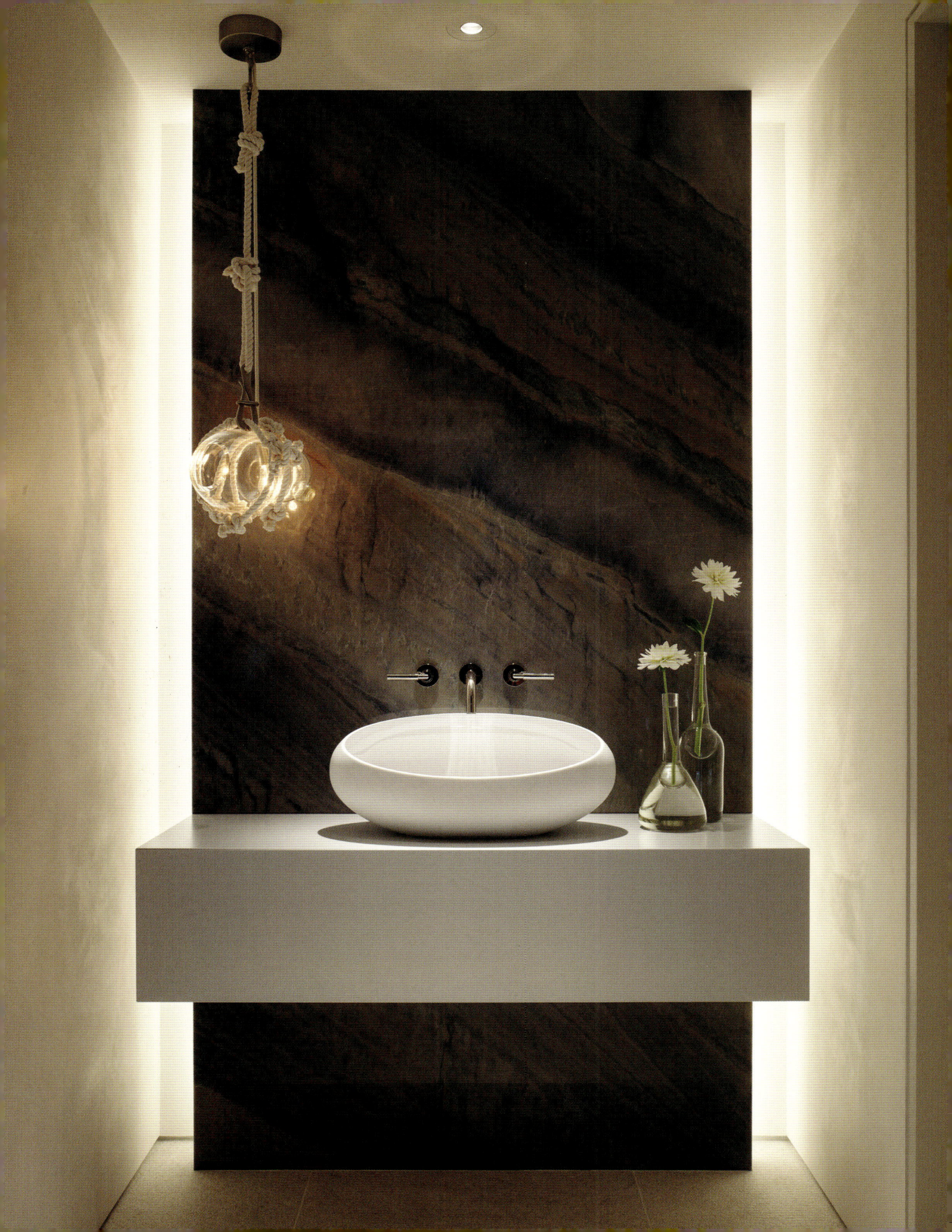

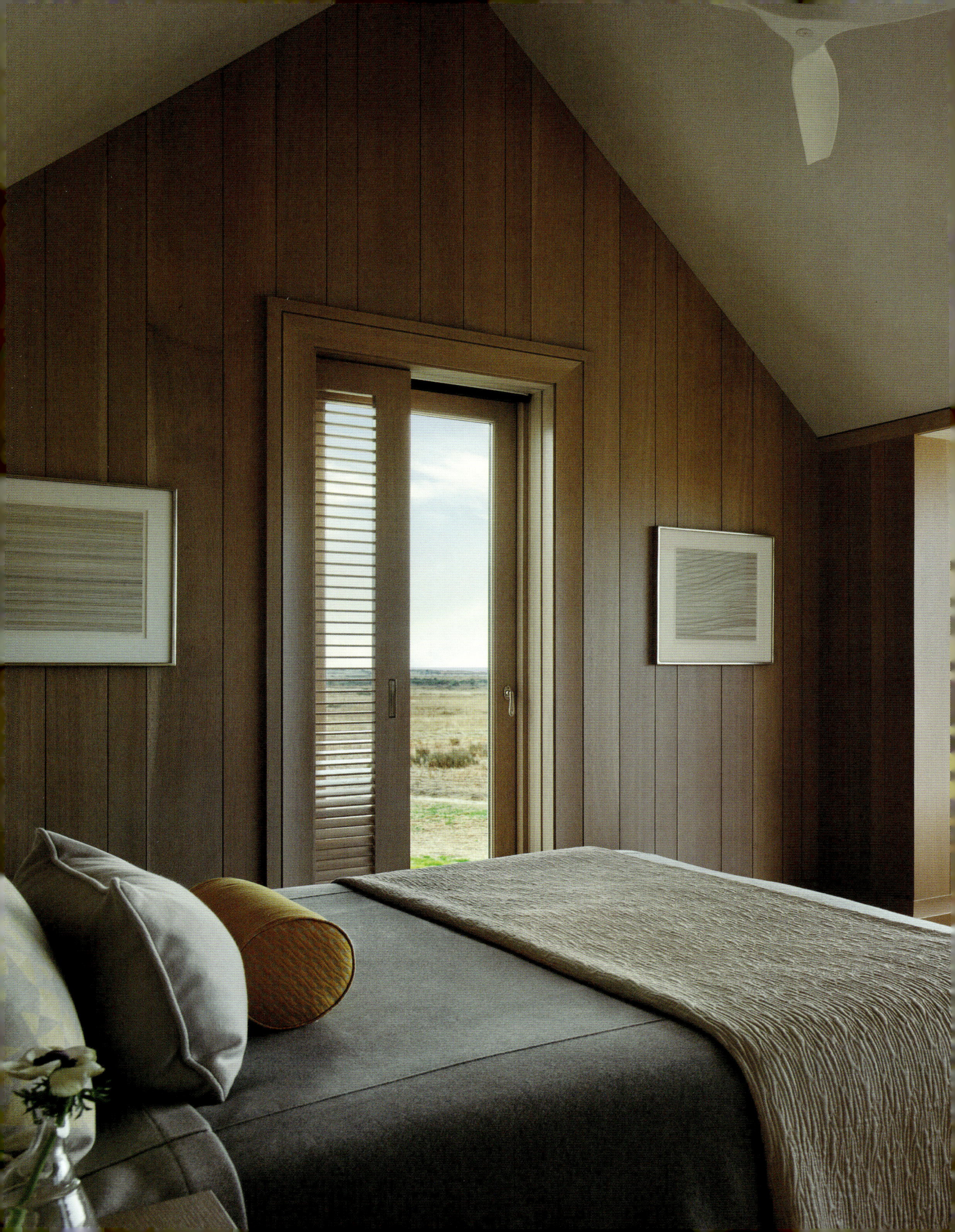

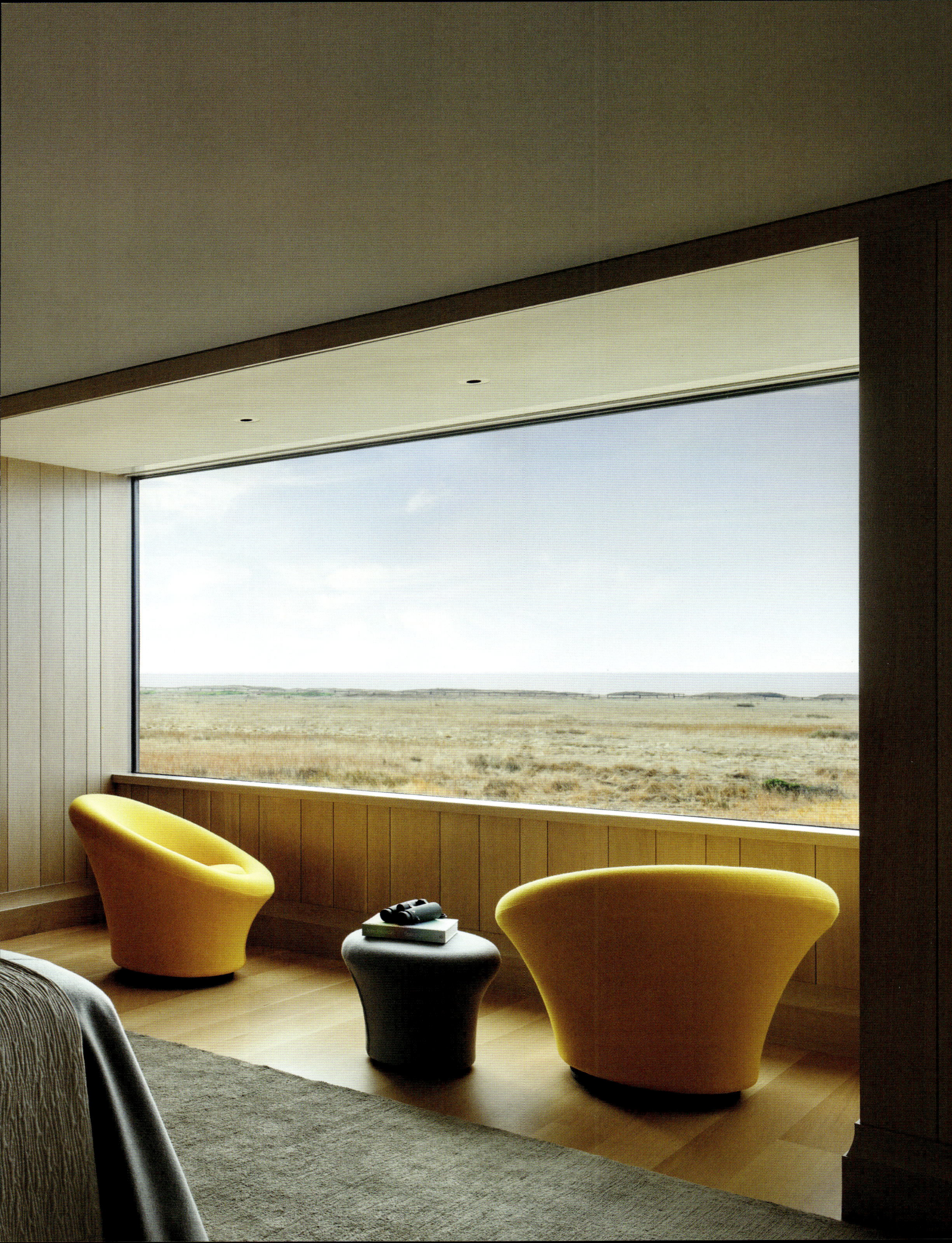

ABOVE: The stairwell to the widow's walk consists of floating cast-glass treads crafted by Bay Area glass artist John Lewis and lit with fiber optic lights embedded in the central spine. The softly graduating color on the walls was created by painter Jamie Stancil. The whole effect is magical.

OPPOSITE: A slim window in the upper-level office frames a slice of the view.

OVERLEAF: Landscape architect Ron Lutsko blurred the landscape immediately surrounding the house into the meadow. Clad in unstained, hand-sawn sinker cypress shingles, the exterior will gray out naturally over time, blending further into the landscape. The whale sculpture on the terrace was inspired by the Winged Victory of Samothrace, one of the Louvre's most famous statues.

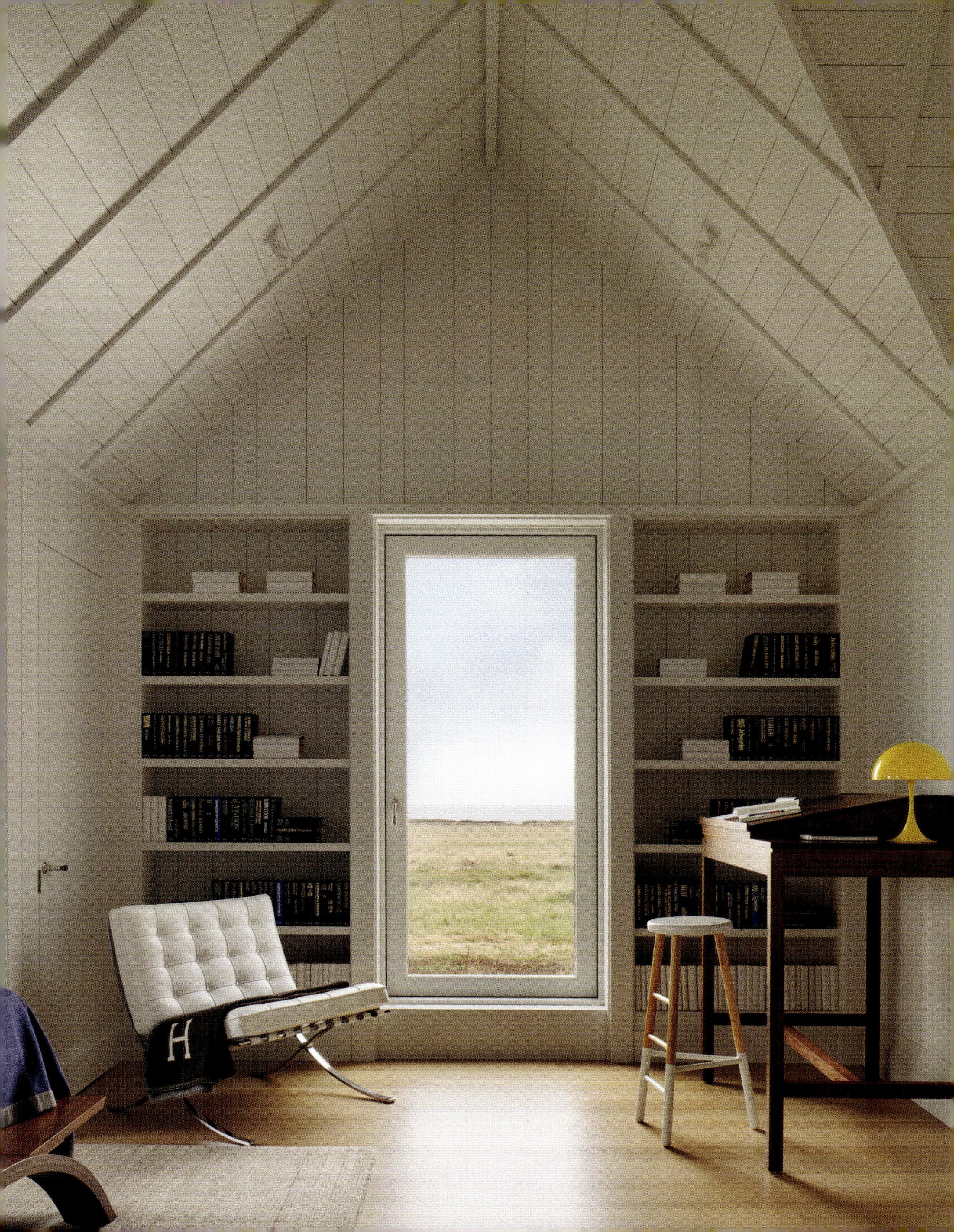

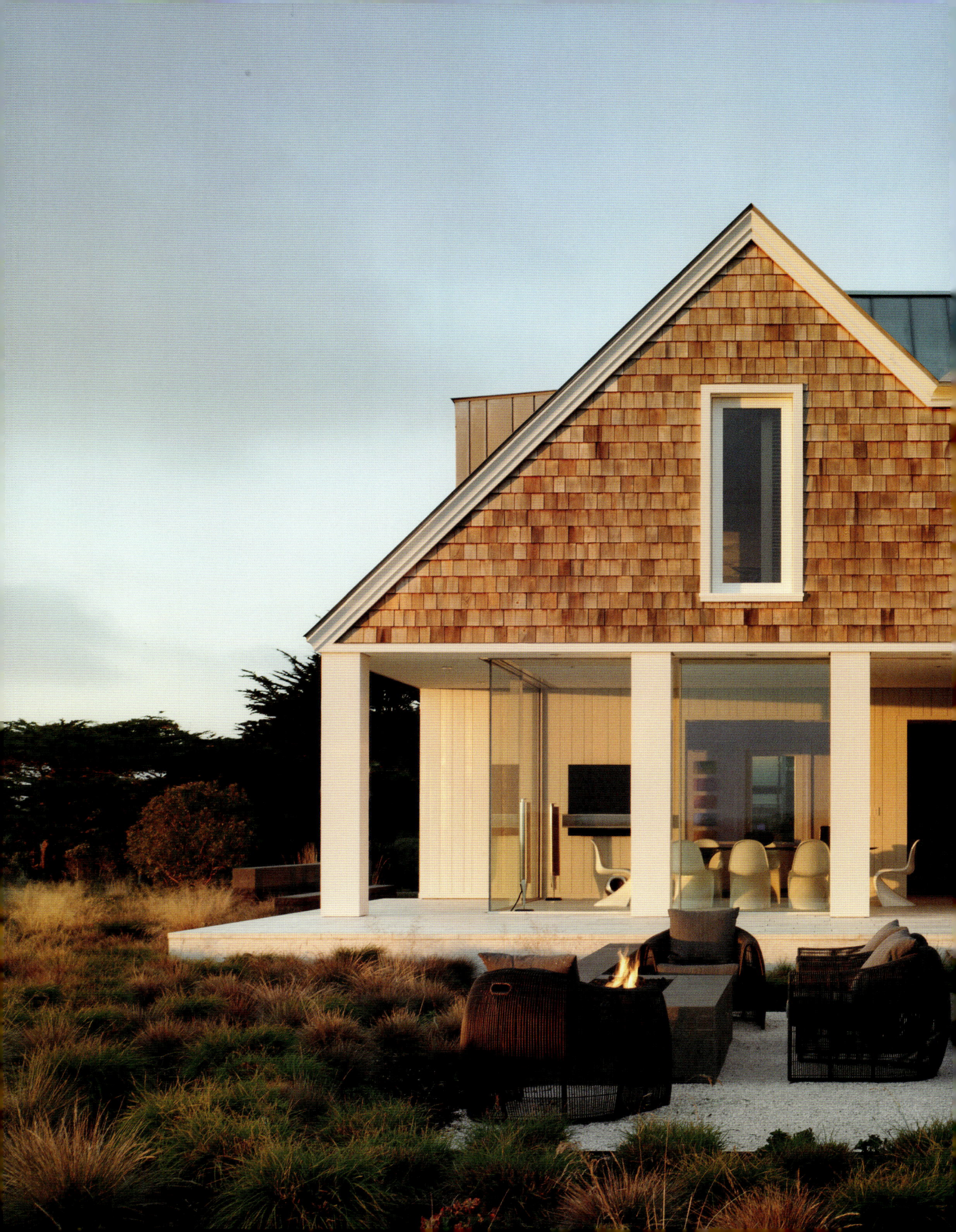

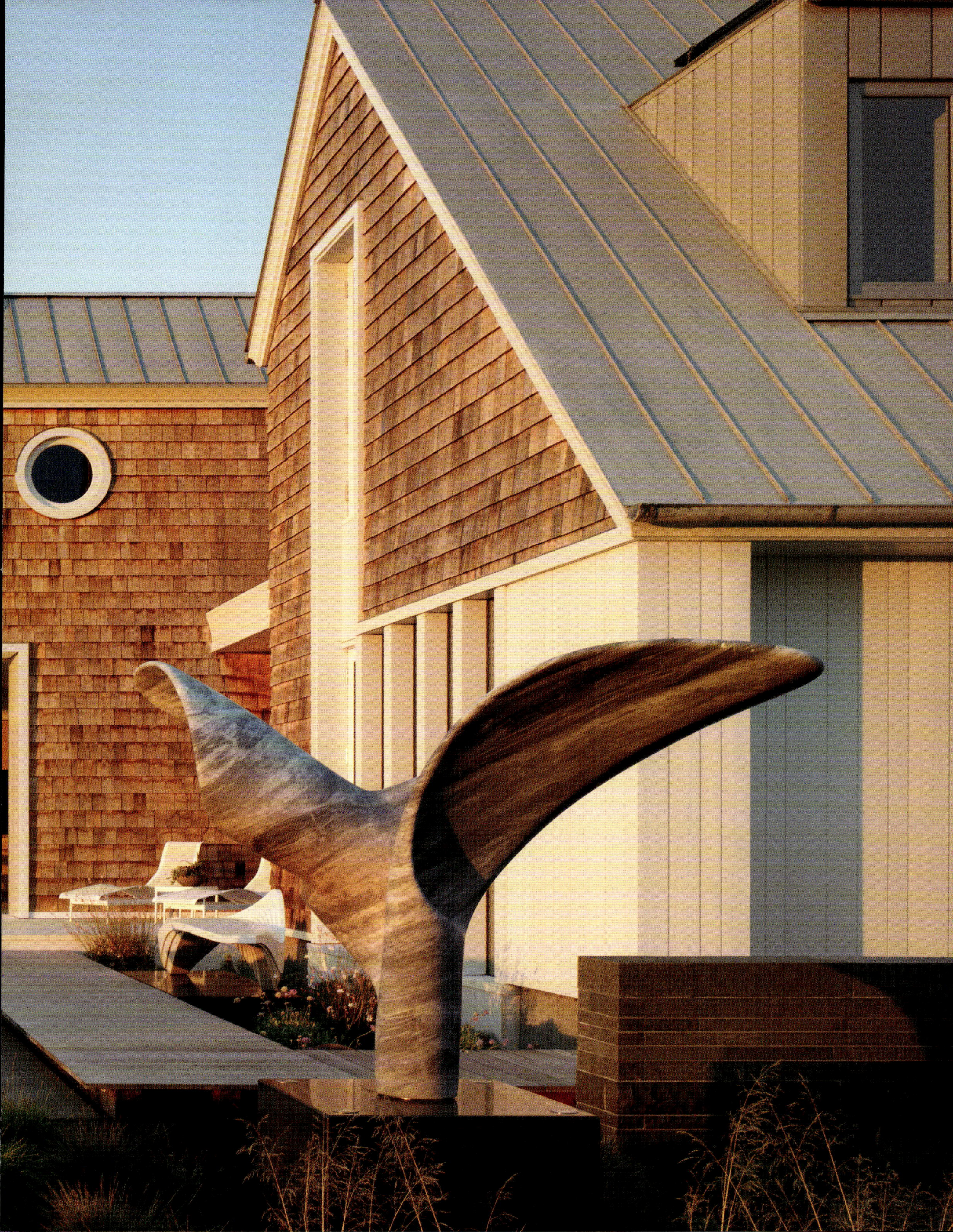

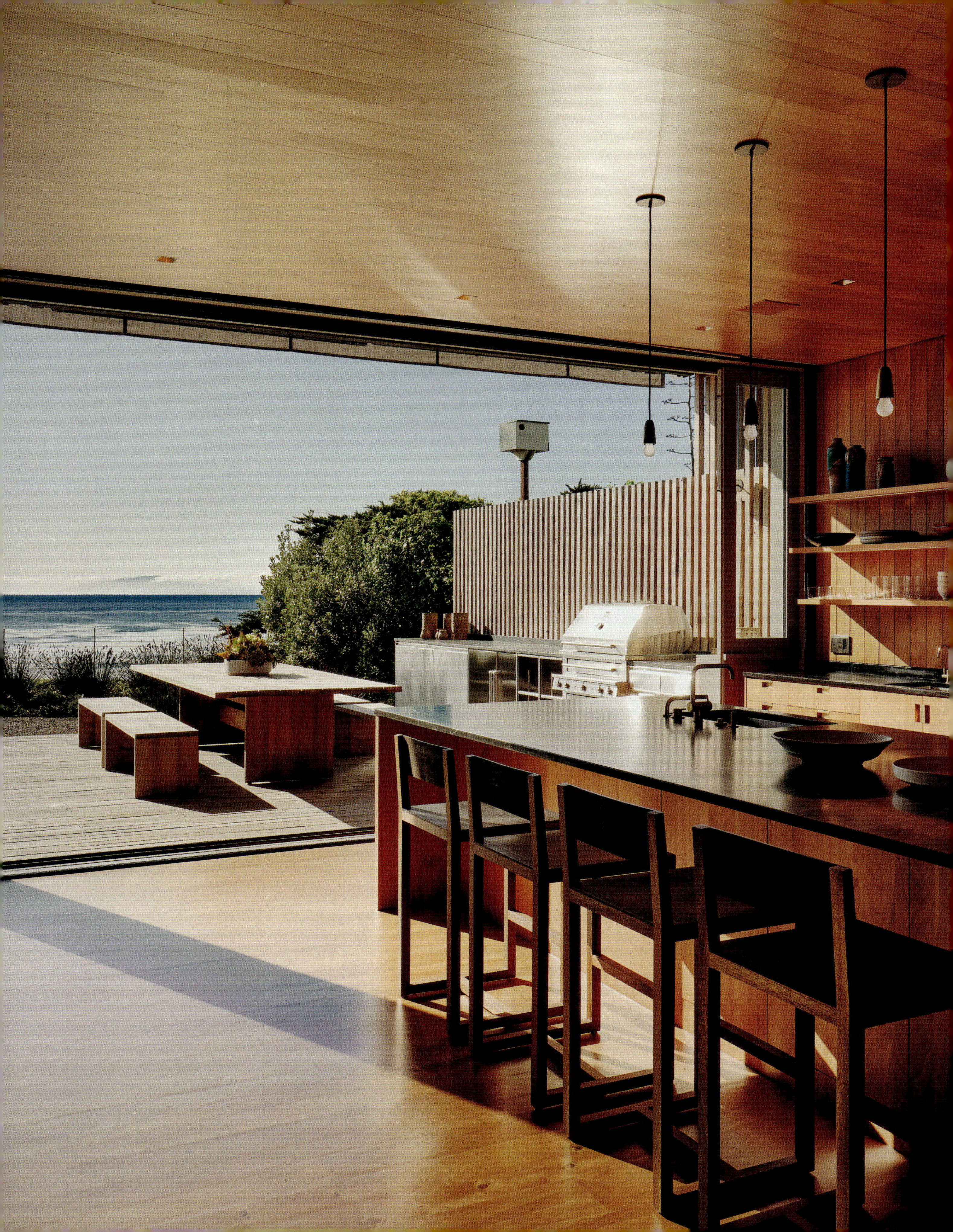

BOHEMIAN SURF HOUSE

/ SANTA CRUZ /

Santa Cruz is renowned for its academic life and beach culture, so the concept of designing a home for "a professor who surfs" wasn't completely out of the box—especially for a prime site positioned above one of the town's most popular surf breaks.

The neighborhood, with its timeless beach bungalow aesthetic, has a laid-back vibe and is immersed in the natural world. Dog walkers raise a hand in greeting to bicyclists with boards tucked under their arms as they coast through the quiet streets on pastel beach cruisers. From nearby overlooks, whale watchers with binoculars scan the surface of the sea for telltale plumes. Closer to shore, surfers and the occasional sea otter bob up and down with the swell, while pelicans dive for fish. So, when a San Francisco-area family with longstanding ties to Santa Cruz and a passion for the ocean approached Commune Design and Feldman Architecture about their project, the initial ask was for a home that was contextual without overwhelming the neighborhood. It would also have to adhere to California Coastal Commission guidelines and a setback requirement determined by the 100-year erosion potential of the oceanfront cliff.

Feldman Architecture partners Jonathan Feldman and Chris Kurrle designed three structures: a main house, a garage, and the "board room"—a surfboard and gear storage structure with a built-in bar. The experience begins at the streetside gate, which is constructed of the same wood as the buildings and joins them seamlessly, forming a sheltered interior courtyard set up for indoor–outdoor entertaining. Even before passing through the gate, one's line of sight extends across the courtyard, through the great room of the house, across the oceanside patio, then straight out to sea and the horizon. The ocean impacts every space in the project; yet, within that setting of expansiveness are a level of handcraftedness and highly refined artistry that demands close attention to detail, resulting in an experience that is at once intimate and infinite. Guests pass through the courtyard en route to the big view, for instance, but not without registering the outdoor fireplace, a striking artwork of stamped clay by ceramic sculptor Stan Bitters.

The house itself, built by True Build Construction, is a masterpiece of craftsmanship, beginning with the wood used inside and out. Evan Shively of Arborica envisioned using Monterey cypress holistically, from the rough wood to the more polished grades, and minimizing waste as much as possible. Chris Kurrle explains, "It became a very elaborate exercise in analytics, which dictated the module of the exterior and the size of the slats we used. The reclaimed Monterey cypress was used 'from tail to snout,' or maybe 'twig to trunk.' The lowest, most abundant grade wood serve as the exterior siding and fencing, while the highest grades delicately grace the interiors, making the home

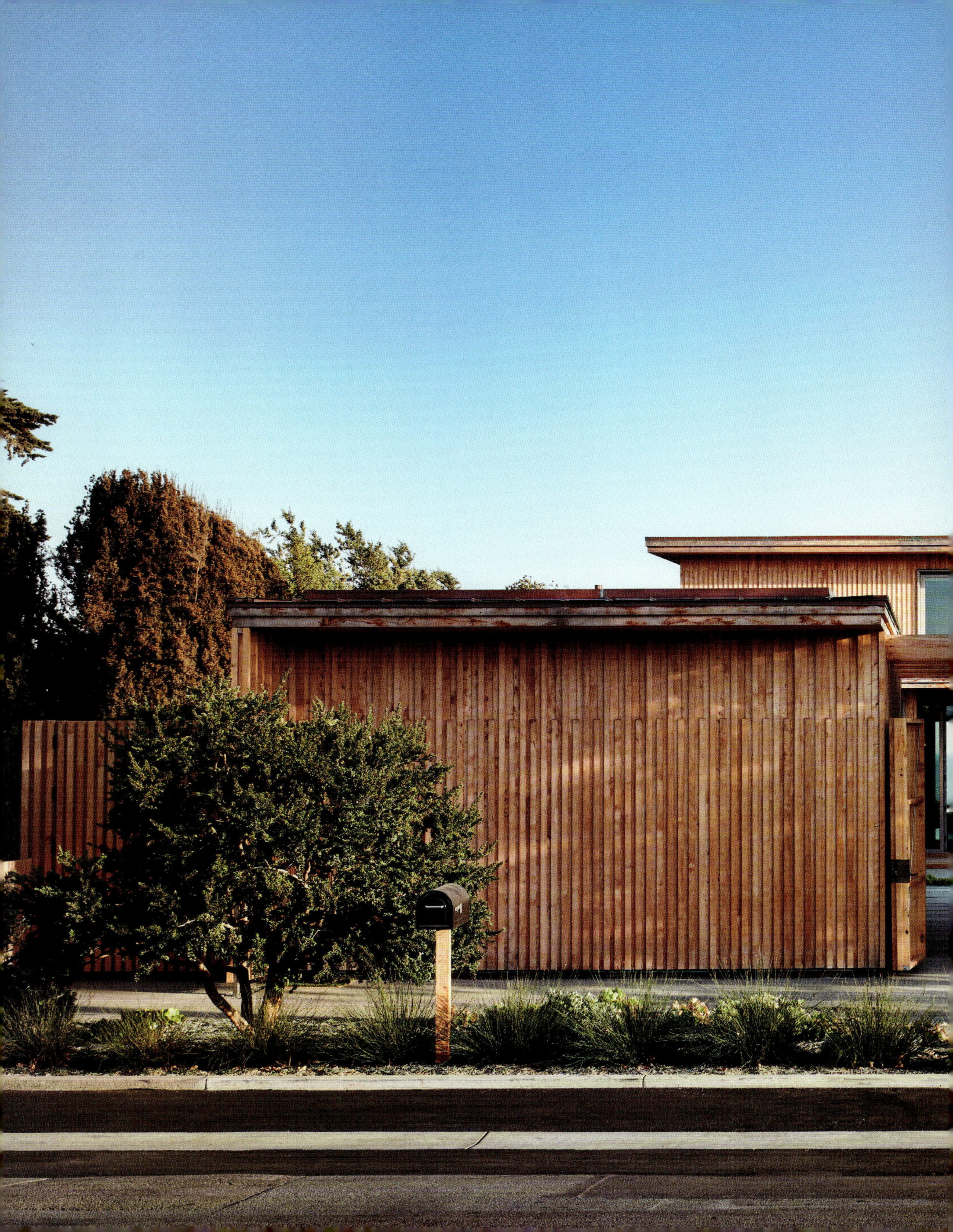

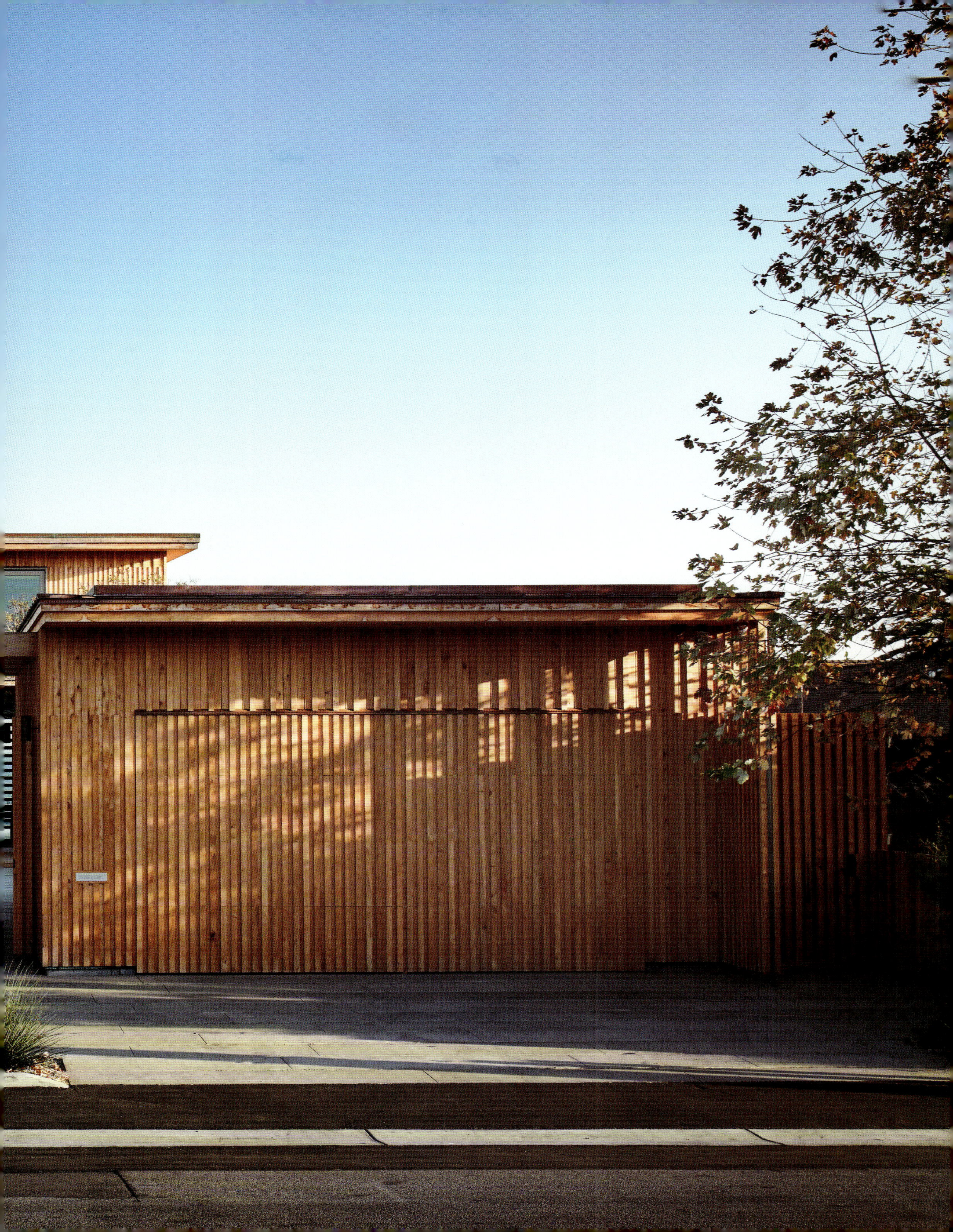

structurally mirror the cypress tree itself." The floors, meanwhile, were fabricated from the clean-grained wood of a fallen tree from a cemetery in Colma, California, one large enough to provide floorboards for the entire house.

The project's bespoke quality carries through from the biggest detail to the smallest; the interiors are filled with commissions from a wide variety of mostly Californian artists, artisans, and designers, including Tripp Carpenter, Doug McCollough, Alma Allen, BDDW, Sam Malouf, and Nakashima Workshop. The living room fireplace combines a concrete hearth with bronze mantel crafted by Chris French and a fireplace screen with woven brass filament by Tanya Aguiñiga. An all-wood bunk room has the carefully crafted feel of a ship's cabin. Details like the custom nook for the owners' guitars inset within a bookcase speak to highly intentional living. Custom seating, vintage furniture, found objects, and masses of books create interiors that feel casual yet elegant, lived in yet soulful.

The modern staircase, its wood treads floating off a steel support beam, leads to private areas where the cypress-clad primary bedroom boasts floor-to-ceiling glass walls that open onto a private balcony and views to surfers below. In the minimalist primary bathroom, it's all about wood, glass, and the white vessel tub. In some private spaces—the cozy TV room, which opens to the courtyard; one bedroom with colorfully upholstered daybeds, another with an artful built-in desk—the walls transition from cypress to plaster, highlighting architectural details. Thoughtfully placed windows yield glimpses of blues and greens, in contrast to the earth-toned interior finishes. Furnishings, meanwhile, have a specificity to place—such as the dining table, made by woodworker Tripp Carpenter from walnut sourced from Arborica—that creates a remarkably holistic feel.

One main goal of the project, explains architect Kurrle, was for the house "to weather, age, and mature and actively respond to its salty coastal locale."

This is already happening, attests interior designer Roman Alonso. "There's something about being in this kind of living structure. It's almost like a musical instrument, and it feels that way when you're in it in terms of the sound and even the smell. The material is constantly changing; the interior will just get warmer and deeper in color as time goes by. All the finishes are live. The soapstones in the kitchen are changing; the plasters are changing as well. The copper and brass throughout the house are oxidizing. It is a space that is shifting. You're in a living piece of architecture when you're inside," he adds, "and that is a very special way to live."

PRECEDING PAGE: As a beach retreat designed by Feldman Architecture and interior designer Roman Alonso and built by True Build Construction, the home presents a quiet facade while enjoying an immediate connection to the water. The home's public spaces emphasize the indoor–outdoor connection beginning at the street entrance and continuing through the light-filled courtyard and open great room-kitchen to the patio overlooking the sea.

OPPOSITE TOP: An unobtrusive gate built from the same wood as the buildings joins them to create a protected interior courtyard—a warmer, less windy, and more private option than the oceanside deck with spa and landscaped garden atop the bluff. This elevated surf shack concept celebrates the good life with a board storage room that doubles as a bar to service the courtyard.

OPPOSITE BOTTOM: The fireplace tile is an artwork by Californian ceramicist sculptor Stan Bitters. Says Alonso, "We wanted the project to have a real connection to the site and to California through its contents."

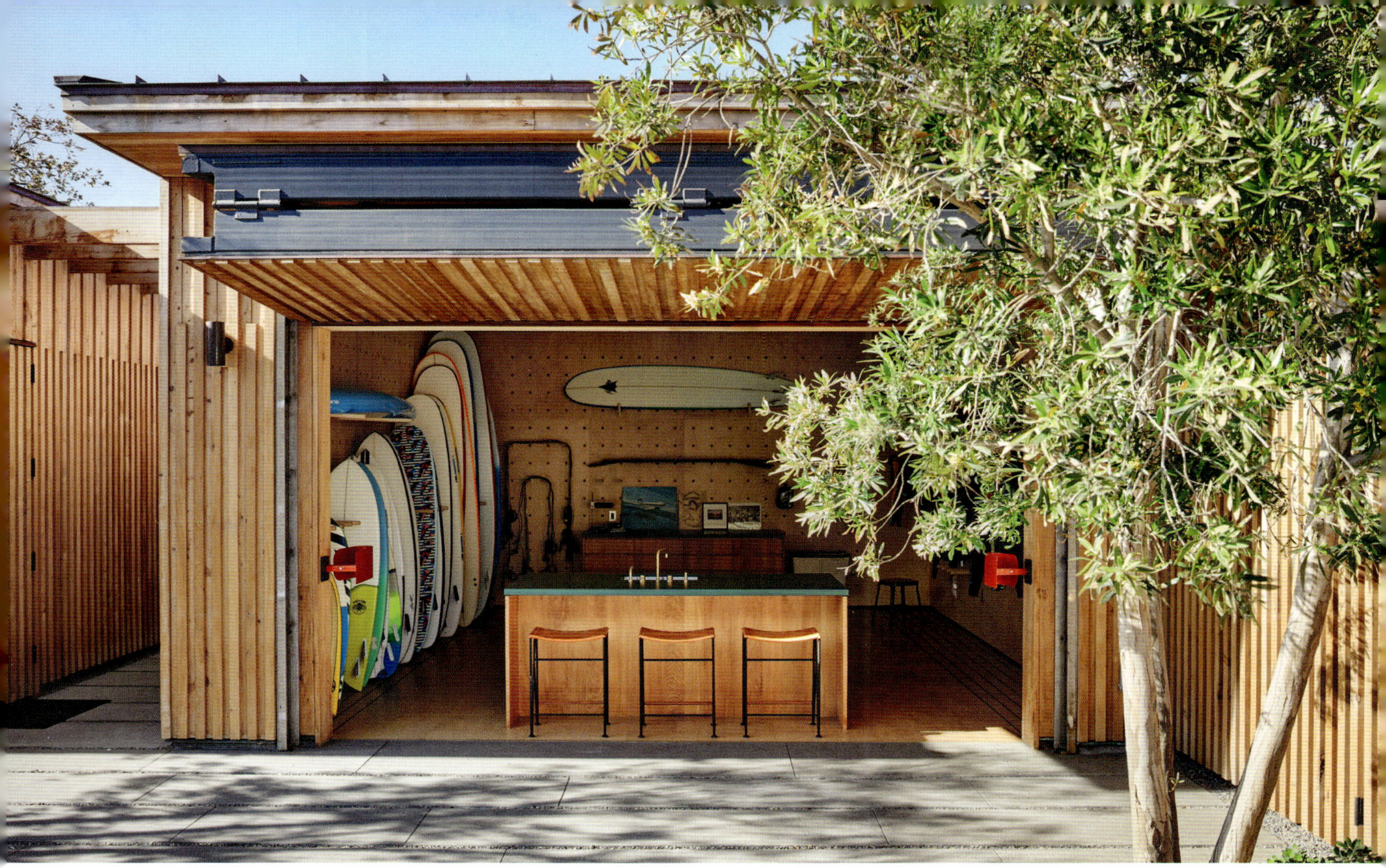

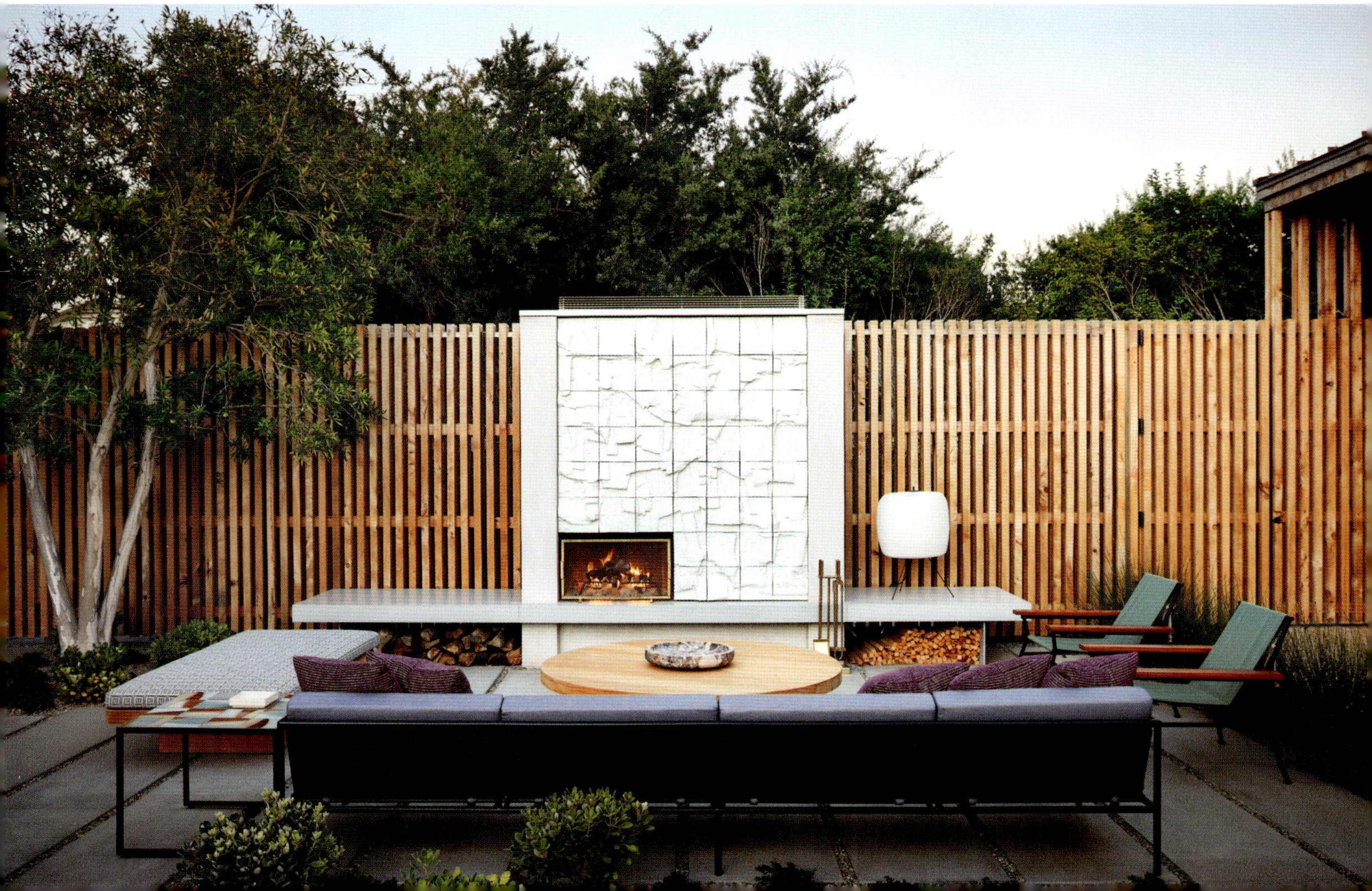

ABOVE: The homeowner, a trained chef, was extremely involved with the layout and all the details of the kitchen, including a wood-fired oven just outside. The countertops are soapstone, the hood is plaster.

OPPOSITE: The wood used throughout the home was sourced by sawyer Evan Shively of Arborica, who provided locally sourced Monterey cypress for the interior cladding and the exterior board-and-batten slats. Floor-to-ceiling doors slide open to a large patio with an in-ground hot tub and outdoor kitchen and dining, effortlessly expanding the space for entertaining.

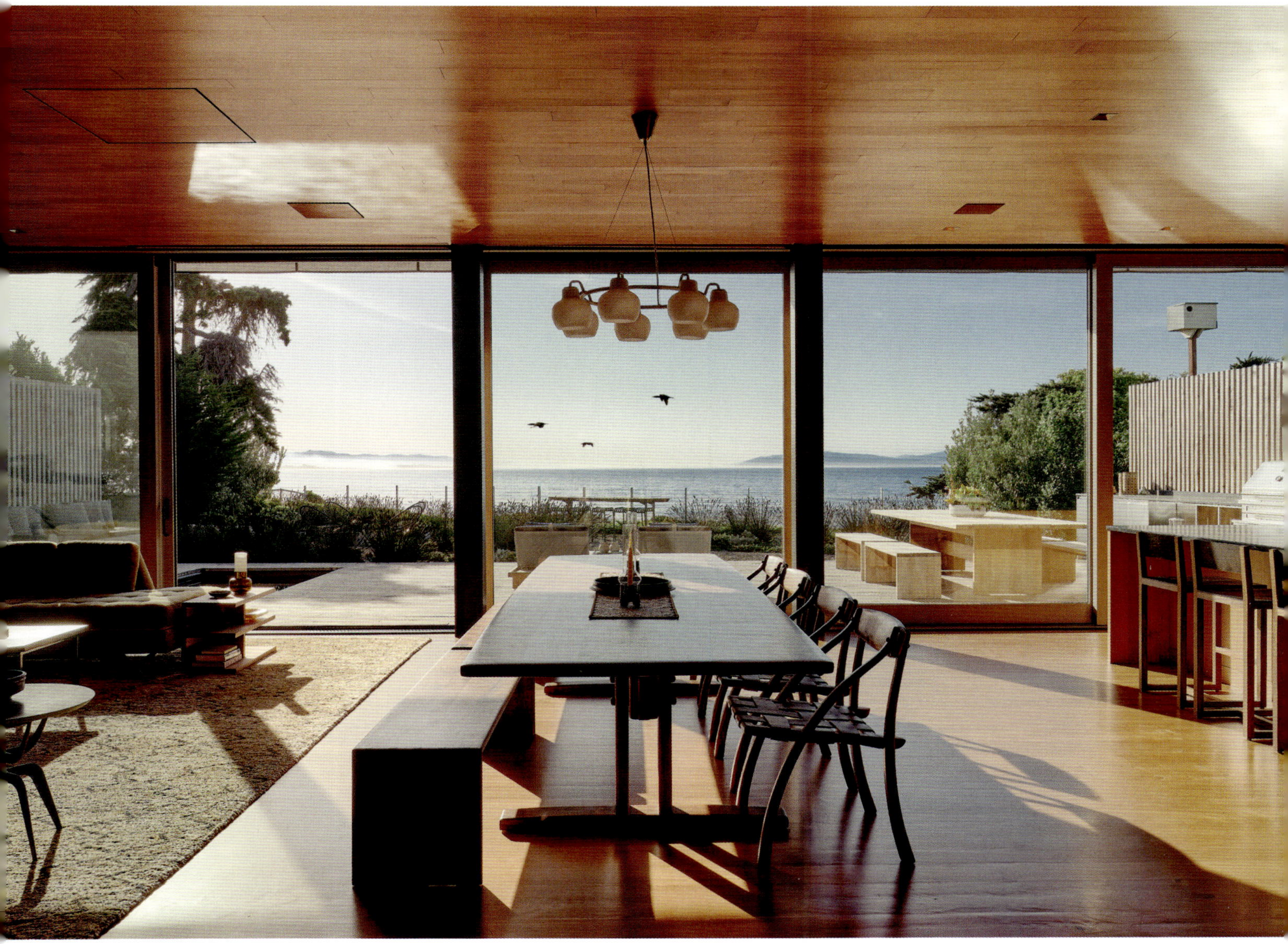

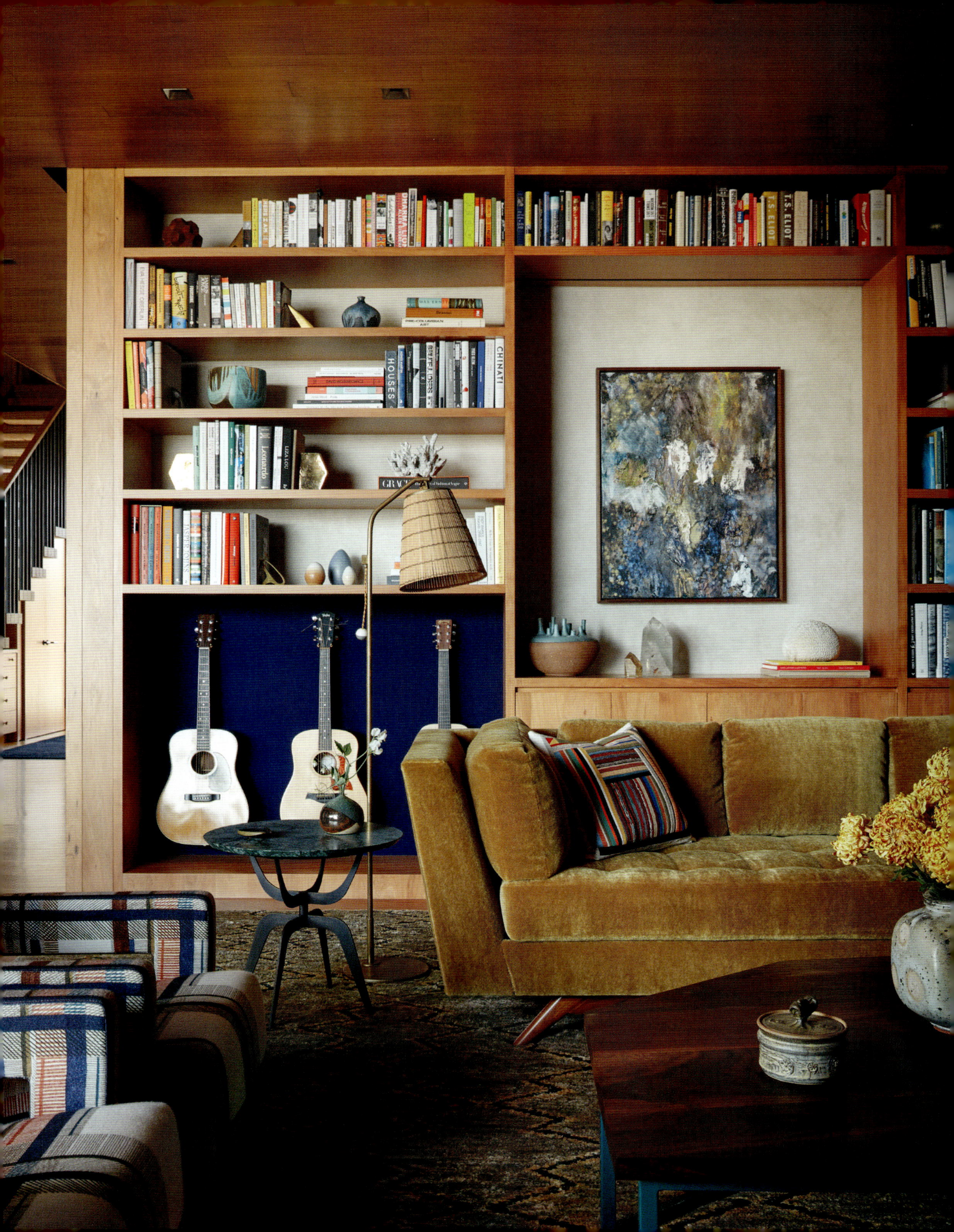
T.S. ELIOT
HOUSES
CHINATI
Leonardo

OPPOSITE: A conceit based on a "professor who surfs" provided inspiration for interiors filled with a number of commissions mixed with custom upholstered seating, vintage furnishings, and found objects. There also had to be room for the owners' books and guitar collection.

ABOVE: "The idea," says designer Roman Alonso, "was to create a space that felt almost intellectual in the way it was conceived, one that was super casual and inviting but also considered. The level of detail in the architecture is mirrored in the level of detail in the furnishings." The hearth is concrete; the mantel is crafted bronze by Chris French. Los Angeles craft-based artist Tanya Aguiñiga made the fire screen out of brass filament.

ABOVE: Art consultant Alison Harding helped the art collector homeowners with pieces for this house, mainly focusing on female artists from California.

OPPOSITE: The primary bedroom's private balcony offers views of surfers below.

OVERLEAF: Siting of coastal houses is a process requiring patience, explains Chris Kurrle of Feldman Architects. "This project took several years to procure approval from the Coastal Commission. The new structure was smaller in massing than the existing and had less of a presence facing the Pacific." With the aid of a local geologist, the project team studied the 100-year erosion potential for the ocean-facing cliff, which drops forty-five feet to the water. This calculation determined the building setback, which in turn helped the team determine the placement and orientation of the home. Landscape designer Ground Studio helped integrate the home into its coastal site.

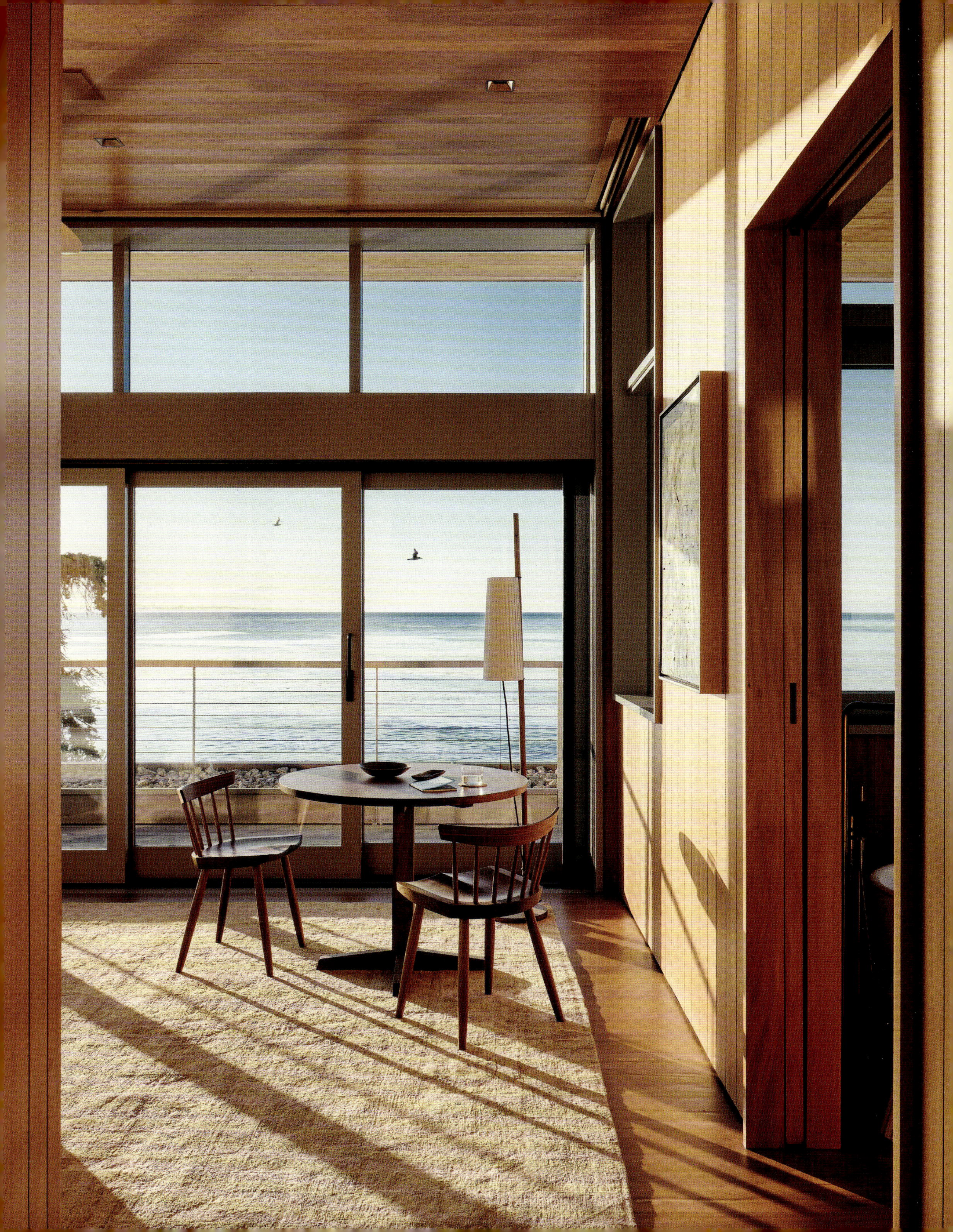

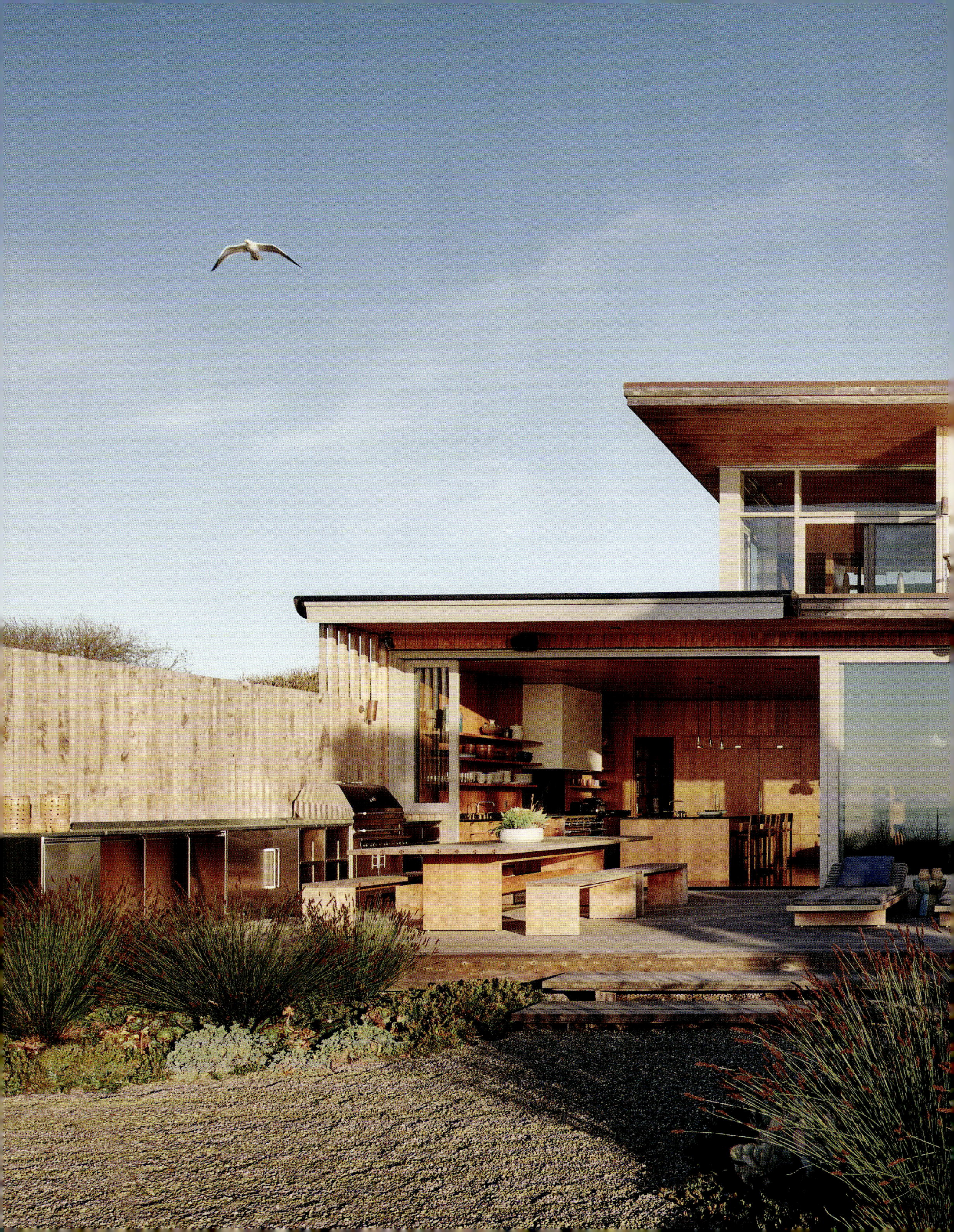

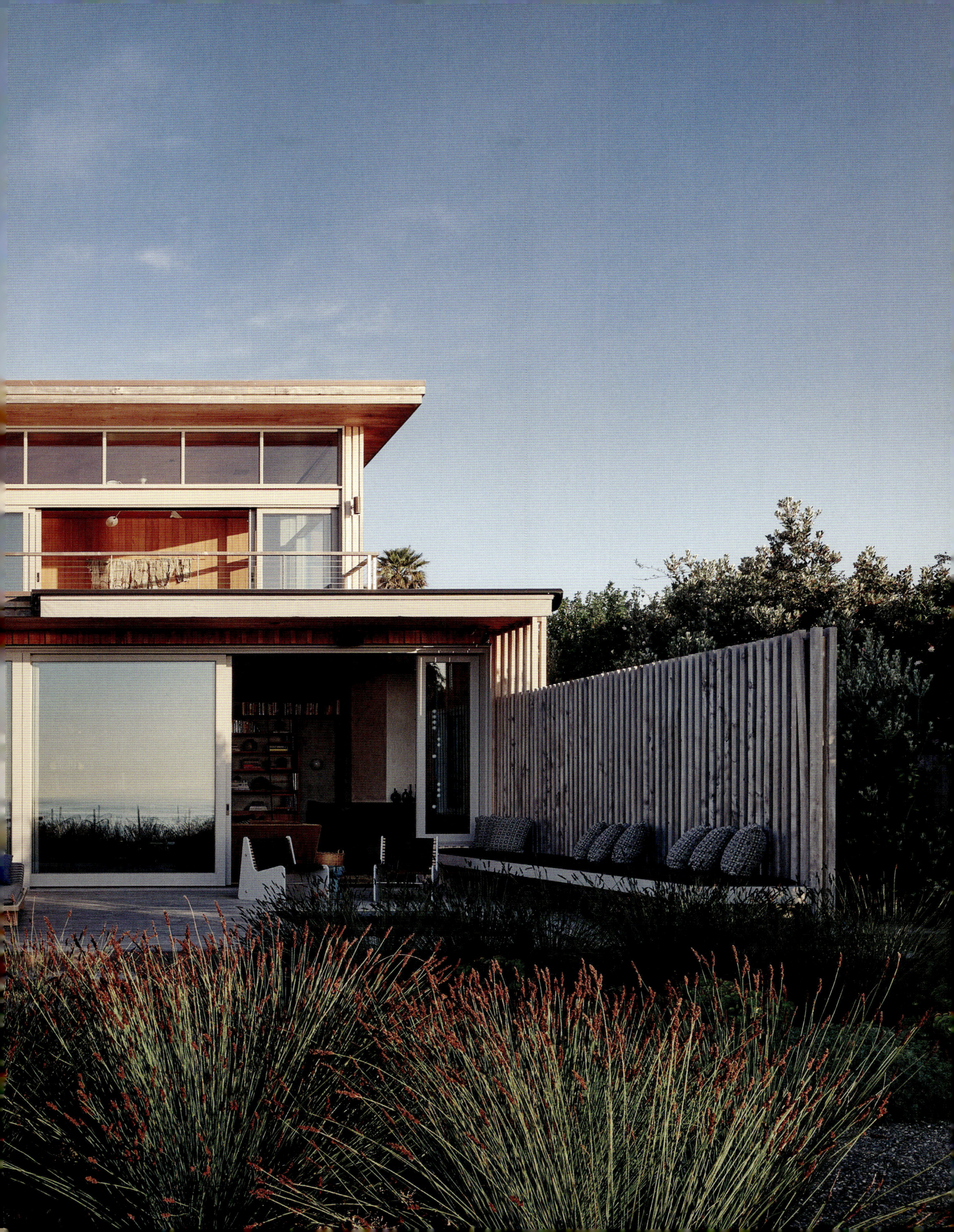

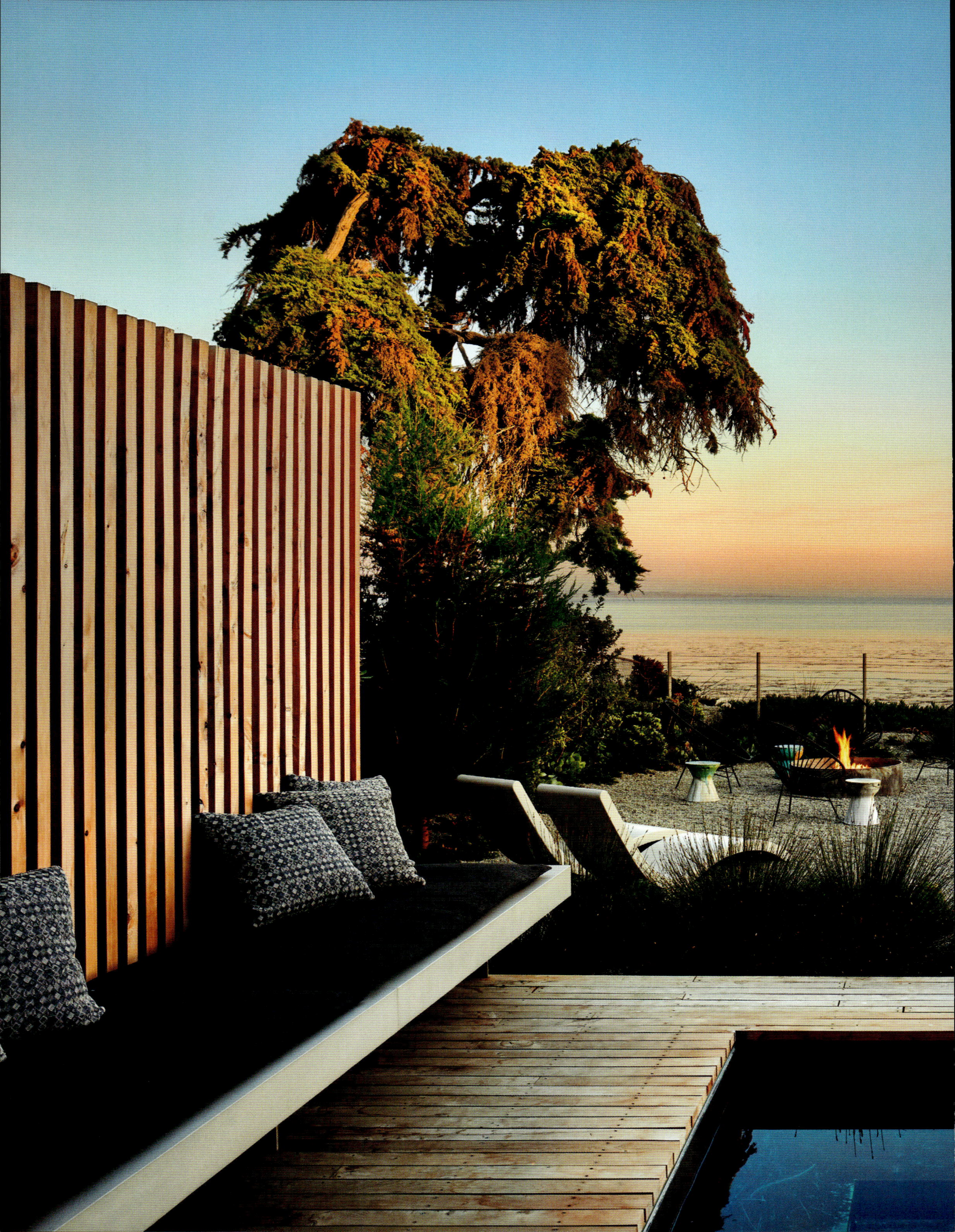

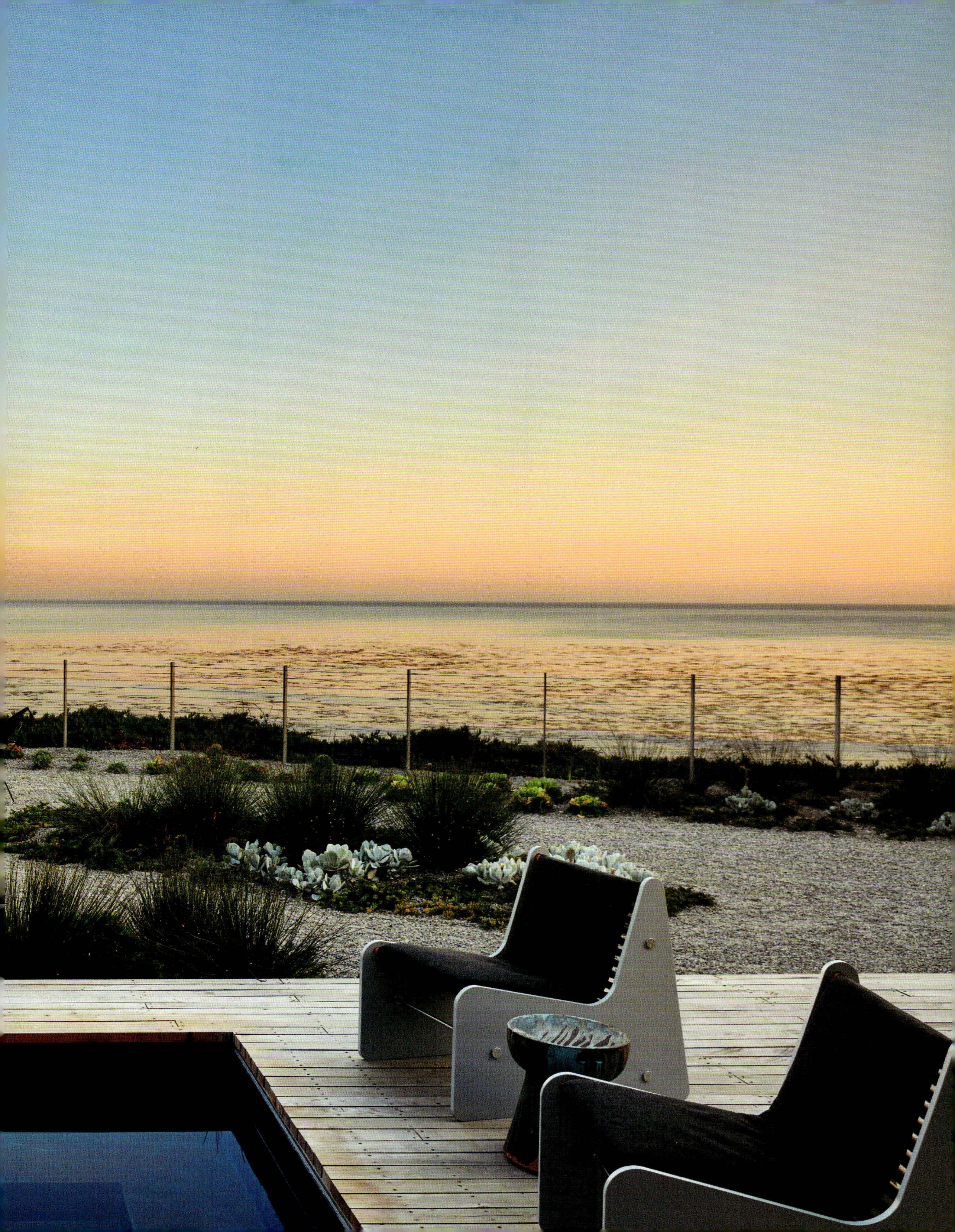

CENTRAL COAST

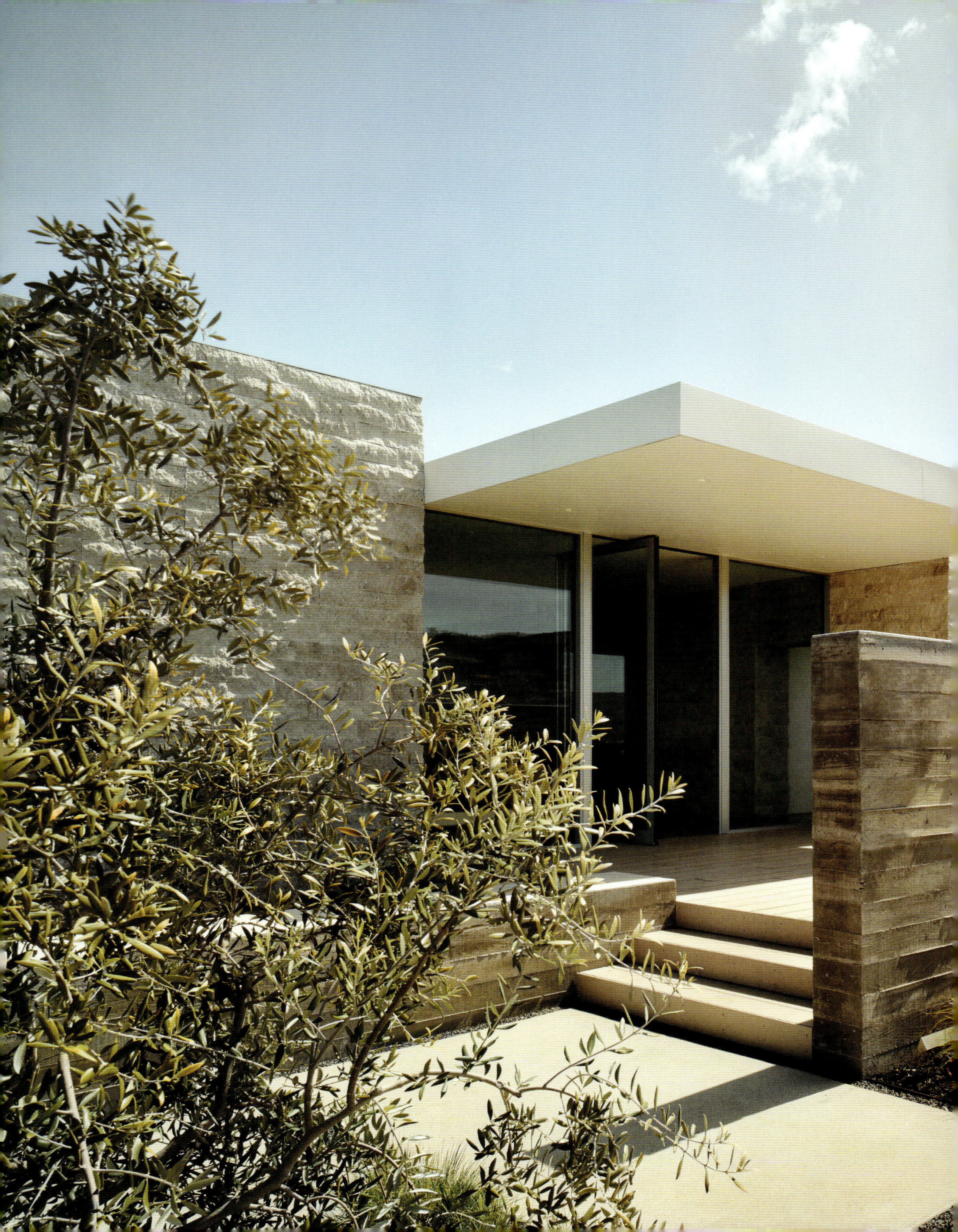

BIRD'S-EYE VIEW

/ CARMEL /

The story of this home is the story of a lifelong dream, a gesture of enduring love, and a monument to family. Owners Max and Linda, who have been married for over fifty years, initially envisioned their second home—set high above the ocean on the Central Coast—as a place to gather their family together. Over time, the significance and meaning of this special place has deepened.

"It's a legacy I'll leave to my children and grandchildren," Max says. "I tell them that when they have parties here after we're gone, they'll think of us. It's the house we built for our family."

Throughout their marriage, Linda longed for a house at the beach, but Max had resisted the idea. Then a health scare for Linda nearly a decade ago shifted his perspective, and he decided it was time to build her a beach house.

Linda's sister Janice, who lives in the picturesque coastal town of Carmel, offered to look at properties on their behalf. The two sisters are the best of friends, so living nearby would be ideal. After months of looking, Janice called with a rare opportunity—a lot with 180-degree views in a charming neighborhood—but Max would have to act fast. He arrived two days later and found it to be perfect in every way except for one thing: it had sold the day before. He put in a backup offer, though he didn't expect to hear from the real estate agent again. One week later, the first sale fell through, and the agent called. "Just like that, the house was ours," he says.

Max, who studied architecture in college, and Linda, an interior designer, met early in their lives as colleagues in the same design firm. While Max has long since segued into real estate, both remain devoted to design. They knew they wanted a contemporary home with an architectural language grounded in simplicity.

In what felt like fate, Ehrlich Yanai Rhee Chaney Architects (EYRC) had just opened a Bay Area office. Takashi Yanai is renowned for his contemporary aesthetic, intentional approach, and, above all, devotion to simplicity in design. Max contacted Yanai and says that initiating the connection between architect and owners was effortless and immediate.

The property was on the edge of a bluff with vast views of the Pacific Ocean to the west and the Carmel River estuary to the north. The lot sat in the interface between suburban and wild landscapes—part neighborhood and part expansive coastal chaparral. To achieve the owners' vision, the team took the existing house down to the foundation and started anew, maintaining the original footprint to ease the process. Building on the California coast is not for the faint of heart, often requiring extended timelines for design and approvals.

The home's fluid indoor–outdoor plan both embraces and protects from the duality of microclimates that converge in this spot. On the exterior, board-formed concrete, stone, and glass absorb

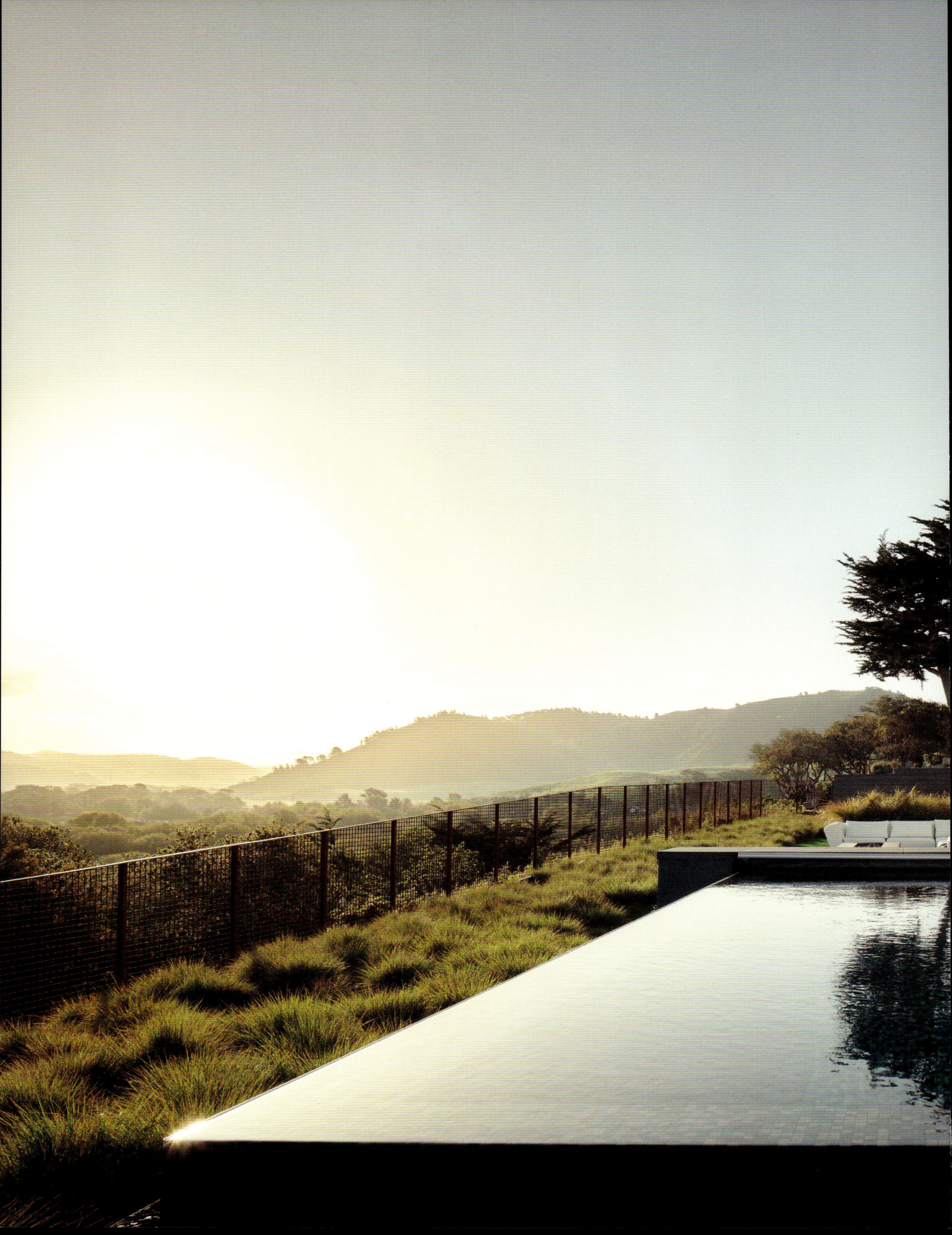

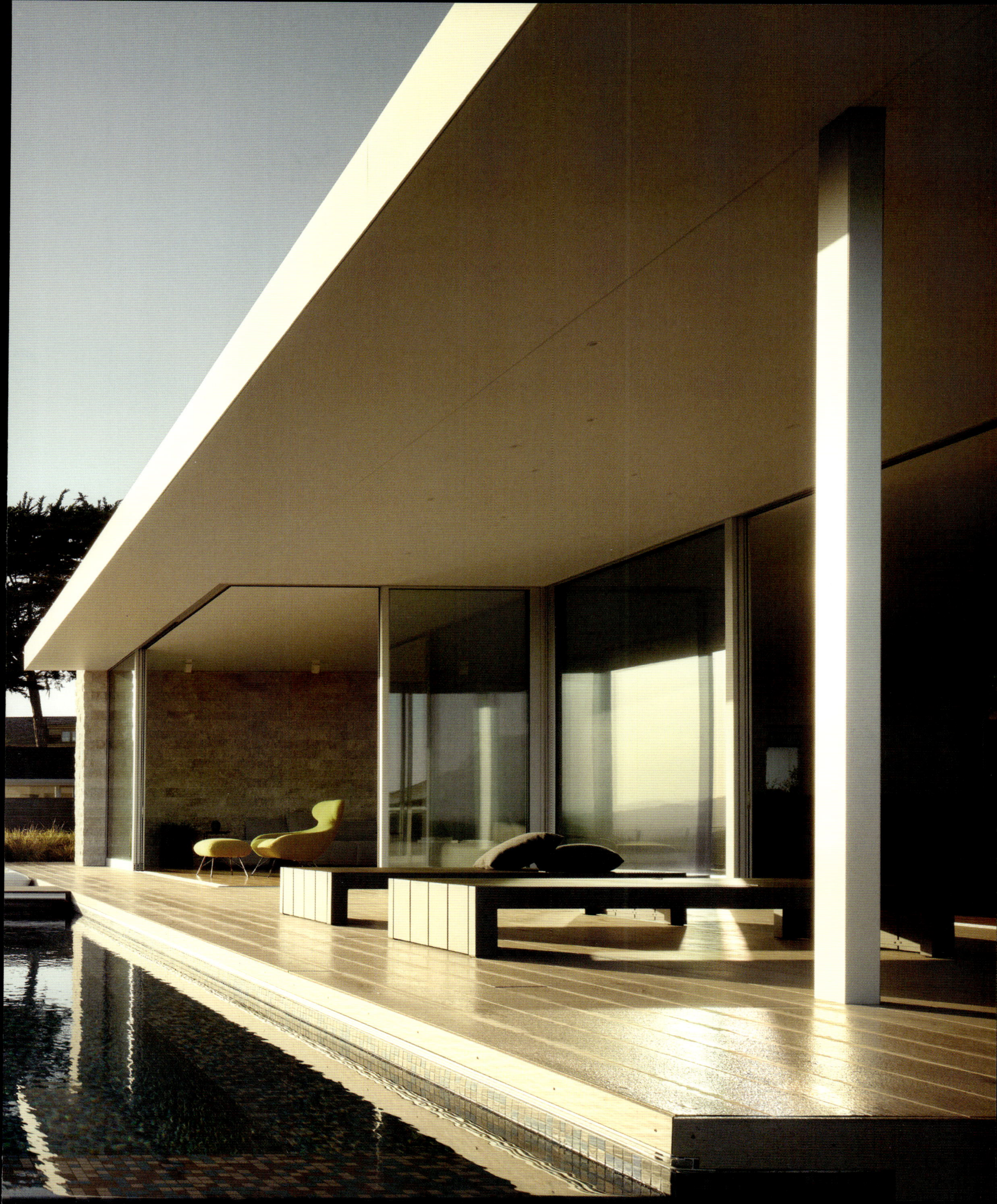

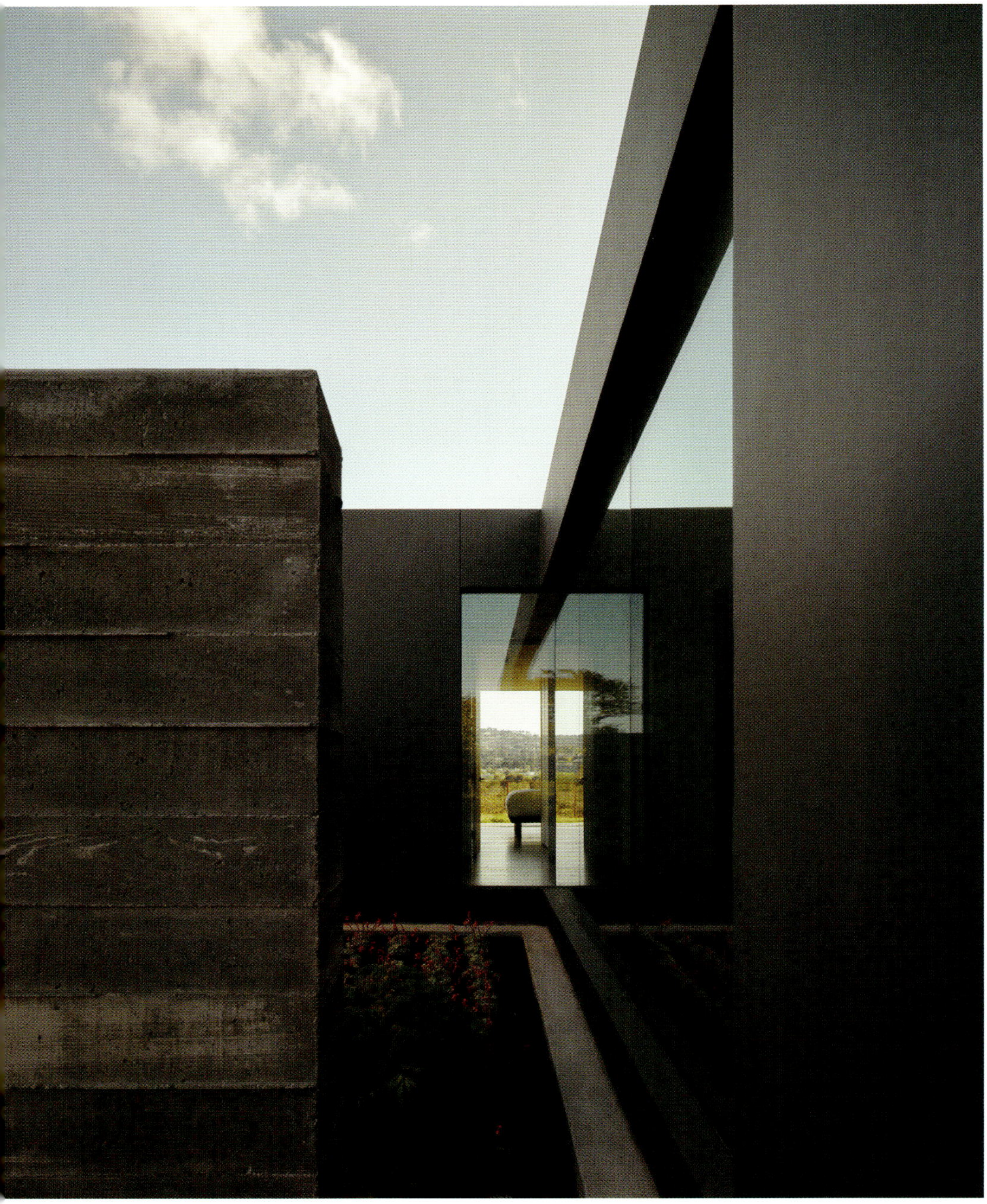

PRECEDING PAGE: The landscape celebrates the fundamental elements of the coast, namely light and wind. "The movement of grasses indicates what is going on outside," says landscape architect Andrea Cochran.

OPPOSITE: Seen from the street, the design of the house is all about layers, with a series of low walls and glimpses of the viewing garden. These fall away one by one along the journey into the home, simultaneously slowing the progression and heightening the sense of anticipation.

ABOVE: The kitchen is open to the view but tucked away in its own volume, with an off-center window oriented toward the street. "It's nice to see who is coming," says the architect.

ABOVE: The home's northerly aspect is serene, taking in the Carmel River estuary and the opposite bluff. In contrast to the wide-open views of the Pacific Ocean to the west, this softer, more layered view highlights the unique nature of the site, where the coastal and estuary landscapes converge.

OPPOSITE: In a house built for family gatherings, the kitchen and dining room seat sixteen at dinner and capacious sofas can be pushed together to sleep a multitude of children.

OVERLEAF: Under the roof's broad canopy, glass walls come together to form two corners that encase the dining and living rooms. The simplicity of the architecture speaks volumes.

PAGES 112–13: Though perched on the edge of a bluff, open to the views of the Pacific Ocean to the west and the Carmel River Estuary to the north, this house feels like a refuge.

and play with light, while the darker shade on the garage and bedroom wing subtly delineates between public and private spaces. Low walls provide privacy from the street and slow the journey from the street to the front door. Gaps in freestanding walls offer sliver views of the carefully planned gardens designed by landscape architect Andrea Cochran. The goal for the landscape design was to form an effortless transition between domestic and wild landscapes. "We wanted it to feel as if the architecture and landscape were accomplished with a single hand," says Cochran.

The walls of the central living area envelope a space that is at once open and sheltered. When the glass doors are slid back, the line between indoors and outdoors disappears. The terrace, set level with the interior, flows directly to the small infinity pool, which in turn seems to melt into the blue ocean view. Set into the landscape facing north, a firepit area is designed around the idea of prospect and refuge, providing connection to the land and safety from the coastal elements.

Yanai draws a careful line between minimalist design undertaken for its own sake and a sense of simplicity that goes beyond architecture to a way of existing in a space and in the world. Asked to describe the spirit of this house, he answers, "It's about restraint. We didn't want to make it more than it needed to be." The result, for these owners, is a home that is just enough.

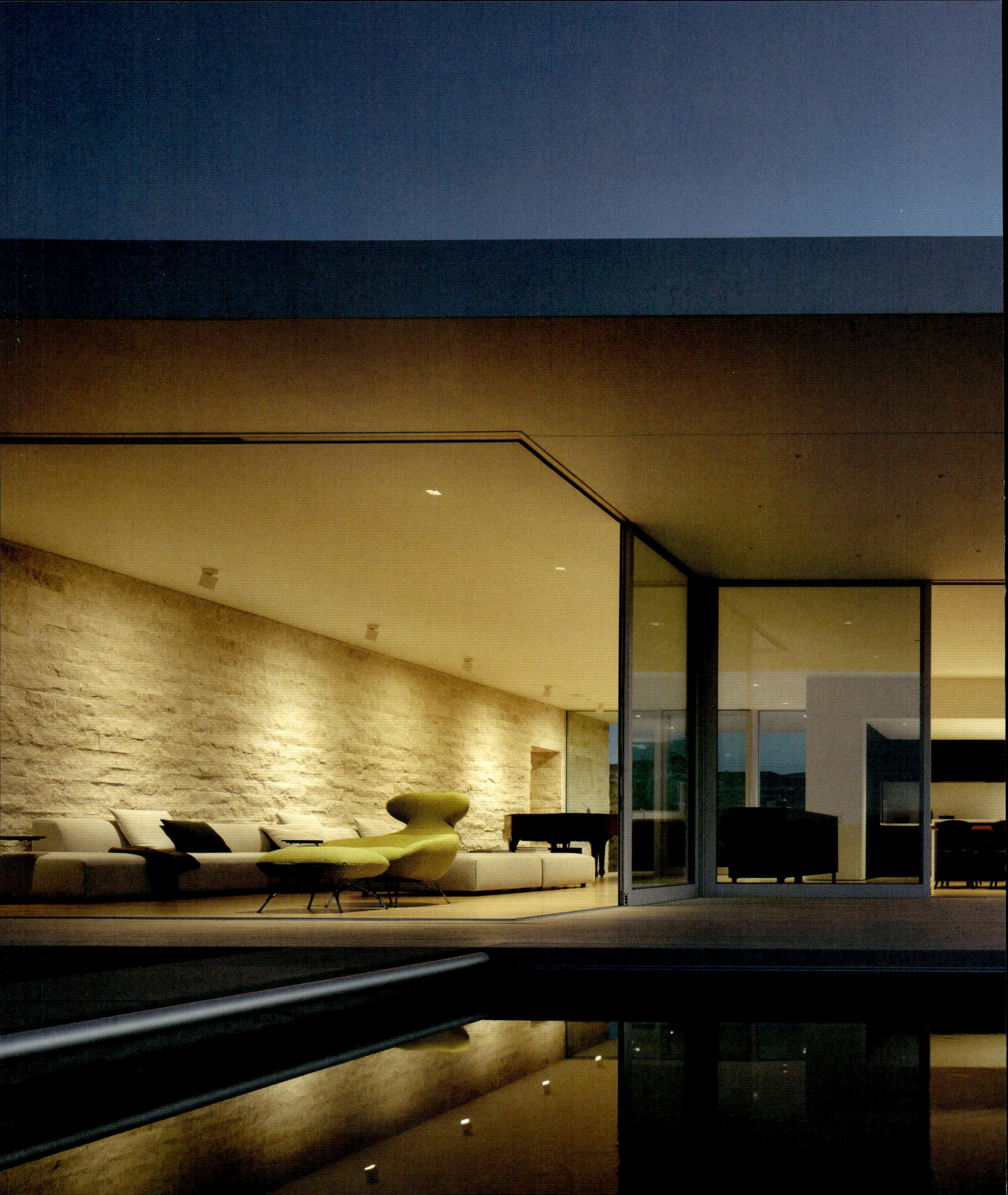

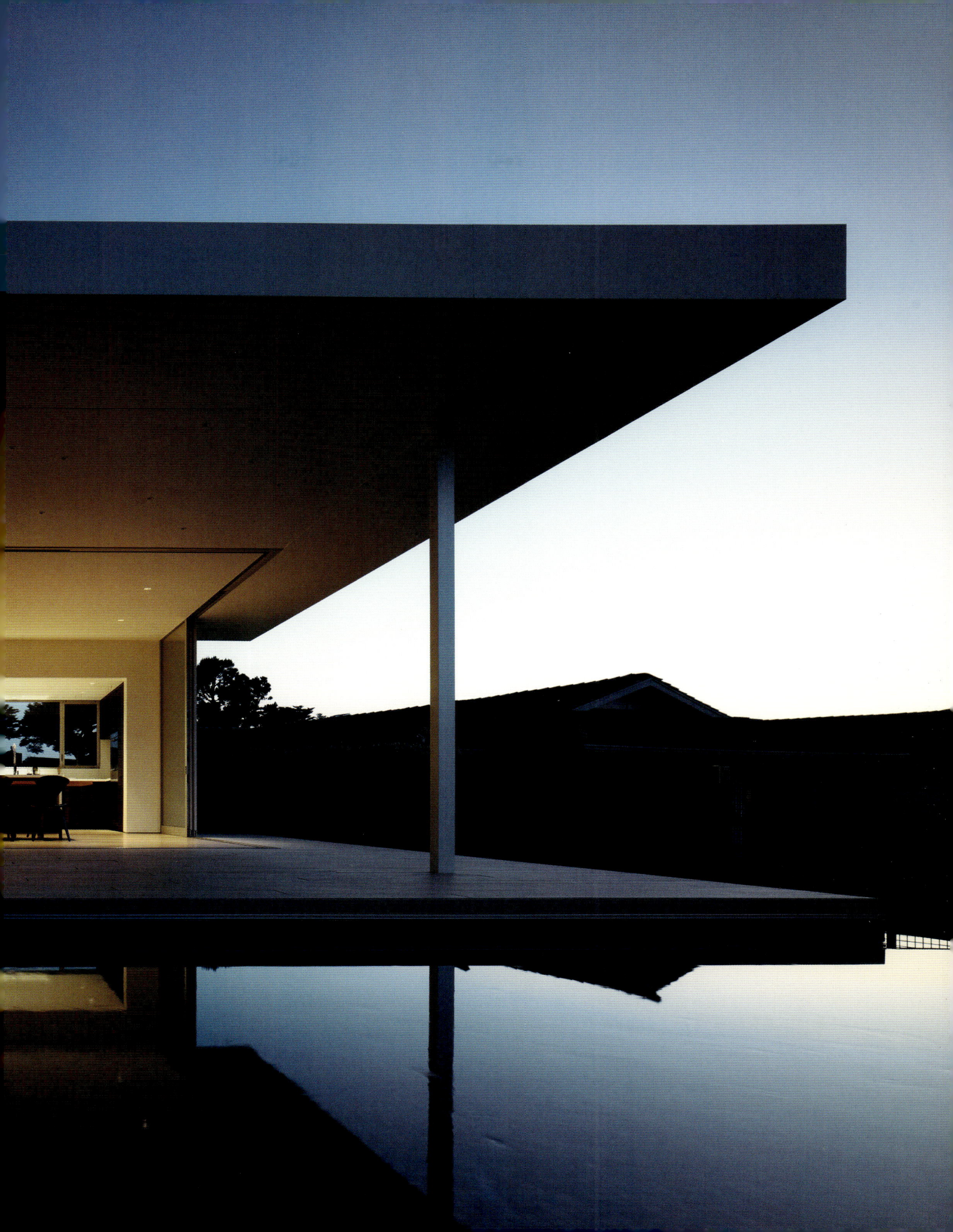

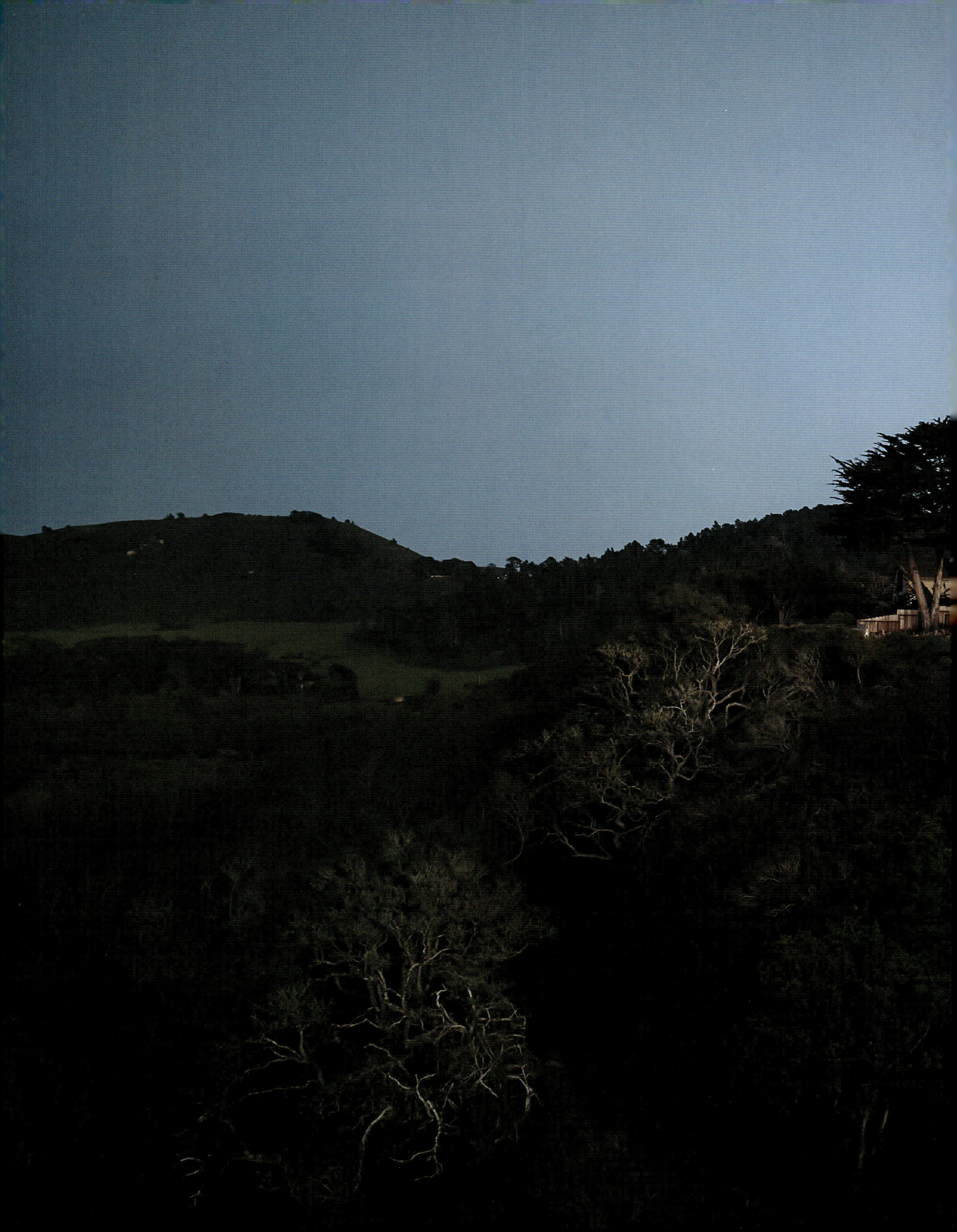

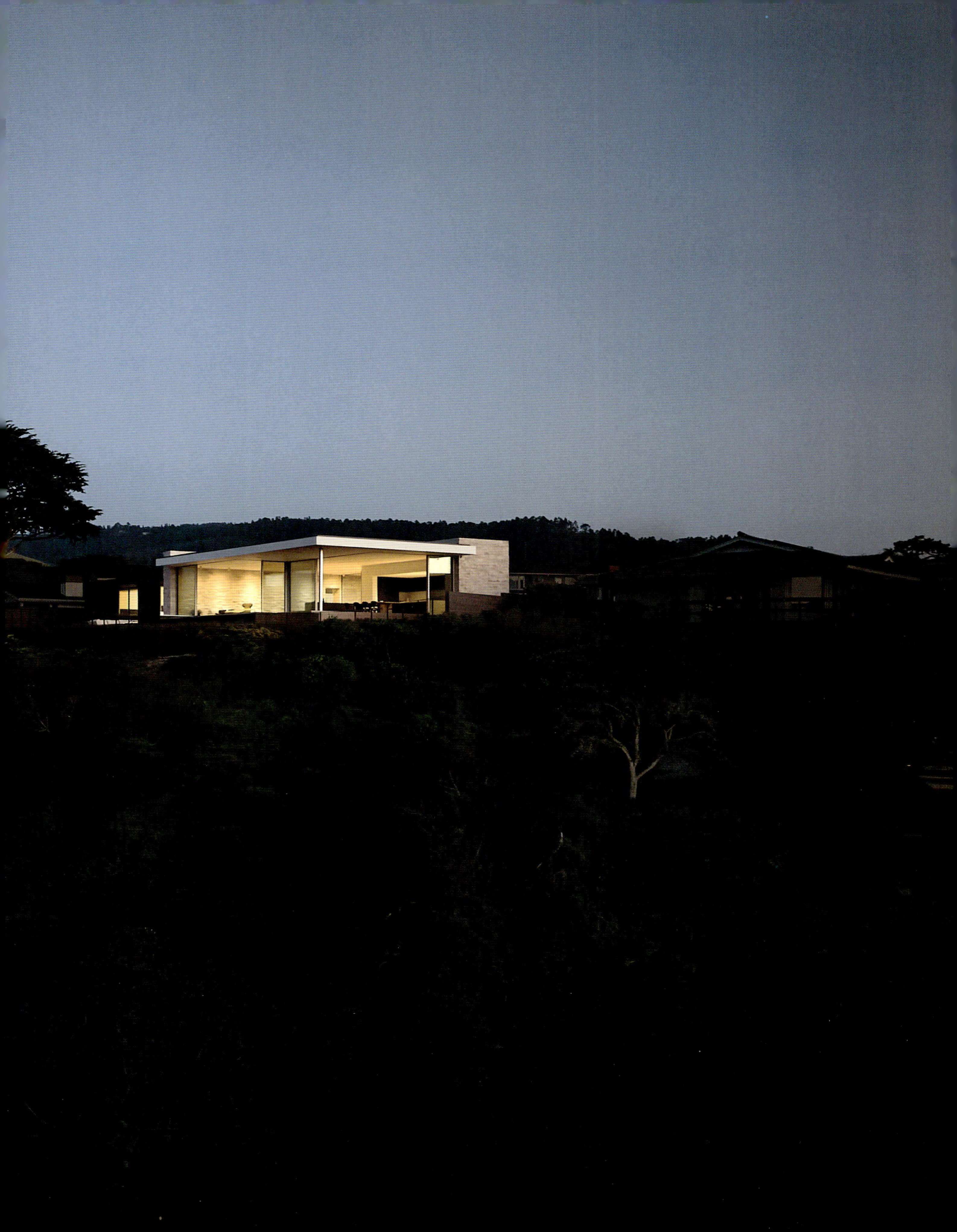

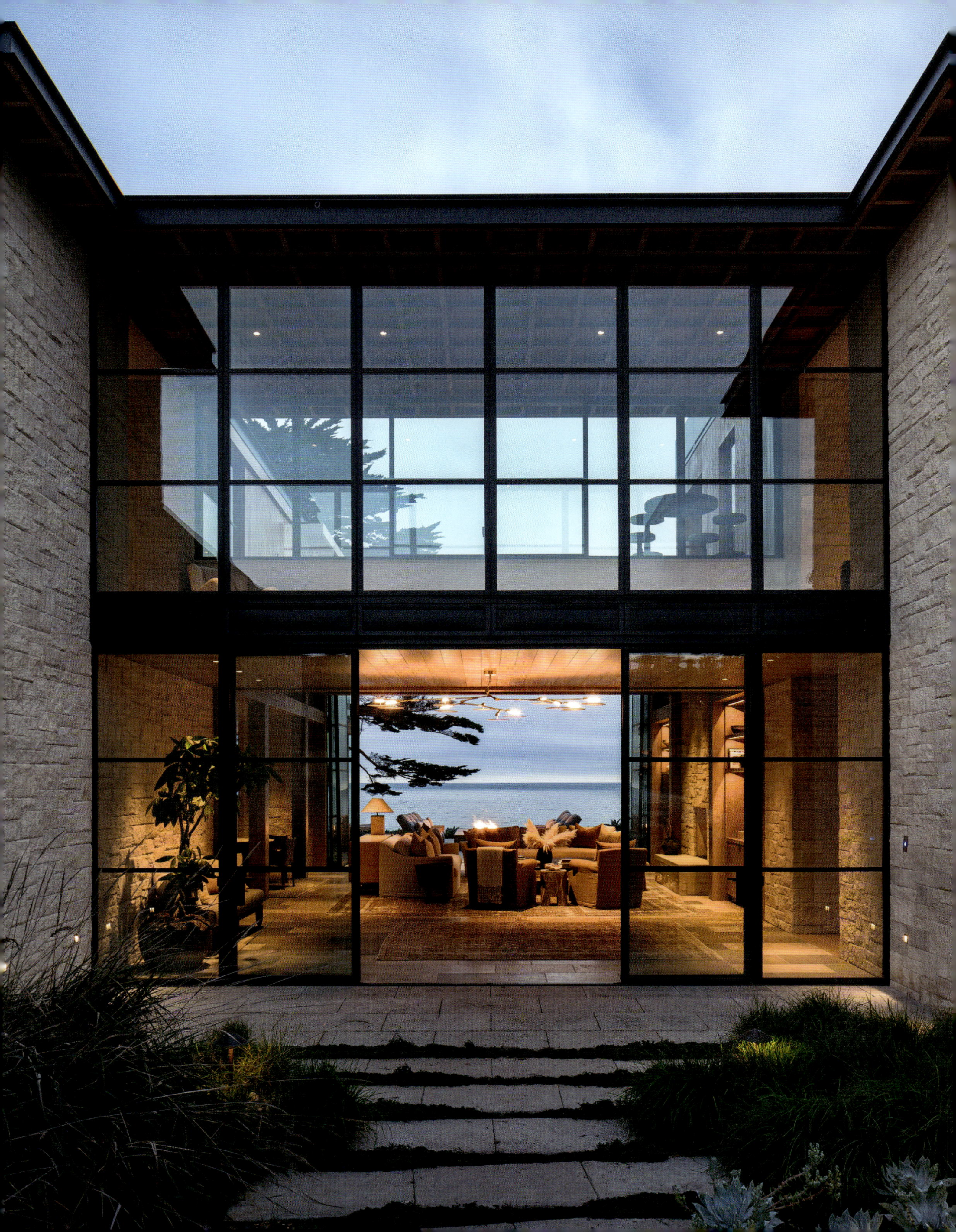

BEACH HOUSE + BOARDWALK HOUSE

/ CARMEL /

The small seaside town of Carmel might be one of the most picturesque coastal communities anywhere, and the site for this pair of homes is very likely the most magical plot of land on this stretch of the coast. At this spot, the coastline bends outward, opening views that span more than 180 degrees. Nestled between the public dunes on the edge of the quaint downtown and the Pescadero watershed, the site enjoys views that sweep from the coastline and Pacific Ocean to the south and west all the way to the famed Pebble Beach Golf Course to the north.

For its owners, a Houston-based couple who are equally passionate about golf and the sea, it was love at first sight. This was the perfect place to gather their large family, which includes three children and a growing brood of grandchildren. Although the plot is just 100 feet wide as it faces the ocean, it is deep enough to accommodate two homes, which they have fondly dubbed the Beach House and the Boardwalk House.

Building on the coast of Carmel is a serious undertaking, but with a deep family history in construction, these clients understood both the opportunities and constraints of designing and building a home on the coast. They assembled an all-star design team—architect Luca Pignata (at the time a principal with Backen & Backen Architecture), landscape architect Joni L. Janecki, and interior designer Amber Lewis—who worked together synergistically.

Pignata did not take the opportunity lightly. "When you are given the chance to design a home on a site like this, there is a huge sense of responsibility and duty to honor the place," he says. "We are obligated to do absolutely the best work we can."

Set one in front and the other behind, the two homes are in dialogue with one another and with the site, linked together by a gently meandering walkway that invites travelers to slow down and take in the surroundings. Unbelievably, every room has a view. Set back 65 feet from the edge of the bluff and framed by two groves of Monterey cypress, the Beach House captures every possible perspective of the Pacific. By pushing the Boardwalk House back on the site and away from the adjacent swale that carries water from the mountains to the coast, Pignata was able to maintain the property's natural contours while expanding views of the golf course to the north, turning a challenge into a golden opportunity.

In a timeless architectural language that marries contemporary massing with rusticated, resilient materials, the two structures share a palette of limestone, glass, steel, and teak. Arranged in a sophisticated pattern with a rough cut (which the architect calls a "magical combination"), the limestone echoes the tones of the sand and bluff, while hardy teak stands up to the coastal elements.

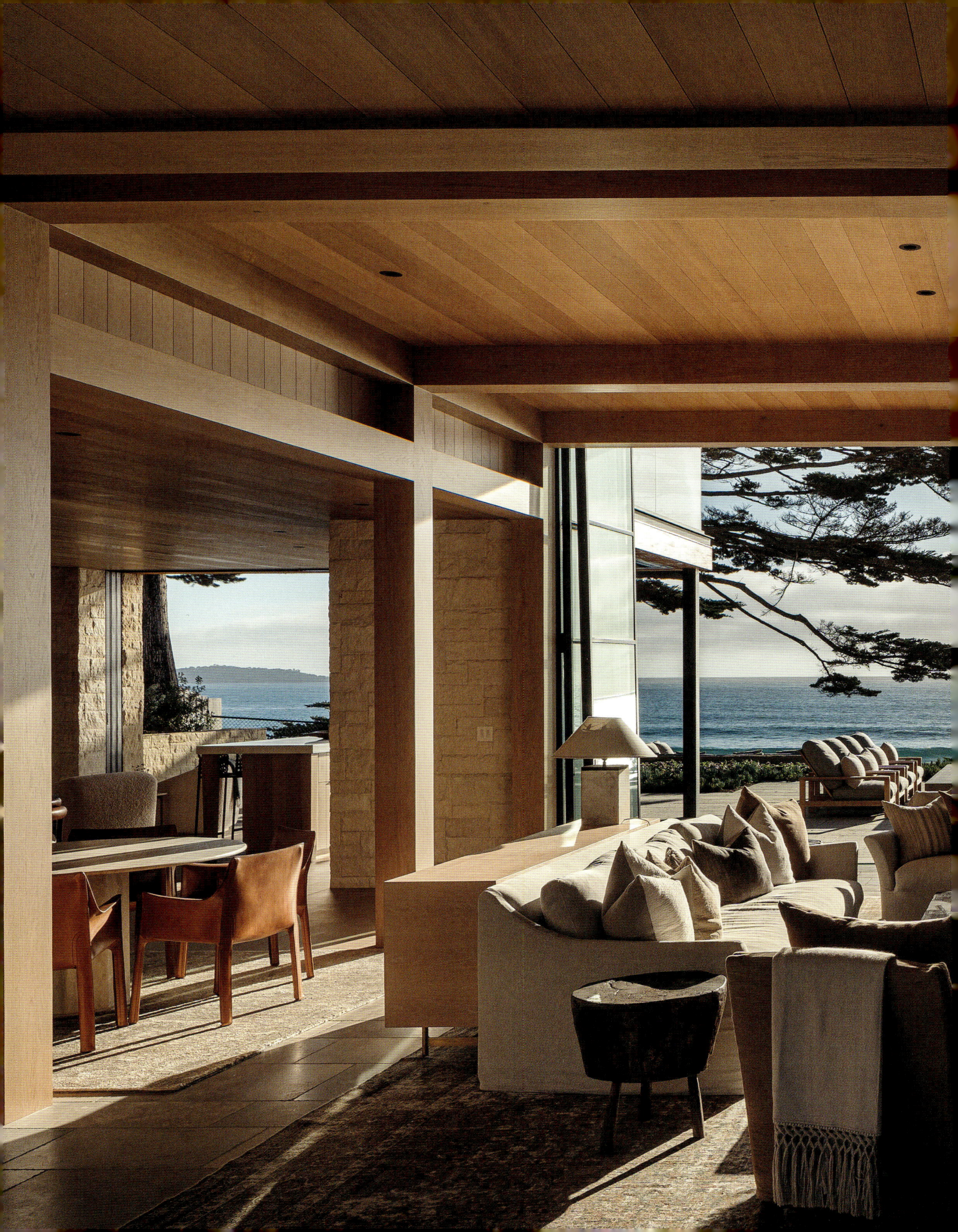

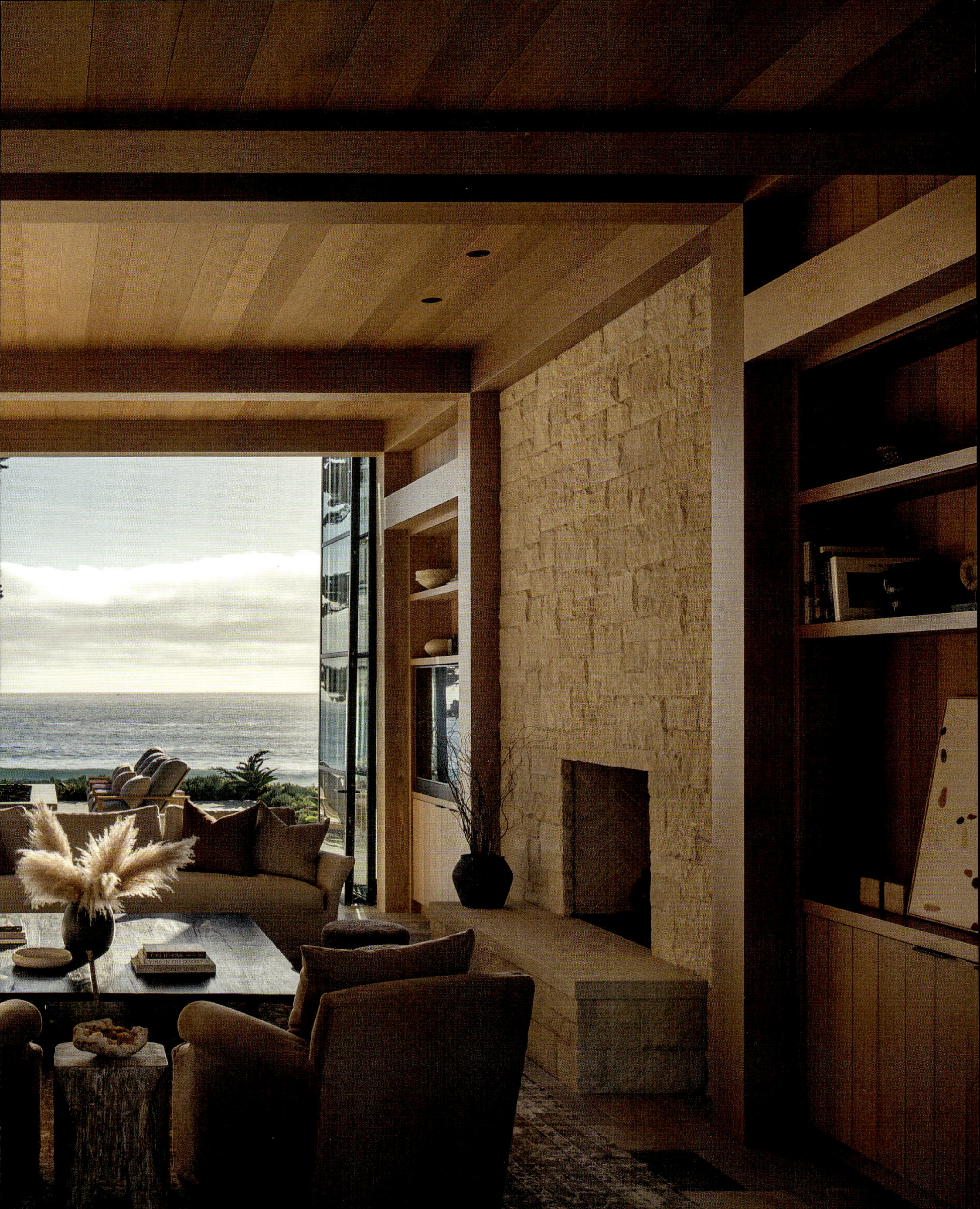
CALL IT HOME
LIVING IN THE DESERT

Each structure employs a unique take on the combination of materials, allowing each residence its individual sense of place.

In the Beach House, the scale and grandeur of the great room matches the impact of the vast ocean view. Walls of glass and steel mirror one another from front to back, and when both are open, the room becomes one with the site and the sounds of the ocean flow through the house. The great room is flanked by a kitchen, dining, and family room on one side and guest bedrooms on the other, all of which open to the ocean views. Numerous oceanfront gathering spaces, warmed by several firepits, step down toward the sea.

Set perpendicular to the Beach House, the Boardwalk House is also defined by a great room. Walls of glass and steel open to two terraces—an intimate terrace on the entry side, where cozy chairs pull up to an outdoor fireplace, and a more spacious terrace facing the golf course, with its own firepit and dining area. On one side of the great room, an expansive kitchen accommodates a crowd. On the other side, three bedrooms provide space for children and grandchildren. Upstairs, a jewel box of a main suite is encased in glass, a world apart from the potentially bustling atmosphere below.

Inside each home, Lewis worked her brand of design magic. Known for her chill California style and interiors that feel inviting and effortless, she is a self-proclaimed "California girl through and through," inspired by the state's myriad environments from coastal to desert.

The two homes share a consistent interior palette, but the unique style choices give each a distinct personality. In both houses, the furnishings and finishes are soft, comfortable, and properly scaled, cocooning the owners in comfort and providing a perfect counterbalance to the straight lines and harder materials of the contemporary architecture. White oak floors, chosen to have a minimum of knots or heavy graining, keep the background simple and soothing. Walls are cloaked in oak and a warm white custom plaster. At sunset everything glows.

The interiors complement the ocean views, keeping the focus squarely on the spectacular surroundings. The color scheme takes its cue from the sandy tone of the beach, the bluffs, and the limestone used in the architecture—a color Lewis considers a true neutral. "We shied away from adding anything stereotypically beachy," says the designer, "but instead created an interpretation of a deconstructed beach."

The team was also inspired by the gray driftwood found on the shore, as well as the shape and colors of the jagged edges of the cliffs, beach rocks, and coastal cypress trees. The effect is entirely natural, comfortable, and welcoming in the most unpretentious way. These are clearly homes meant to be lived in and enjoyed.

"This is not just a pair of beautiful houses. This is a work of love and a family legacy—a beautiful merging of vision and passion," says Pignata.

PRECEDING PAGE: The view from the Beach House front door, straight through the great room to the sea, invokes a feeling of pure awe.

OPPOSITE: The buff-colored limestone continues from the exterior into the interior, laid out in a sophisticated pattern with a rough cut, in an arrangement the architect calls a "magical combination."

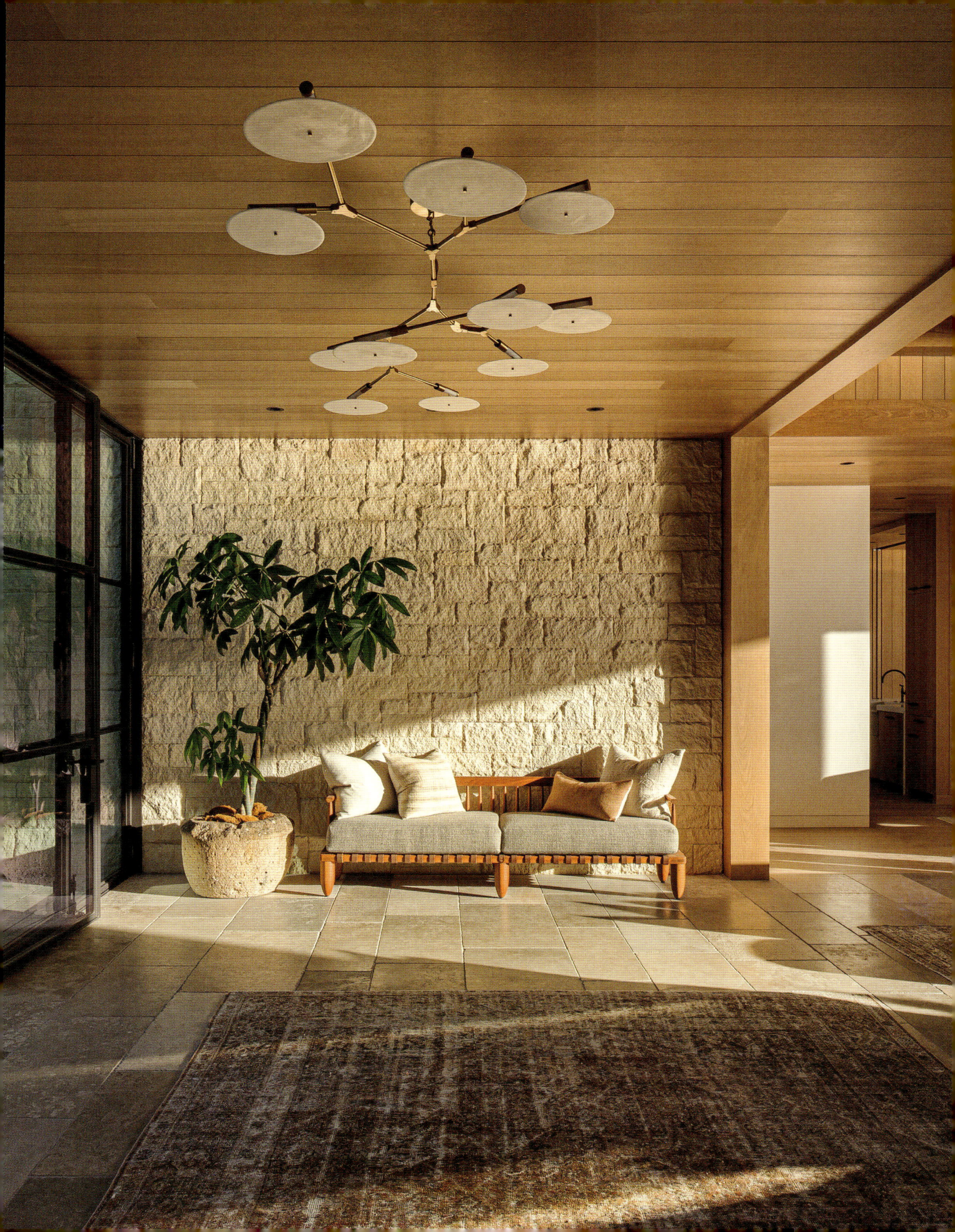

ABOVE: The glass walls of the family room and bar peel back from the corner and pocket into the walls. "When the doors to the terrace disappear, that is where the power of what we are doing becomes apparent," says Pignata.

OPPOSITE: An integrated cabinet divides the dining room and kitchen. Doors discreetly hidden within the cabinetry slide closed to hide any mess.

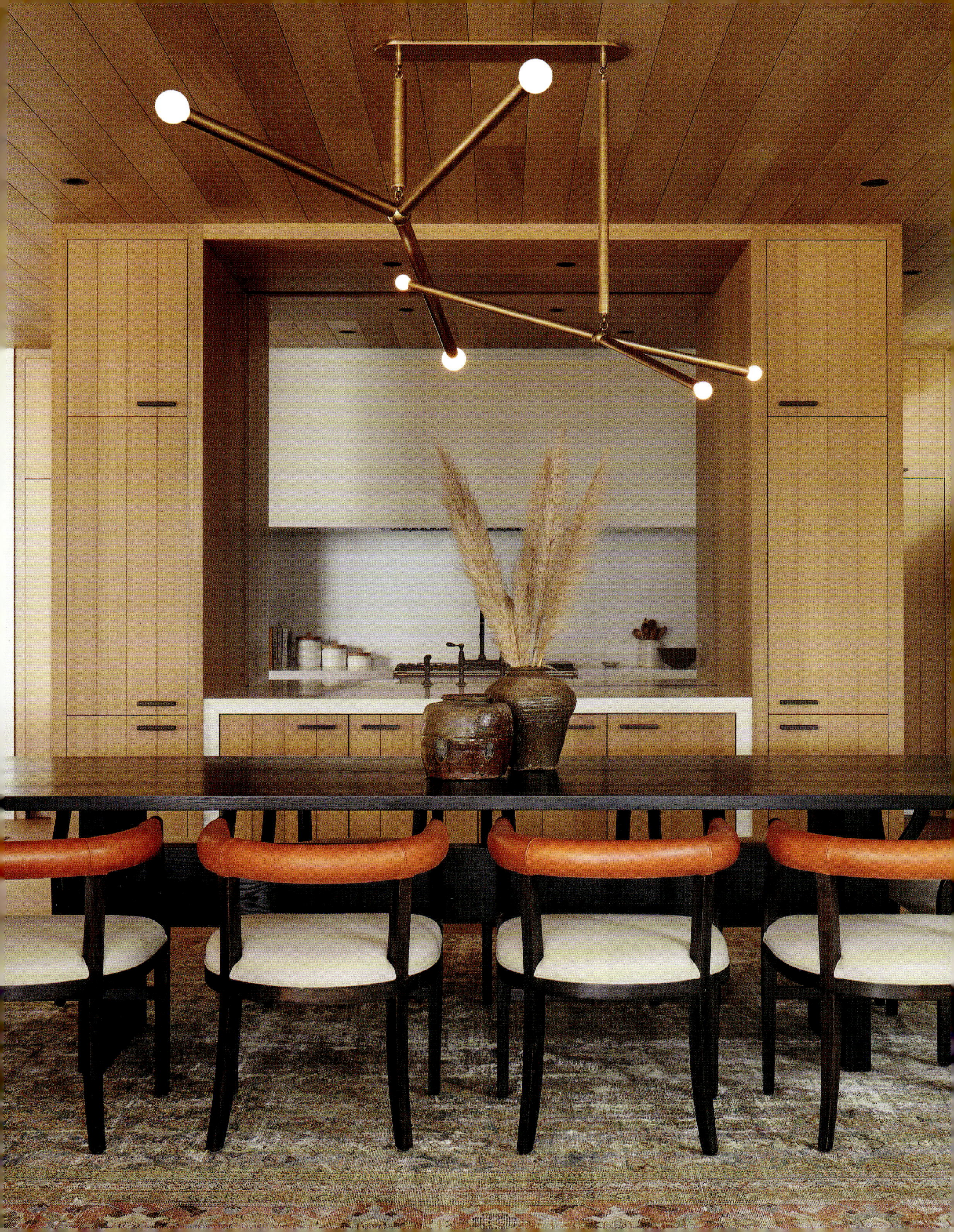

The bedrooms are private and restful yet open to the views through groupings of Monterey cypress, which shield the private terraces from the beach.

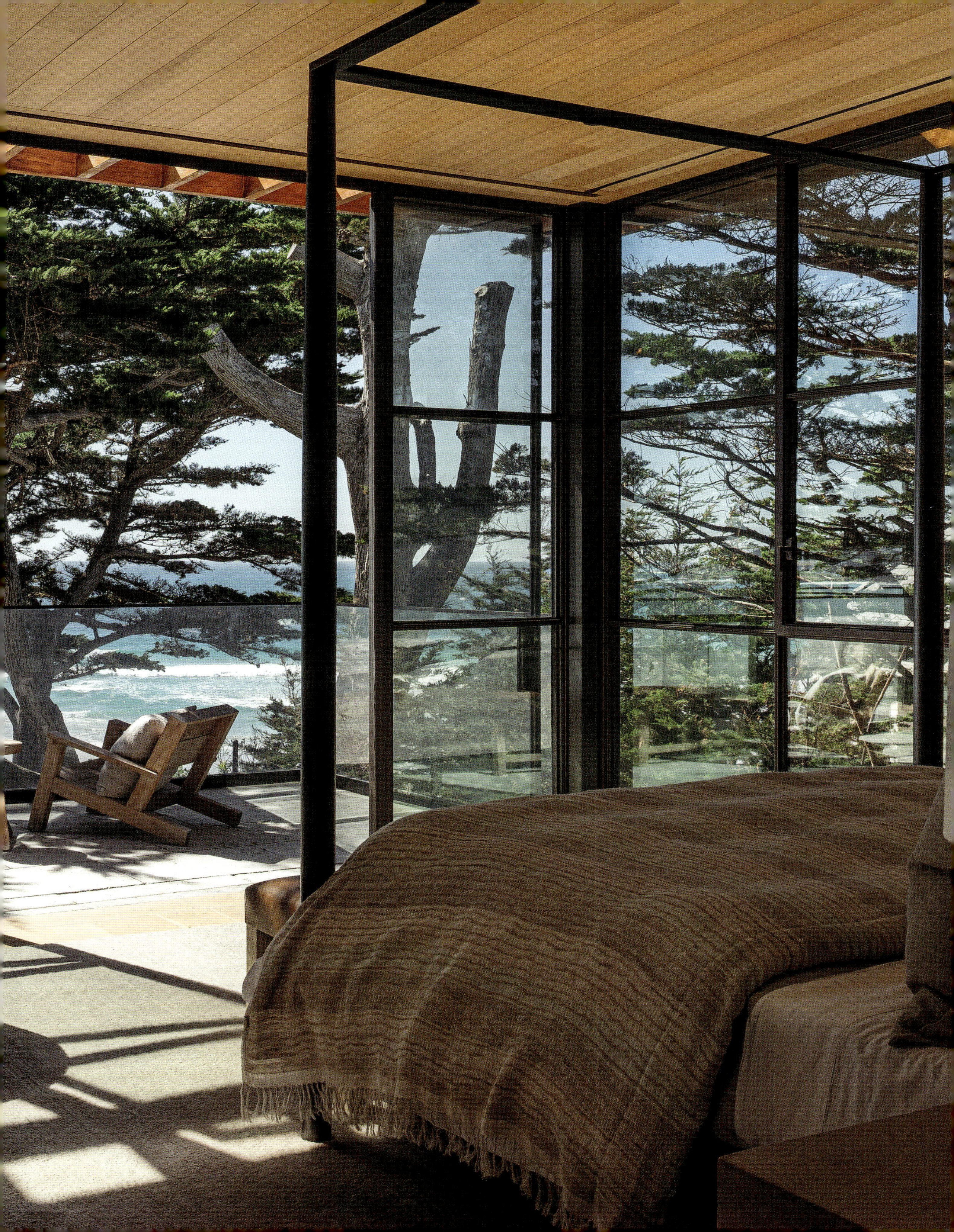

ABOVE: The garden path forms an essential connection between the two homes. The landscape knits the houses into the land, where native plantings abound and multiple microclimates influence the varied planting palette, as does the clients' love of flowers and color. "The coastal environment is specific and can be harsh. Nothing is going to do well here unless it is native to the place," Janecki points out.

OPPOSITE: Set perpendicular to the Beach House, the Boardwalk House hinges in the middle to follow the contours of the site. The building's turning point provided an ideal opportunity for a glassed-in primary entry that not only connects the two halves of the structure but forms a perfectly framed through view of the golf course to the north.

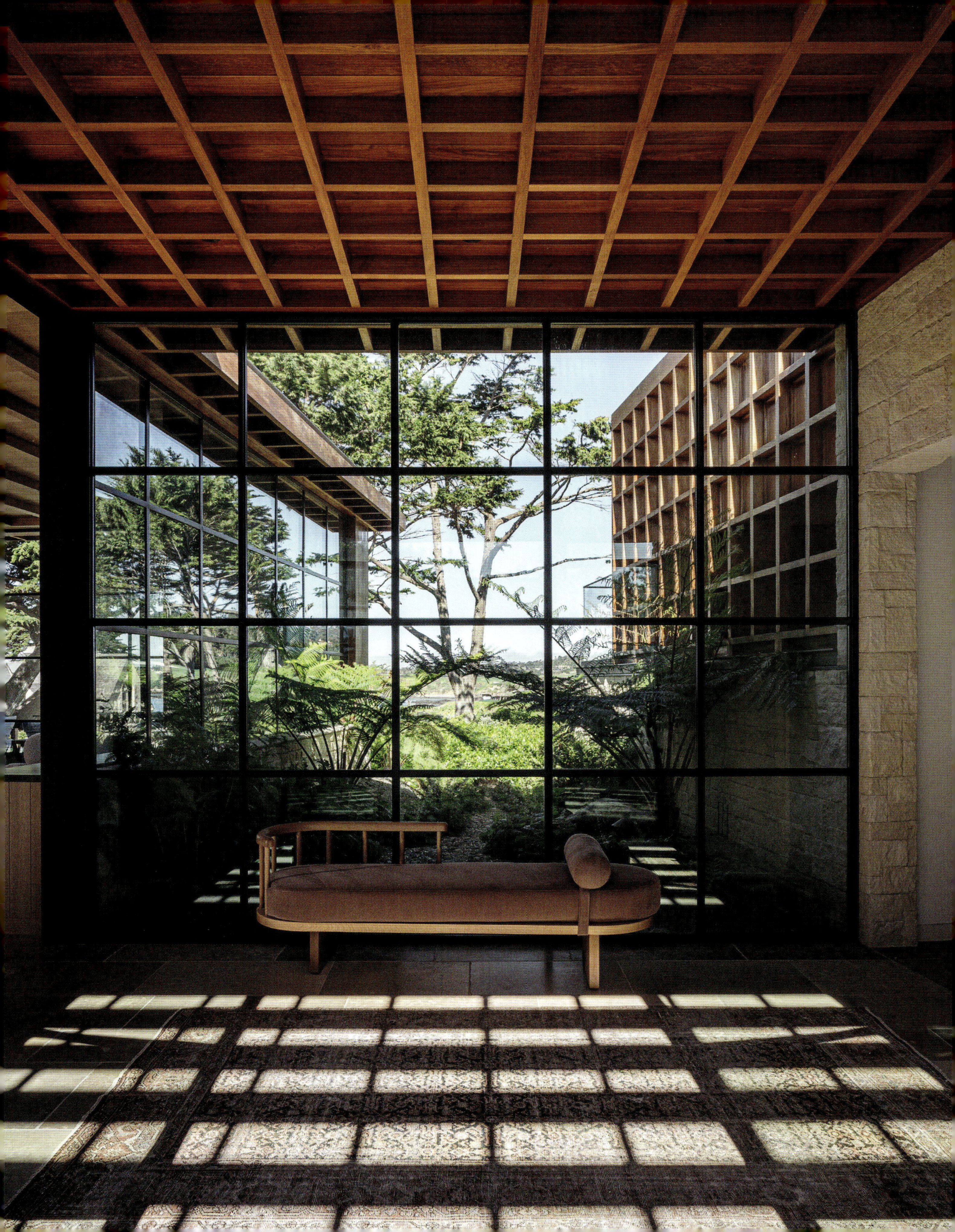

ABOVE: The kitchen in the Boardwalk House is large enough to host a crowd. Its simple palette consists of white oak cabinetry, light marble counters, leather bar stools, and brass fixtures.

OPPOSITE: Lewis calls the living–dining room in the Boardwalk House "the ultimate hangout room," and it's designed to stand up to wear and tear. Vintage Pierre Jeanneret caned dining chairs with custom pads in a performance fabric surround the long table. Glass doors pocket away to form a seamless indoor–outdoor space.

OVERLEAF: Fires are a much-enjoyed amenity in frequently chilly Carmel, and this property boasts seven of them: four firepits and three outdoor fireplaces. Positioned to warm the many decks and terraces, they also act as beacons on the journey through the property. Set into the native landscape, the bluff firepit is the owners' favorite spot on the property.

BEACH HOUSE + BOARDWALK HOUSE

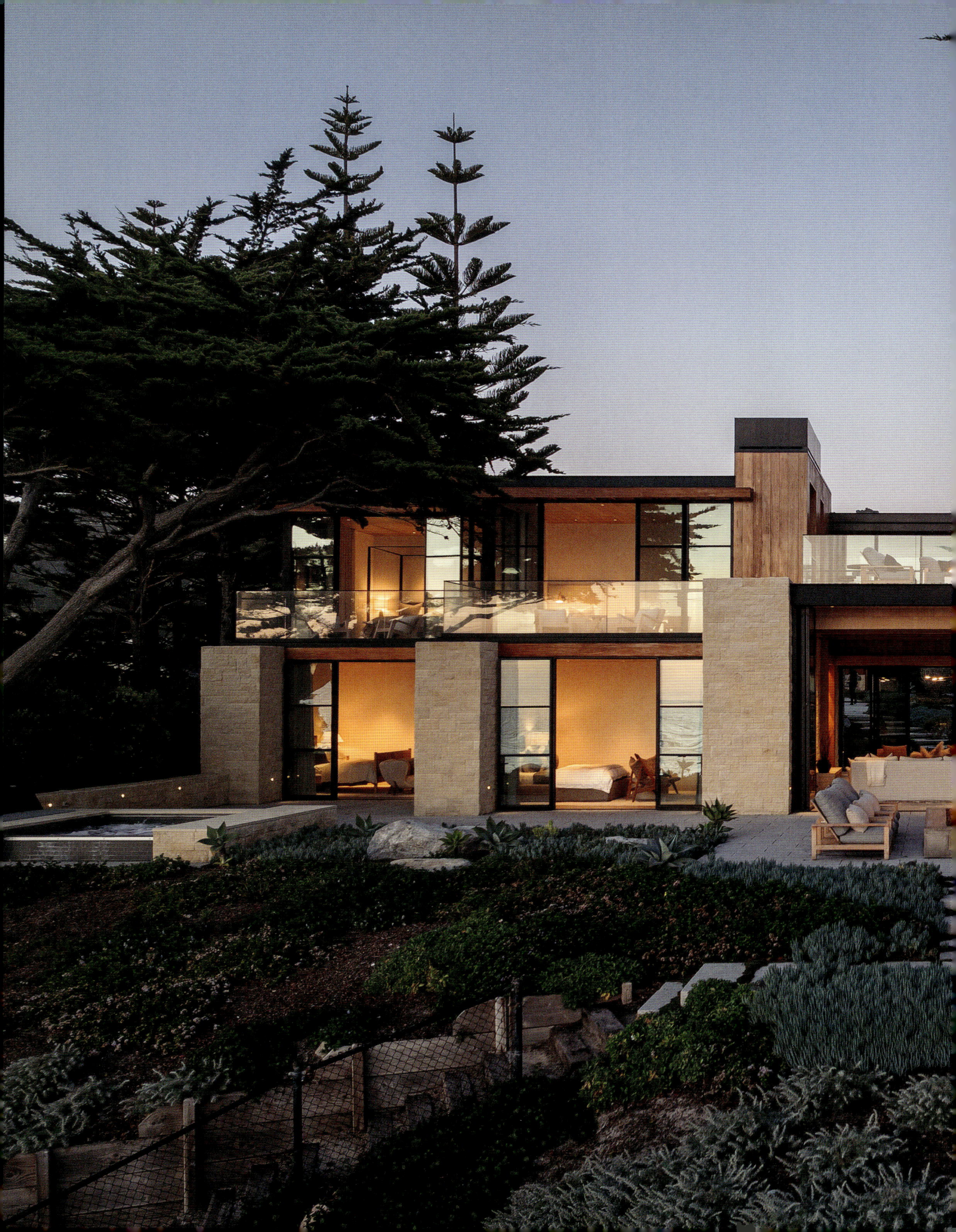

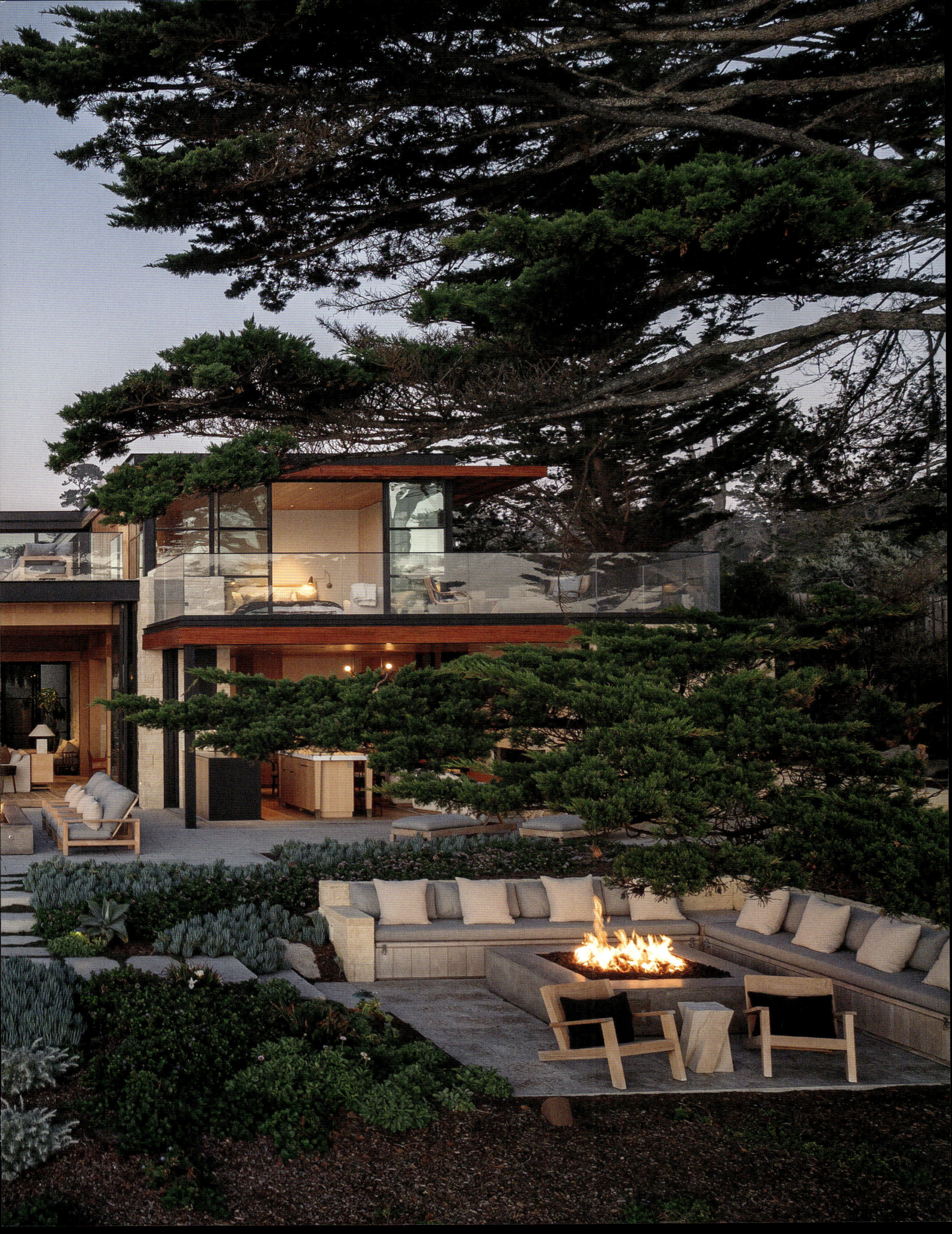

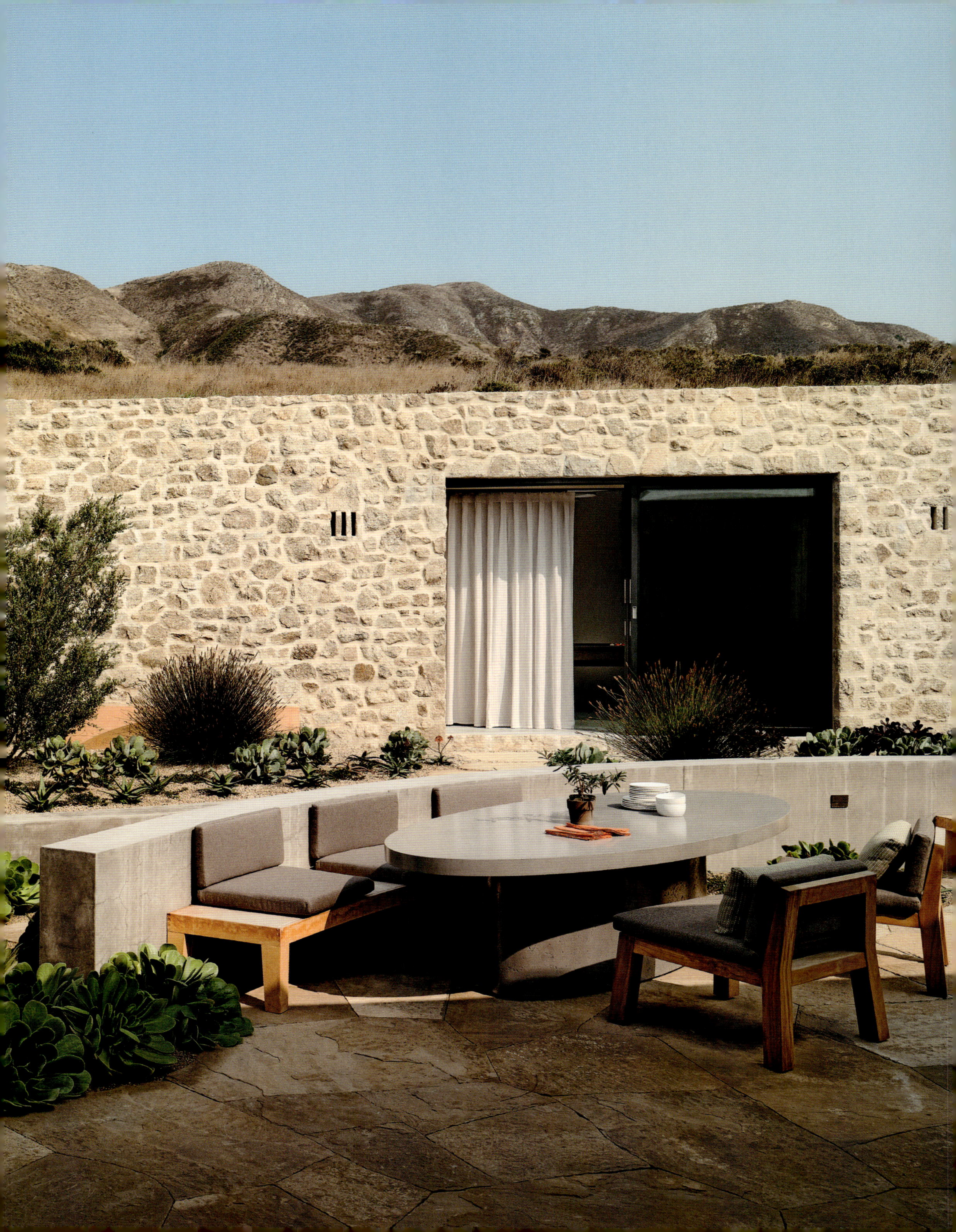

GROUNDED IN PLACE

/ BIG SUR /

The phrase "once in a lifetime" is usually employed hyperbolically, but when it comes to the fabled Big Sur coastline, it just might be literal. In an exceedingly rare move, three contiguous parcels owned by The Nature Conservancy were offered on the market, sparking an unparalleled opportunity for new construction in one of the most iconic and protected regions of the entire coast. This exquisite landscape attracted the perfect landowner—one who would not only buy all 160 acres but would build only minimally.

For architect Mary Ann Schicketanz and her design-savvy clients, a Bay Area family of three generations, the goals were twofold: to capitalize on the extraordinary setting and to meld into the environment as much as possible. They envisioned a multi-pavilioned home that would embed into the ocean-facing landscape of rolling hills and open native grassland. In conceptualizing the design, explains Schicketanz, "We tried to be respectful of the land, to have as small a footprint as possible, and to lock the buildings into the landscape as best we could. The 175-foot-long retaining wall starts at zero, slowly curves up to full height to accommodate the building, then goes all the way back to zero again. We tucked a wedge into the hillside and put as much of the building underground as we could. We then folded the hill, so to speak, back over the house and added green roofs."

The effect is sublime. As the access road winds its way uphill from Highway 1 to arrive at the parking court, the long retaining wall seems to carry through that line as it turns to arc across the hillside. It then embraces and shelters the rectilinear volumes of stone and plaster. Other than the house and the minimalistic pool, interventions are virtually unnoticeable; the native landscape comes right up to the edge of the structure, while external support systems like power lines, transformers, and water tanks are buried. With minimal hardscaping around the pool, the only additional landscaping is found in the interior courtyard carved out between the house and the hillside. There, Bernard Trainor, Ben Langford, and David LeRoy of Ground Studio planted Mexican lily, Australian tea tree, manzanita, and succulents to add color and texture to the outdoor gathering area, which offers warmth and sunshine even when high winds are blowing off the Pacific. Uniform paving materials of Sonoma buff sandstone in the parking area, courtyard, connectors between buildings, and pool coping create consistency. These harmonize with the local granite used for the building's stone walls and Venetian plaster interiors, reclaimed oak and concrete floors, and ceilings made from reclaimed wine barrels.

The residence was designed to be intergenerational, with four separate masses comprising one wing for the owners, one for the children, one for extended family (the grandmother lives with the family much of the time), and another for guests. At the light-filled entry connector, frosted glass at

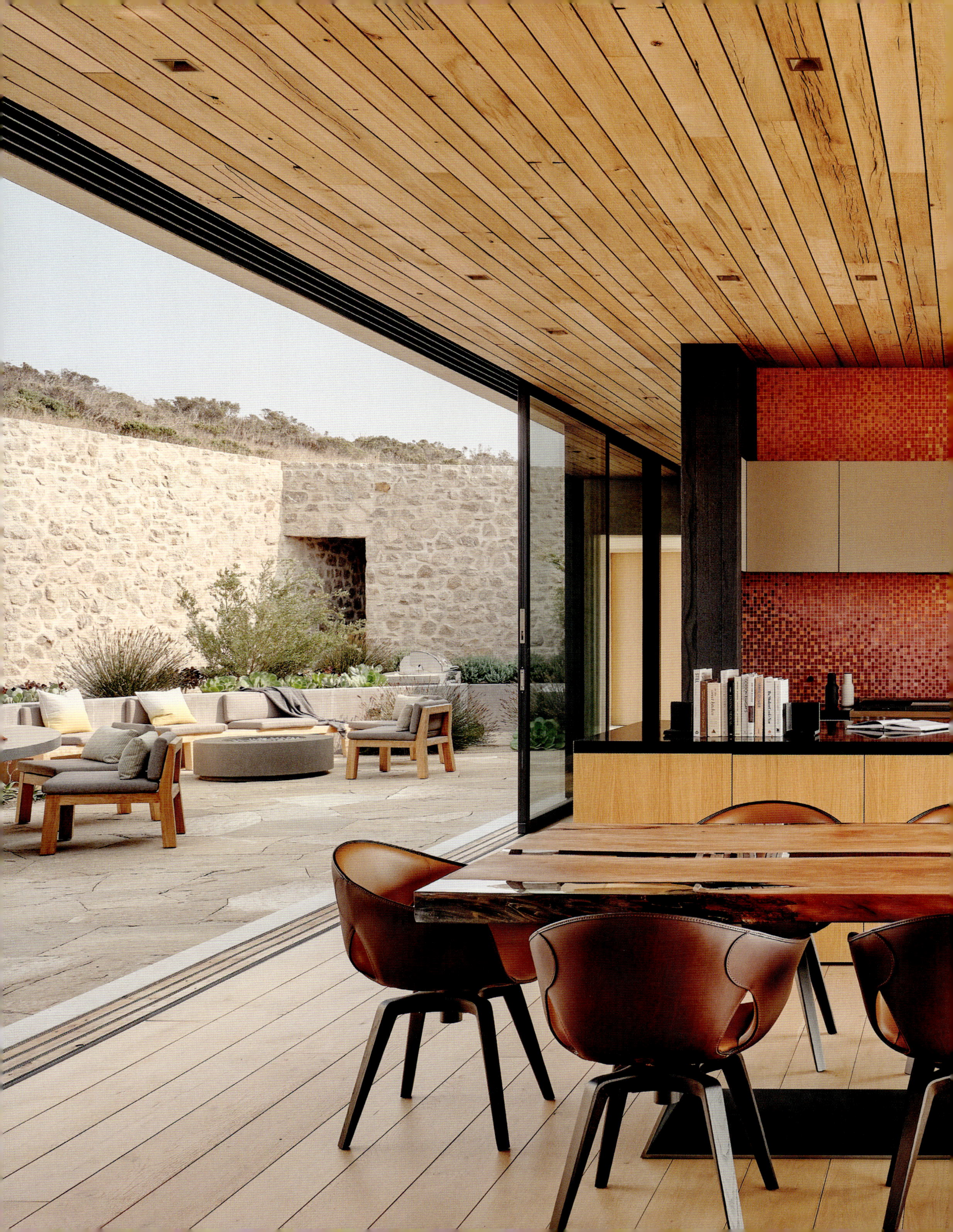

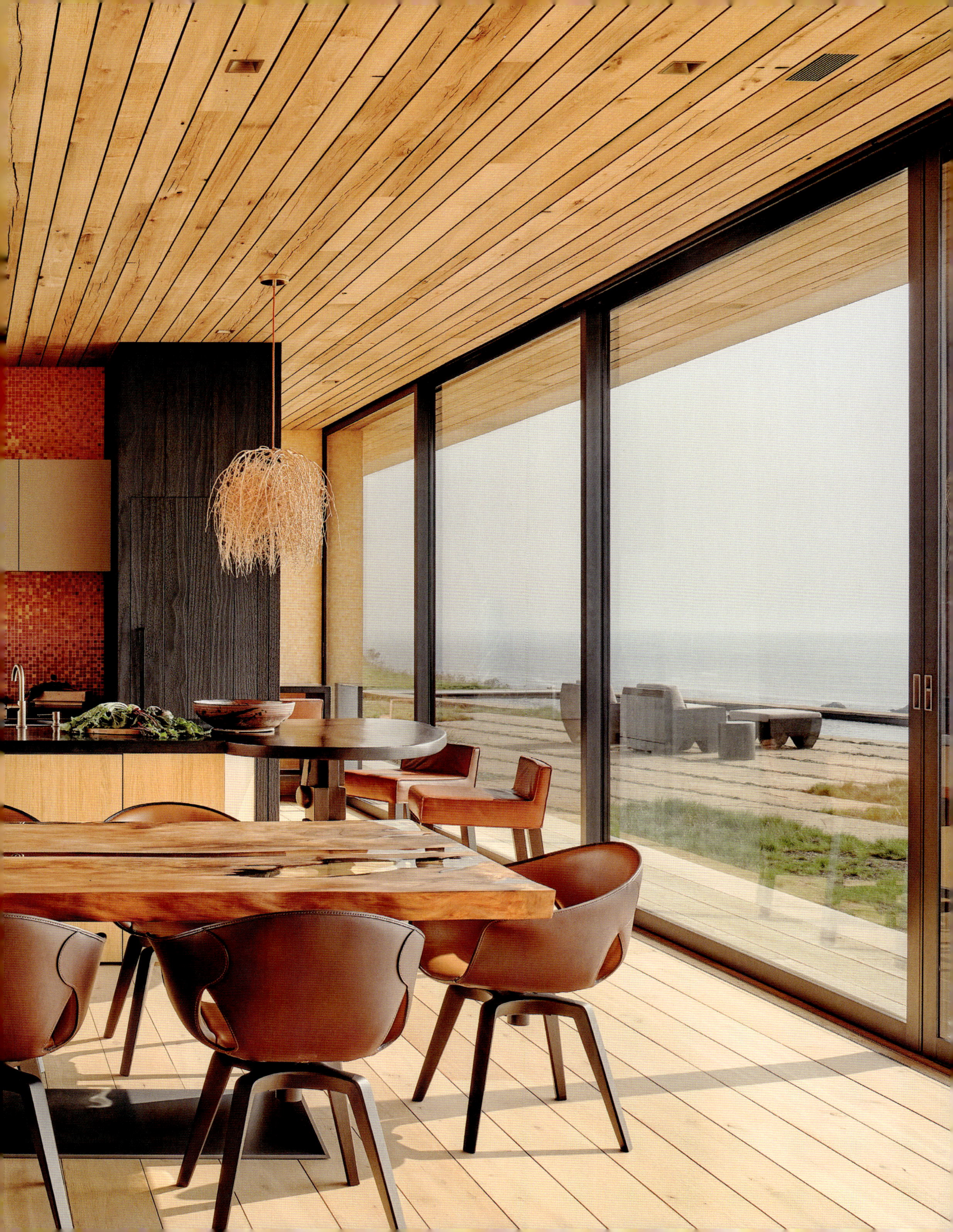

the doorway creates privacy for those inside, while clear glazing provides a full view into the interior courtyard. Three of the primary volumes have floor-to-ceiling sliders on their western walls to maximize views of the Pacific and create a connection to the pool. The guest suite, positioned against the stone retaining wall carved into the hillside, inhabits the fourth volume; it has a view into the courtyard through sliding doors for a more contemplative experience.

It is in the primary living, dining, and kitchen space where sliding doors open wide on either side, that the integration of house into hillside is most impactful. There you feel at once part of the environment and protected from it, explains Trainor. "Resilience and refuge are the two words that come to my mind. It's harsh out there. It's beautiful, but it's not for the fainthearted. With 40-to-50 miles-per-hour windstorms, you need incredible fortitude to enjoy it. But there's this layer of landscape that slices between the buildings and the courtyard. And when you're in the house, it feels like the landscape is sweeping straight through."

Respect for the land is inherent in this project and is no doubt the only approach that was acceptable to the California Coastal Commission. For Schicketanz, it was a given. "I felt it needed quiet architecture rather than something that makes a big to-do," she says. "The curved retaining wall very much belongs to the land, then we have this very quiet, still meadow. There was also this incredibly beautiful long, flat horizon, and the house responds to that. Looking out, you see a light blue strip of sky, then the dark blue strip of the ocean, and then the green strip of the meadow. It looks like a beautiful landscape painting."

Although the Big Sur coastline is world famous for its visual iconography, it is when the fog rolls in, as it so often does, that the experience feels its most immersive. When the house becomes enshrouded in mist and visibility is limited to the immediate grasslands, life is reduced to the sounds of waves lapping and sea lions barking. For a home nestled in the hills on the edge of the continent, it is the ultimate grounding in place.

PRECEDING PAGE: For a home set in the pristine hills of the fabled Big Sur coast, the team — Studio Schicketanz with Anderson Construction and Ground Studio Landscape Architecture — took inspiration from the surrounding landscape, while the project's main design challenge served as catalyst for its most innovative feature. In accordance with local planning laws, the new building had to remain invisible from Highway One. The building site was created by cutting a shelf into the hillside and building a curved, fifteen-foot-high retaining wall to blend with the land. The layout incorporates two freestanding pavilions whose connectors have floating roofs and glass on two sides; a third volume contains the parents' wing. Schicketanz says of the clients, who were both educated and involved, especially in the architecture, "They couldn't have been better stewards of the land."

In designing the interiors, the designers wanted to honor the homeowners' Indian heritage with a considered infusion of color. The Bisazza custom tile mosaic in the kitchen is an interpretation of a Rothko painting. The Kauri dining table by Riva 1920 and Poltrona Frau chairs are centered within the dining room and between ocean views to the west and the interior courtyard to the east. Cabinetry is by Sozo Studio.

OPPOSITE: Bernard Trainor, Ben Langford, and David LeRoy of Ground Studio designed the landscape for the interior courtyard. "By having a large courtyard," says Trainor, "you can satisfy the desire for a garden or decorative plants without seeing out or redirecting the native landscape." On the hillside their approach called for minimal intervention with a mix of low shrubs, native pine trees, and wildflowers and grasses.

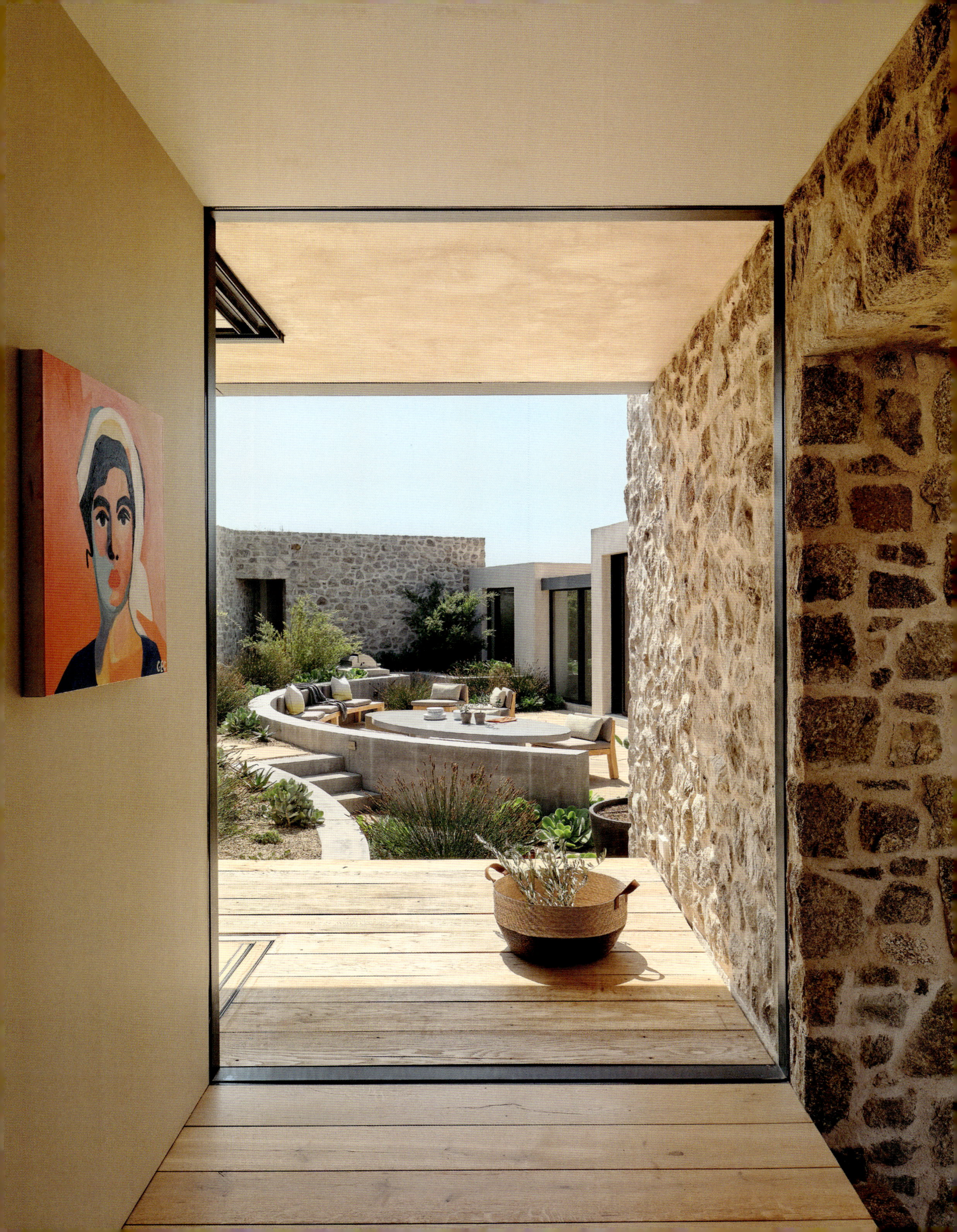

ABOVE: The design and detail of the house was crucial for its long-term viability, explains architect Mary Ann Schicketanz. "This location is so exposed; it is completely out in the open. Storms from the south and north just pound this location, and it's very windy. Having robust detailing was crucial because it rains sideways and uphill. Having a house that's really low was very important for all those reasons."

OPPOSITE: Ceilings made from reclaimed wine barrels add warmth and texture throughout the home, while furnishings were selected for shape and comfort and kept neutral as a reflection of architectural finishes. In the media room, a Flexform sectional is paired with B&B Italia poufs and backed by a dark Phillip Jeffries wall covering.

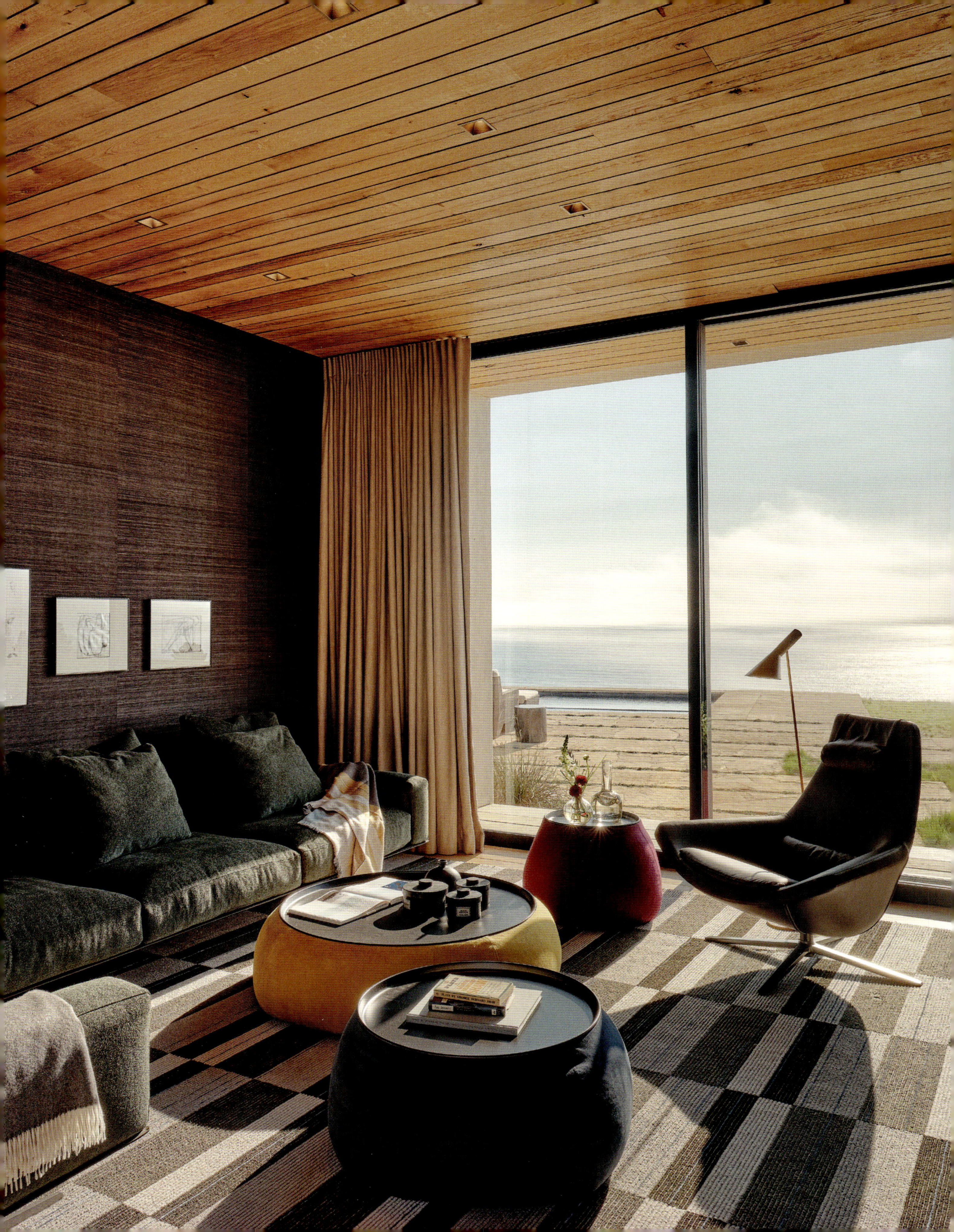

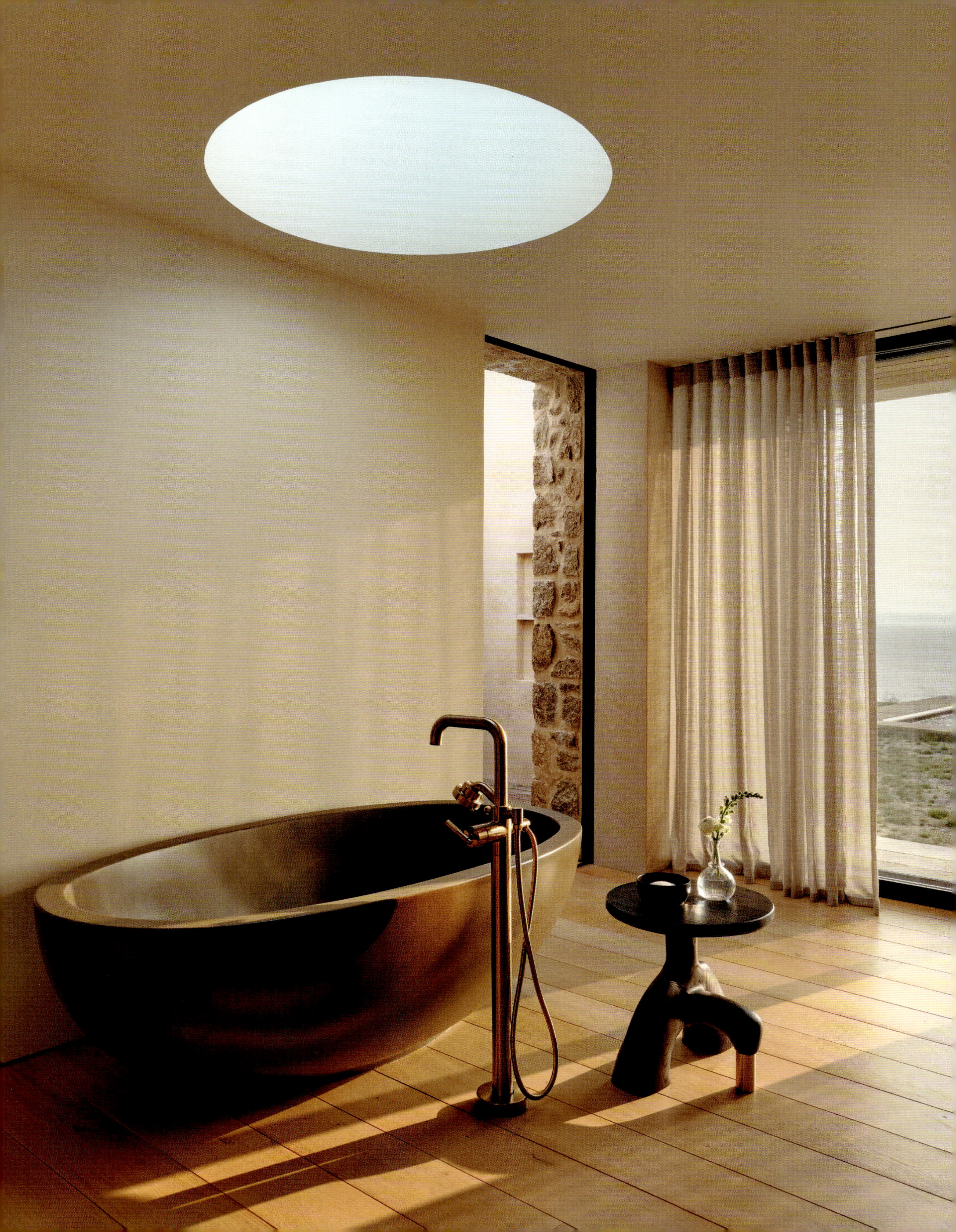

OPPOSITE: A round skylight pulls light down onto a Vegas tub from Concreteworks, which in turn faces out to the Pacific.

ABOVE: The primary bath features custom cabinetry with Litze Collection fixtures by Brizo.

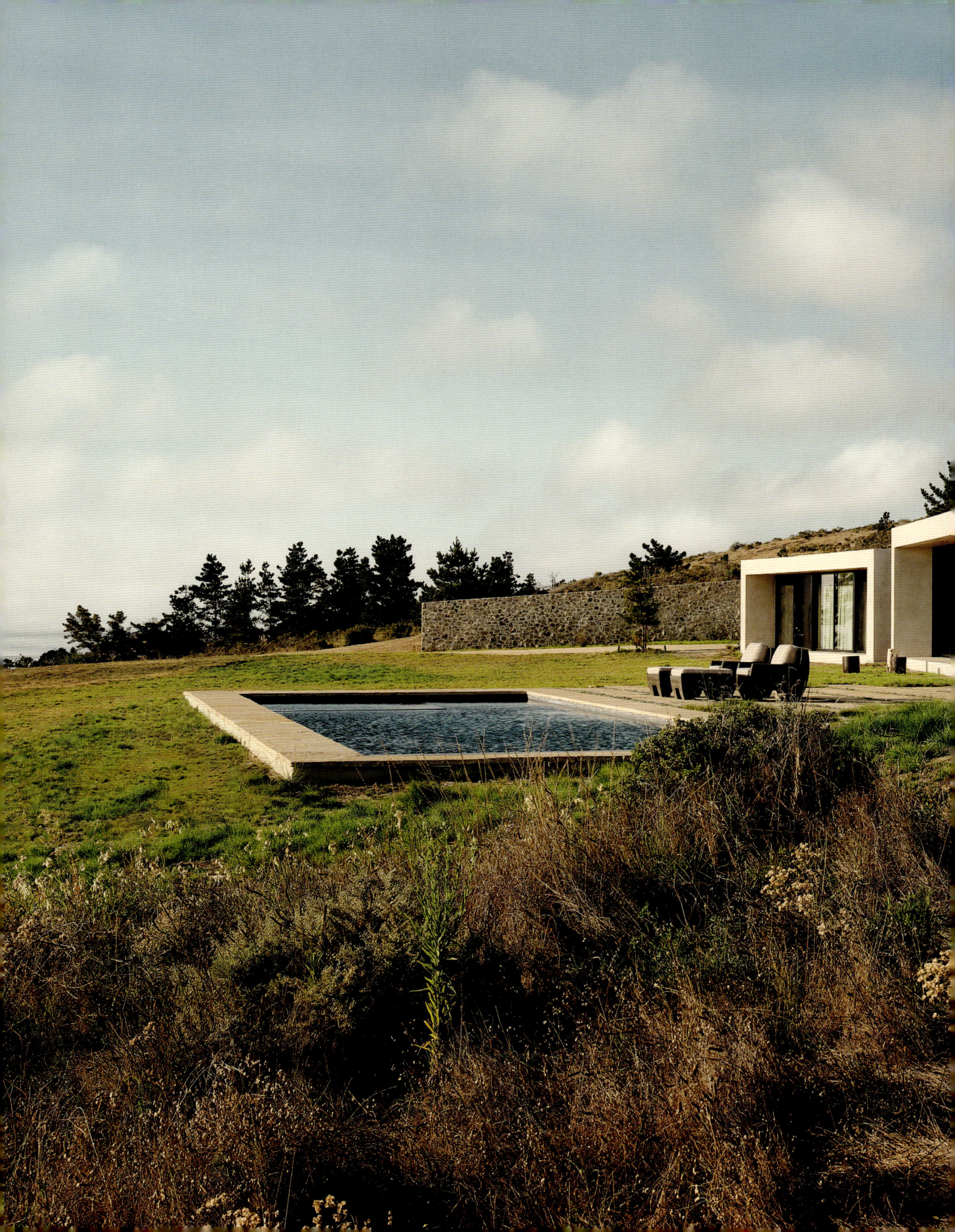

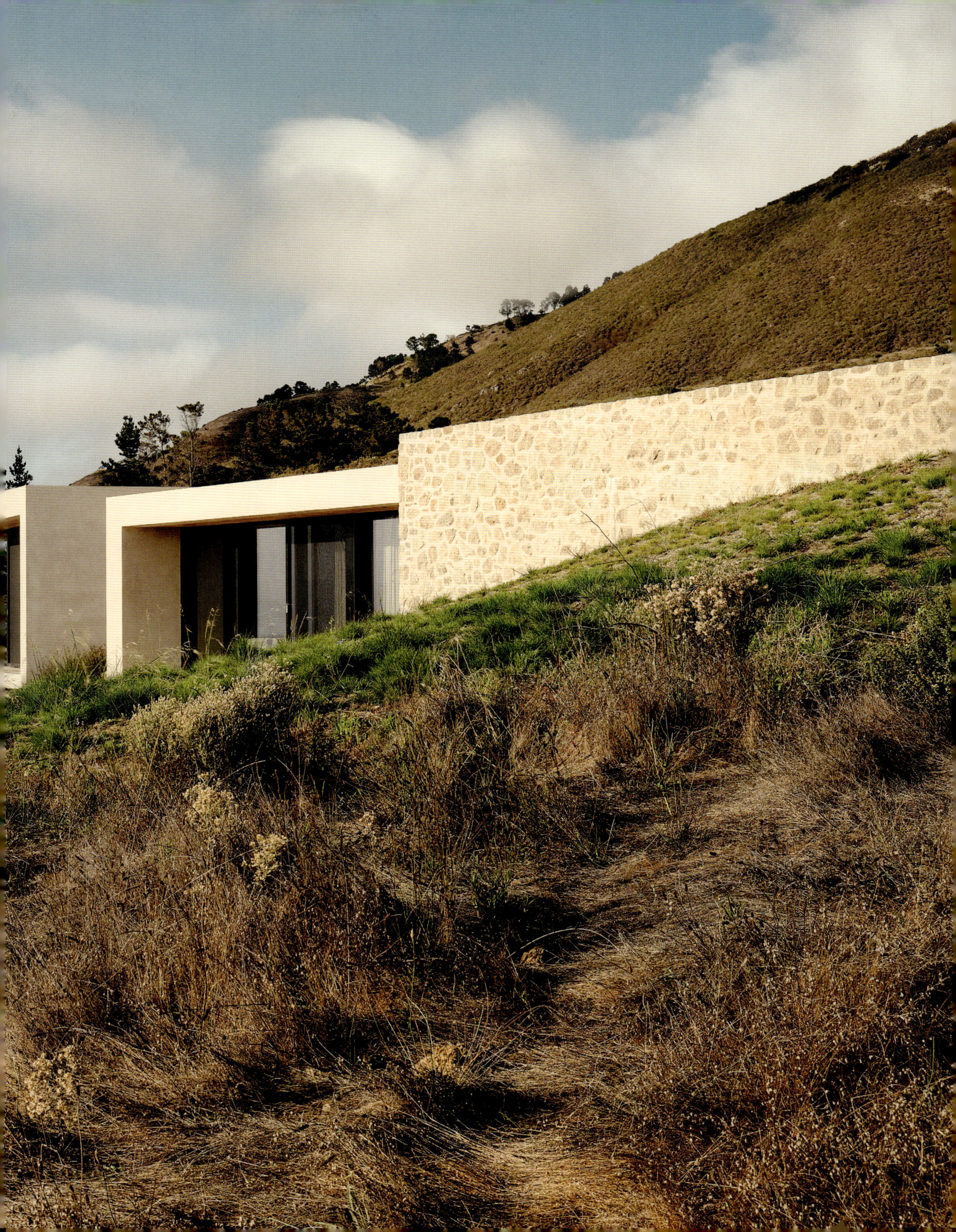

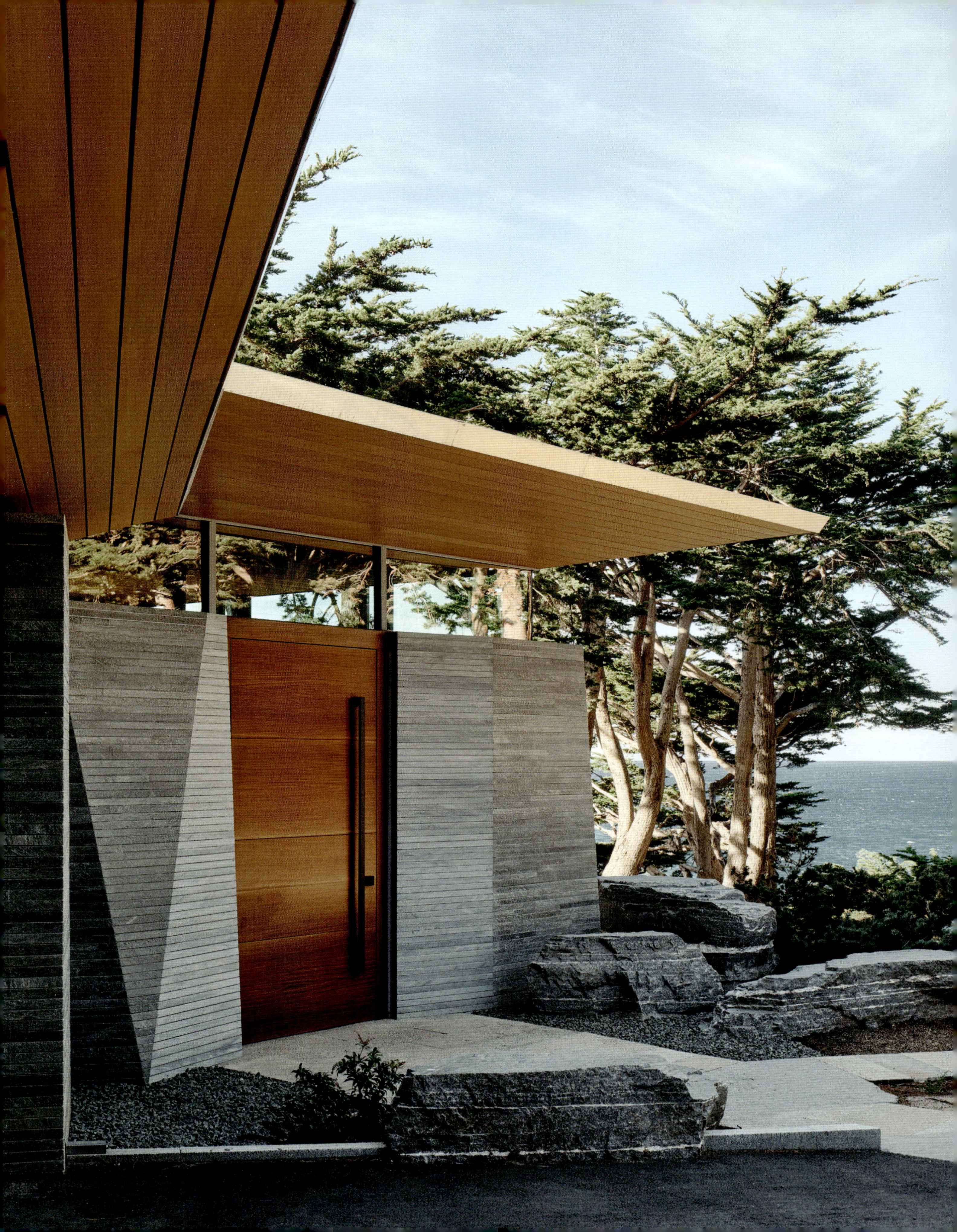

PROSPECT + REFUGE

/ BIG SUR /

Architect Jess Field loves the California landscape, particularly its coastline. "We have to form a personal connection to the place in order to create what it means to be there," he asserts.

Jess sits at the helm of Field Architecture, a firm founded by his father, Stan, on the premise that architecture belongs to the land and at its best can become the conduit for an intimate and meaningful connection to nature. If there is a throughline to the work of this firm, it is derived from the art of listening to the land.

As surfers who have spent thousands of hours walking the shores of California and swimming in its waters, Jess and his father have a decades-long relationship with the cliffs of Big Sur, which epitomize the rugged grandeur of the state's Central Coast—raw, powerful, and shaped by the unmitigated strength of the sea. "Big Sur is the soul of the California coast," says Field. This is one of the steepest interfaces between mountains and sea on the West Coast, and the impact of the Santa Lucia Range cannot be overstated. "The topography is constantly changing where the power of the ocean collides with the edge of the land," notes the architect. The ethos of this home set on the jagged cliffs is—more than almost any other—one of intention and discovery, an authentic architectural response that comes from paying attention and hearing what the land has to say.

The house is a second home designed for clients who are equally passionate about the region and site. It occupies a plateau on which an aging wood-frame structure once stood. Simply incapable of withstanding the forces of nature here, the original structure had outlived its useful life. The new home, like the property it occupies, displays a balance of elegance and power. Field describes his design process as an attempt to carve out the architecture in response to the elements, in much the same way as the cliffs are carved out by the sea, so the architecture and land abide by the same laws of nature.

The structure is equally defined by its architectural concept and the emotions it evokes. Combining immersion in the coastal environment and protection from the elements, it forms a balance of prospect and refuge that often repeats itself in the best of California coastal architecture. Embedded into the landscape, the architecture has the gravitas of an anchor.

Set high above the ocean, the site is varied—folding and hollowing out into ravines and fingers of ground that reach out into the ocean. On an early site walk, a suspect squishy spot revealed an ancient seasonal stream that had been filled in with decades of leaf litter. Working with landscape architect Joni L. Janecki, who calls the collaboration a "delightful meeting of the minds," Field cleared the ravine and restored the stream, honoring the naturally occurring topography by moving

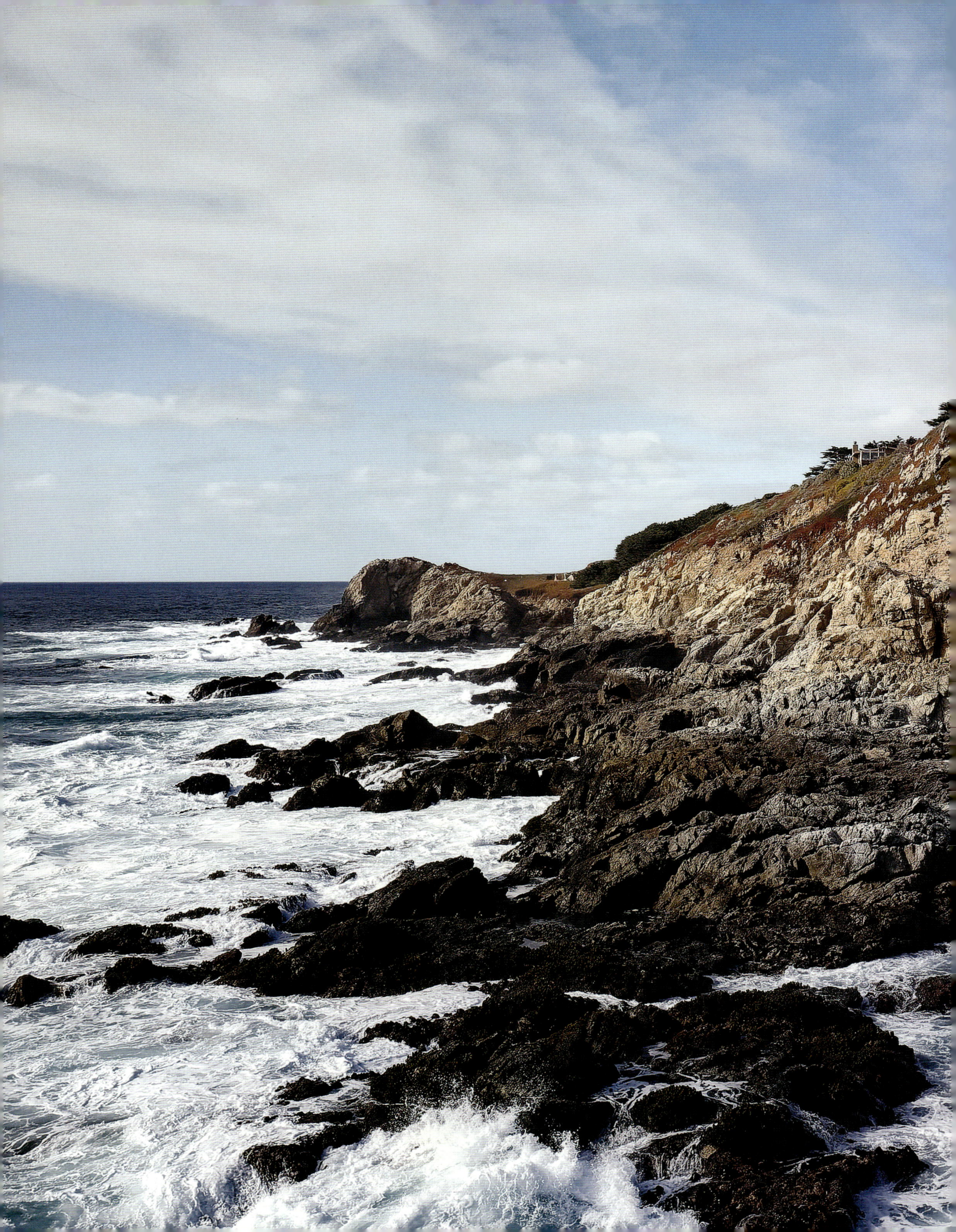

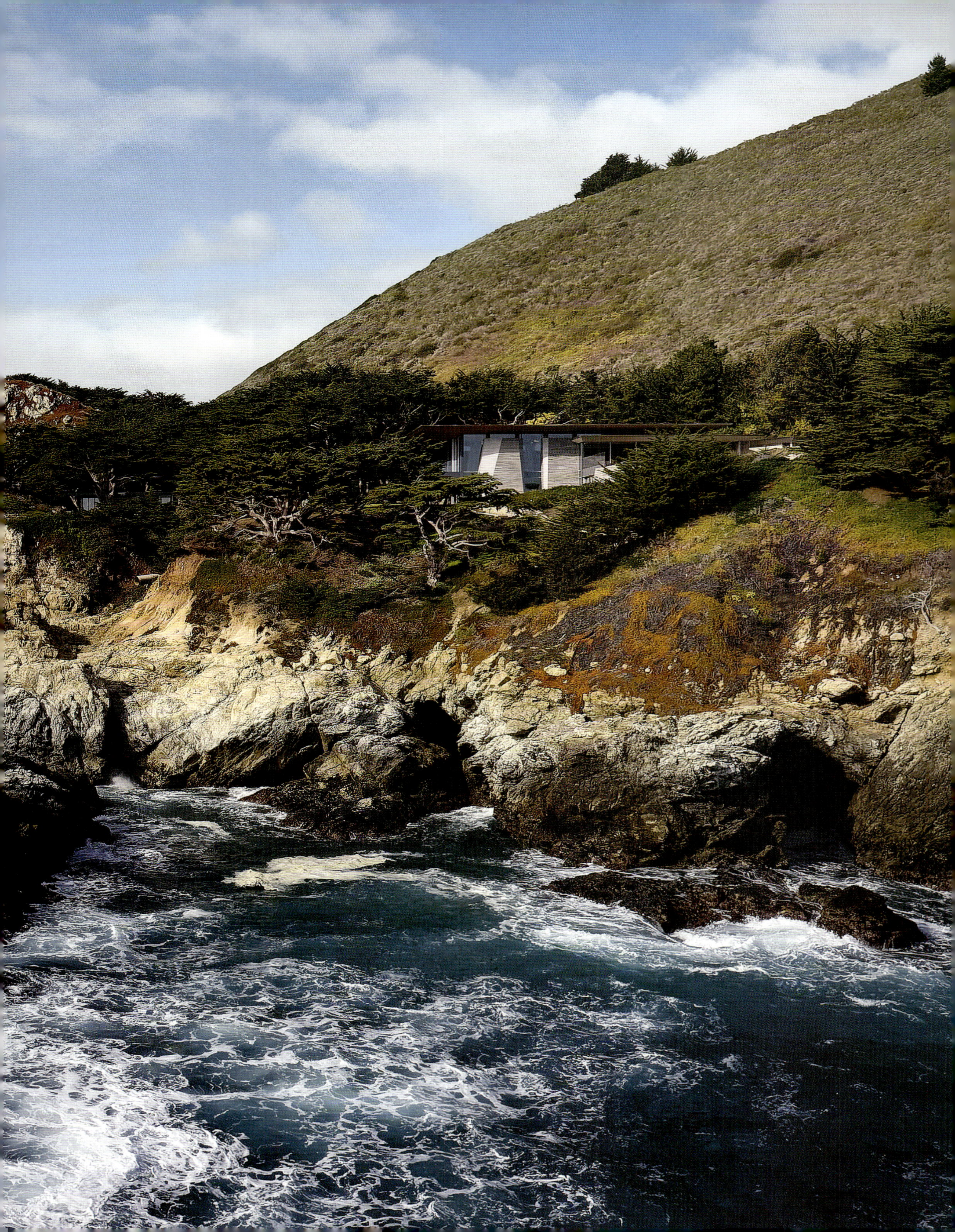

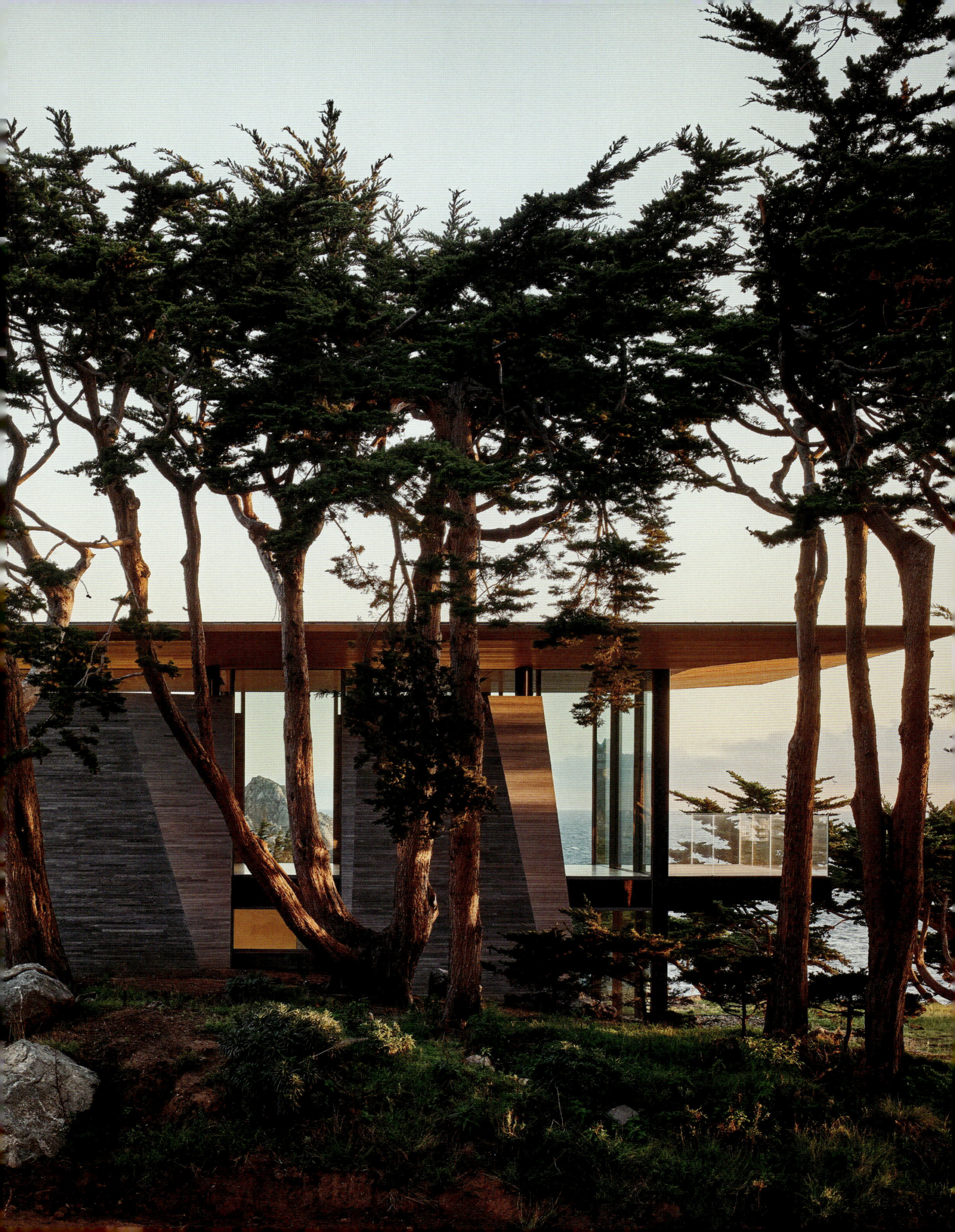

the building out of the pathway of nature. A bridge now spans the ravine, linking the entry structure to the main house and forming a carefully orchestrated journey that urges visitors to slow down and appreciate the surroundings.

Tucked behind a cypress grove, the house is sheltered from the winds that bear down from the north. These iconic trees also frame the ocean view, bringing a sense of scale and perspective to the broad expanse. The more protected southern facade is designed for indoor–outdoor living, with an infinity pool carved out of the site like a tide pool.

The most stable components of this constantly evolving environment are the rocks, which, as Field puts it, "have staying power." The home's stone walls, visual echoes of the fractured coastal cliffs, form buttresses that provide both visual and actual strength, collecting the sun's warmth during the day and then dispersing it through the interior at night. Apertures are carefully curated to frame specific views of the sea, the rising tide, or the setting sun. The extended rooflines are calibrated to shade from the high summer sun while allowing the low winter sun in. The clerestories complement this effect by allowing daylight deep into the spaces, as well as views of the surrounding hills and treetops. As the building ages, it will take on the patina that the landscape imparts, becoming ever more stitched into the fabric of the coast.

Wanting the entire environment crafted by the same hand, the clients asked Field Architecture to extend their work to the interiors, which are cloaked in wood, filled with light, and immersed in the beauty of the surrounding natural environment. The design team integrated their clients' collection of art, some of it commissioned for the house, and worked with local artisans to craft custom furnishings, such as living room chairs made from a single piece of walnut and a headboard meticulously carved to evoke the movement of light on the rippling water.

In this home, the language of the architecture distills the language of the land down to its most basic geometric forms. There is a careful distinction to be made here between learning from and echoing the wisdom of natural forms and simply mimicking them. In this place of prospect and refuge, the design team has listened to the land, incorporating nature's adaptations into the human environment. The effect is extraordinary.

PRECEDING PAGE: "They are excited every time they arrive," says landscape architect Joni Janecki of the home's owners. "They are in awe of the majesty of the site."

OPPOSITE: The house both nestles into the site and lunges outward. Architect Jess Field extended the datum line of the floor toward the horizon to create a sense of prospect and echo the dead flat plane of the horizon. Inspired by the wind-formed Monterey cypress, the roof's tapered form enables more light to enter through the clerestory windows.

ABOVE: The entry bridge is the beginning of a carefully orchestrated journey, which Field describes as a "series of moments," drawing visitors over the ravine and toward the main house, where the ocean view is revealed.

OPPOSITE: The interior is a dialogue between the warmth of oak and beech, the cool gray of the quartzite walls, and the greens and blues of the landscape visible through the many windows. Darker wood furnishings in the dining room, living room, and primary bedroom deepen the experience.

OVERLEAF: Beech is the predominant material in the kitchen. Inspired by rocky coastal outcroppings, the tapered geometry of the three islands narrows as they delicately touch down on the floor.

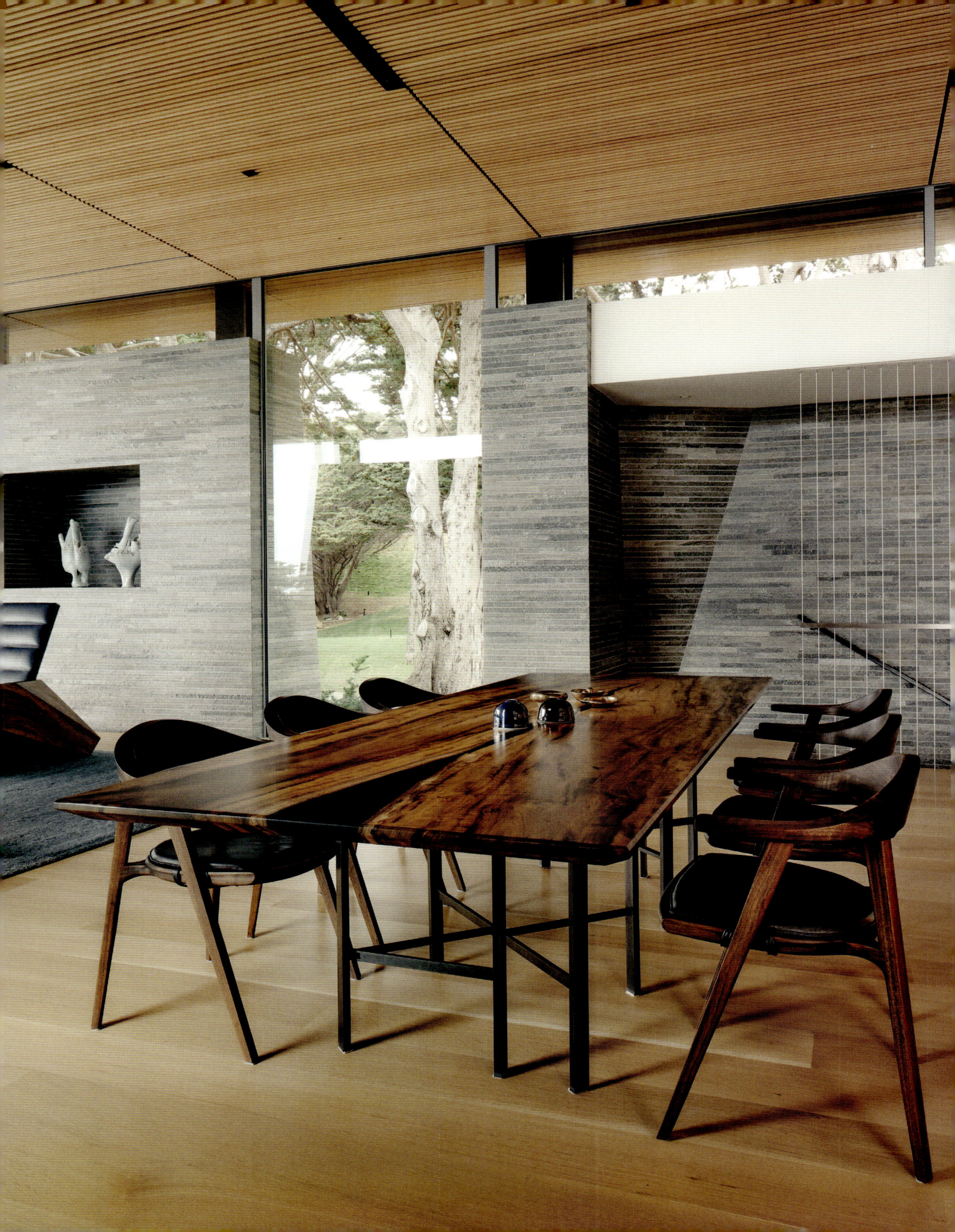

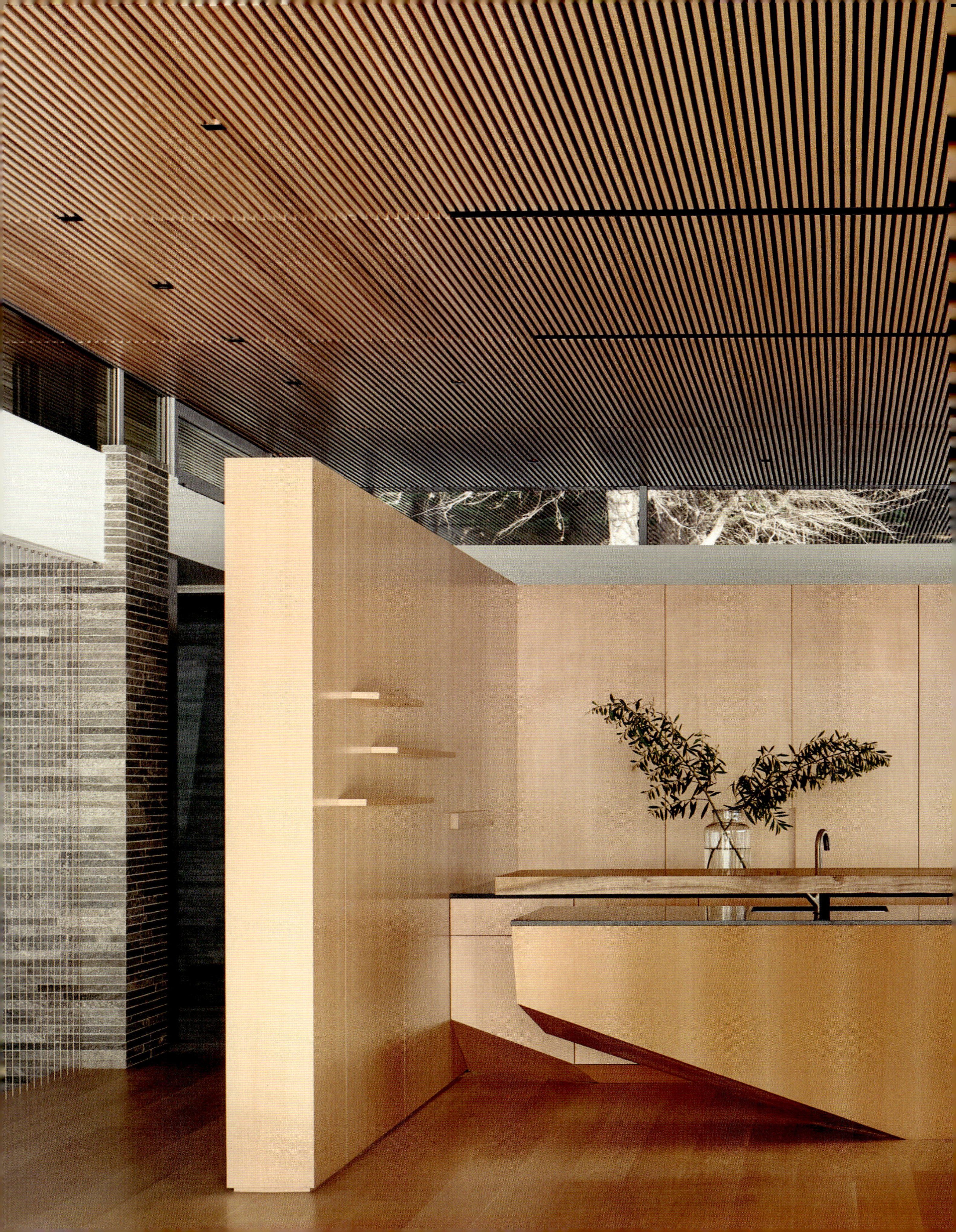

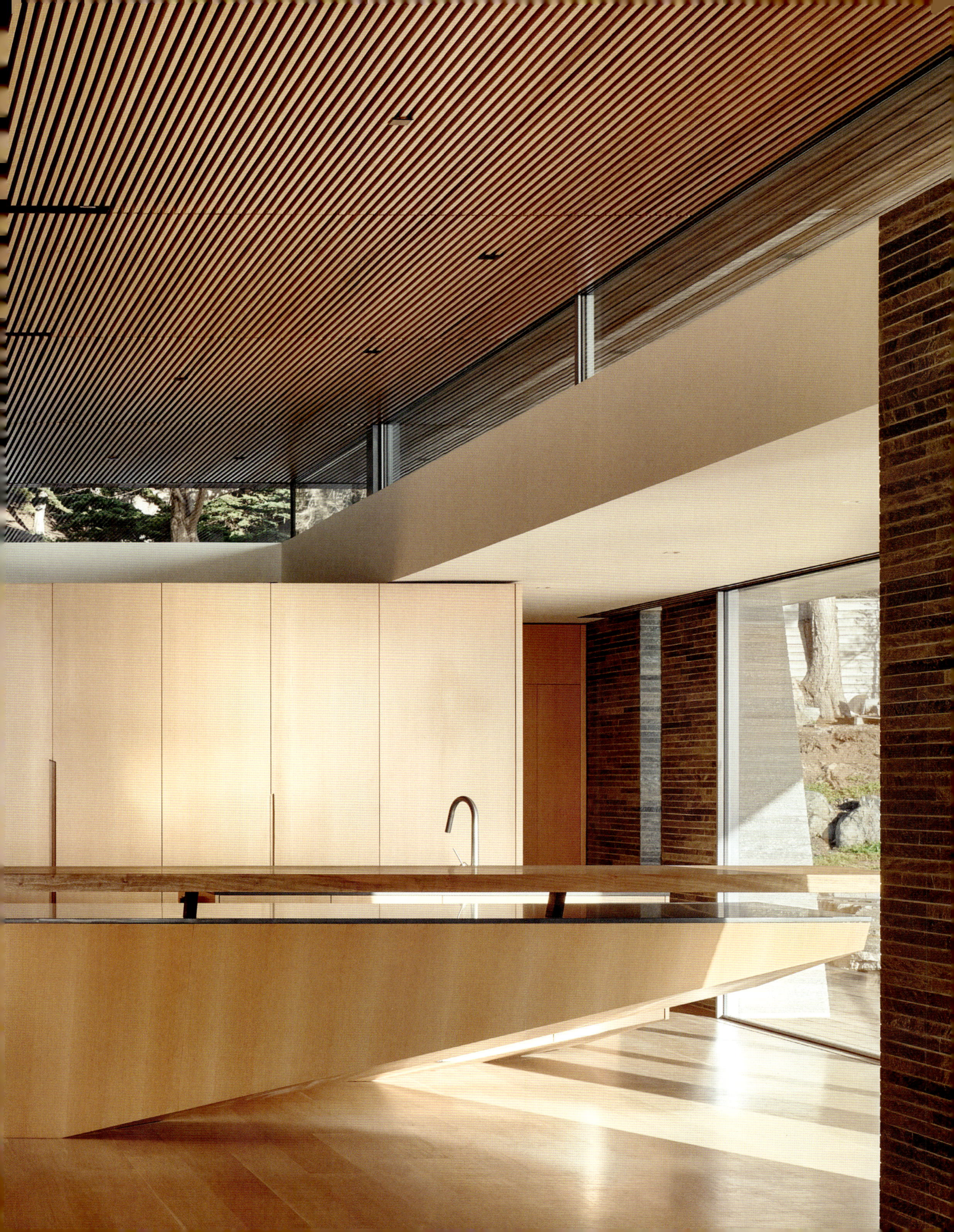

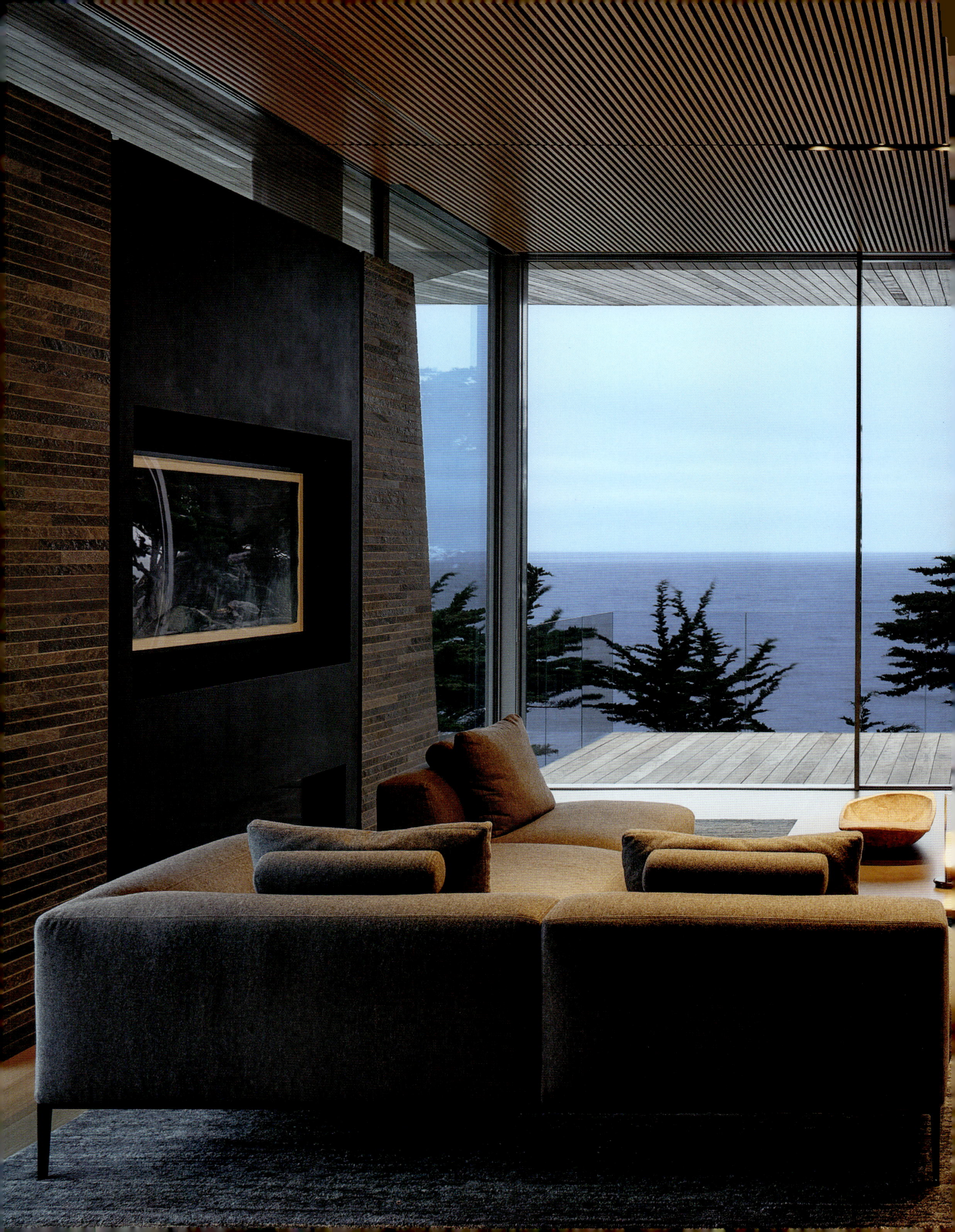

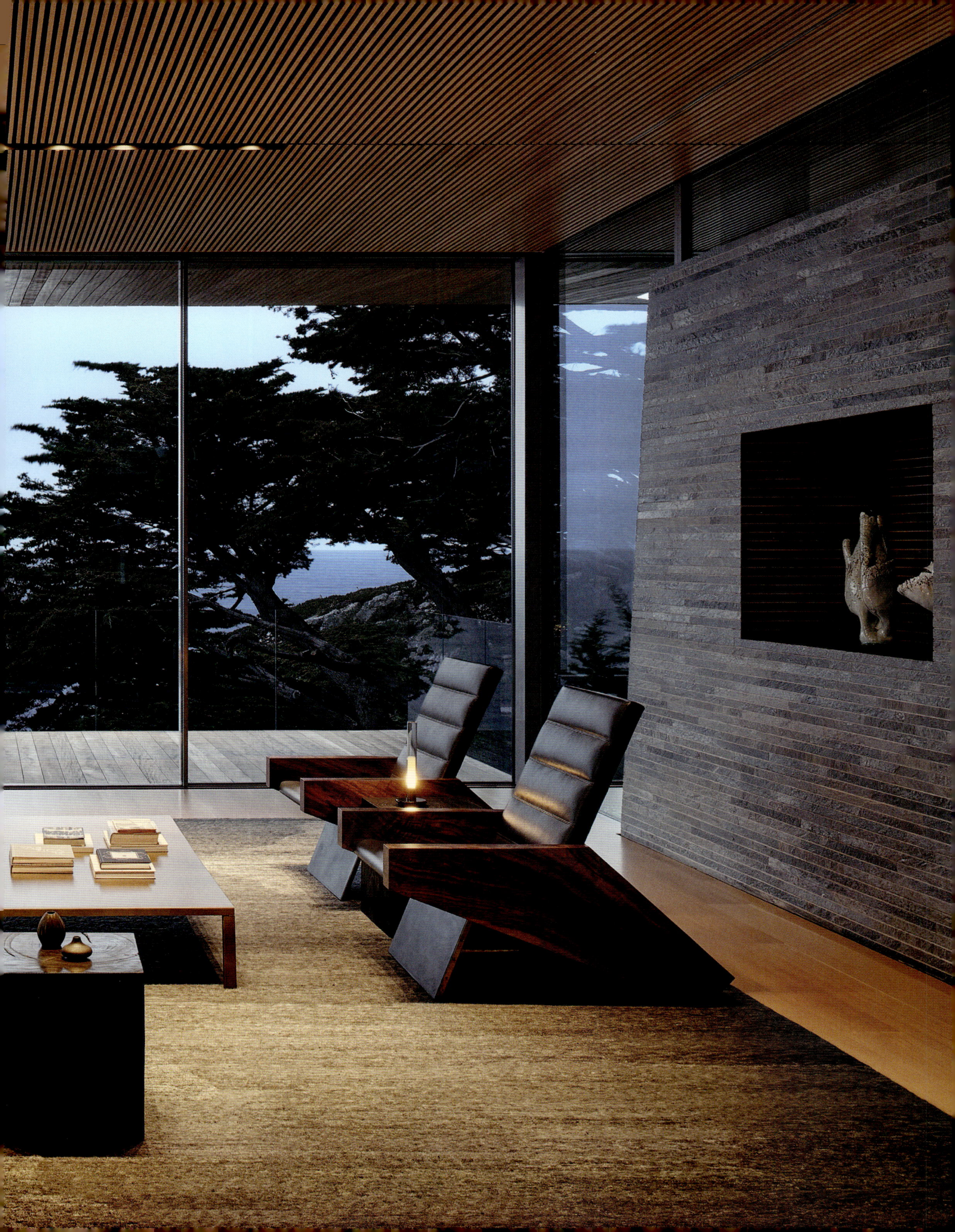

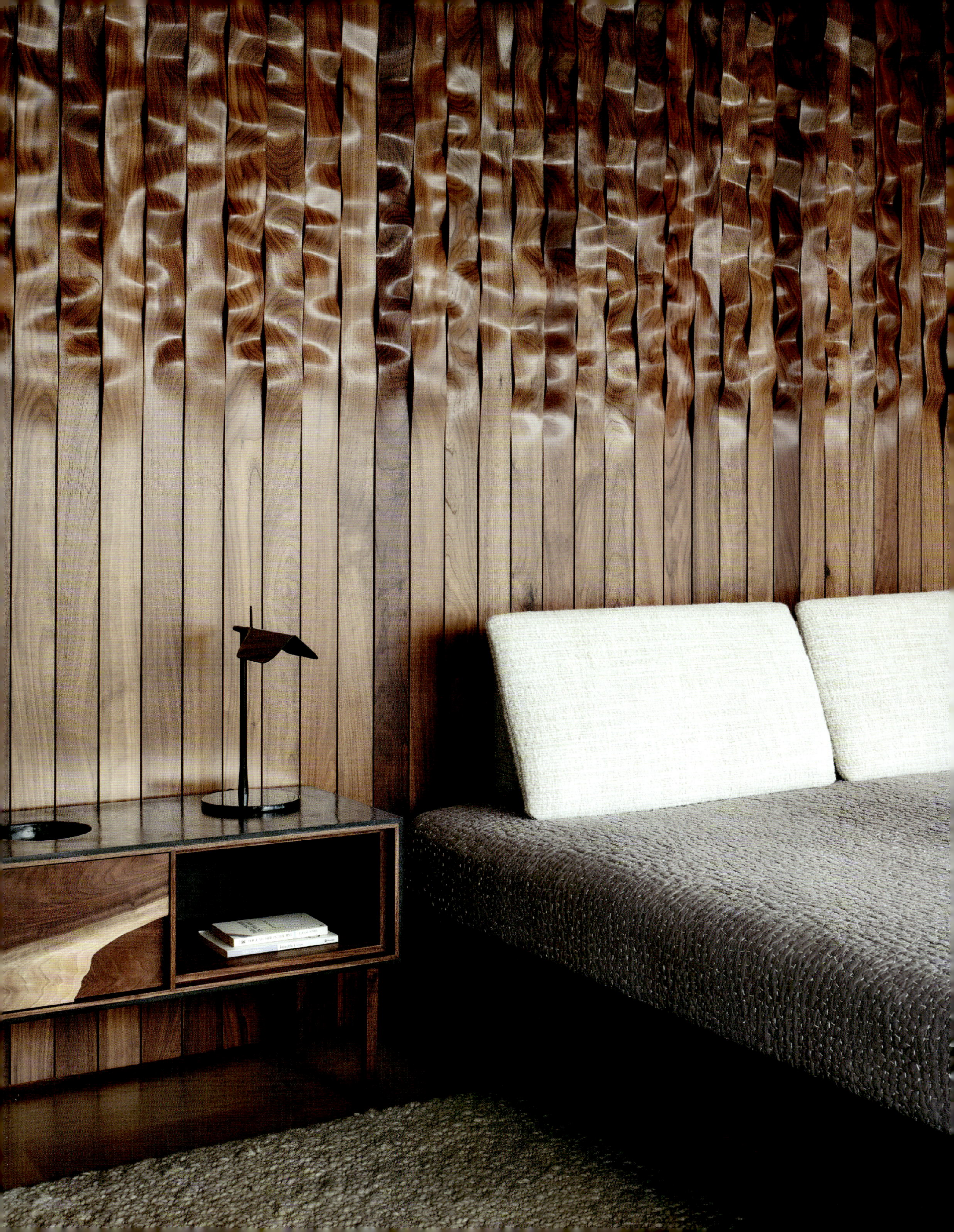

PRECEDING PAGE: The chairs in the living room were custom designed for the home, carved out of solid slabs of walnut, each with a hidden cubby in the base just large enough to hold a blanket.

OPPOSITE: In the primary bedroom, fifty-two strips of walnut were hand carved to reflect the annual tidal chart. The effect is that of rippling water, which glistens when hit by the sun's rays.

ABOVE: In the primary bath, a Japanese soaking tub takes in the view. Gray quartzite walls and loose stone underfoot extend from the exterior to the interior to form a singular experience.

OVERLEAF: The language of the land becomes the language of the architecture, distilled down to its most basic geometric forms. The central idea is to learn from nature's adaptations and incorporate them into the human dwelling.

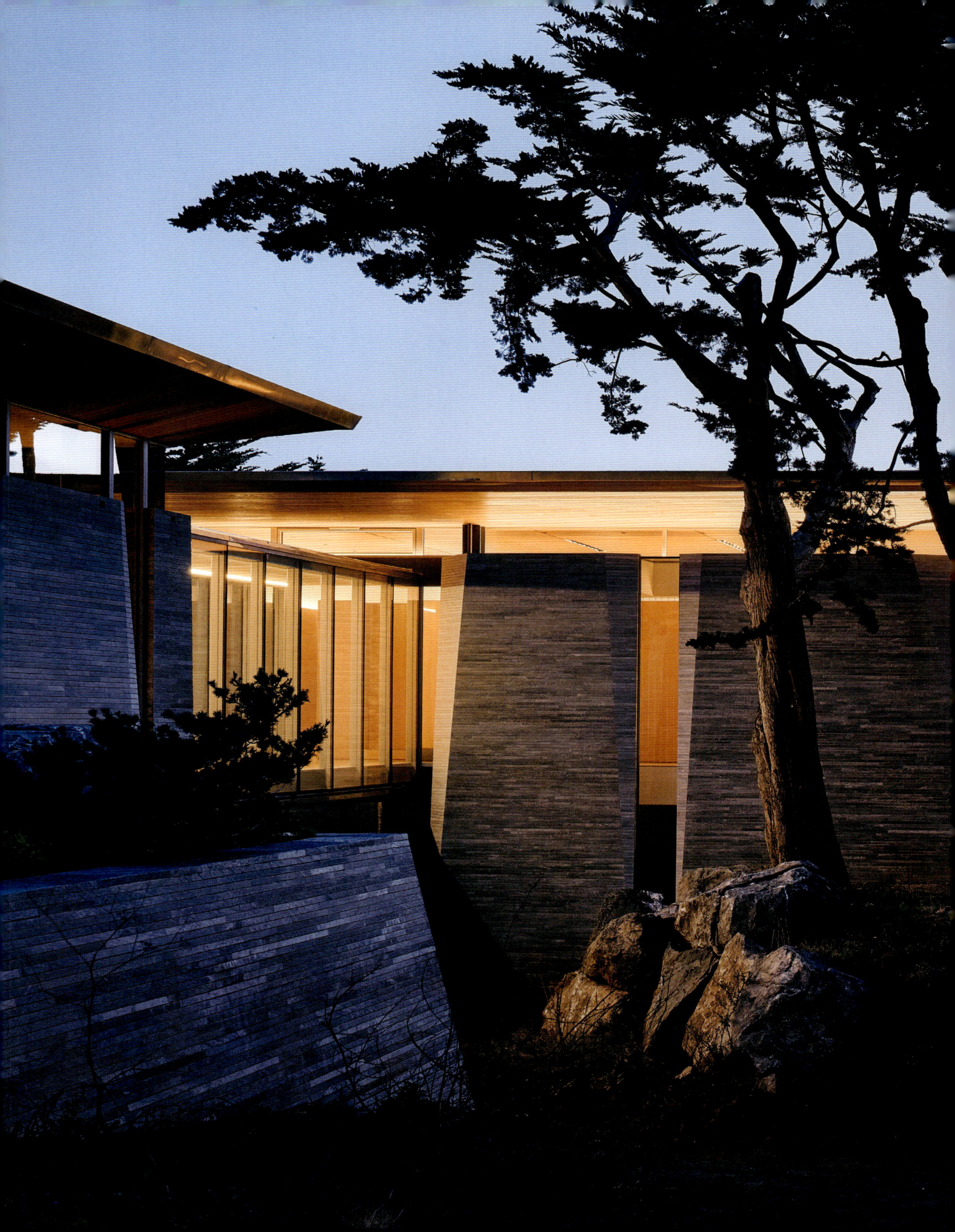

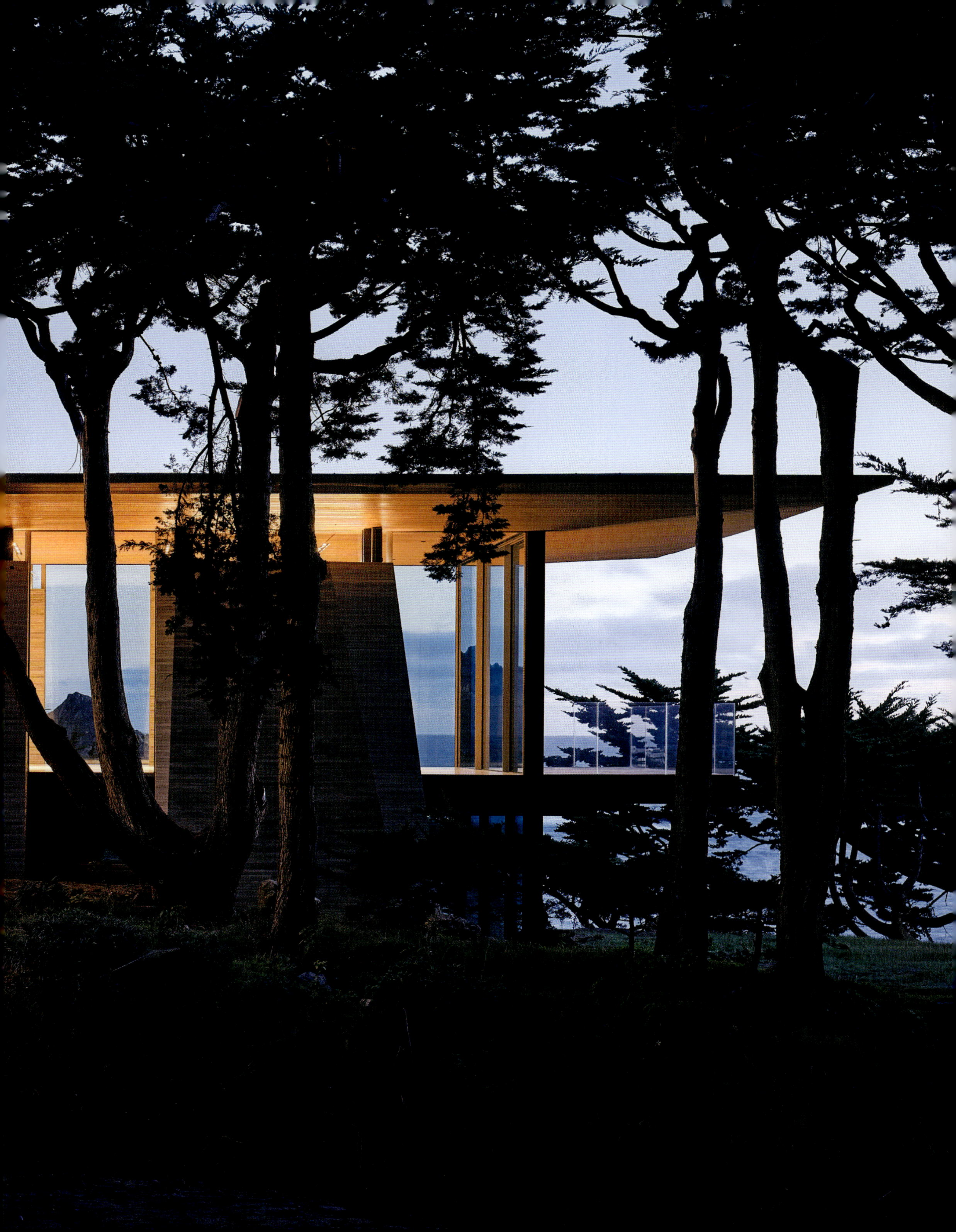

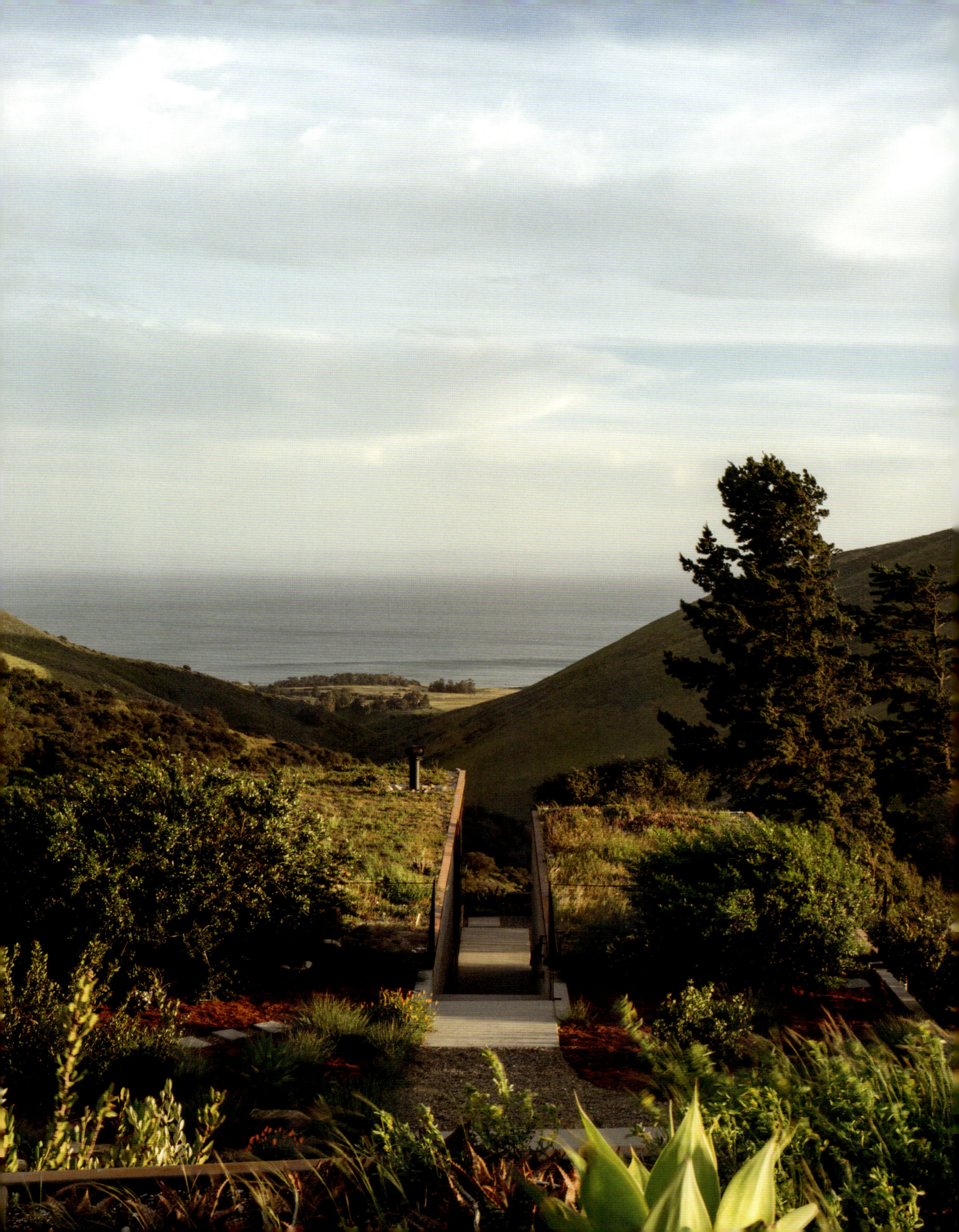

OFF-GRID GUESTHOUSE

/ SANTA BARBARA COUNTY /

Set on a large cattle ranch on the Gaviota Coast north of Santa Barbara, this guesthouse is tucked into the hillside high above the coastline. With its proximity to Point Conception—the point at which the state's northern and southern terrestrial and marine ecoregions meet and the long coastline turns eastward from its north-south axis—the site for this small dwelling feels symbolic of central California's wild coast.

This property is part of a hundred-acre parcel owned jointly by three families of entrepreneurs and adventurers who years ago formed a partnership to acquire this special piece of land. Steve and Margaret Cegelski—one of those three original families—built their home on a beautiful plateau just down the slope from where the guesthouse now rests. They soon needed a place for their adult children to visit and settled on a site set upslope from the main house. The partnership with their architect, Dan Weber of Anacapa Architects, came about by chance after their daughter fortuitously glimpsed drawings of another of Dan's projects in the ranch office.

Weber describes the site they chose as a "radical ridge with a rusting tank and some wire . . . and impossibly beautiful." His feelings about building here were admittedly mixed. On one hand, this site offered a spectacular opportunity, and on the other, it felt a shame to build a house here at all. Those mixed feelings, shared by the owners, resulted in a design philosophy that dictated minimal visual impact and intrusion on the land. Together they set out to create a structure that felt almost as if there were nothing there at all.

To protect the integrity of the coastal landscape and ecosystems, environmental regulations governing the state's coastline are extensive. "I'm a big fan of regulations," says Dan, viewing them as critical to preserving the immense biodiversity on this stretch of the coast. The process was lengthy, but the team accomplished something that might have seemed nearly impossible—building a house on an exposed bluff in this highly protected region. The resulting design—set into the slope with a low profile and landscaped green roof—nearly disappears into the hillside. In this secluded setting, the guesthouse is off the grid both by design and by necessity. Solar arrays, a well, a septic system, and 100 percent native landscape minimize impact on the land.

"We had so much fun building this well-designed work of art on the hill," says Steve Cegelski. "We lived up top for about a year and a half and loved it, but we found ourselves returning to the garden, fruit trees, and horses of our main house down below." So, in time, they sold the guesthouse and in so doing gained a partner. For its new owner, who lives on the property part-time, it is a place to retreat and recharge, live in the moment, and gain perspective. When he visited the property and

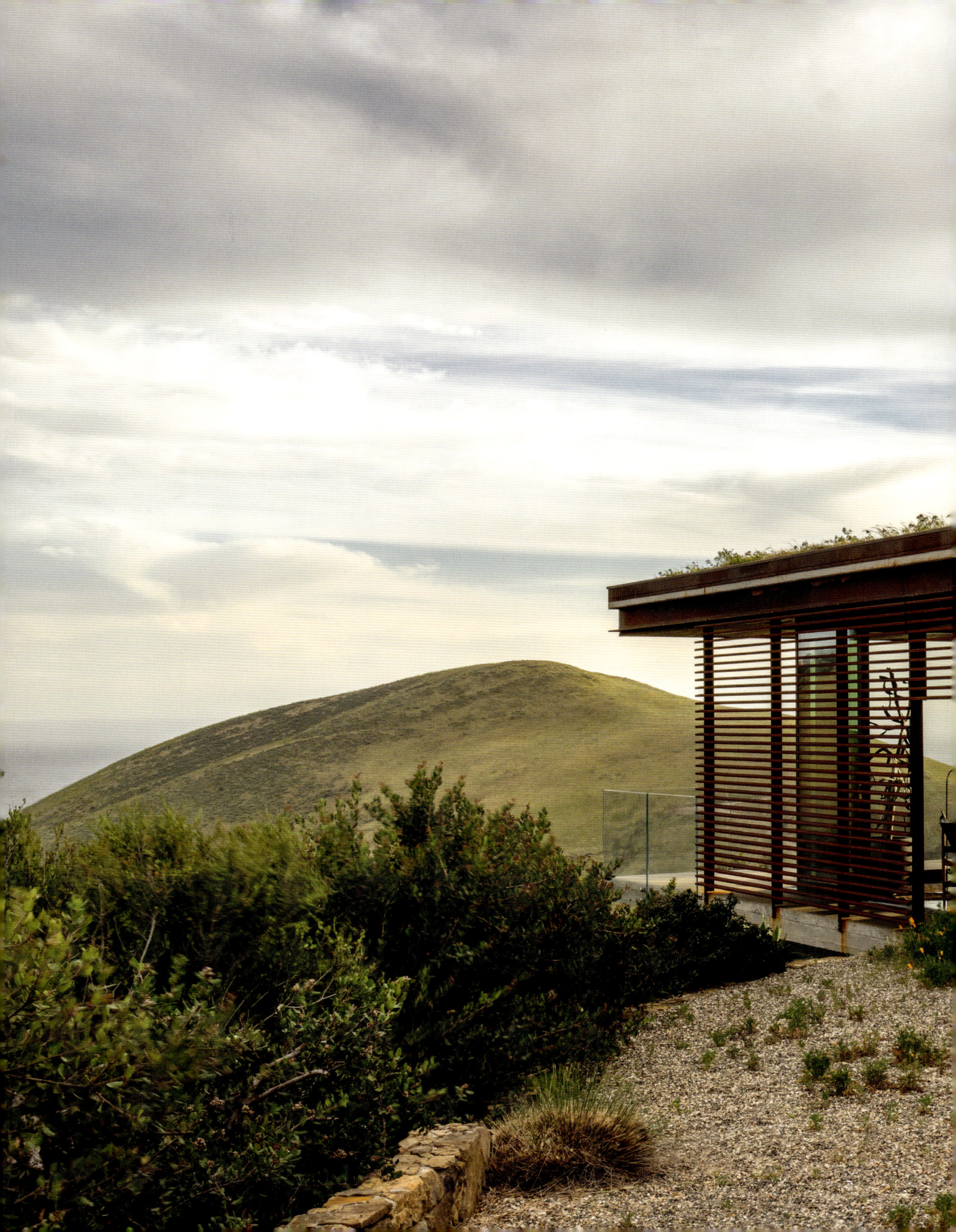

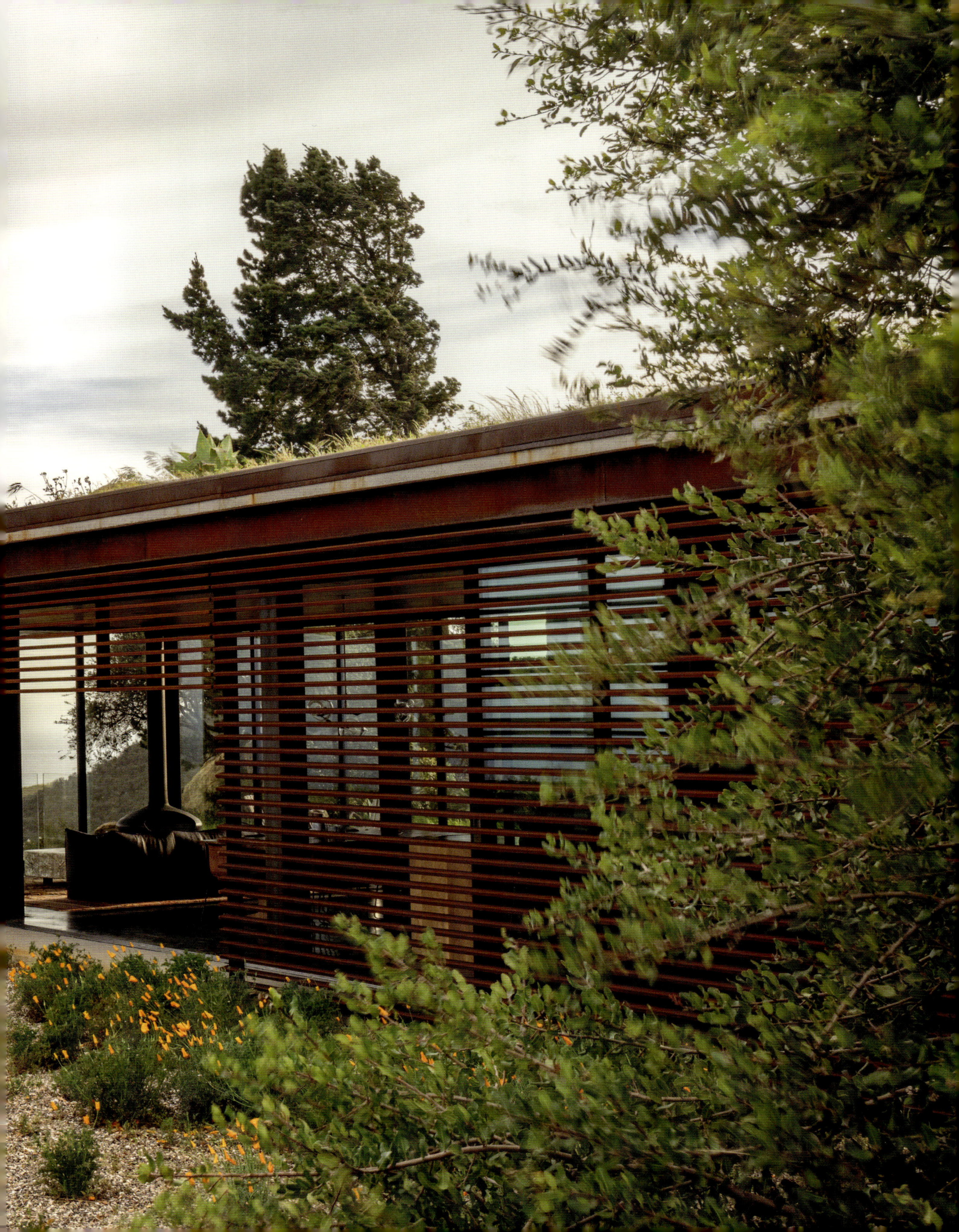

met the Cegelskis, who would become his neighbors on this isolated land, he knew that he had found his place. The people who live on this part of the coast share a mindset; they view themselves as stewards, independent thinkers who cherish and respect the land.

"There is a certain type of person who chooses to live in an area as remote as this," he says. "The sky is huge, the stars are bountiful, the wildlife is wonderful, and on a big day we can smell the ocean."

Set a mile from the coastline, with sweeping views of the ocean, the house is at once transparent and womb-like. Large expanses of glass expose the immensity of the view, while slatted steel screens on the north and south provide buffers from the wind and deep overhangs shield the terraces from the low-angled afternoon sun. Actually, the guesthouse is a pair of structures, separated by a central entry stair that dives down through the center, temporarily constraining the huge view and acting as a portal where visitors can let go and disconnect from the world.

The wind is a physical presence here, with an artistry evident in the form of the land and trees, the movement of the plants and the sounds in the air. The offshore winds that sweep down the hillside toward the ocean can be fierce. Shielded by glass walls, which provide both transparency and protection, occupants can follow the weather patterns as they arise and change. It was imperative that the architectural materials be rugged, durable, and nearly maintenance-free. The constrained palette of wood, steel, and board-formed concrete—inspired by the concrete troughs, rusted steel gates, and old wood barns of traditional coastal cattle ranches—ensures that the structure, while contemporary, feels entirely native to this coastal range.

Tucked into the hillside and covered by a living roof, the interiors provide a feeling of safety—a place of retreat from the elements and a rest from the grandeur of the views. For the design team, extending the concrete retaining walls to form the outer walls felt like a natural decision. Enclosed within their embrace, the house is, both metaphorically and literally, embedded in the land.

PRECEDING PAGE: Breathtaking landscape views are seen from every angle in the home. Wild California poppies that dot the site are volunteers.

OPPOSITE: This part of the coast carries deep meaning for native Chumash people, who considered it the Western Gate, through which departed souls passed from earthly to heavenly realms.

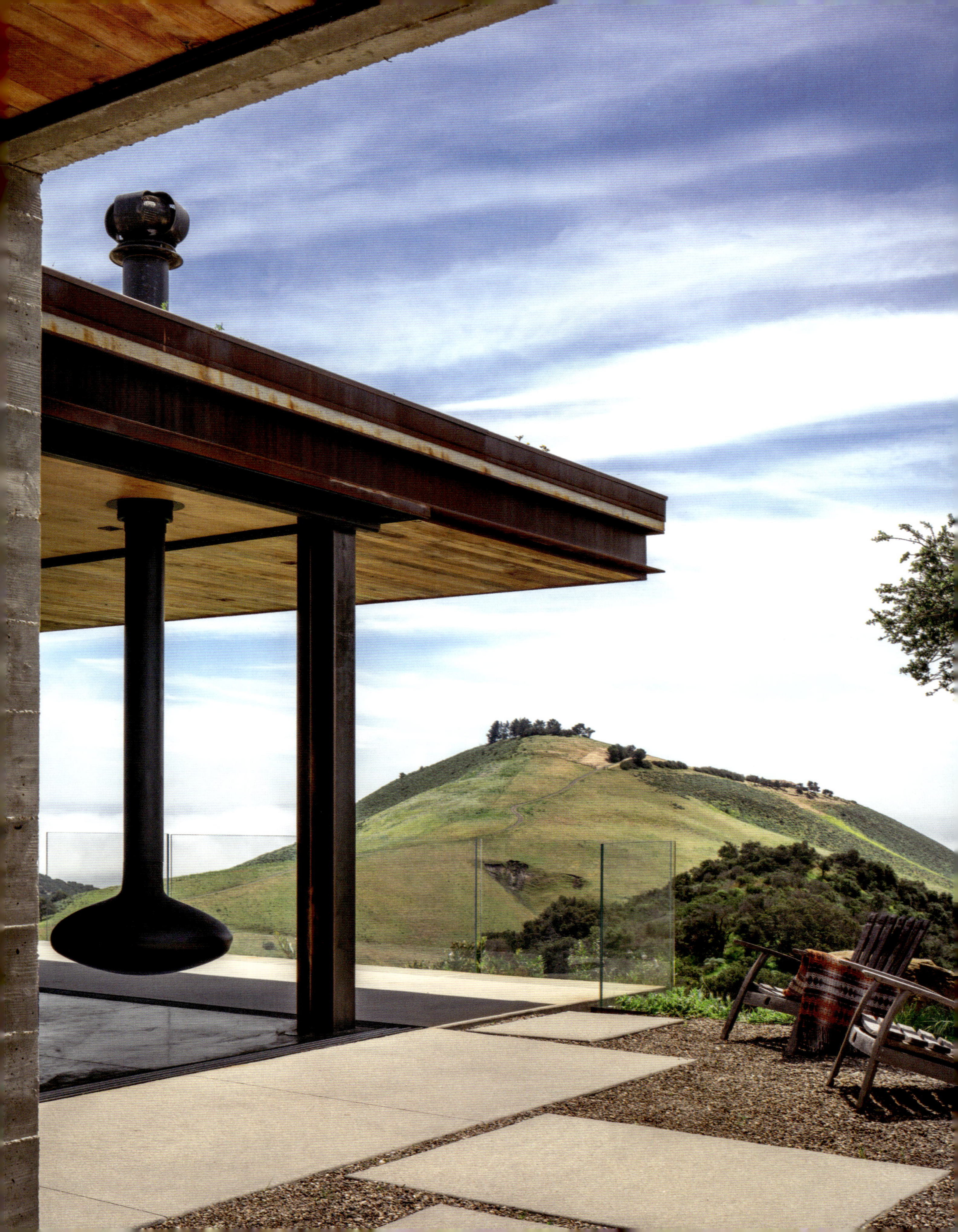

RIGHT: The vistas are deep and layered, looking down the canyon to the coast, encompassing the coastal hills with their native chaparral, scrub, and grasslands. Two adjacent hills form what architect Dan Weber calls a "martini glass" view. "It's so much more interesting to be set back from the water, so you see the whole coastal environment," he says.

OVERLEAF: Slatted steel screens shield the north- and south-facing facades from the elements while allowing in the view of the surrounding terrain. The palette of wood, steel, and board-formed concrete is inspired by the concrete troughs, rusted steel gates, and old wood barns of traditional coastal cattle ranches.

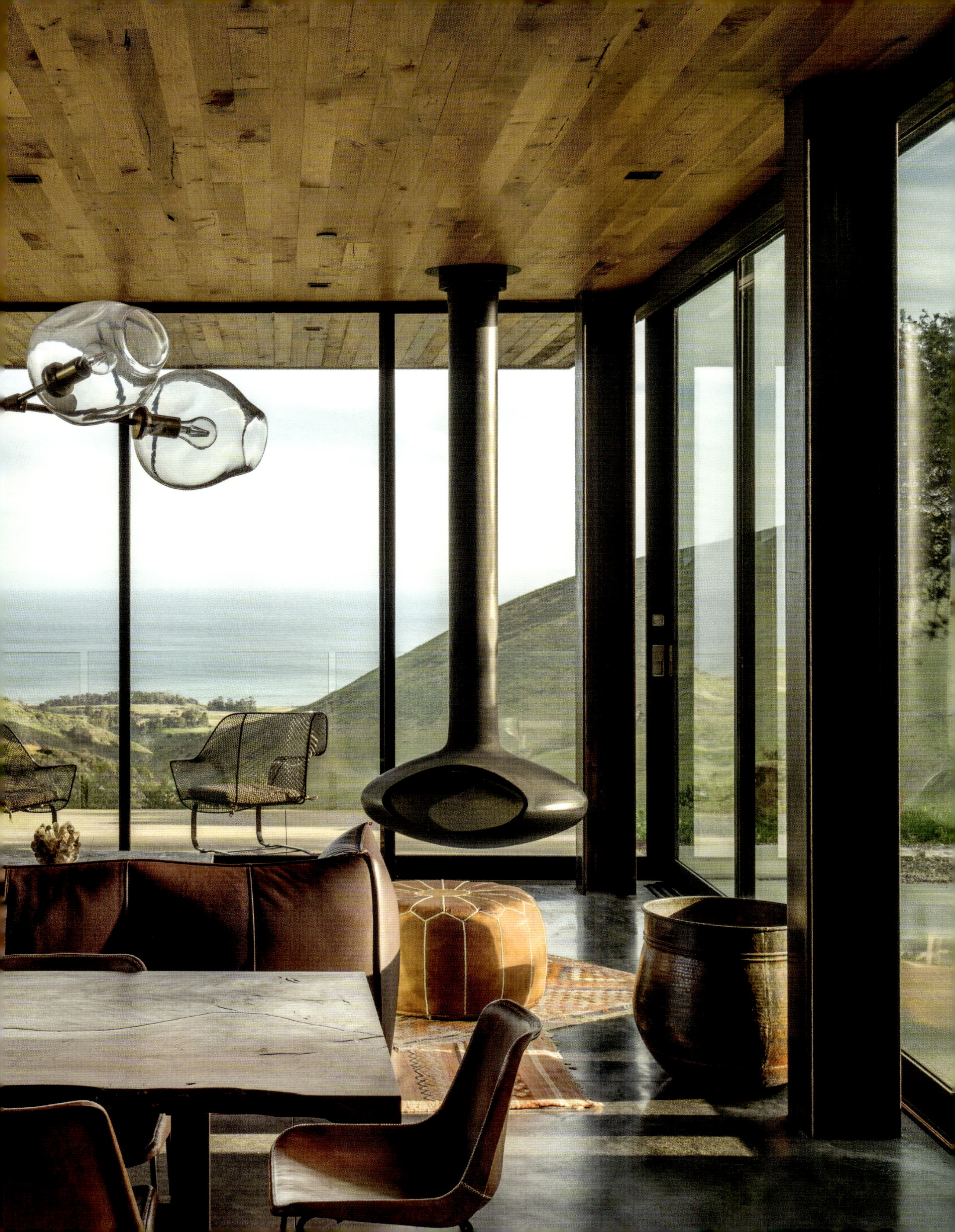

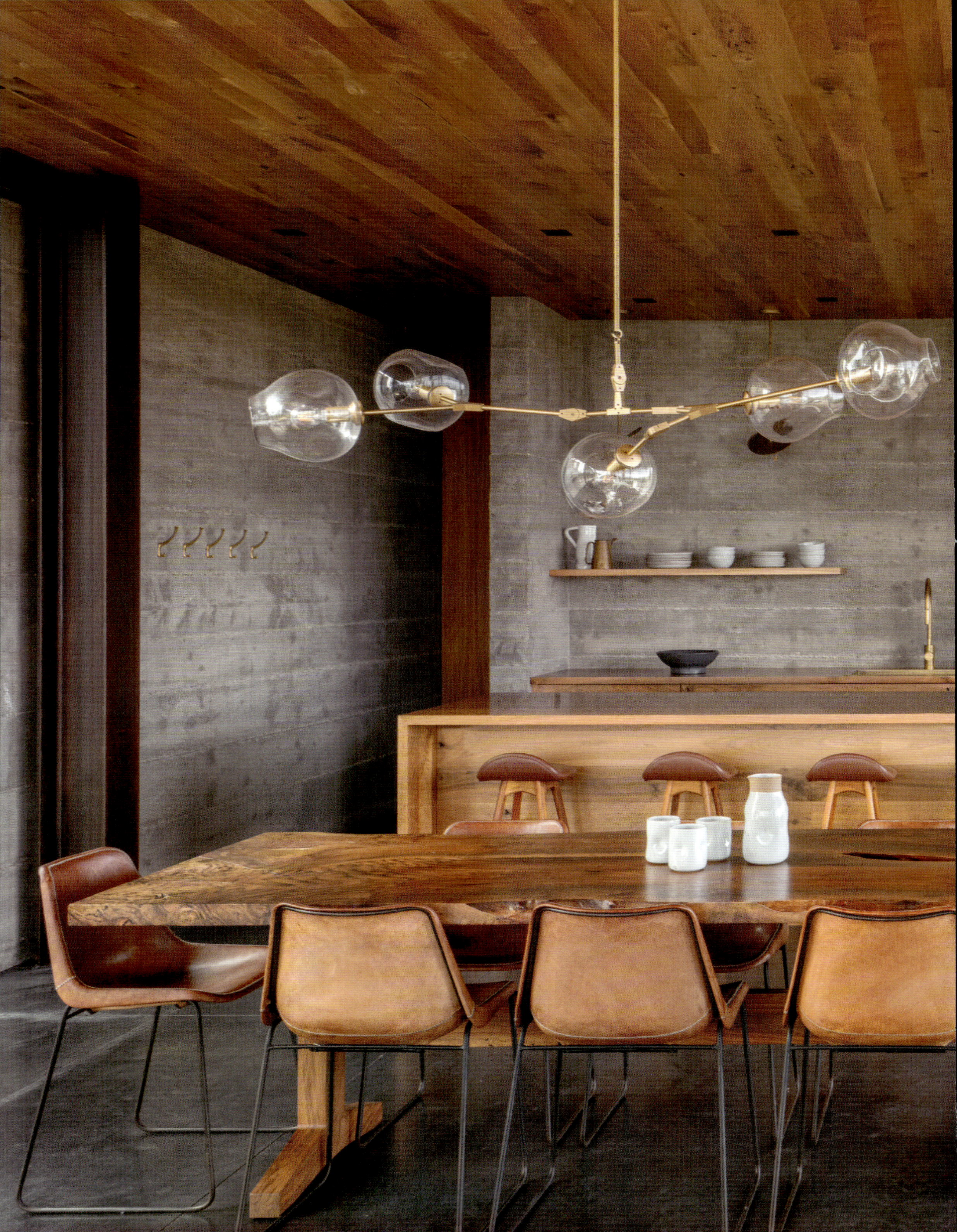

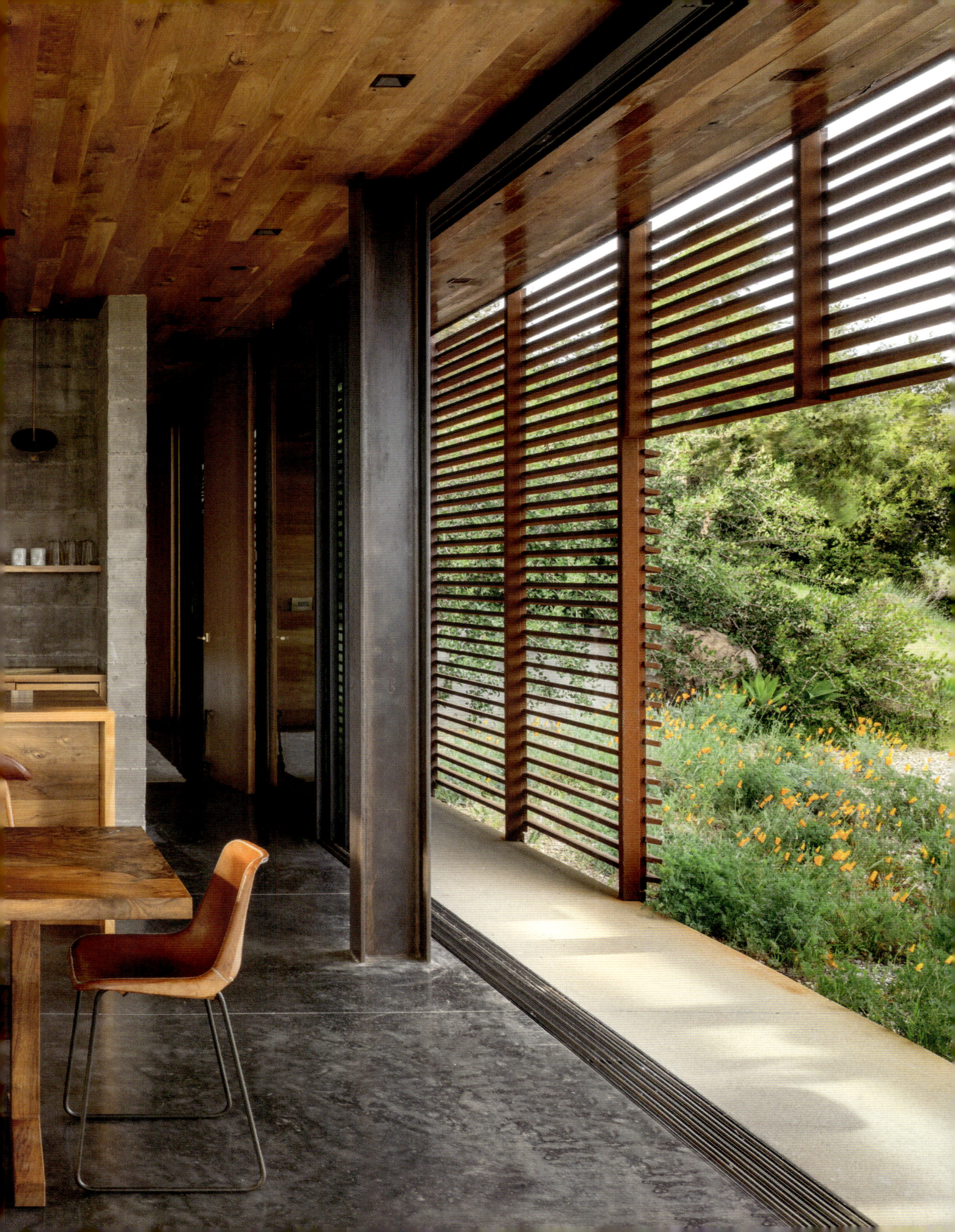

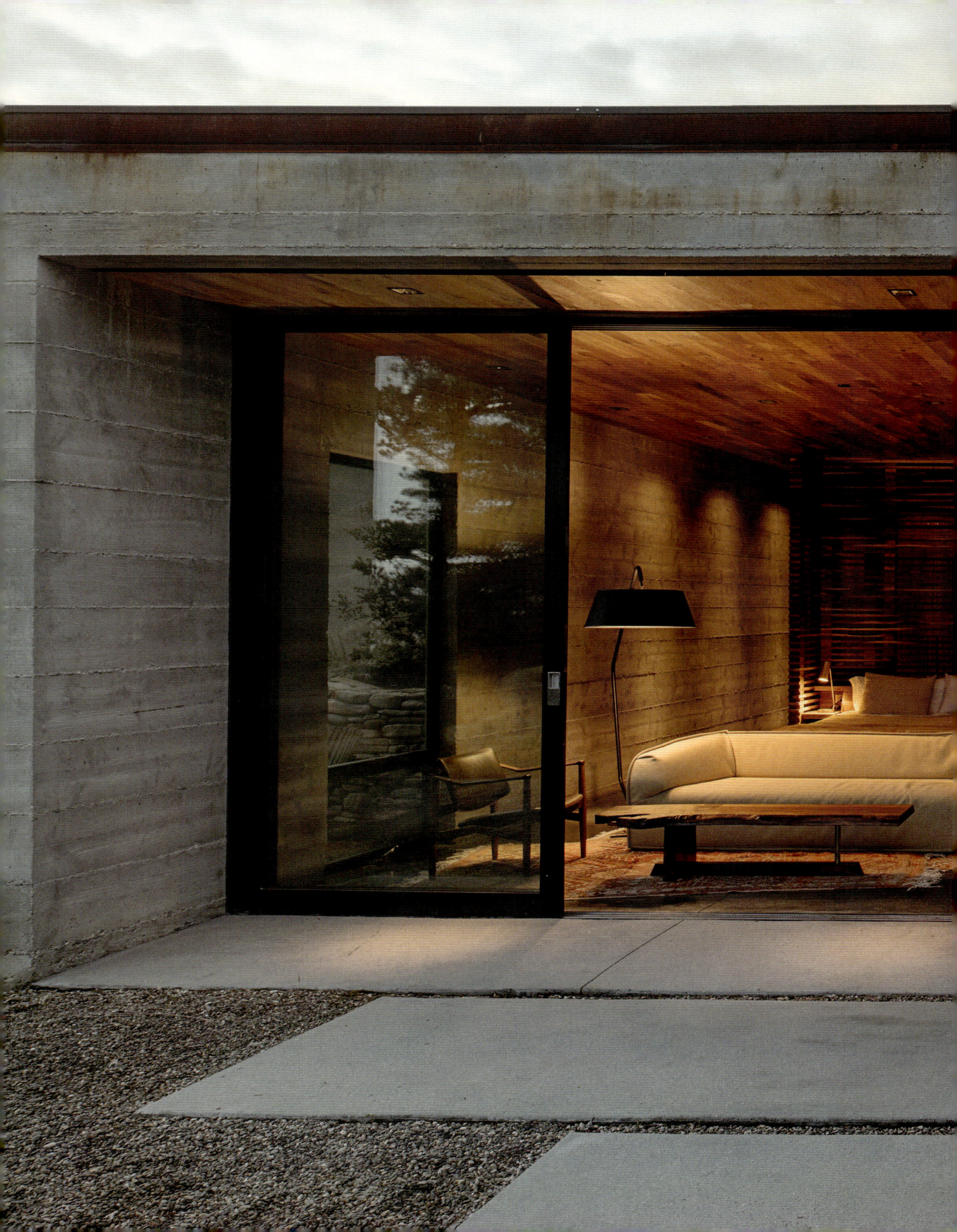

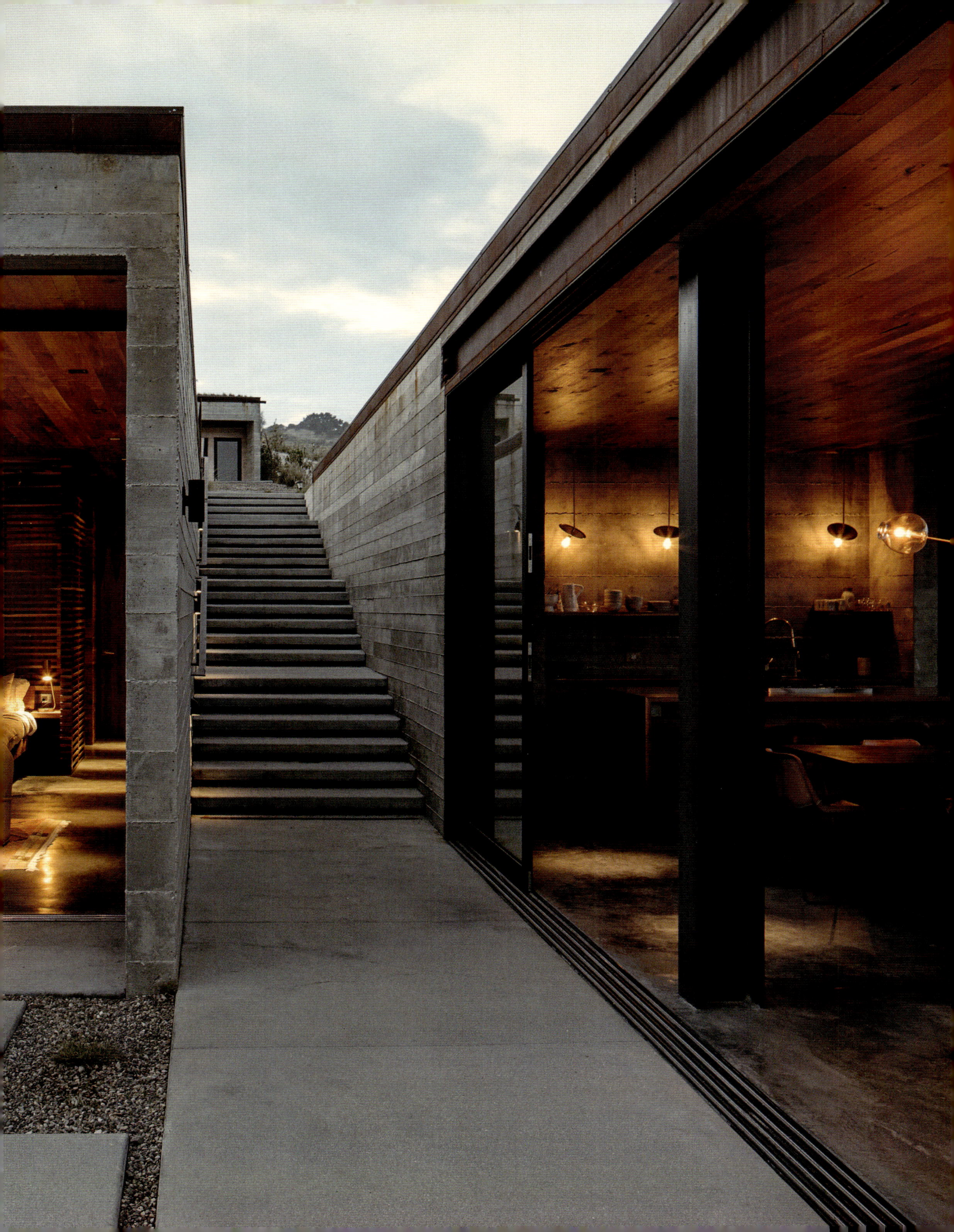

PRECEDING PAGE: The entry stairway's sense of compression and release is acoustical as well as visual; the concrete walls block the sound of the wind and waves, invoking a sense of decompression and serenity.

ABOVE: The homeowner loves waking up here. "The sky is huge, the stars are bountiful, the wildlife is wonderful, and on a big day we can smell the ocean," he says. When asked how it feels to live here, he answers, "I feel held."

OPPOSITE: Extending the concrete retaining walls outward to form the walls as they rose above-ground was a natural decision. The gray concrete walls are balanced by the warm tones of wood and brass.

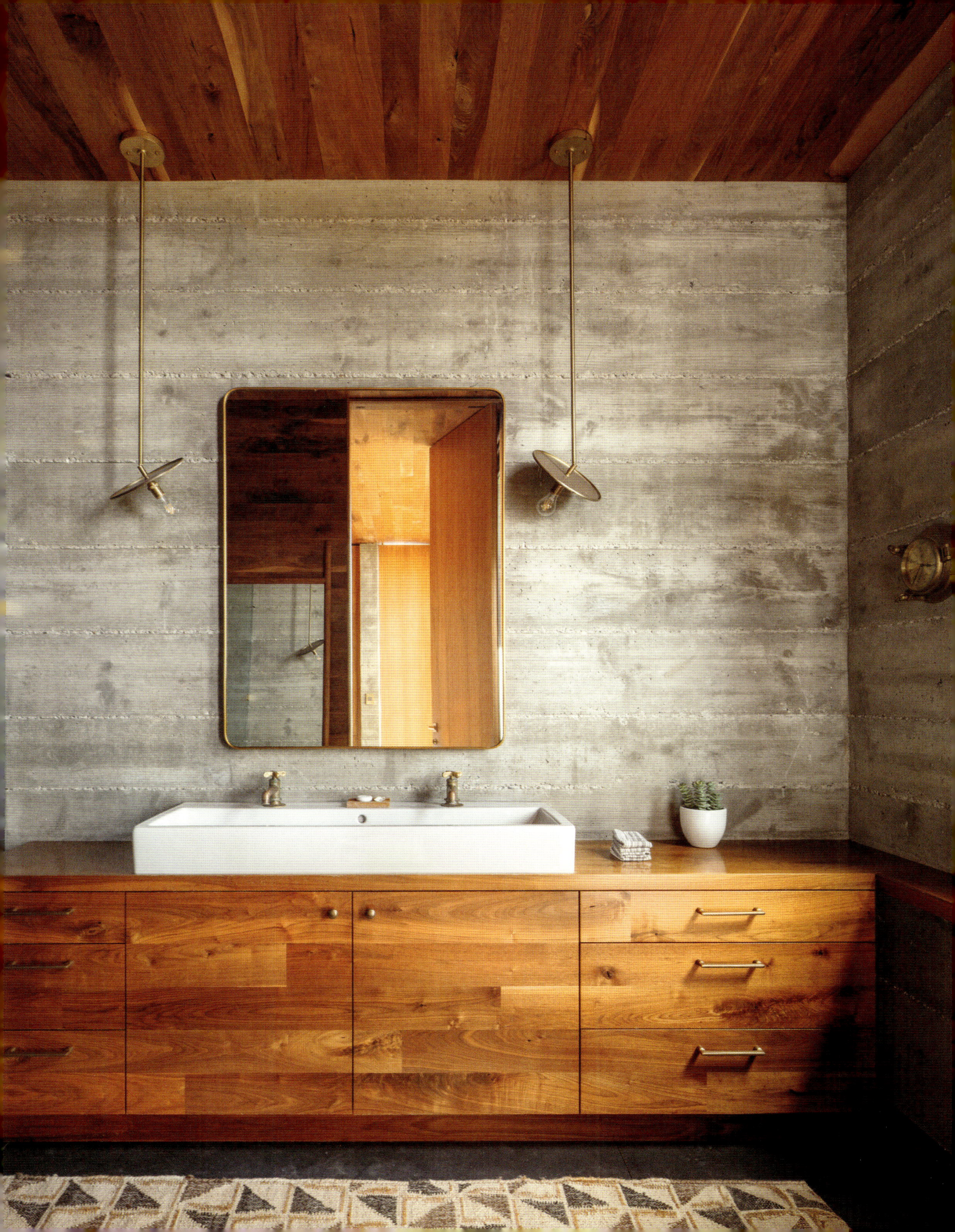

SOUTHERN COAST

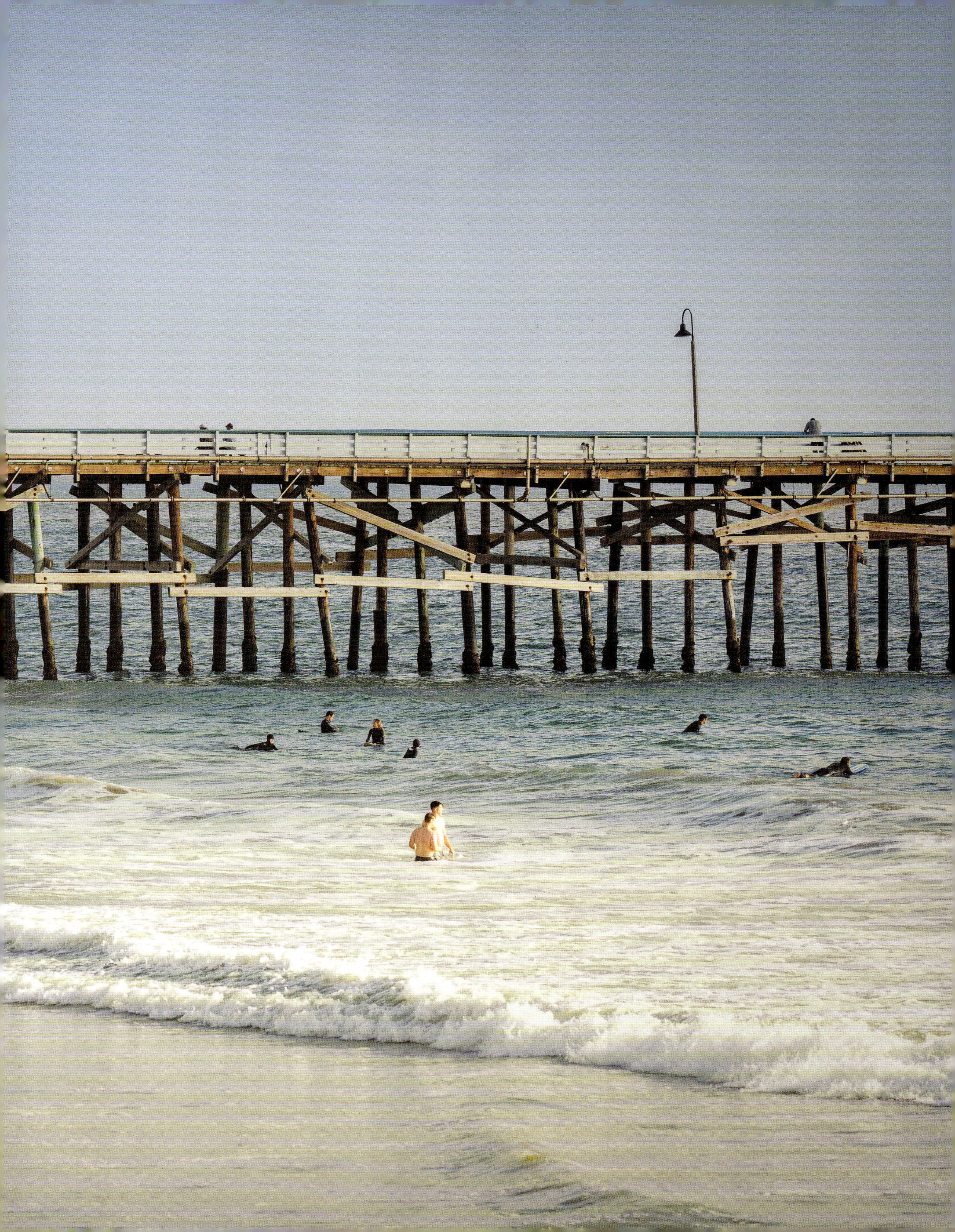

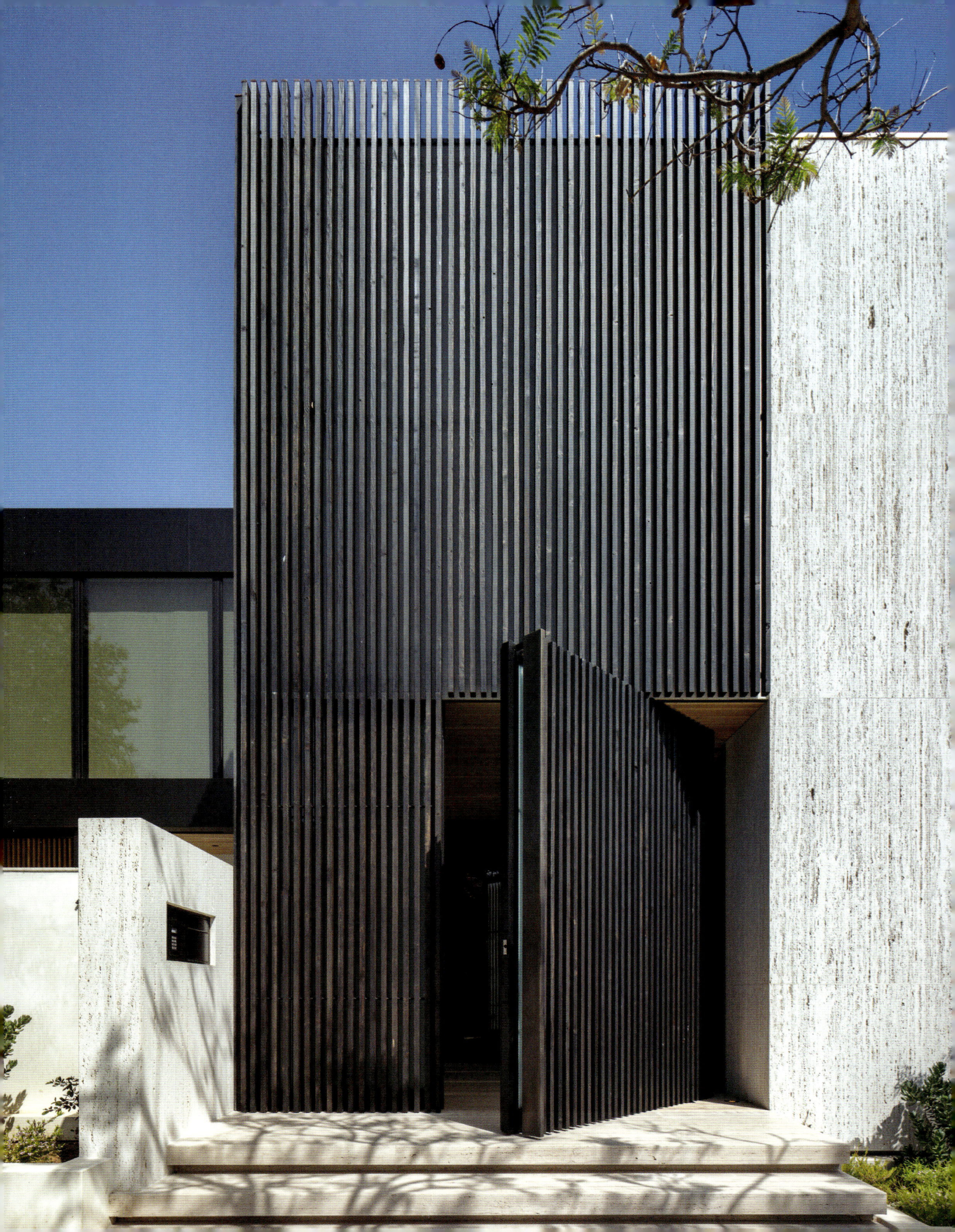

ATABEI

/ PACIFIC PALISADES /

Blake and Karina Mirkin are kindred spirits—gregarious, open, and nearly inseparable after twenty-seven years of marriage. They share a deep love for beautiful, one-of-a-kind places, a passion for the ocean, and an unbridled enthusiasm for their home.

It took them a while to get there. Their first house, set in the hills of the Southern California enclave of Pacific Palisades, seemed perfect at the time, but as their children grew, it felt isolated. They then bought a house in town that was family friendly and close to everything. However, it didn't have a view, so it didn't last long, and they soon found themselves house-hunting again.

Then they found it—a partially completed spec house in a small neighborhood on an idyllic bluff with uninterrupted views of the Pacific. Nothing separated the house from the water but the landscape and a private pedestrian street. They bought it before it was completed and put construction on hold to reimagine the design of the house to make it their own. This is where designer Jae Omar came in.

In forming a new vision for the house, Jae took his cues from the couple's openness, their shared passion for the water, and Karina's Puerto Rican heritage. He designed an environment that is so uniquely suited to the couple that it has taken on its own character and sense of place. Composed of a series of interconnected but independent spaces—what Jae calls "a collection of emotional vignettes"—the flow of the house is easy and effortless. Every vantage point captures a special moment in relation to the ocean views or the water that forms the defining feature of the design. Inspired by the Taino goddess of fertility, water, and the moon, he called it Atabei.

Set in a connected, active neighborhood, the home nonetheless maintains a sense of privacy. The front entry is at once dramatic and reserved. Masterfully integrated into a slatted wall whose unbroken lines extend up two full stories, the enormous pivot door is virtually indiscernible, gliding open to reveal an entry. It is the home's defining moment.

Inside the entry lies an inner sanctum that exudes a visceral sense of serenity. In rethinking the design of the house, Jae had tucked a pool into the home's interior courtyard, but he drew it into the entry to form an innovative and deeply meaningful integration of exterior and interior environments. As one crosses the meticulously placed stepping stones, the outside world disappears. Jacaranda trees that line the street outside the entry cast shadows visible from inside the glass door, forming an ever-changing work of art visible from nearly everywhere on the entry level.

"It's Jae's version of walking on water," Karina laughs. "It's a truly magical experience."

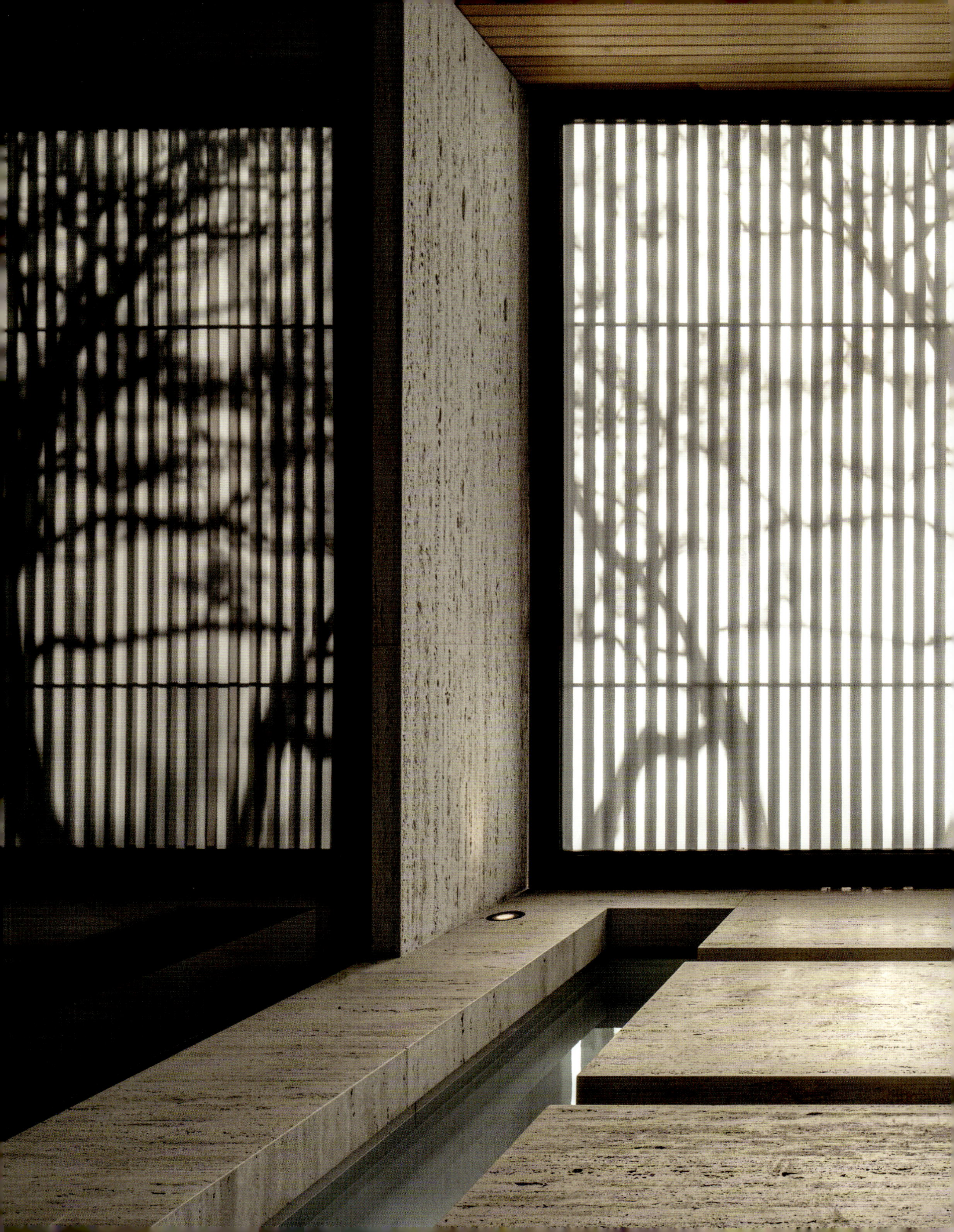

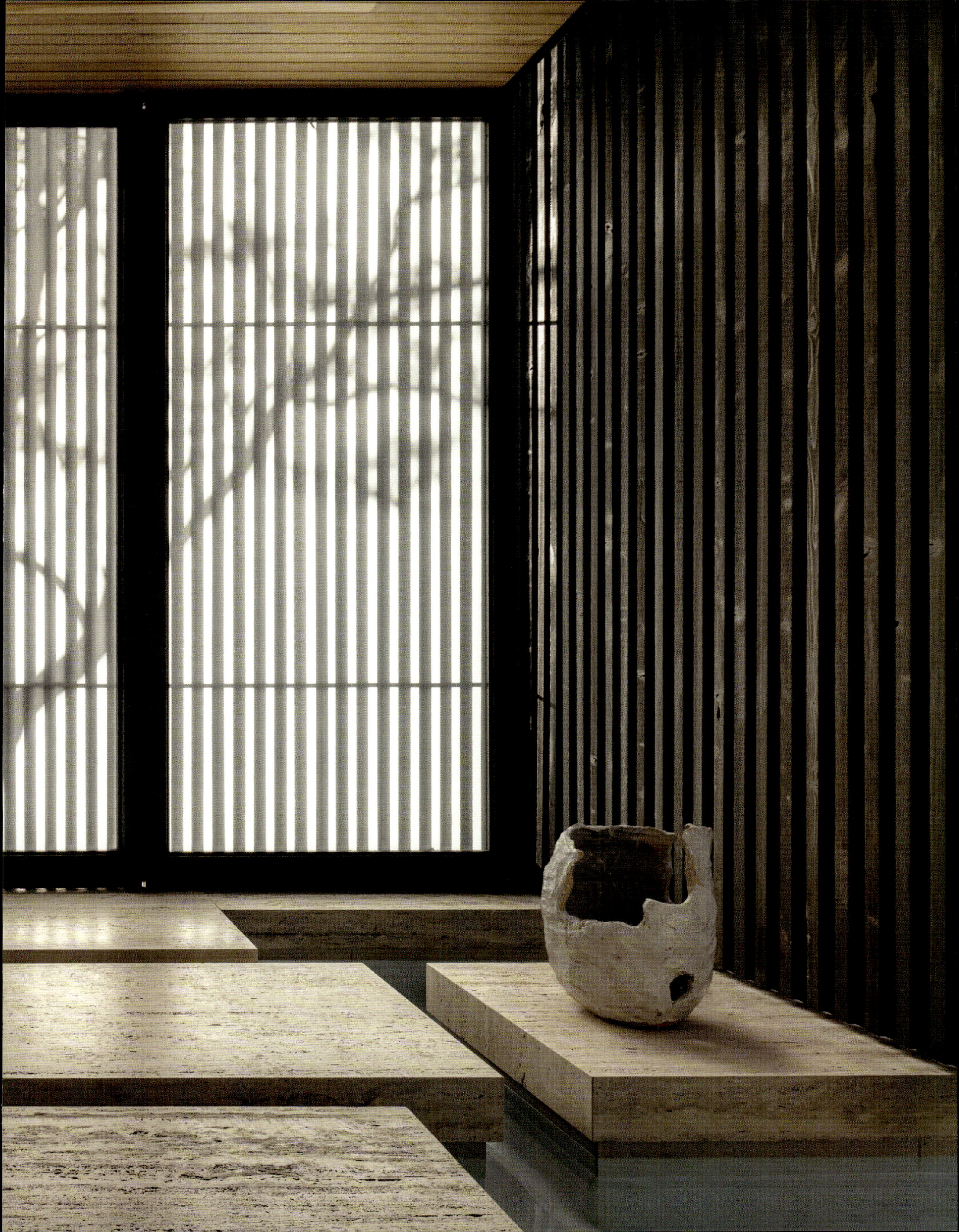

The journey from the street plane to the view plane is carefully scripted, with vertical slatted walls of oak partially screening internal views while allowing natural light deep into the interior. The double-height screened wall that defines the central stair extends to partially shield the kitchen, which reveals itself slowly, creating what Jae calls "a little bit of mystery." The contemporary but warm white oak ceiling planks echo the scale and materials of the screened walls and draw the eye out toward the ocean view. Oak ceilings and unfilled travertine floors extend to the outdoor terraces, blurring the line between inside and outside.

The material palette is restrained and cohesive. In an intentional approach, Jae likes to use the evolution of a single material through a space—in this case oak—progressing from unfinished to a more manipulated state. Blackened oak screens on the exterior take on a light finish on the interior. In the kitchen, cabinets fashioned from oak logs with a dark patina due to spending 200 years submerged in an Italian lake are left unstained but have a matte clear coat. The glass backsplash reveals a view of the greenery outside and brings light into the kitchen, providing a counterbalance to the dark cabinets.

The expansive primary bedroom suite—a sanctuary of its own—is the couple's favorite spot in the house. The journey from the sitting room through the dressing space to the cocoon-like bedroom is like a walk to the sea. A private terrace, warmed by an outdoor fire, allows them to continue the journey outdoors.

"Karina and I have always been in love with one-of-a-kind locations," says Blake. Even on the storied coast of California, with its multiple awe-inspiring vistas, Pacific Palisades stands apart, with views from the Santa Monica Pier south to the "Queen's Necklace"—the homes that sparkle like jewels in the evening along the Malibu shoreline. For this couple, whose enthusiasm for their designer is as infectious as their passion for the house he helped them envision, this is home.

"Someone was looking out for us," Karina concludes. "Jae shared our passion for this place, he saw things we didn't see, and he thought of every single thing. That's what makes the house so magical."

PRECEDING PAGE + OPPOSITE: The pool, which flows from exterior to interior to create the water-filled entry, is viewable from nearly every vantage point on the main floor. The pool courtyard cleaves the massing, ushering light deep into the house.

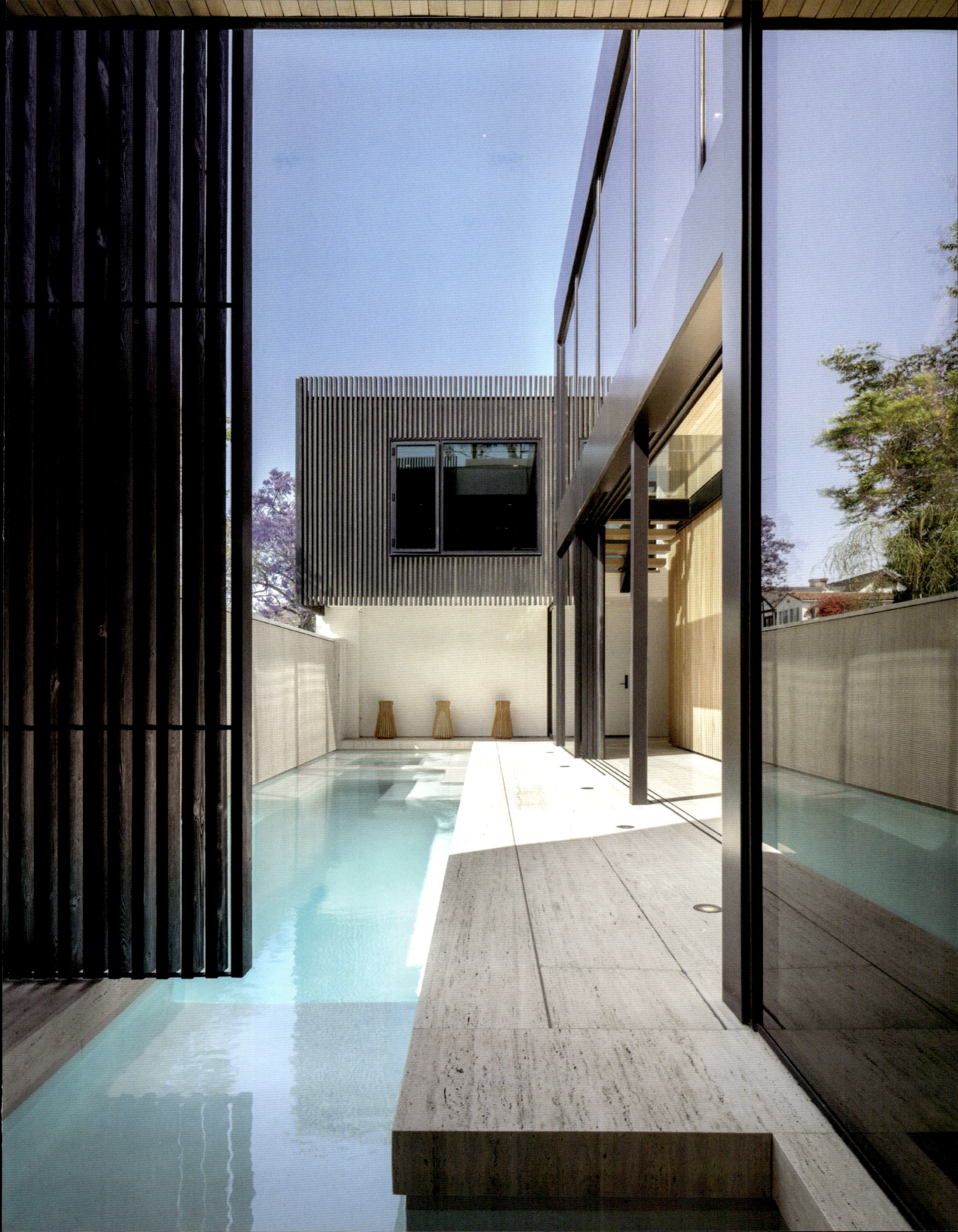

ABOVE: The island in the kitchen, topped with Calacatta Paonazzo marble and lined with a breakfast bar fashioned from a salvaged oak sinker log supported by a single bronze leg, is an interactive sculpture in its own right. Under the bar, the channeled marble enhances the sculptural quality, and the sink module, nestled at the end, is slightly raised.

RIGHT: Vertical slats made of white oak extend deep into the house, providing a strong sense of design continuity, particularly when echoed by ceiling boards of the same material. The curvilinear form of the pendant fixture from Henge, which hangs above the dining table, provides a gentle counterpoint.

ATABEI

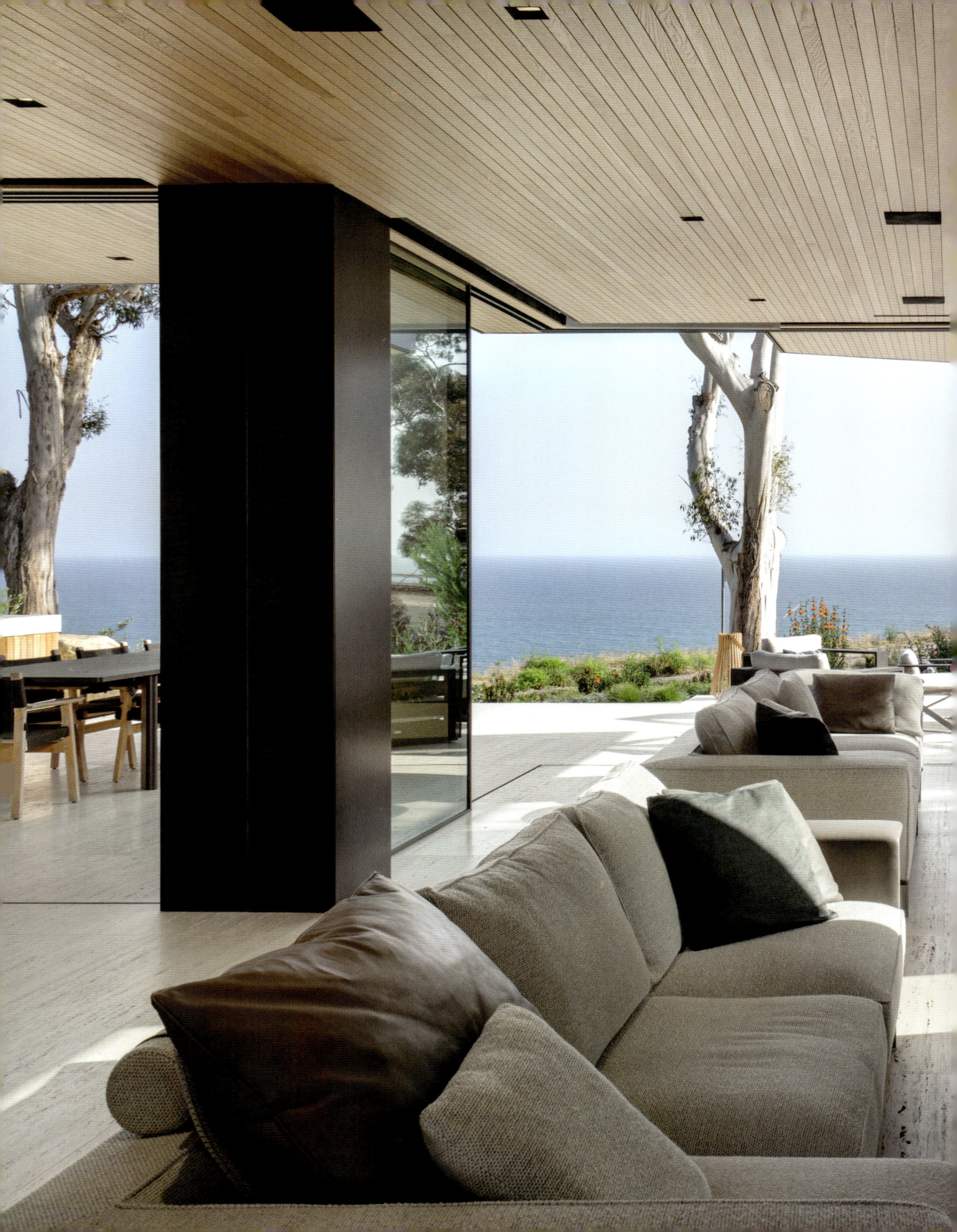

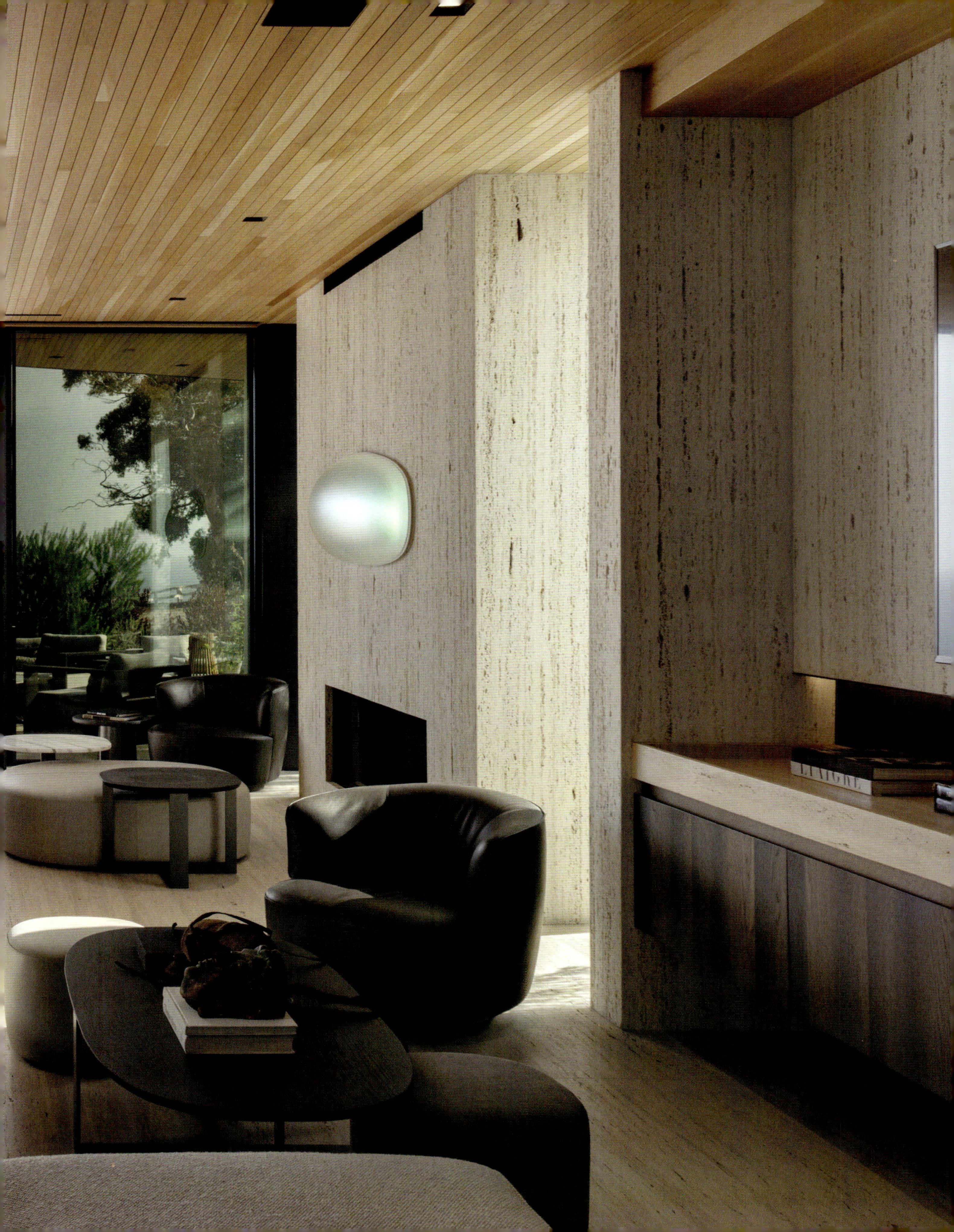

PRECEDING PAGE: The house, in its simplicity, calls out for great art, but the selection is kept to a few impactful pieces. The organic shape of the iridescent artwork above the living room fireplace, sculpted by Karina's sister Gisela Colón, as well as the curves in the furnishings (mostly from Italian furniture company Molteni & C), soften the lines of the contemporary architecture.

ABOVE + RIGHT: The expansive primary suite includes the ocean-facing bedroom, primary bath, dressing room, sitting room, and view terrace.

ATABEI

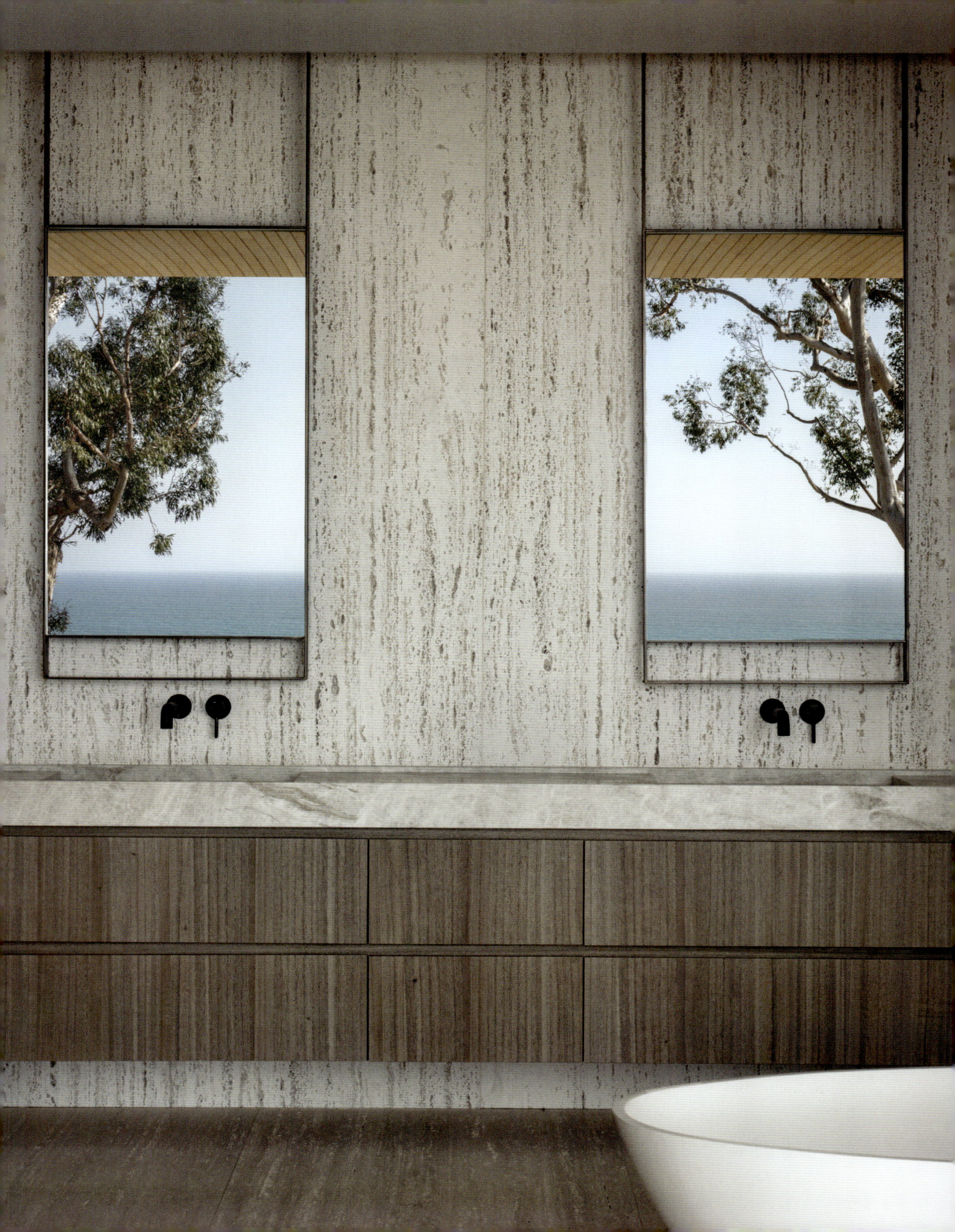

OPPOSITE: In the master bath, twin mirrors hover over the travertine wall. Gray eucalyptus cabinets are topped with a counter of Taj Mahal quartzite; Jae looked at 50 slabs to find the one with just the right undertones.

ABOVE: A rectilinear skylight provides the primary shower, cloaked in sand-blasted travertine, with its own source of natural light.

OVERLEAF: The view terrace off the master bedroom feels private and secluded yet enjoys an expansive ocean vista.

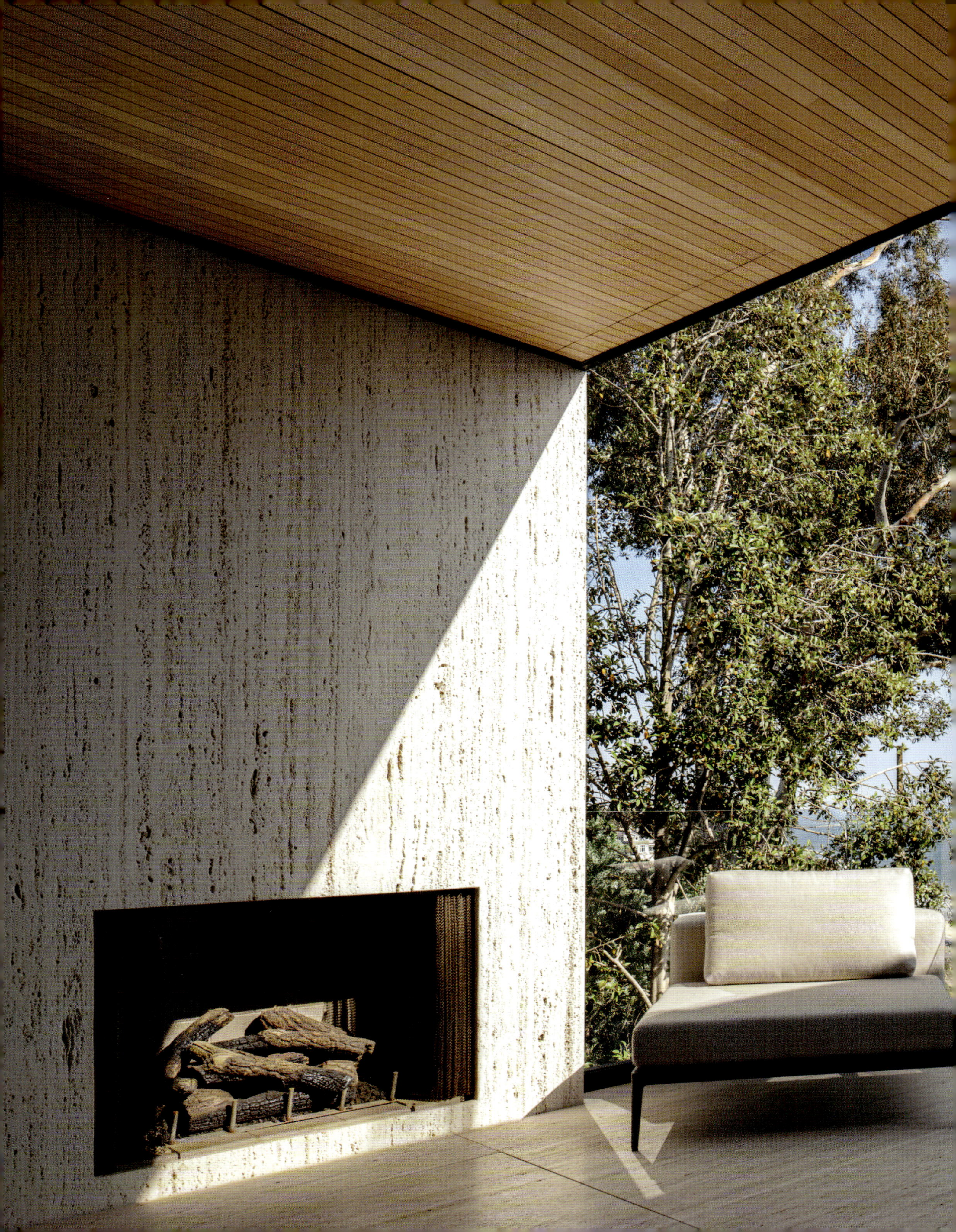

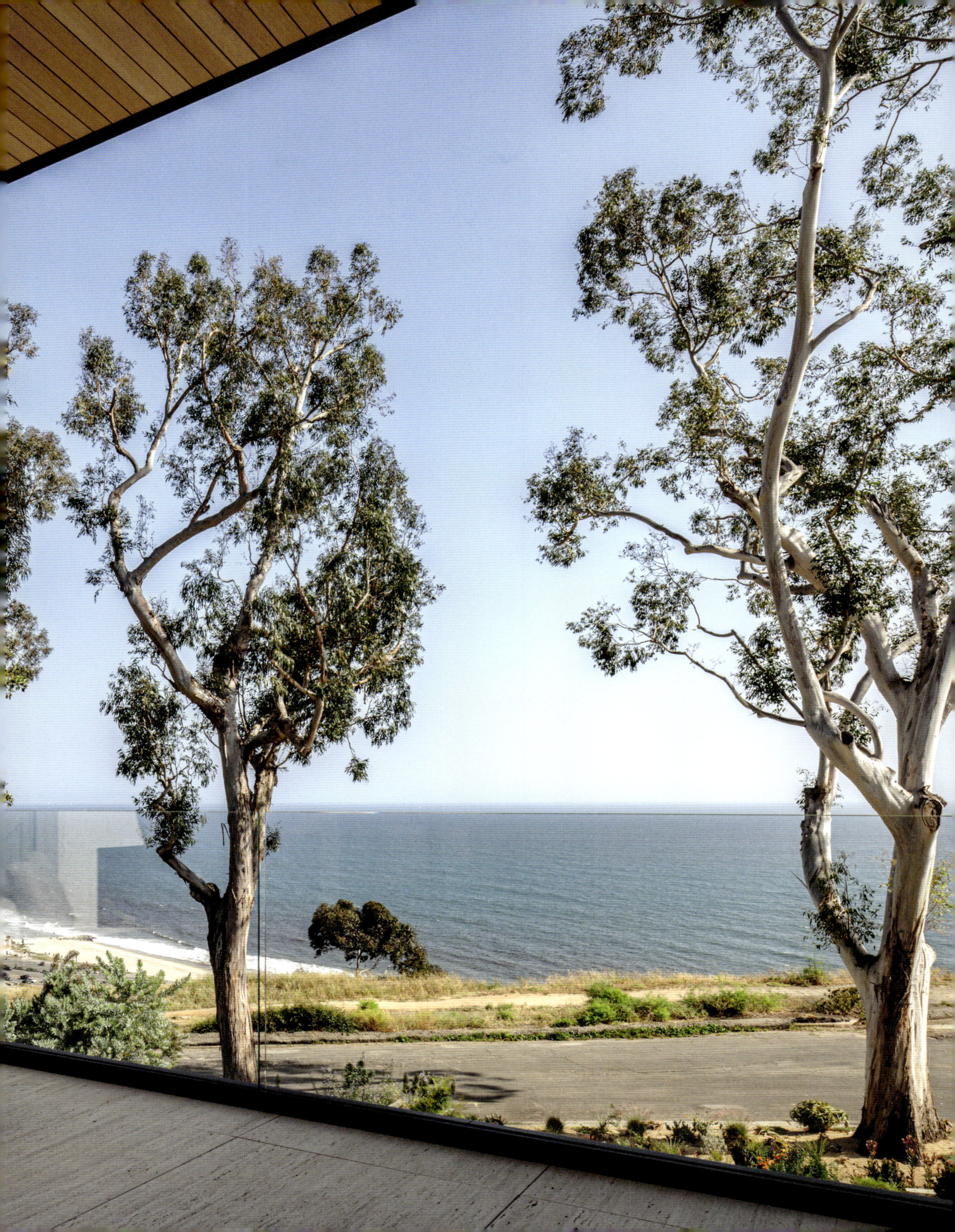

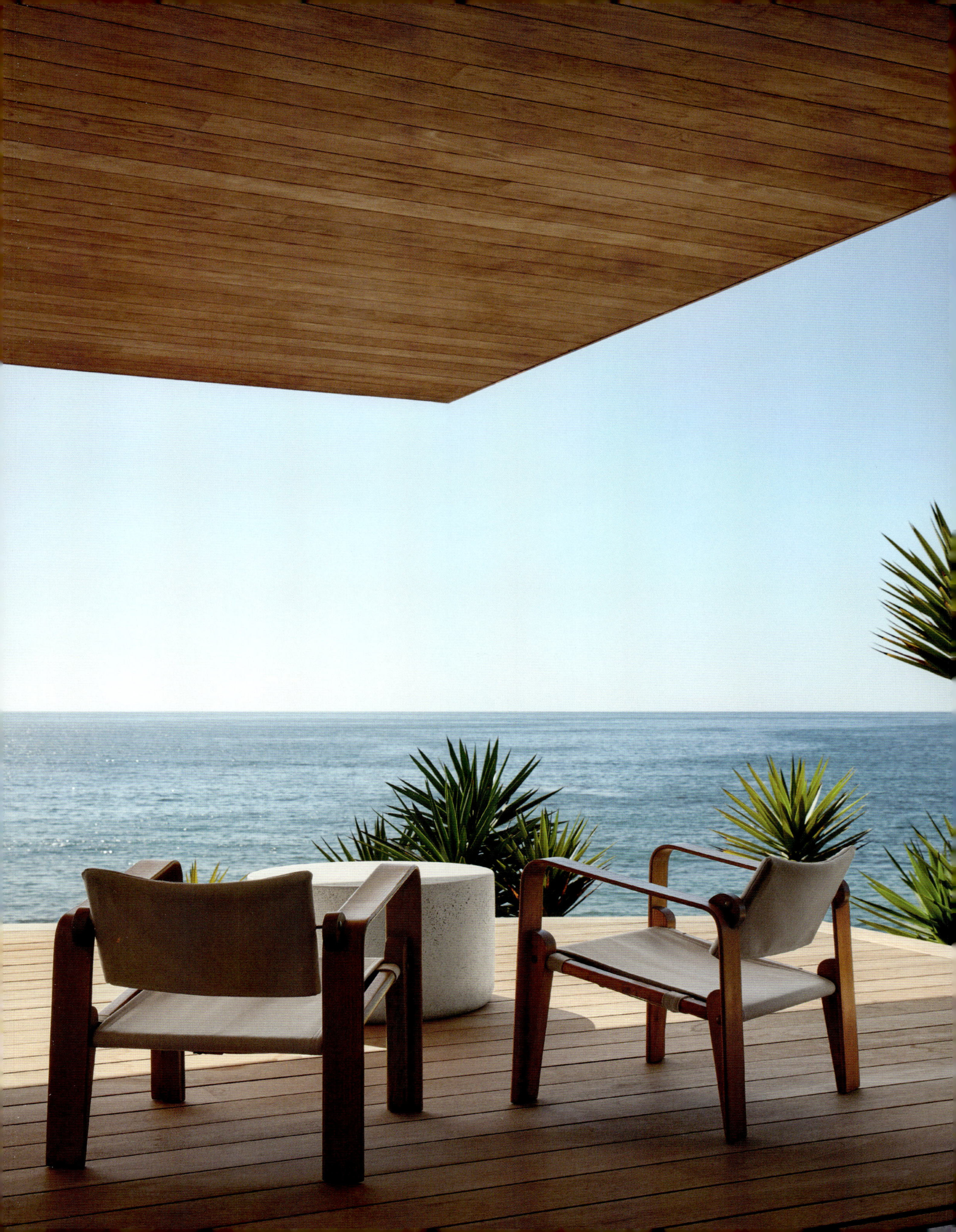

COASTAL SERENITY

/ MALIBU /

When his longtime clients asked him to look at a house they had found in Malibu, architect William Hefner was surprised by what he described as its "conquistador modern" aesthetic. The home was a mix of wood, stone, and orange glass capped with a shingle roof. But the new homeowners, with whom Hefner had worked on a series of Spanish Colonial homes in Los Angeles, had chosen it for the location. The husband and wife had grown up surfing in Malibu. Their vision was of a weekend retreat where they could spend quiet time with the family, entertain friends, and teach their own kids to surf. With a high, vegetation-covered hill screening it from the road behind and the building just steps from the sand, the house enjoyed that exquisite and rare balance of immediate beach access combined with a sense of removal from the world.

"There aren't a ton of houses right on the beach in this part of Malibu," explains Hefner. "Given the approvals process and potential complexities, we decided it made sense to do the project as a remodel rather than new construction. We replanned it and rejiggered the floor plans on all levels, expanded it some, and changed it stylistically to be more decidedly modern. The inspiration, for me, was nautical. There's something about the materiality of that style—the teak and the silver metal, the decks and the railings—that to me seemed like being on the deck of a boat where you have these wide-open views and you're right on the ocean. That was the influence. And where the house before was kind of heavy and more solid, this would be more open, with wide, expansive glass to take in the views. Because it's not about one sight line but the whole setting."

The house encompasses a main level for living; a lower level with two bedrooms, a TV lounge and direct beach access; and a view-filled aerie for the primary bedroom. Constructed by Hanover Builders, it is rendered as a sleek structure of wood, glass, and split-face limestone whose sandy texture speaks to its setting and creates a dynamic contrast to the crisp lines of the other materials. The limited materials palette carries inside, with a generous use of teak on walls and ceilings maintaining a sense of serenity.

New York–based designer Billy Cotton, who also had a long history with the homeowner, embraced the opportunity to define a fresh California coastal aesthetic. "We were always talking about this idea of modernity," recalls Cotton. "That's a huge theme when building in California. We ended up mixing things from Scandinavia, midcentury and contemporary pieces, and pieces from France and Italy to come up with our own modernist language." The owners contributed works from their extensive art collection, including a neon Tracey Emin piece titled *I Listen to the Ocean and All I Hear is You.*

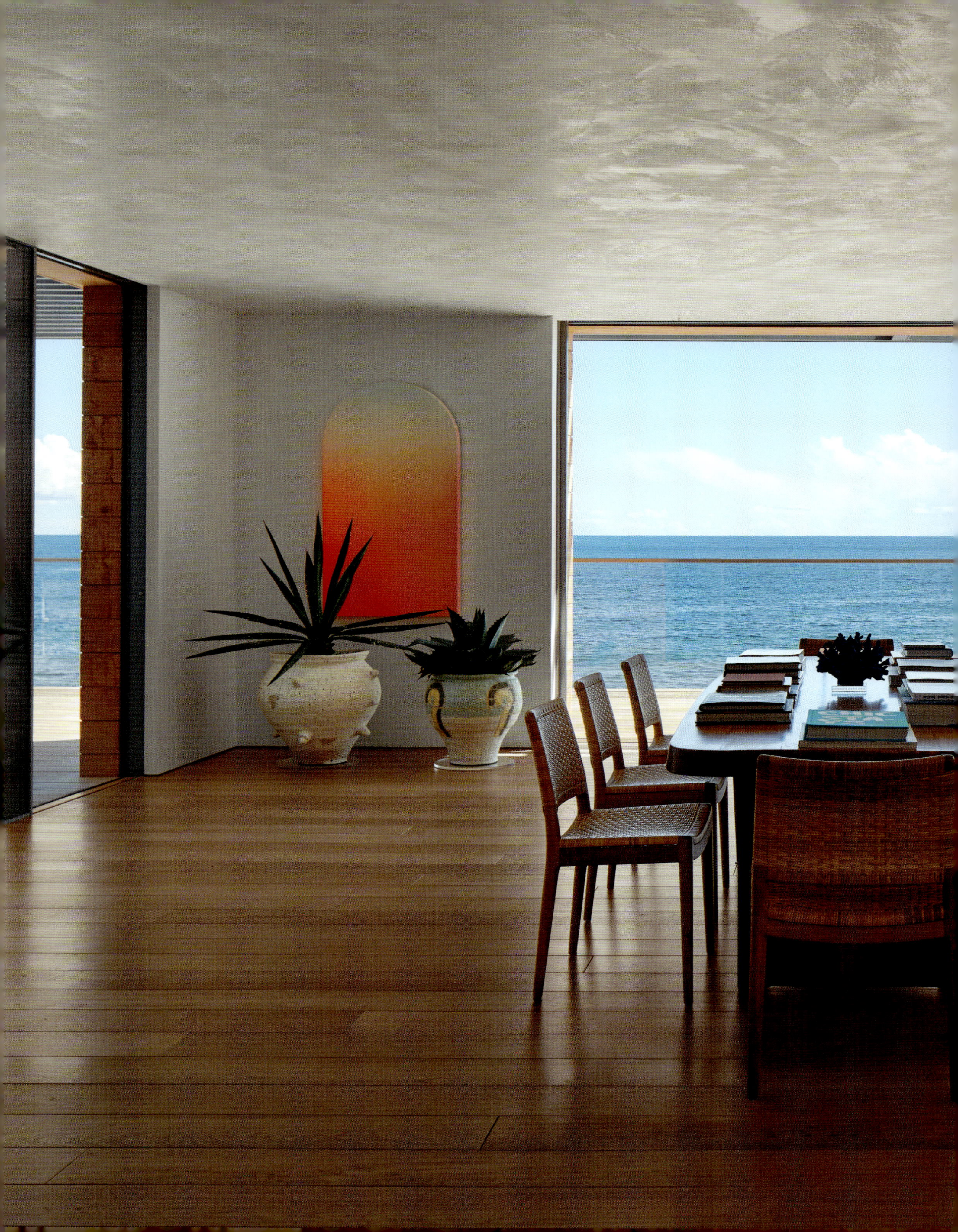

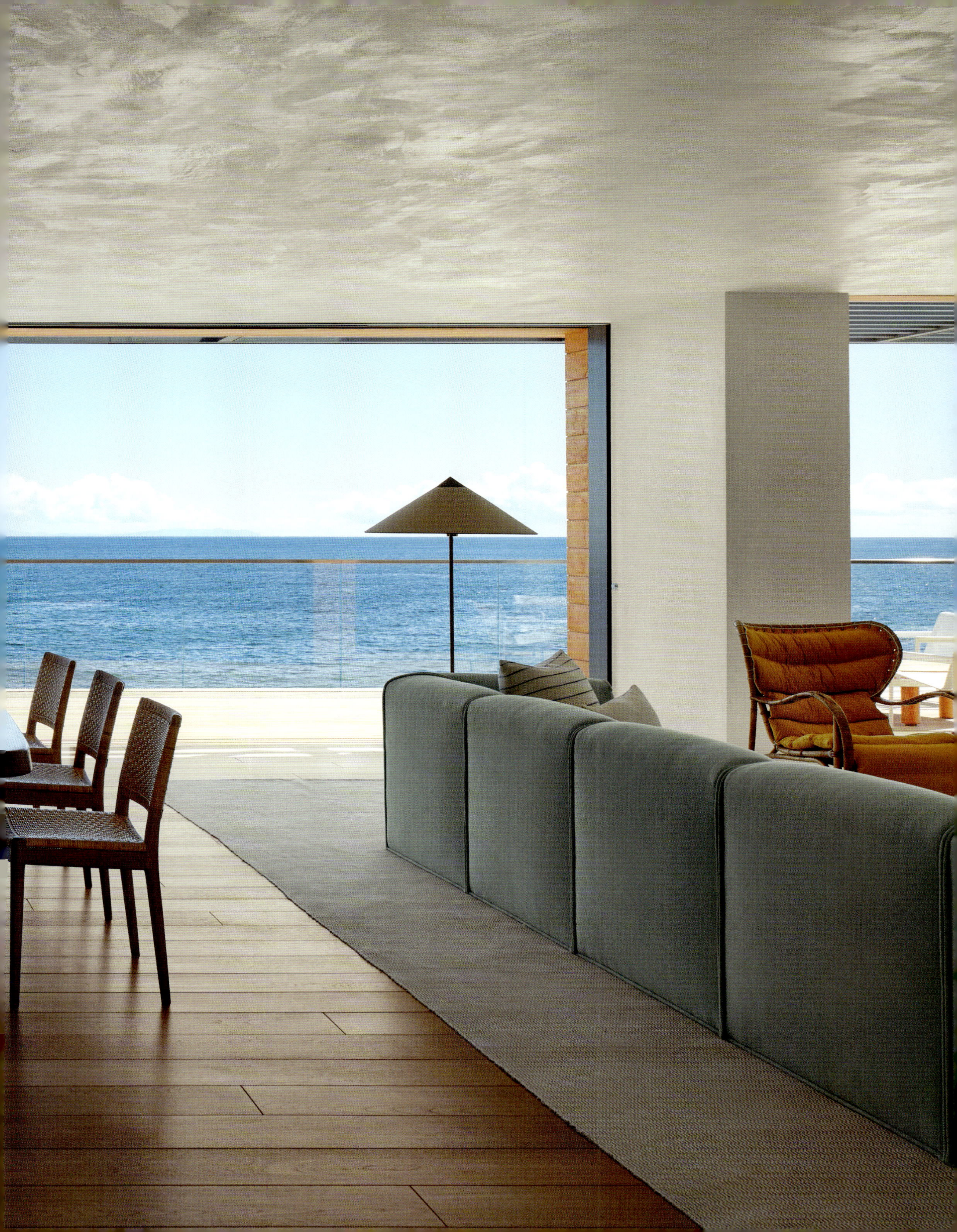

A laid-back vibe is established through inviting furniture with rounded edges in soft sky blue and complementary yellow, a palette that is carried through both living areas. "Colors found in nature led the way—"the blue of the sea, yellow of the sun, and greens of the flora," Cotton explains. The family-friendly feel extends throughout the home: the rectangular dining table has rounded corners and upholstered chairs have a bulbous quality. Sconces from Ingo Maurer take the shape of fans, while in the living room two leaf-shaped tables nest together for an organic feel. Natural and sustainable materials were prioritized to harmonize with the home's deep immersion in the natural world.

In this oceanfront home, every space maintains a strong connection to the outdoors, with generous decks on all three levels, glass doors that slide out of sight, and transparent deck railings that allow unobstructed views to the horizon. The beachside facade offers sheltered alcoves, carved from the building itself, outside the living room and between the dining area and kitchen, to create protected outdoor areas for times of high winds or relentless sunshine. Nestled into the hillside, where native bushes and succulents soften its edges, the house is at one with its setting, embodying that enduring dream of California beach life.

PRECEDING PAGE: The storied beaches and surf breaks of Malibu drew architect William Hefner's longtime clients to this site and prompted a radical remodel in collaboration with Hanover Builders and New York designer Billy Cotton, who had worked with the homeowners before. The house features a strong art program with works by Matt Connors, Alex Israel, Jonas Wood, and Catherine Opie, among others. The homeowners, says Cotton, "weren't afraid of color, so we used it."

OPPOSITE: A skylight over the island brings light into the kitchen with its windowless wall. The round table is custom, with handmade ceramic tiles.

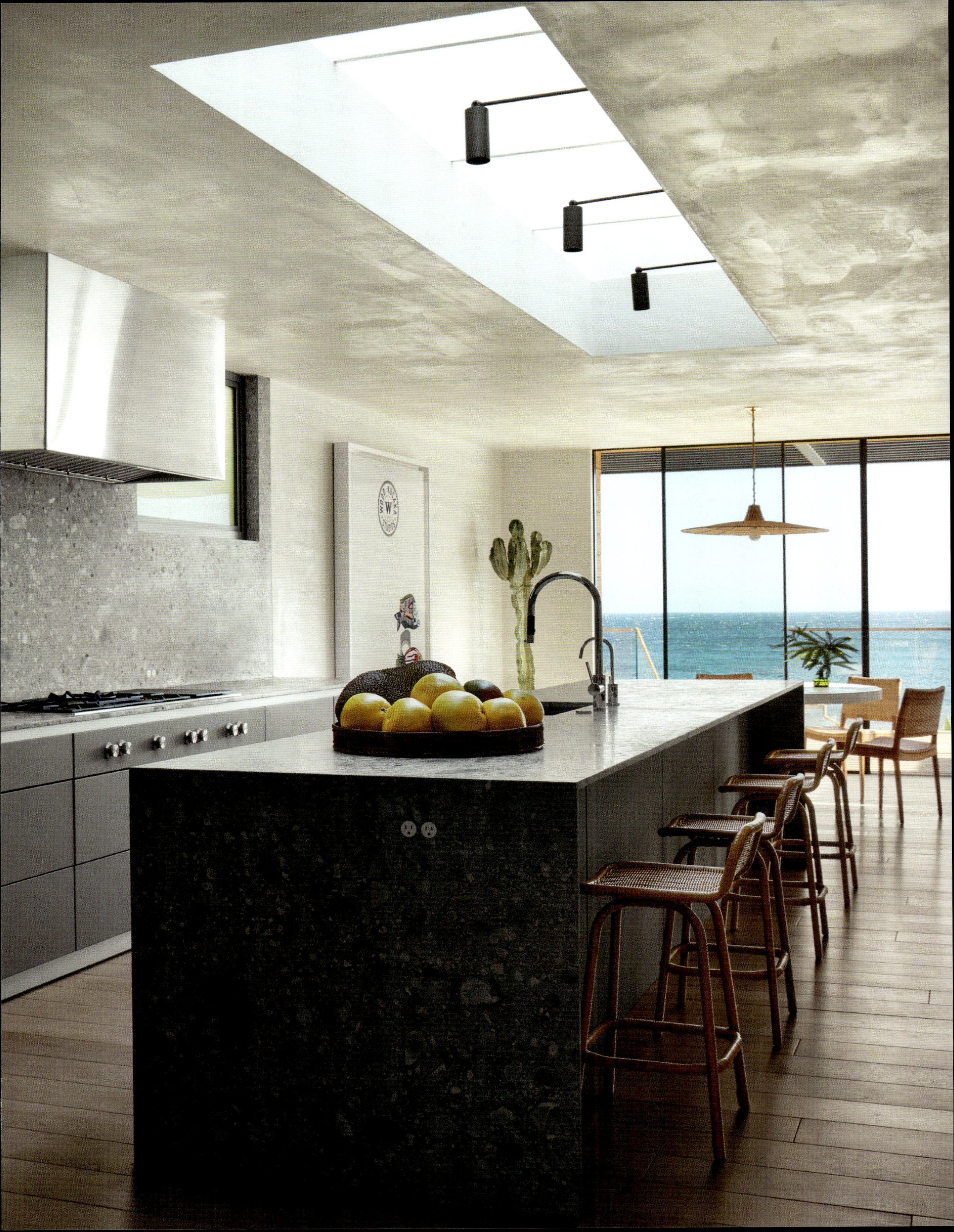

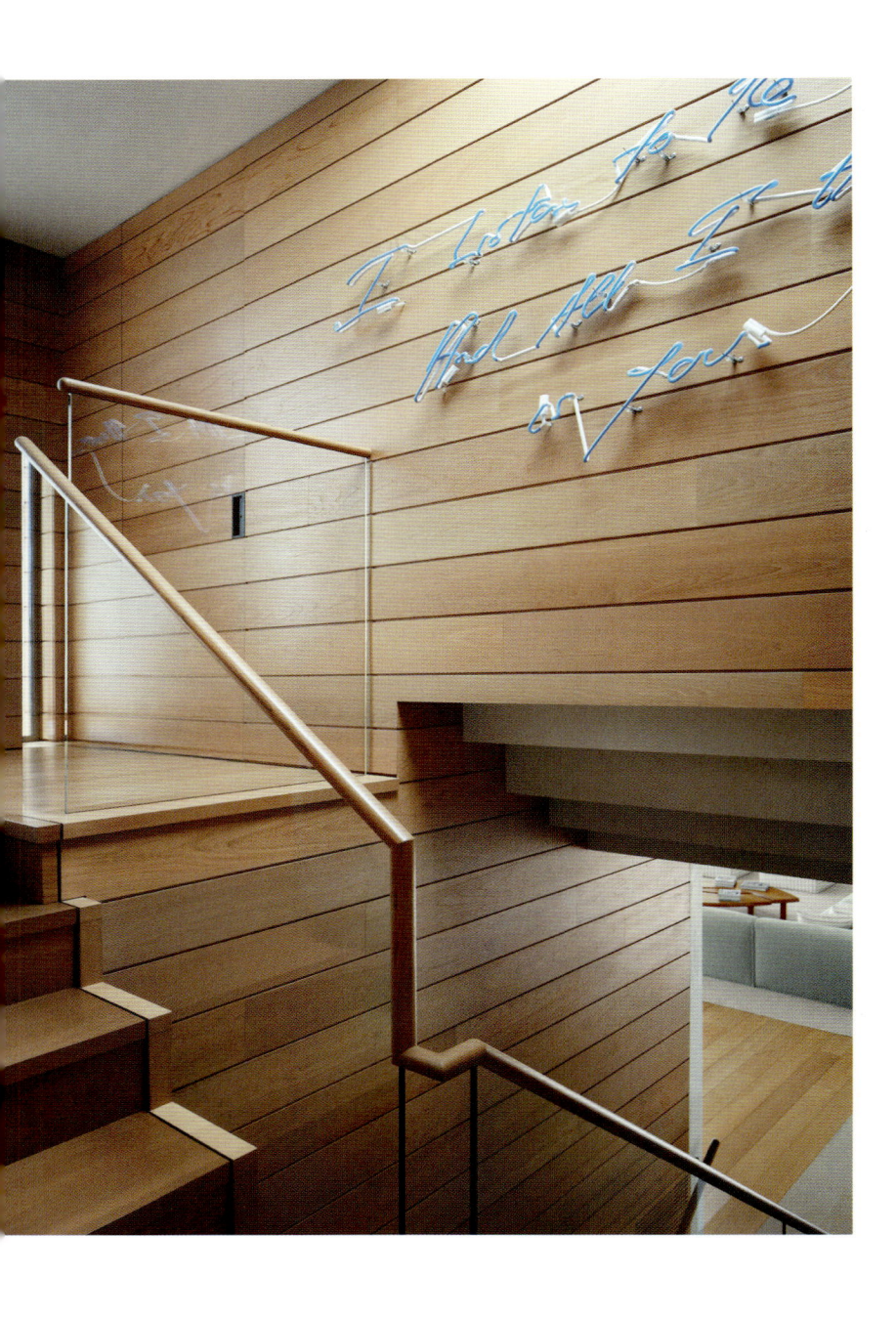

ABOVE: A Tracey Emin piece in neon light in the stairwell captures the spirit of the house: *I Listen to the Ocean and All I Hear is You.*

RIGHT: In fabrics and furnishings, Billy Cotton prioritized natural and sustainable materials, resulting in a comfortable, beach-appropriate feel. The fan sconces are by Ingo Maurer.

COASTAL SERENITY

ABOVE: The primary bath is a serenity-infused space with floating vanities and a stand-alone vessel tub.

RIGHT: Special attention was paid to light fixtures in this light-filled house. In such cases, says Cotton, "minimal is better, to add to the serenity, light, art, and function."

COASTAL SERENITY

Architect William Hefner's design with Nathalie Aragno includes insertions, setbacks, and carve-outs on the beach side for dining out of the wind or sunbathing out of eyesight of beachgoers. Beach-appropriate landscaping was overseen by Dennis Hardesty of Studio William Hefner. Minimal drought-resistant plantings were added to provide some privacy, soften the edges where the architecture meets the environment, and help stabilize the site.

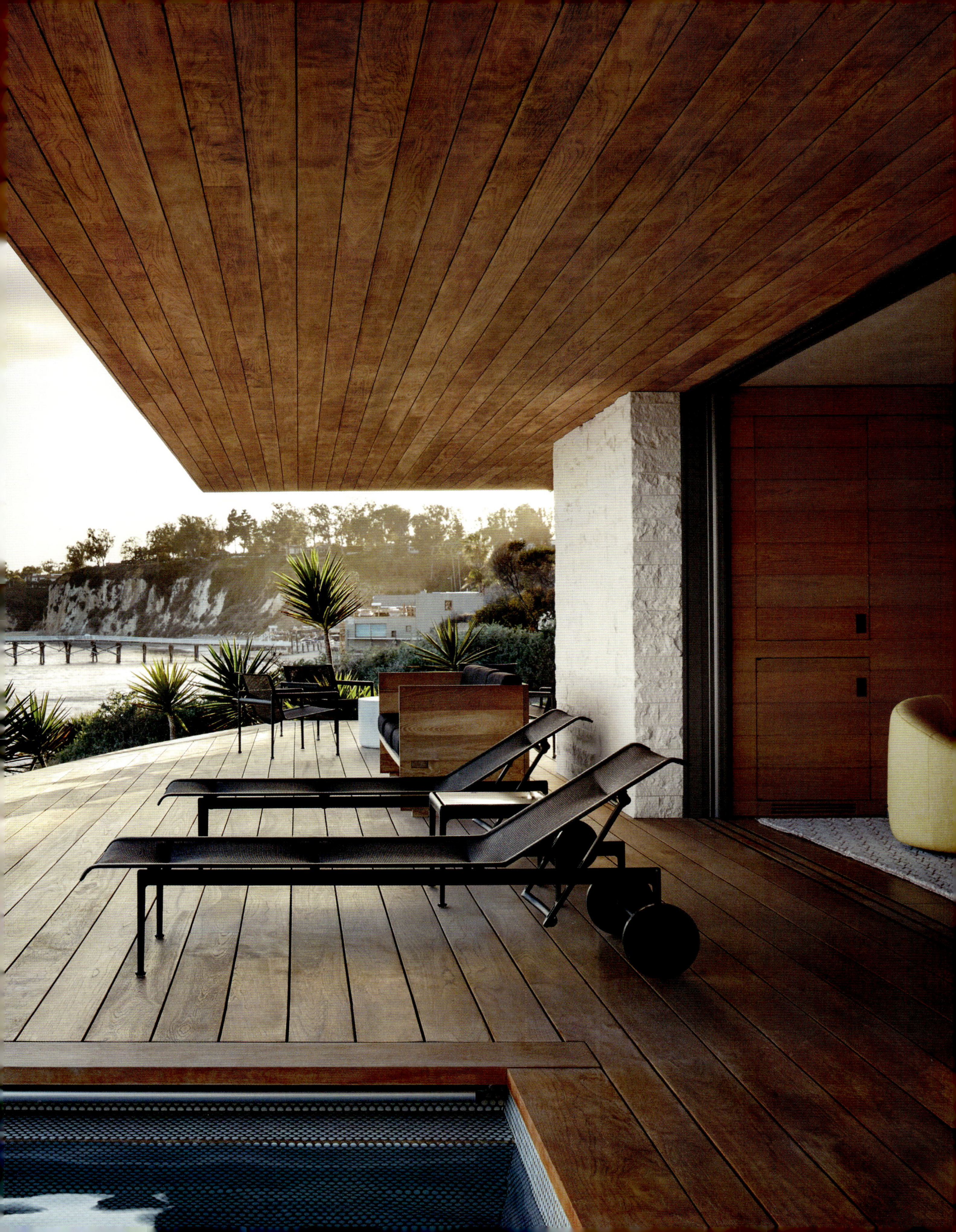

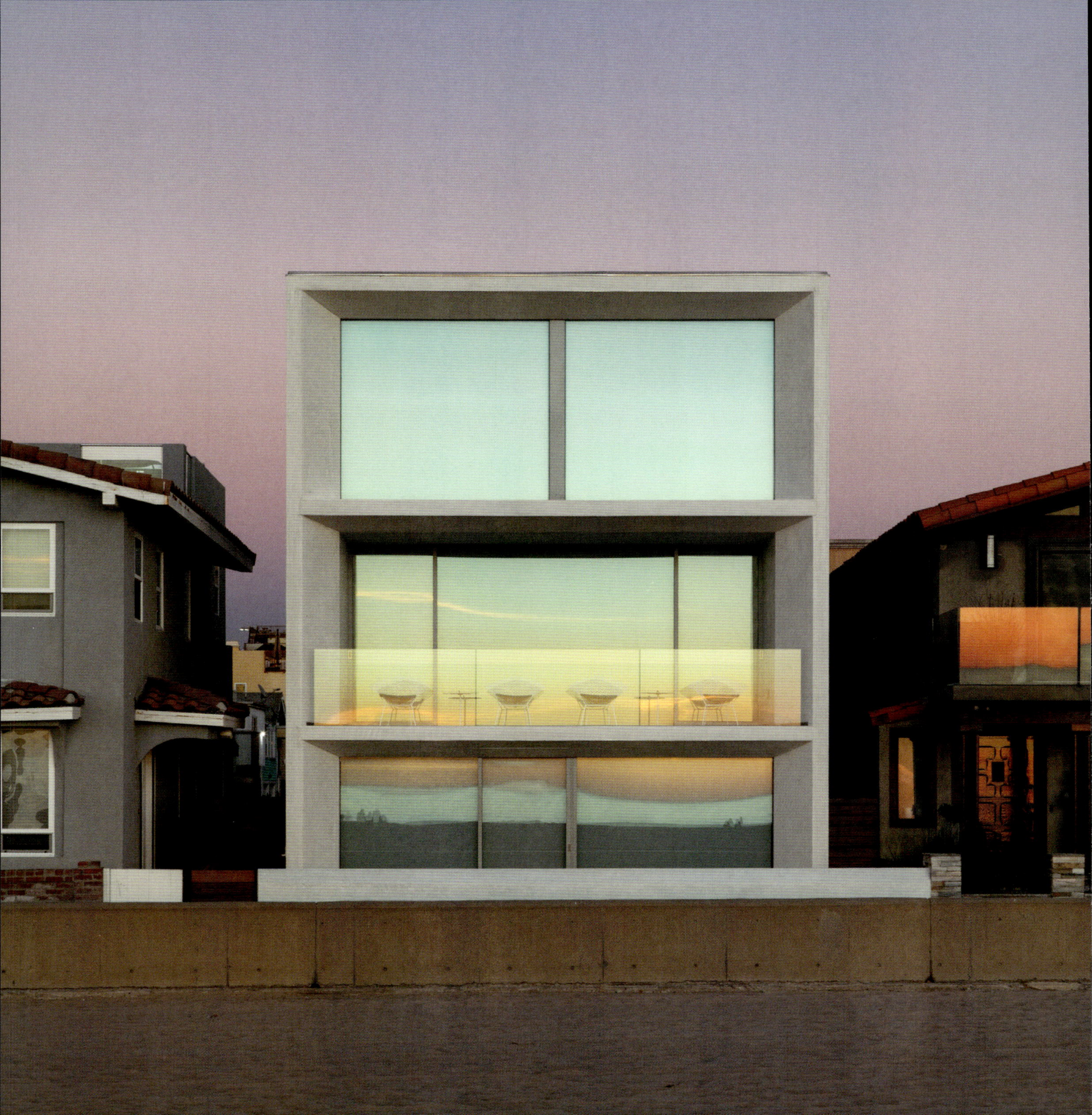

BEACH, OCEAN, SKY

/ HERMOSA BEACH /

In L.A.'s Ocean Cities, the Strand is like an oceanside version of the town square. It's the place that never sleeps, the place to which all roads lead, and, for a family that has maintained a home there for multiple generations, it can feel like a place where everyone knows your name.

When a couple contemplated building a new house on the lot next door to the family bungalow, their goals were twofold: to maximize usable space on a constrained lot and to create zones of experience so they could participate in the community along the Strand without being constantly one with it.

XTEN Architecture's Monika Haefelfinger and Scott Utterstrom designed a three-level home in rectilinear form that presents from the beach as a white outline framing broad panes of glass. The glass in turn reflects the limitless expanse of sea and sky, maintaining a constant dialog with an ever-changing environment and turning the structure into its own contemporary art piece. Within the house, each floor has a distinctly different living experience, Utterstrom explains. "The lower level belongs to the beach, the main living level belongs to the ocean, and the upper level belongs to the sky."

At the ground level, it's all about the neighborhood. The street entry, guest bedroom, bath with indoor and outdoor showers, and modern staircase are arrayed around an art installation. This area leads to the Beach Room, a multipurpose hangout, work, and overflow bedroom space opening to a patio, which is separated from the Strand by a low wall. Beyond the pathway lies white sand and surf, but the foreground hosts a ceaseless parade of bikers, surfers, strollers, and dog walkers backed by an upbeat beach-life soundtrack: cheers from volleyball matches, shouts of children, snatches of music, and the call of seabirds.

The activity of the Strand fades away as one ascends the stairs and emerges into a serene space filled with light. Across the top of a low, white, L-shaped sofa is a framed view of beach, breaking surf, and the receding depths of blue of sea and sky. On the street side lies the kitchen, warmed with wood and designed for hosting, the pantry and laundry room hidden behind a camouflaged pivoting door. A sheltered patio extends the space and provides an out-of-the-wind spot to dine or grill.

The top floor is a sanctuary. The lot is just wide enough to accommodate two ocean-facing bedrooms, each with undivided glass panels framing views that encompass mostly sky. "The rooms are pretty small," says Haefelfinger, "but one large opening expands the space. It is a lesson in how you can maximize the effect in having one wall disappear and the space expand."

On each level, a palette of white, gray, and black allows the focus to remain on the views while creating the perfect backdrop for contemporary art. "We created a neutral palette so that it would

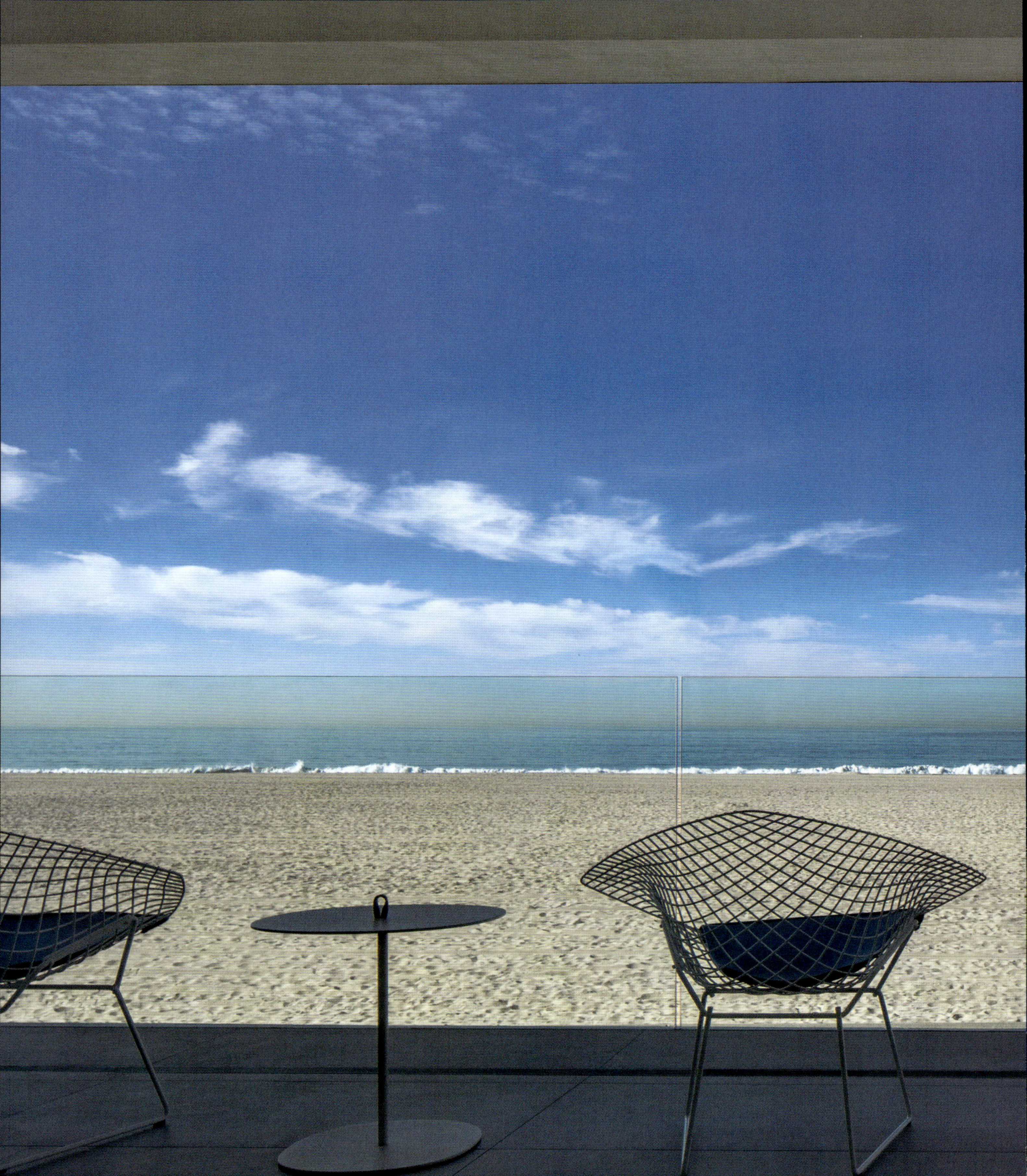

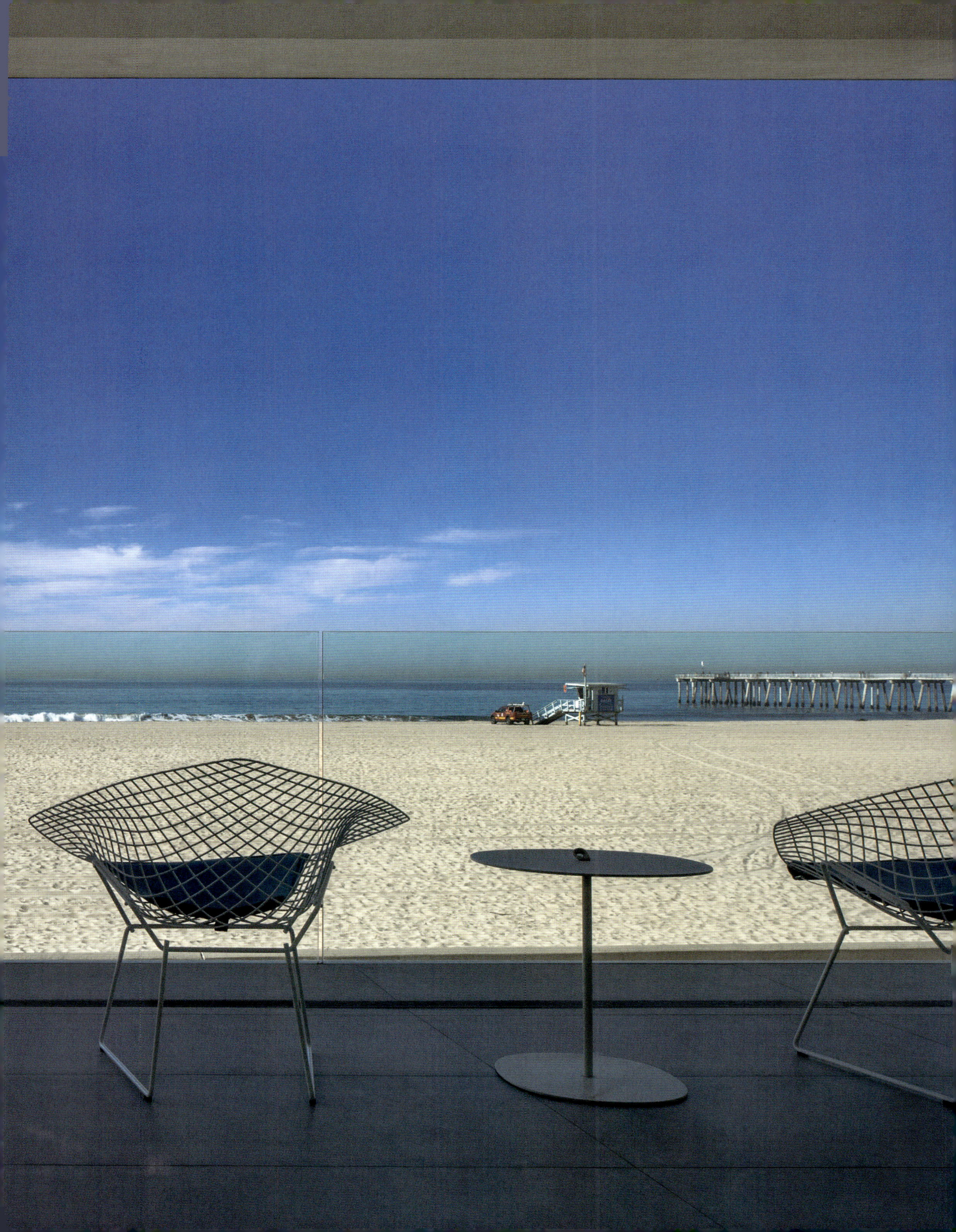

be flexible in terms of any art that came and went," explains interior designer Jorie Clark. "If we used the art for color, it could adapt as the art changed over time. The palette is very subdued to let the view be the main aspect. The oak has a lot of natural character to warm it up. All the fabrics and finishes are virtually bulletproof. The dining table is made from a European textile that's self-healing, and I spent a lot of time making sure that whatever you set a drink on, whether ceramic or dark marble or Fenix, wouldn't be damaged. Our thinking was that you want people to relax and have a good time."

The house performs exactly as designed, whether for one couple or the extended clan flowing back and forth between neighboring homes. And it allows the owners to be part of their beloved community while also permitting them to retreat from it, whether they want to access beach life or quietly gaze into the cerulean sky.

"The patio at the Strand is lively," says Haefelfinger. "We had a lot of discussions about whether we should build higher, but the clients really like being in the action. Neighbors walk down the Strand in the evenings; everyone moseys along and chats. Downstairs it's about the theater of the beach, while upstairs it's about the serene quality of the Pacific."

With the right design team, it seems, you can have it all.

PRECEDING PAGE: Hermosa Beach, one of southern California's "Ocean Cities" (several beach communities linked together by a thoroughfare called The Strand), is known for its laid-back, family-friendly atmosphere. For a homeowner who had grown up vacationing there, XTEN Architecture designed a strikingly modern home immediately next to and in sharp contrast to the 1940s-era bungalow that still belongs to the extended family. From a deck off the second floor, the view vividly illustrates the designers' concept of beach, ocean, sky.

RIGHT: Decidedly neutral interiors in the open living space are warmed up in the kitchen with oak paneling, where a pivot door leads to the pantry and powder room. The countertops are user-friendly stainless steel. Sliding doors open to a protected deck on the side of the house, perfect for grilling and dining on windy days. Frosted glass windows along the side of the house bring light into the space while maintaining privacy.

BEACH, OCEAN, SKY

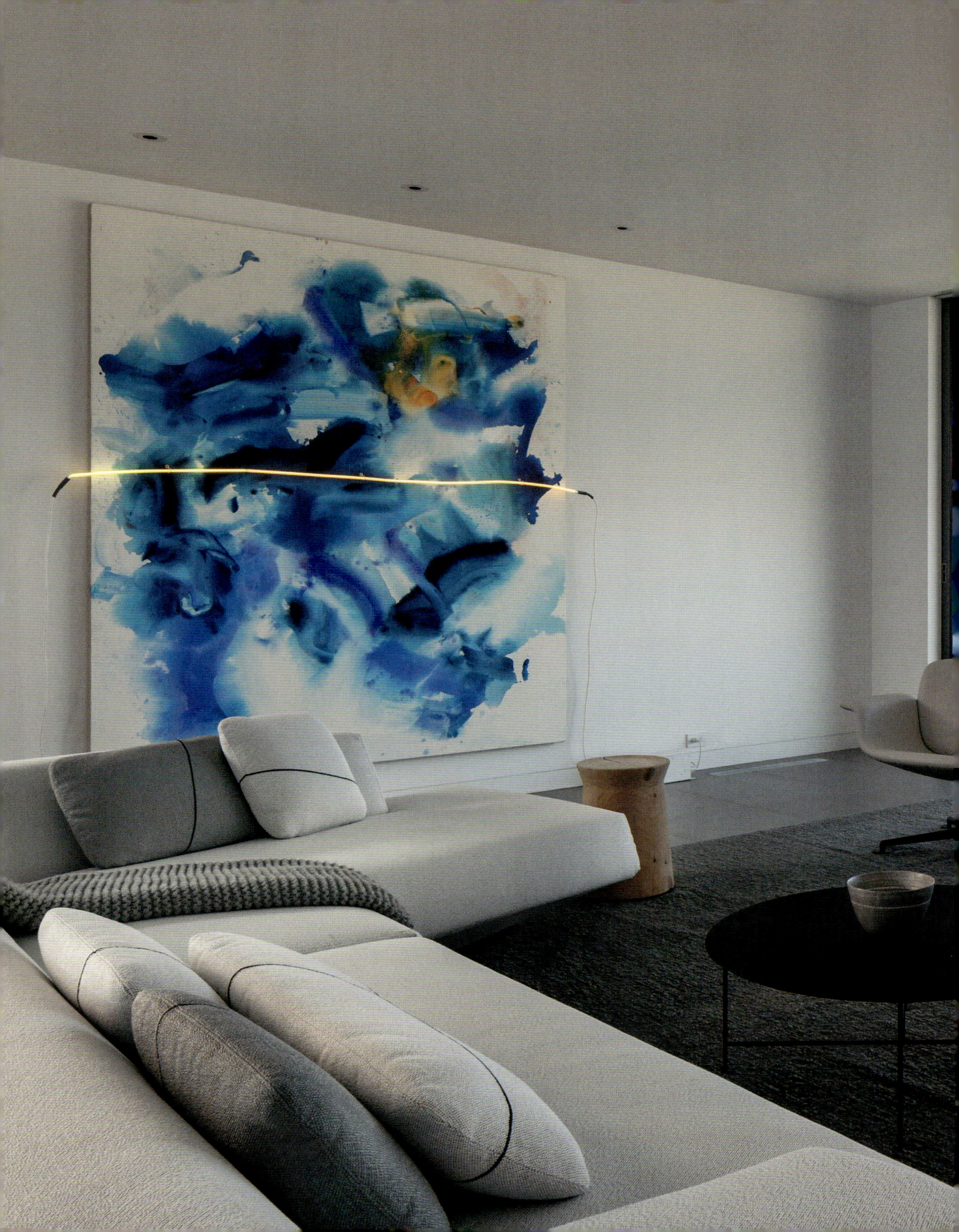

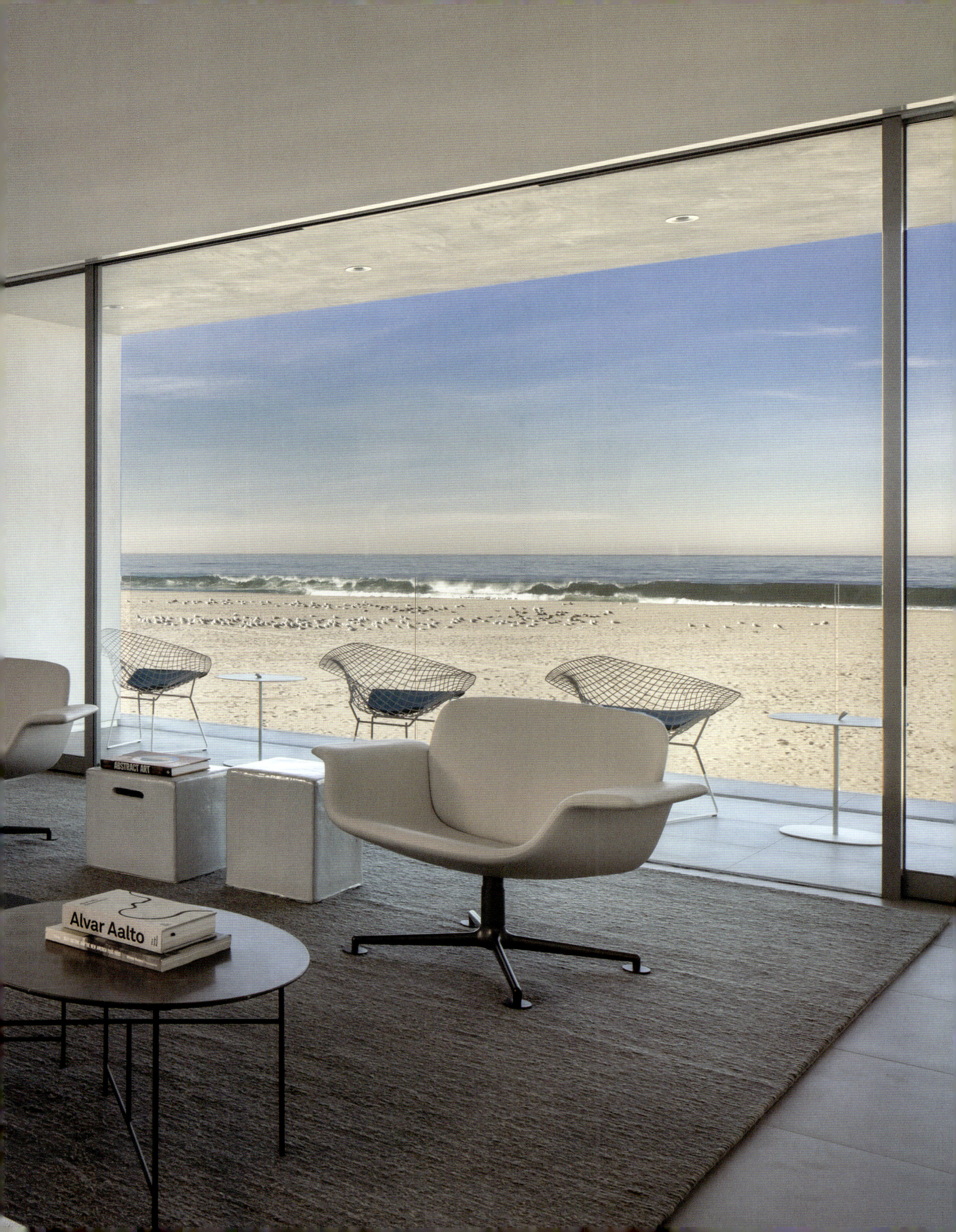
ABSTRACT ART
Alvar Aalto

PRECEDING PAGE: The clients knew they wanted a modern form and an achromatic palette to create a backdrop for contemporary art, such as the large piece by Los Angeles artist Mary Weatherford. "The color is so vibrant, it felt just right," says the homeowners' longtime interior designer Josie Clark. The chairs are from Pierre Luzon; the sofa is by Poliform.

ABOVE + OPPOSITE: Two upstairs bedrooms were kept small, spare, and equal in size. Simplicity reigns in these rooms, with furnishings and wide plank oak floors all deferring to the views. "I think what's unique about our strategy," says XTEN's Scott Utterstrom, "is that fixed glass became a priority; we kept it mullion-free to preserve the views. There are a few sliding doors for cross ventilation, but the rest was designed to capture the ocean as best we could."

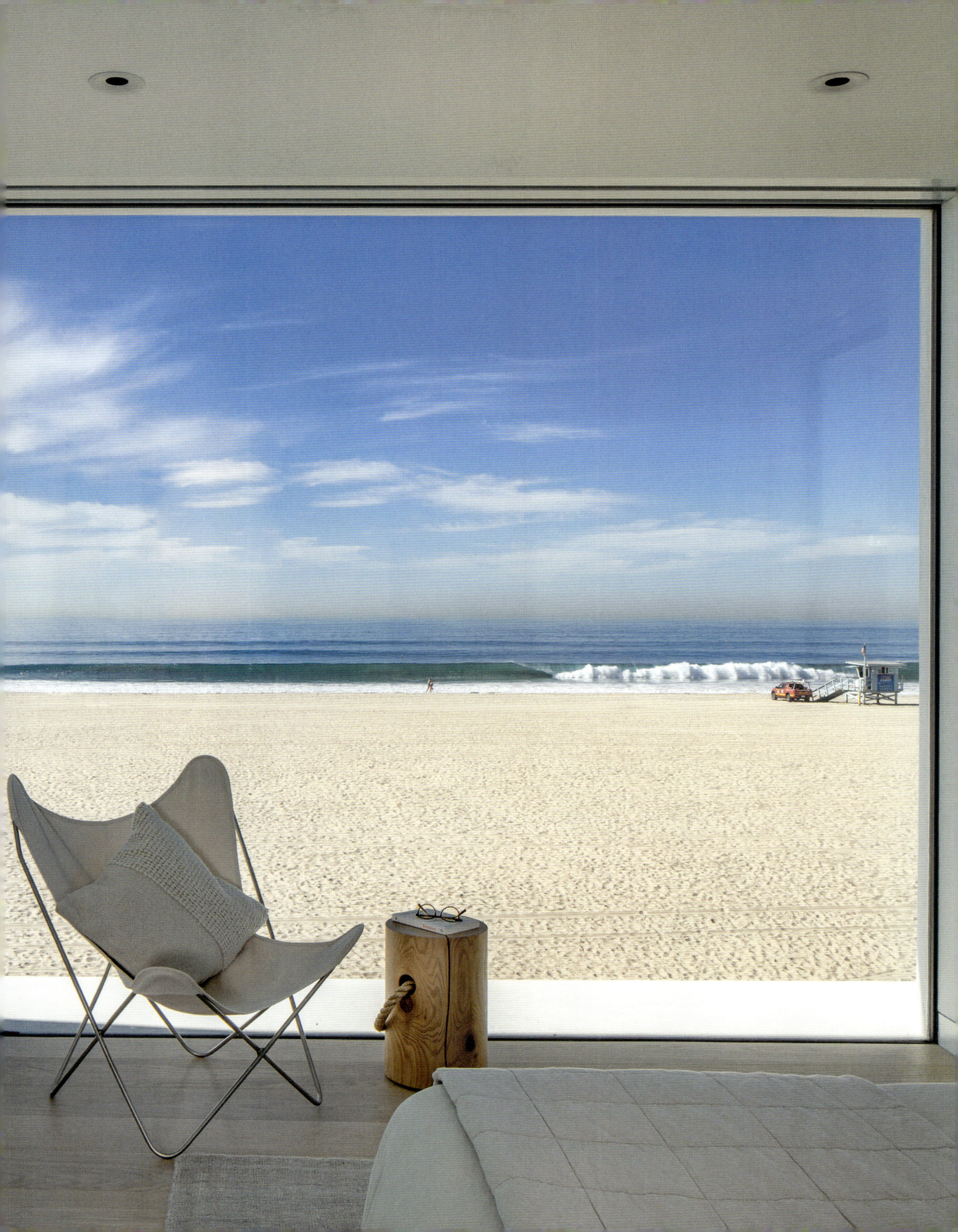

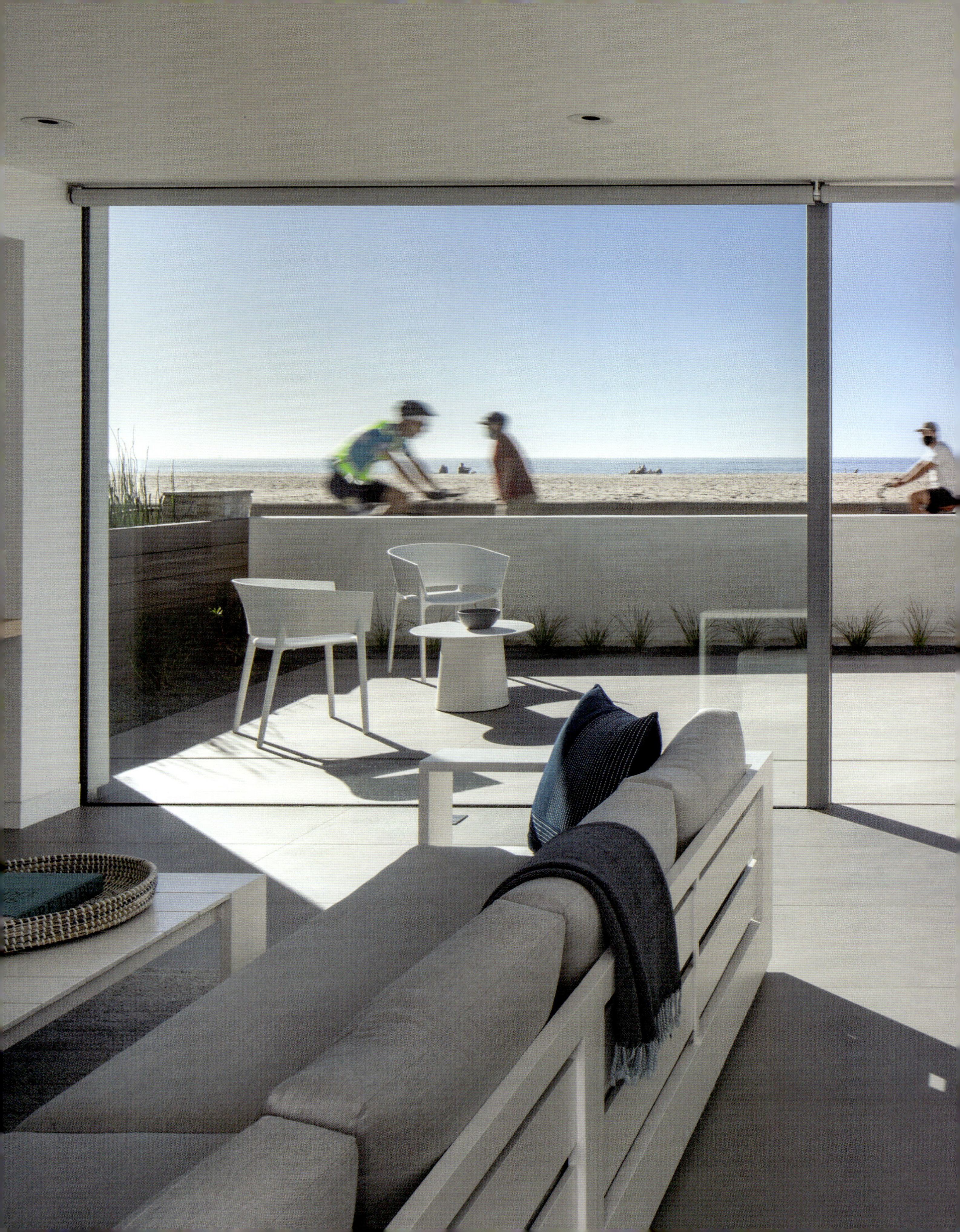

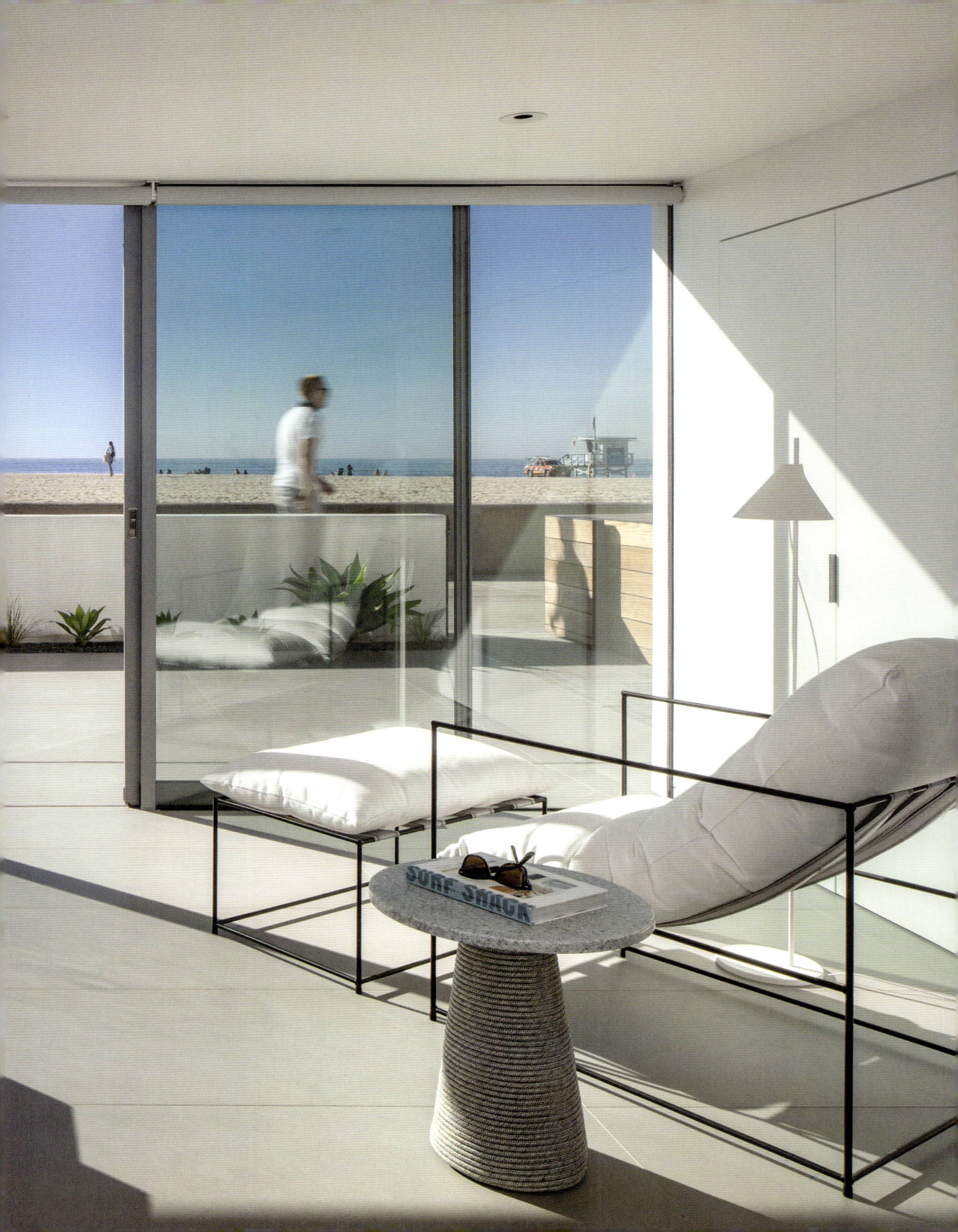
SURF SHACK

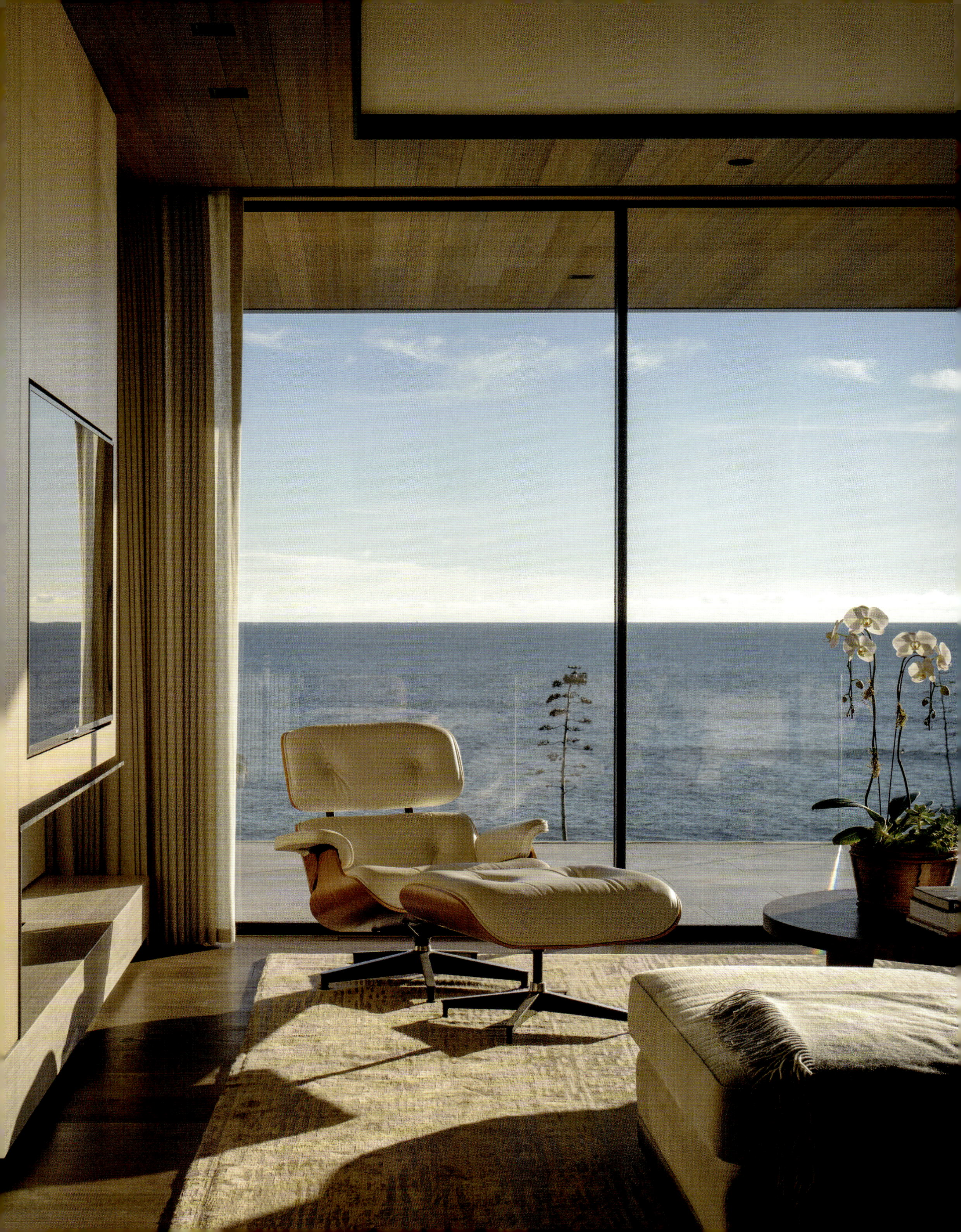

SEASIDE SANCTUARY

/ LA JOLLA /

The seaside community of La Jolla, in northern San Diego County, is one of the most popular beach destinations in California, known for its dramatic coastline, picturesque beaches, rich cultural offerings, and friendly village vibe. It's a small town, where everyone knows everyone, and relationships are the key to doing business. The team behind this home on a protected seaside bluff is no exception. Architect Mark House has known the client for nearly three decades, having worked with him on several projects over the years. Sibling interior designers David and Suzie Lucas have a well-deserved reputation for creating some of La Jolla's most beautiful houses, even though they are headquartered in Seattle. Together this team envisioned a residence for their very private client that provides him not only a sense of sanctuary but a deep connection to the site.

"Of all the houses we've worked on together, this is my favorite," says Mark. "It's peaceful, tranquil, and connected." This, he feels, is his client's forever home; in fact, the team is in the process of designing a guesthouse and spa on the adjacent lot.

Located in Bird Rock—a seaside neighborhood named for its views of the famous bird-shaped rock just off the coast—this home sits just where the coastline curves outward to form a cove. Facing southwest rather than straight toward the sunset, the site is largely shielded from the winds that blow in from the north. It is also part of an active, close-knit neighborhood.

Set downslope of the road, with neighbors on each side, the house achieves a feeling of privacy without being entirely closed off from the street. Board-formed concrete walls are low enough to enable passersby to view the water through the upper windows, while landscape and permeable paving soften the lines of the architecture. From the street, the house appears as a single-story home, with the second level below the entry—what is commonly referred to as an "upside-down house."

A carefully orchestrated journey down a set of free-floating concrete stairs and past a sculptural water wall leads to a central courtyard that feels like an oasis. Thoughtfully landscaped and surrounded by transparent window walls, the courtyard sets the tone for the rest of the home: softly sophisticated and deeply intentional, the very essence of tranquility.

Beyond the courtyard, architecture and interiors are layered, with a strong sense of continuity. Walls of windows that line the entry and ocean-facing walls retract into the walls to create an unrestricted flow from the entry courtyard through the house to the oceanfront terrace. When the weather is blustery or the fog rolls in, the ocean-facing facade can be closed, and outdoor life can continue in the protected courtyard. The backbone of the house is a board-formed concrete wall running from the entry plane through to the exterior terrace. The board forms are exaggerated, drawing the eye outward toward the water view.

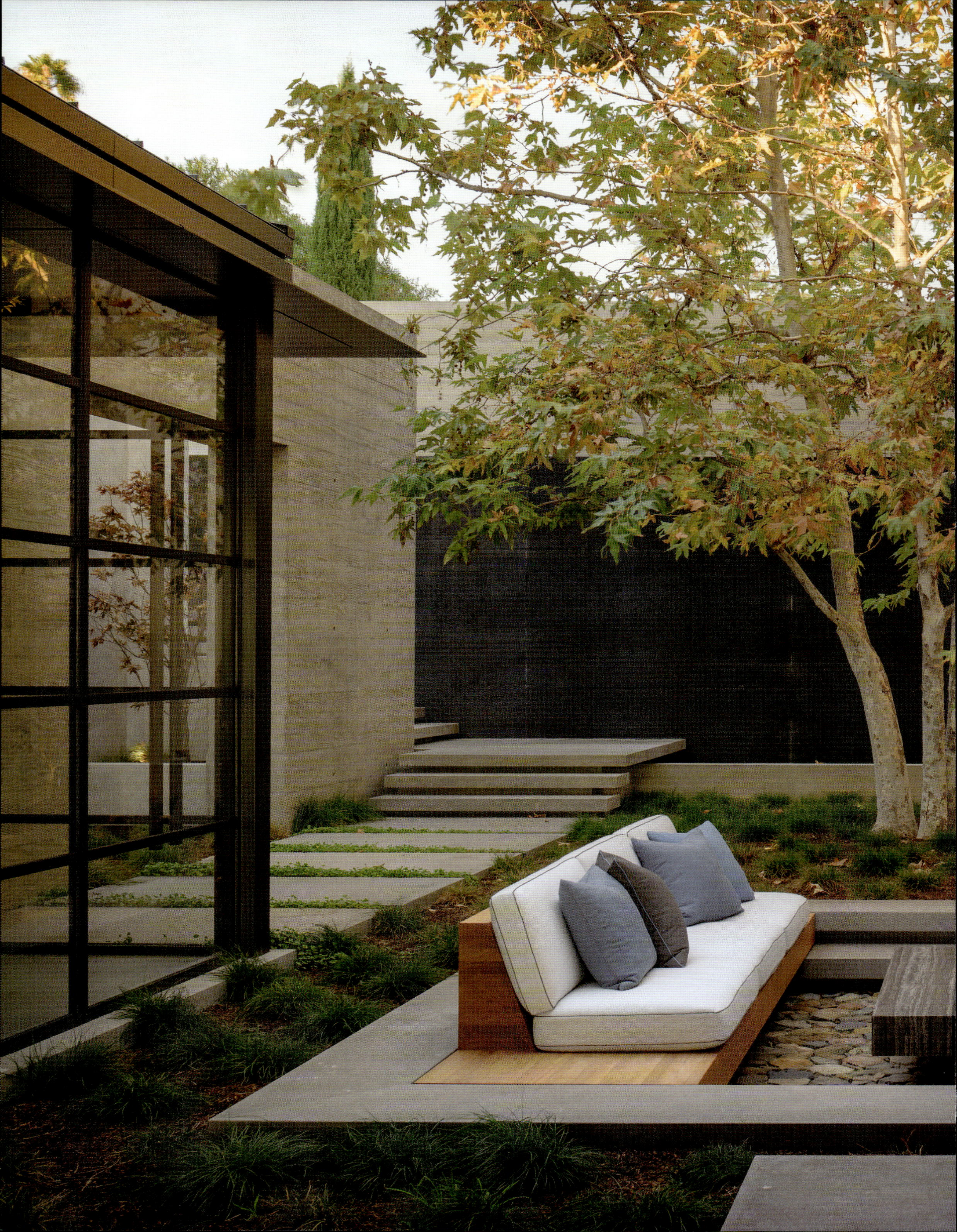

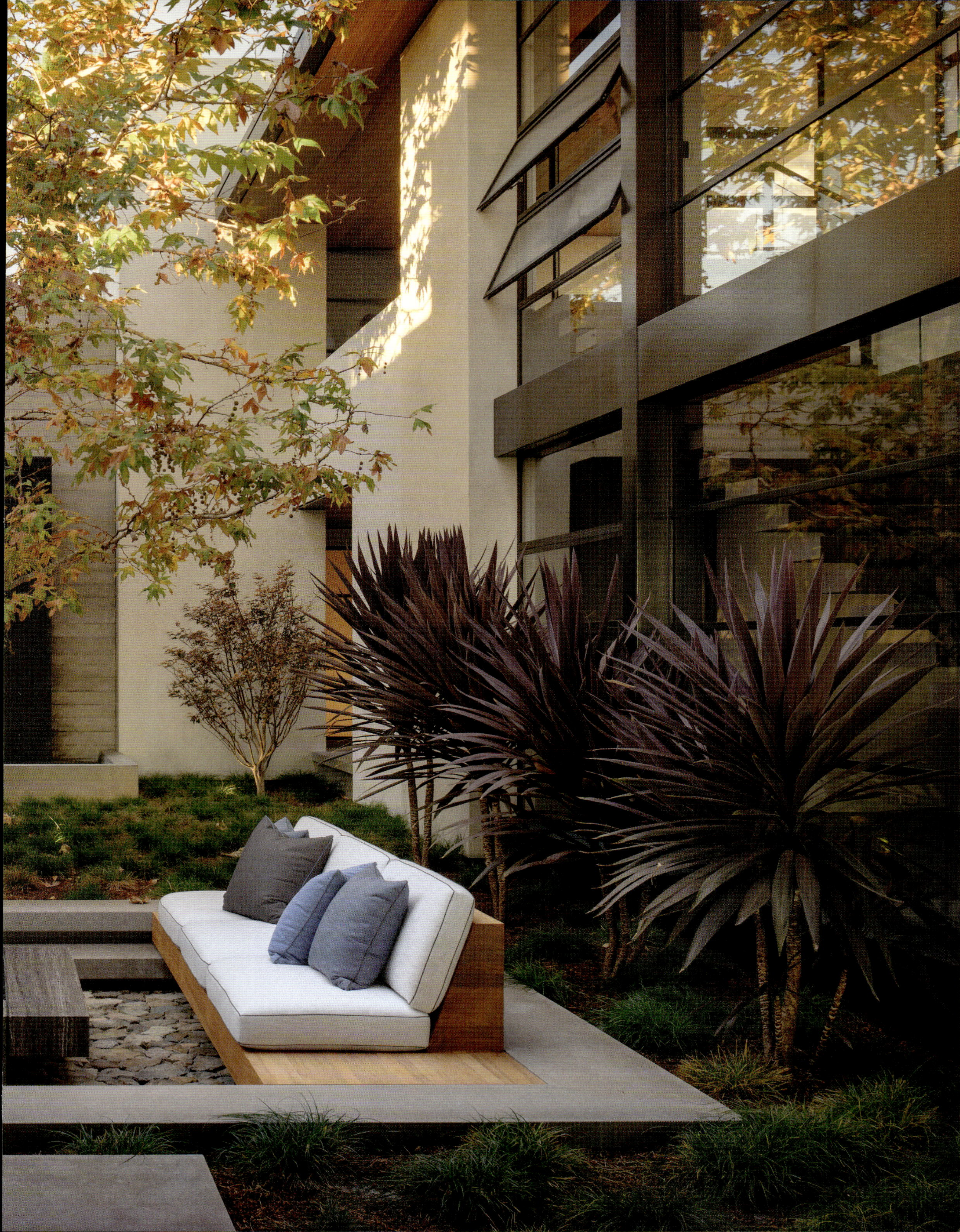

"What interests me is the blurred space where the architecture ends and interiors begin," says David, who directed the design of both the interiors and the landscape.

Set far back from the edge of the bluff, the house feels protected. A large wall of translucent glass lining the south side of the terrace can be pushed forward to provide privacy from the neighboring homes or pulled back to expand the view. A strong sense of horizontality in the architecture—and the shoji-like window panels in particular—speak to a Japanese sense of order and tranquility. Flooring and ceiling materials flow from interior to exterior, weaving them together into a single experience of place.

Both architect and interior design team design coastal properties with materials that are as low-maintenance as possible. Concrete and limestone stand up to the elements, bronze windows and doors are finished with a simple oil finish, and the only exterior wood is in the protected eaves. The team received an assist from contractor Hill Construction, a frequent collaborator. "We helped select materials that will last and look as good ten years from now as they did when the project was completed," says Ryan Hill.

On the interior, the material palette is crisp and tailored but warm and tactile, with hemlock ceilings, limestone floors, board-formed concrete, rift sawn white oak cabinetry, and details rendered in steel and dark walnut. Deeply involved in each of his projects, the client worked closely with David on every detail. Inspired by yacht design, he requested as many built-in furniture-quality elements as possible. There is very little artwork; instead, the artistry plays out in the details, environment, and views.

Architecture and interiors come together in a single vision—a peaceful sanctuary that is tailor-made for its owner.

PRECEDING PAGE: Designed with a built-in seating area surrounded by greenery and filled with the soft sounds of the water wall, the courtyard is an oasis that sets the tone for the rest of the house.

RIGHT: In this cohesive environment, windows and doors have a minimal profile and run flush to the ceiling to restrict the expanse of the views as little as possible.

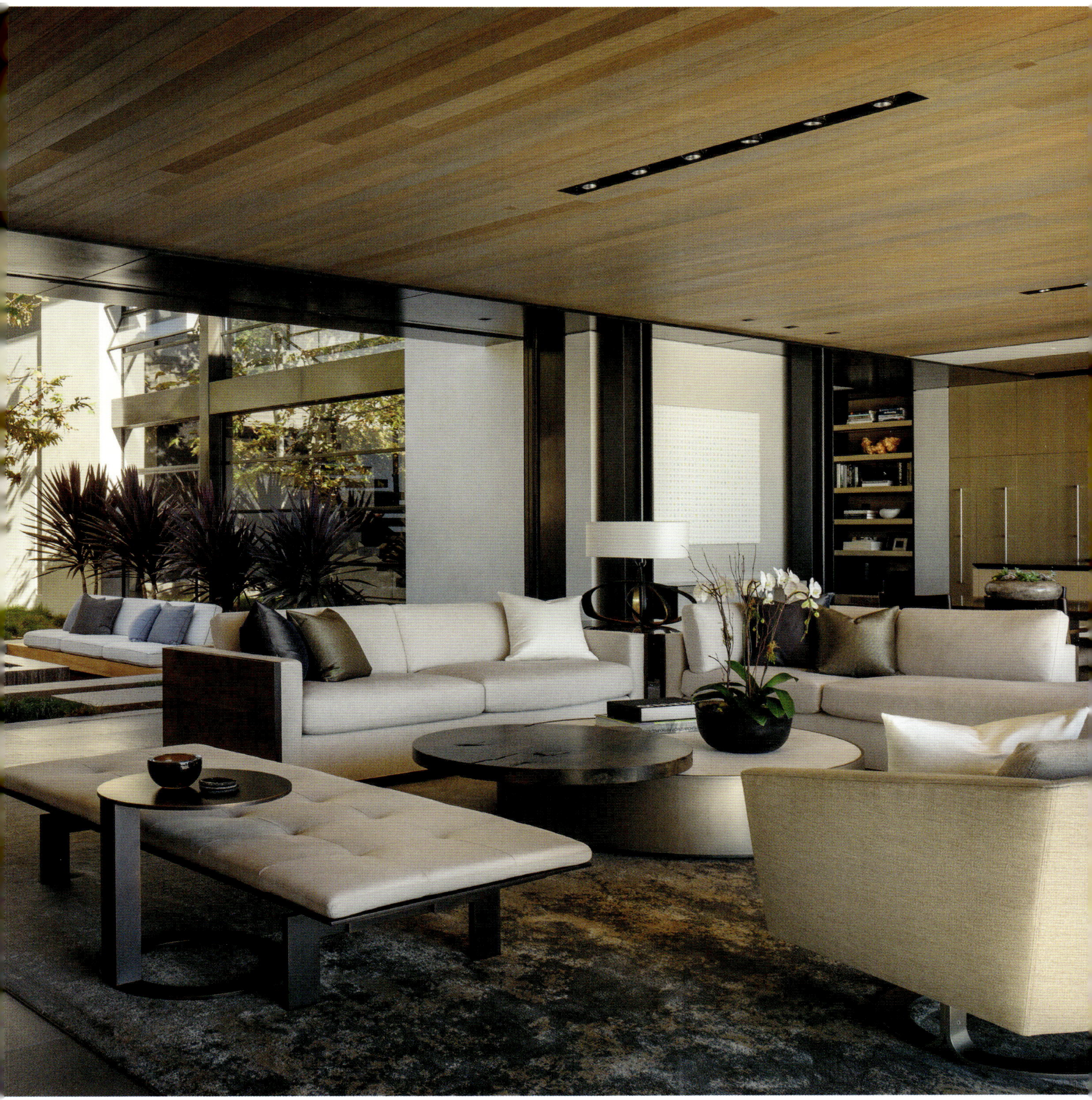

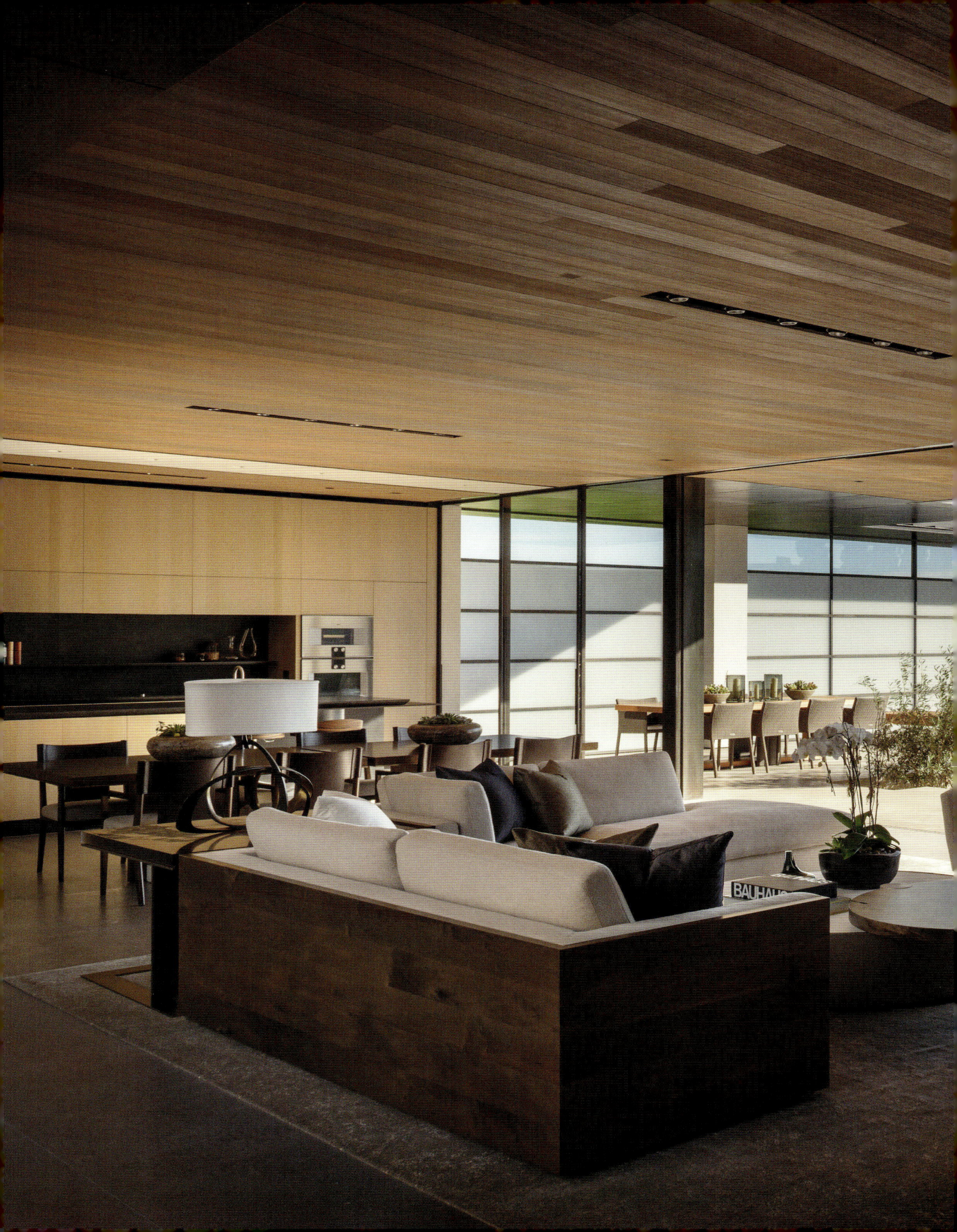

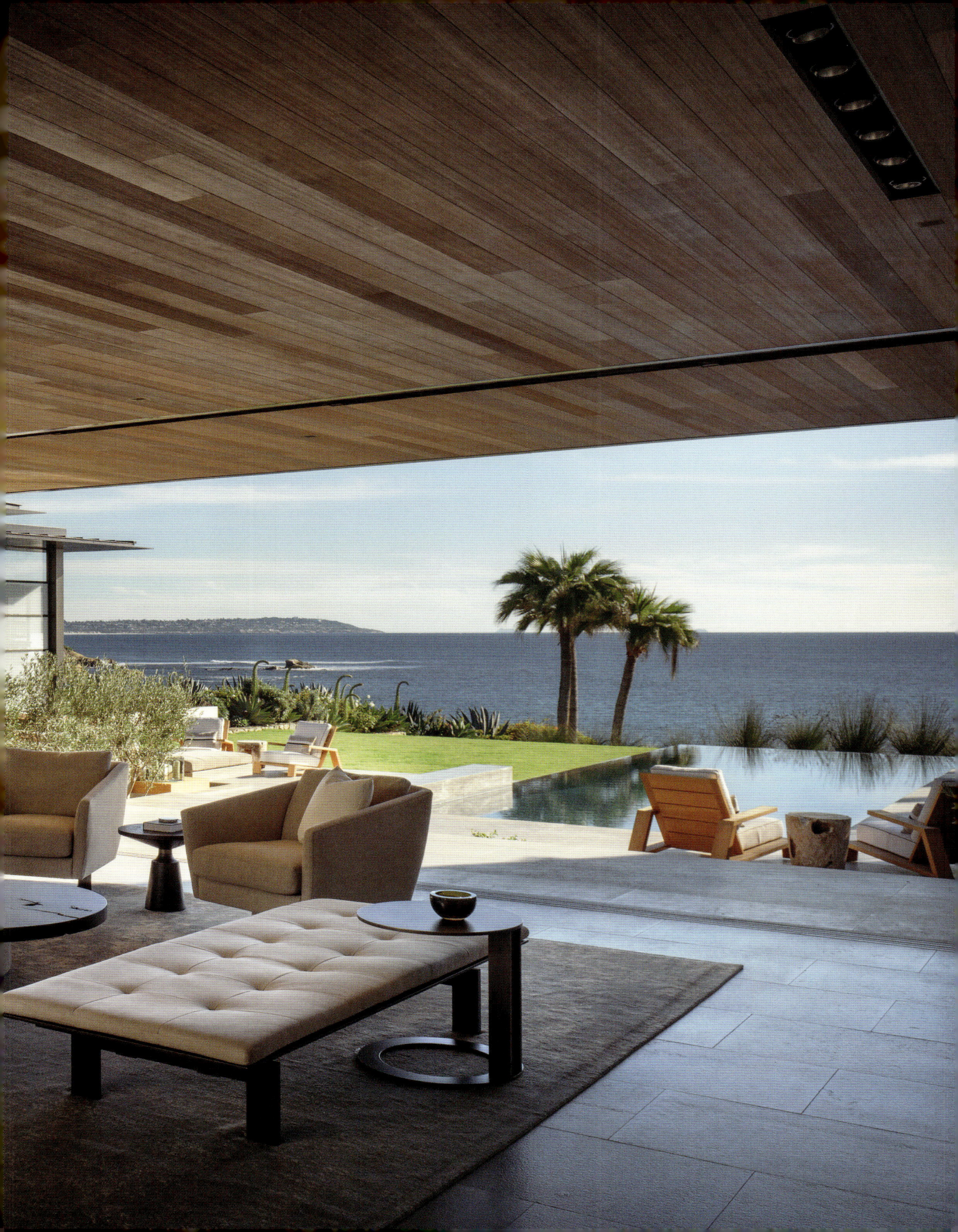

PRECEDING PAGE: The terrace off the great room is relatively narrow, giving more of the land over to the pool and hillside. A dining terrace off the kitchen, covered by a metal canopy, is a perfectly situated entertaining space, with translucent screens that pull back to reveal a full outdoor kitchen.

ABOVE: Influenced by yacht design, the details in the kitchen are seamlessly rendered: cabinetry of rift white oak, bleached and stained a custom color and set against a backsplash and countertops of London Black Granite, is nearly free of hardware.

OPPOSITE: On the kitchen island, custom designed by Lucas Interior, the sinuous curve of blackened stainless steel provides a touch of understated drama. Bar stools are from Usona.

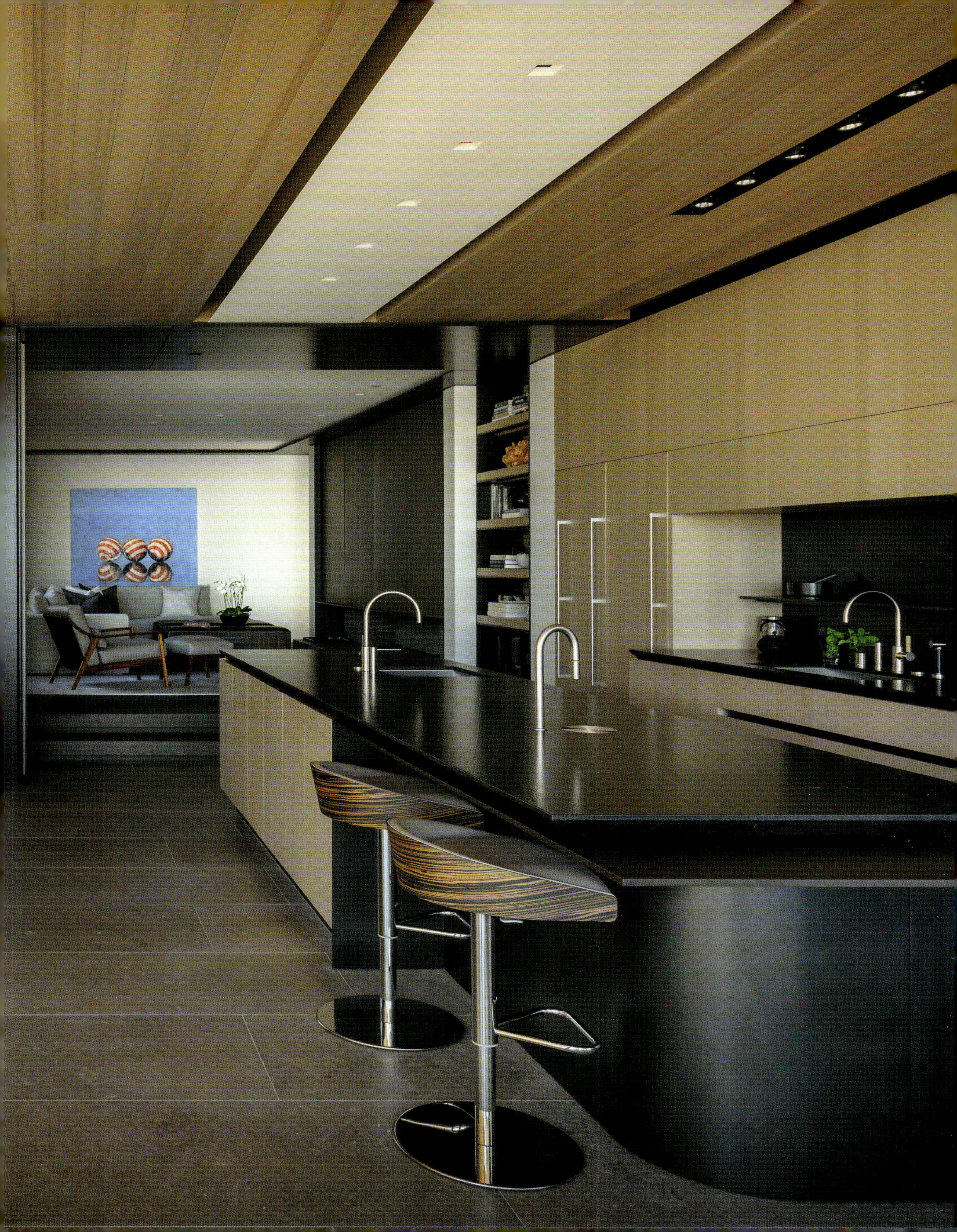

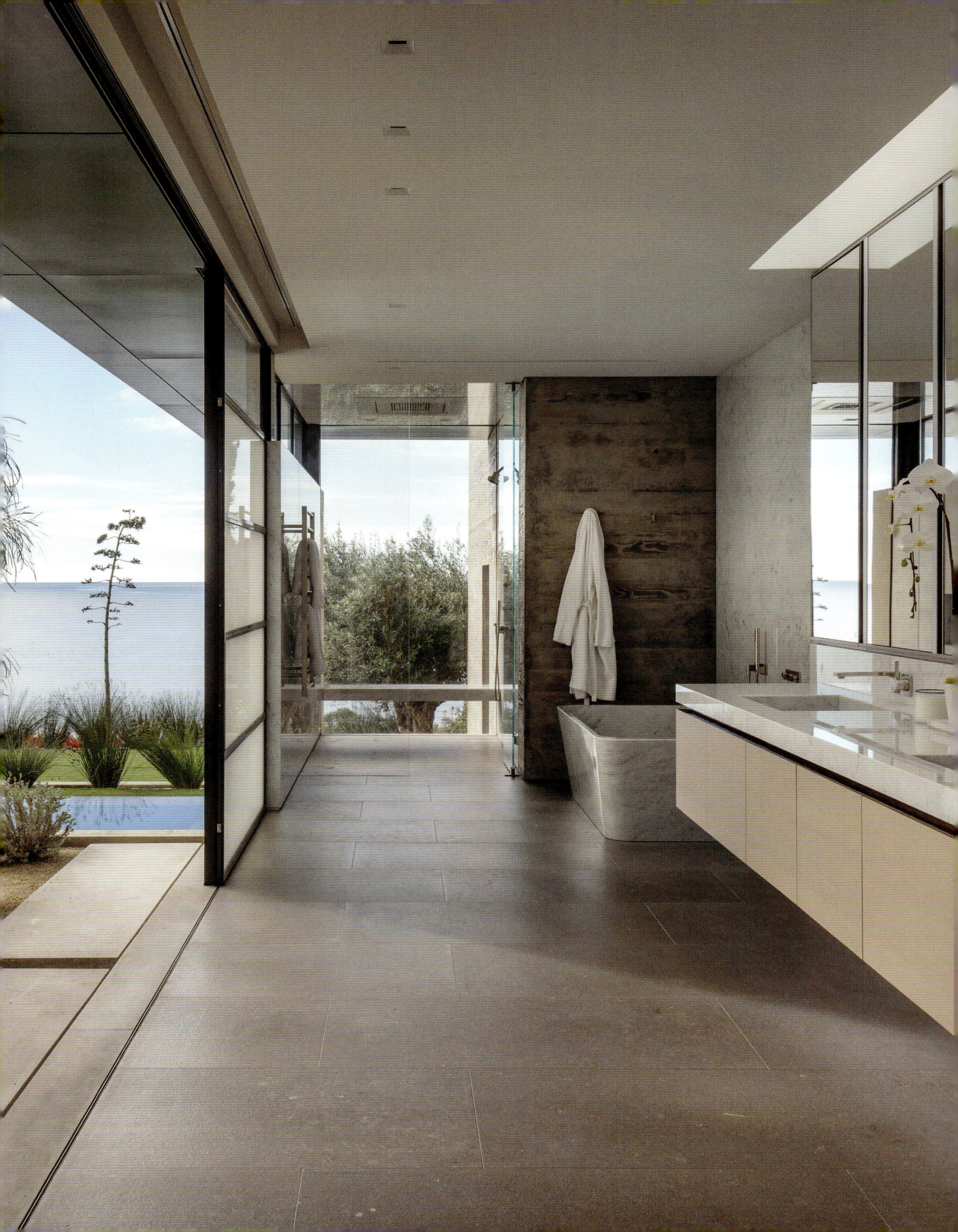

OPPOSITE: Translucent window walls—reminiscent of traditional shoji screens—slide open to connect the primary bath to the rear terrace.

ABOVE: In the primary bedroom, intricate design elements are seamlessly composed, featuring a wall of suede panels in a nickel framework, built-in bedside tables of ebonized wood and nickel, a stone ledge, and a bed frame that forms an integral bench.

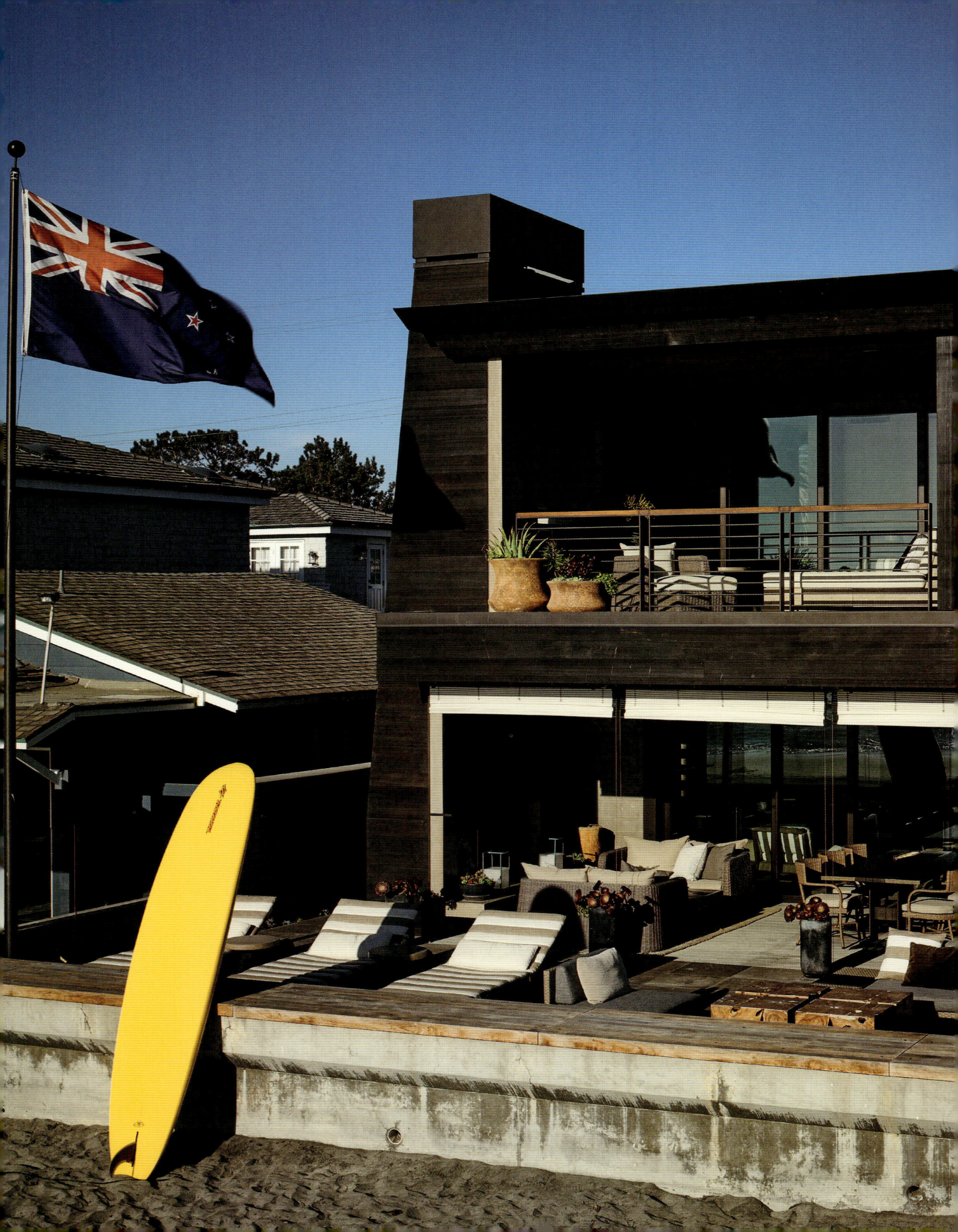

BEACH RYOSHA

/ DEL MAR /

The Asian philosophy of yin and yang is based on the concept of separate but interconnected beings possessing opposite characteristics that, when combined, become greater than their parts as each complements and completes the other.

A pair of New Zealanders based in Newport Beach put this philosophy into practice when they created a home of paired structures in the Southern California beach town of Del Mar. The oceanfront house, built on the site of the bungalow they had owned for two decades and had outgrown years earlier, represents the lively, outgoing character of the duality. Light-filled and open to the action on the beach, it's where kids spill in fresh from the ocean, where neighbors stop by, and where family meals take place—sometimes with as many as twenty-four seated in a space specifically designed to accommodate that number. The secondary building is located across a small road that runs parallel to the beach. With its darker palette and more private spaces, this home is a place of quiet and retreat. When paired as a unit, the two structures indeed transcend the sum of their parts.

The owners, parents to two sets of twins, loved the concept of duality and in fact named the property for it; the Japanese word ryosha suggests "two," "pair," "both persons," and "both things." It's only fitting, then, that sibling designers David and Suzie Lucas of Lucas Design Associates were deeply involved in every aspect of the project, along with architect Chris Light of CJ Light Associates and Sweig General Contracting. "The clients loved the idea of the back house and main house being fraternal rather than identical twins," says David Lucas. "The houses speak to each other and have a lot of the same details, but each has its own personality. The front house is the main gathering and entertaining space for the adults. The back house is a little more reclusive, a little moodier. The two houses are like the introverted and extroverted children."

A highly creative approach to space planning drove the project from start to finish. Exterior stairwells and connectors augment the allowable square footage; likewise, the main entry, although exterior, is covered and flanked by functional spaces. "This house really blurs the inside and the outside," explains Lucas. "And by tucking all these necessary things in like a jigsaw puzzle, and having that experience be really beautiful, when you're walking into this space it feels like you've entered another world, though in reality you might have the laundry on one side and the garage on the other. It's very practical, but the experience is elevated and sets the tone for living in the house."

In both buildings, lines are blurred in every way—between indoor and out, between one room and the next—such as in the pivoting window that creates a pass-through from the kitchen in the beachfront house to an exterior dining counter with stools. In place of solid interior doors, slatted screens impart a sense of airiness and permeability. The one interior staircase is presented as a sculptural art piece and is integrated into the design of the living room, with two levels of poured concrete forming the platform for sofa cushions. Rooms that would traditionally be found inside a structure—for example, TV-watching lounges, a bar and game area—are instead outdoor spaces that have a sheltered feel. Meticulously designed bedroom sitting areas cleverly morph into extra bedrooms with the press of a button (to convert sofas to futons) and the sliding of partitions. "Rather than separate rooms, it's like every space takes space from every other function," says Lucas, "and it just depends on what you're doing as to what the room is." The result is a series of flowing, dreamlike spaces, perfectly in keeping with the languid days and family-forward bonhomie that epitomizes California's beach lifestyle.

Aesthetically, the prevailing influence in both homes is a strong Japanese sensibility, seen in the dark cedar reminiscent of fire-blackened shou sugi ban of the beachside house—the material repurposed from the boards of the board-formed concrete walls in the back house—and in wood screens and futons. Bedrooms are graced with handwoven custom throw blankets. A custom bed cover designed for ease of housekeeping was inspired by the sleeves of a kimono. In keeping with the Asian aesthetic, furniture is simple and minimal, sculptural in form and beautifully crafted. A consistent palette of earth-toned organic and natural materials includes brown granite in the kitchen, a teak slab for the dining table, and works commissioned from Japanese textile artist Hiroko Takeda.

With three bedrooms and baths in the beachside house and four bedrooms (one a bunk room) and baths in the secondary house, plus additional areas that convert to sleeping spaces, the owners are now able to host the entire family, numbering close to two dozen—a remarkable feat given town-imposed constraints. Architect Chris Light reflects, "We could only enclose 2,000 square feet in the main house, so it was very challenging in terms of what they wanted to do, but we came up with concept of a covered courtyard in the middle. With big doors opening, we added another 2,000 square feet of covered indoor–outdoor space, so the house doubles in footprint the minute you open it all up. They have a big family, so that was the goal."

When guests prepare to leave the repose of the secondary house to join in the activity of the main house, they might stand for a moment in the doorway, contemplating the perfect alignment of entrances across the narrow street and a line of sight that connects and unites the structures while passing straight through to the endless depths of the ocean beyond. It's the perfect final note to the yin and yang, the push and pull, the harmonious duality of a contemporary California beach home born of two worlds.

PRECEDING PAGE: Sibling designers David and Suzie Lucas of Lucas Design Associates, with architect CJ Light Associates and Sweig General Contracting, reimagined two houses in a southern California beach community for longtime clients who had more than outgrown their vintage bungalow. The two structures—one on the beach and one across a road that's more like an alley—are designed to function separately as well as together.

ABOVE: For the beachfront house, David Lucas explains, "We tried to set our clients up for how they wanted to live in the house because it is really exposed; it just gets hammered. The exterior is a dark-stained hemlock that can be easily touched up; we used teak on the handrails, and there's a lot of concrete." For maximum flexibility and livability, he says, "the whole house is designed with the theme of letting spaces flow into each other. The outdoor eating area has a wood floor that flows inside; it also has a dining space where the tables connect. The second dining table has a drop leaf they can move to get all their numbers around the table—though their numbers keep growing."

ABOVE: The beach house is set up as two volumes with a courtyard and staircase between, effectively blurring the lines between indoor and outdoor spaces. A living wall introduces an organic element to the design. The concrete lattice with turf creates an artistic lawn-like area for parking.

OPPOSITE: An entry passageway with fumed oak flooring and shou sugi ban–style darkened panels in the beachfront home directs the eye to the courtyard of the secondary house across the drive. The name of the home (*Ryosha* means "two" or "pair" in Japanese) speaks to the twinned nature of the structures.

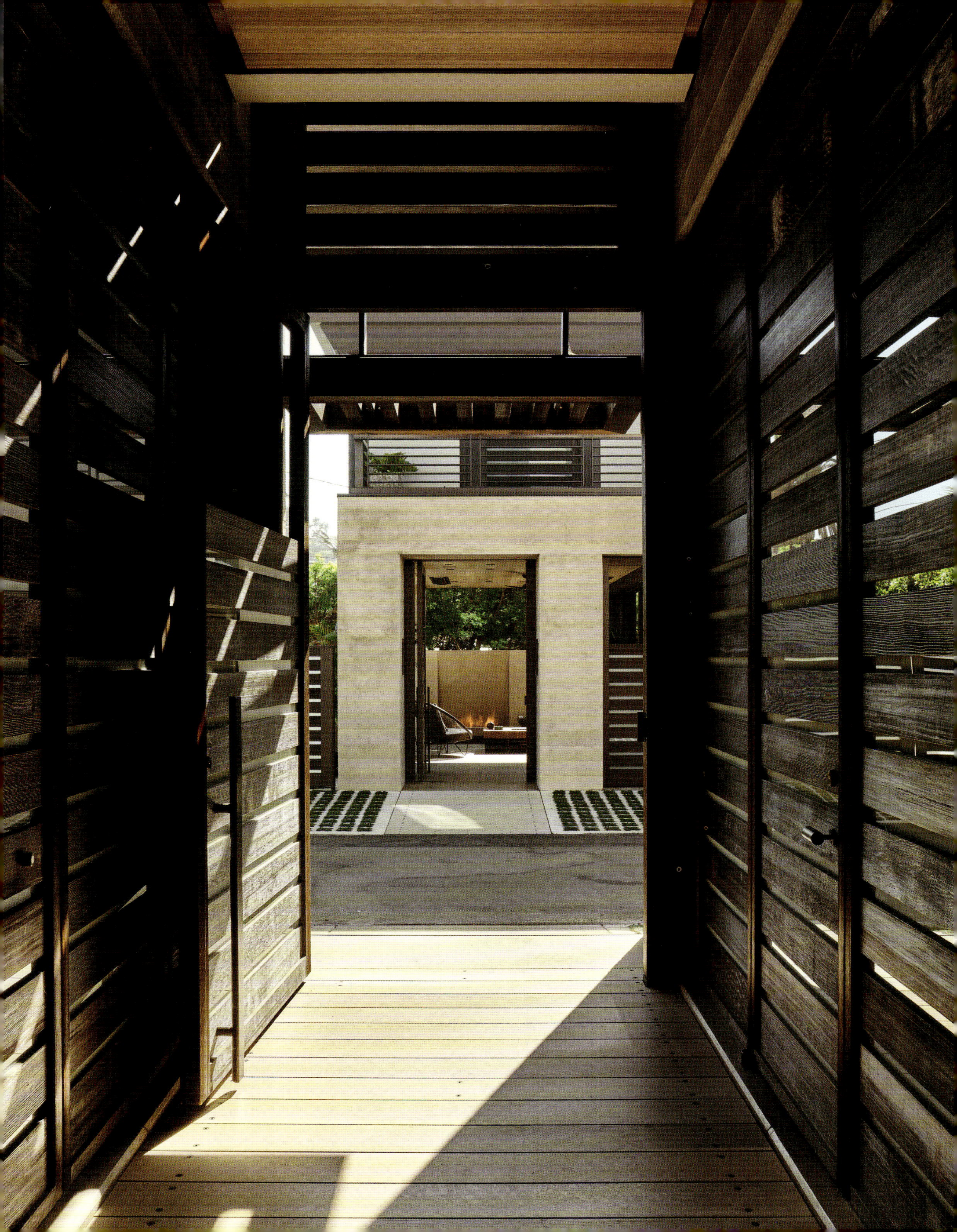

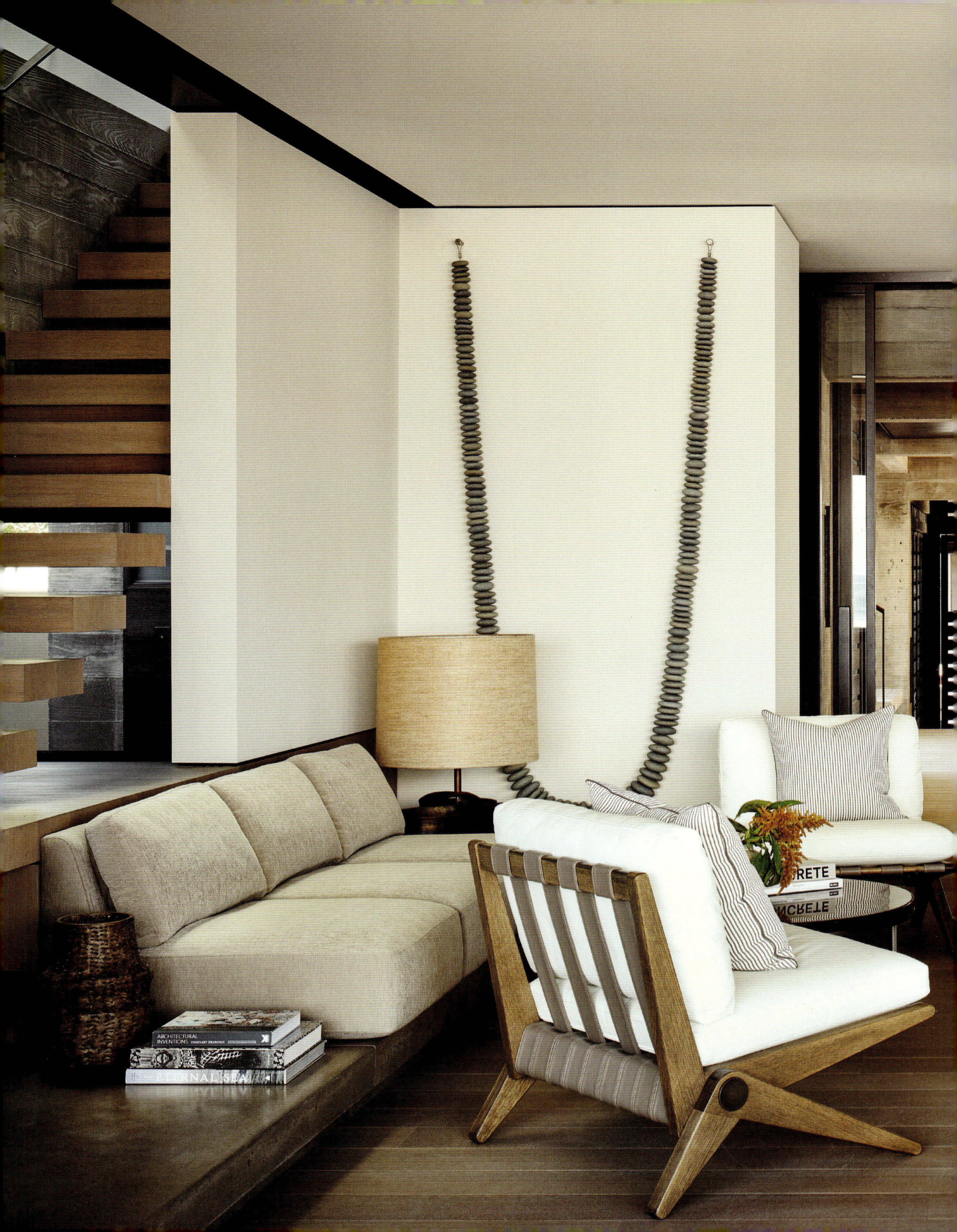
ARCHITECTURAL
INVENTIONS
ETERNAL SEA

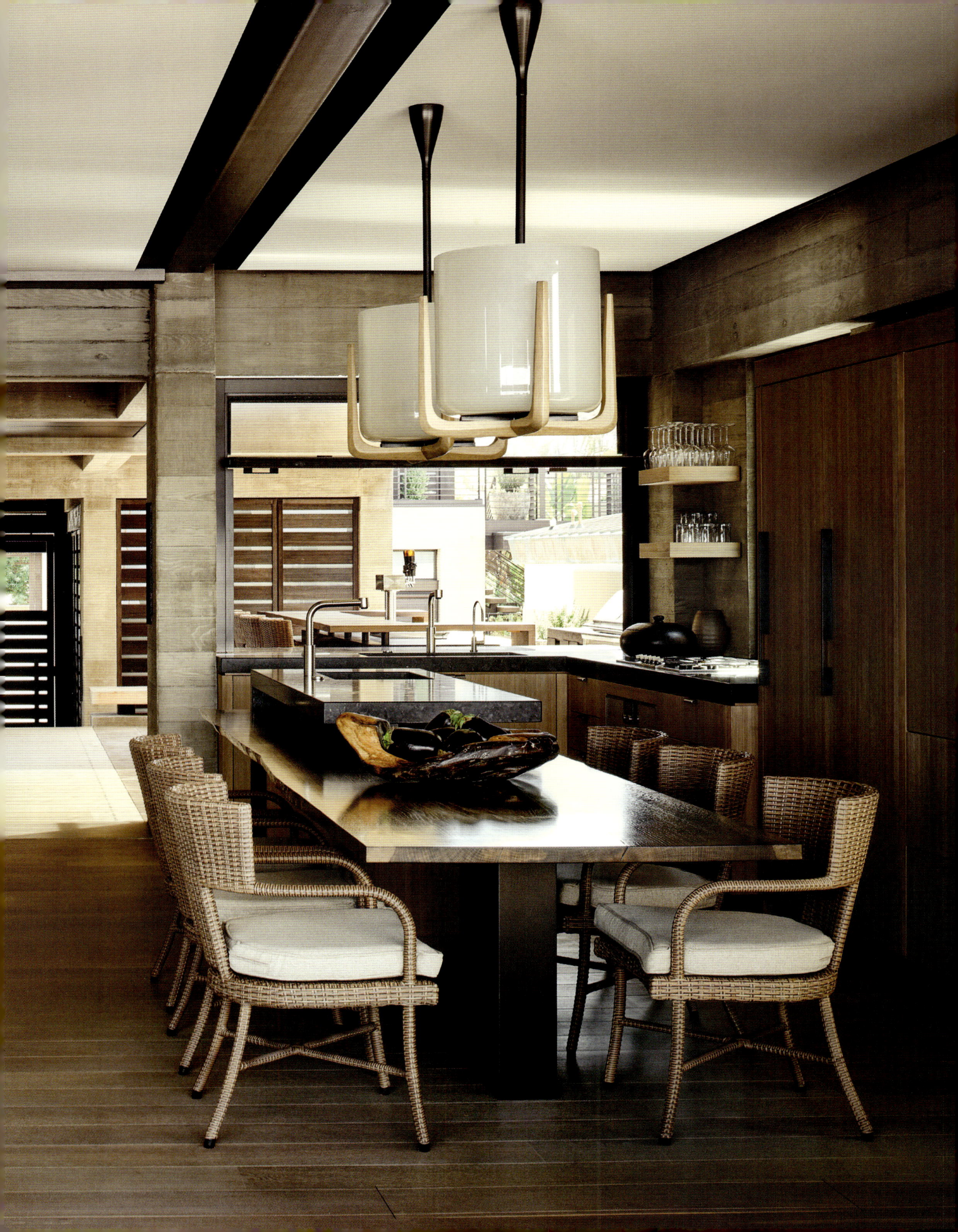

PRECEDING PAGE: The main living area in the beachfront house has an integrated sofa built into the base of the staircase. The striking necklace artwork is by Chris Chateris. The scissor chairs are by Saturn with BC Custom, the round table is from Mayer Designs. The kitchen opens to additional dining areas in the interior courtyard as well as on the beach-side patio.

ABOVE: In both homes, much of the circulation is exterior—an efficient use of space that also serves as a constant reminder of place. An open-air bridge connects the upstairs living spaces of the secondary home. Concrete pavers carry through from the lower to the upper floor.

OPPOSITE: The barbecue terrace has a pivoting window that creates a pass-through to the kitchen. The wood counter stools are from Kitchen Window, the pendants above the kitchen island from Fuse Lighting.

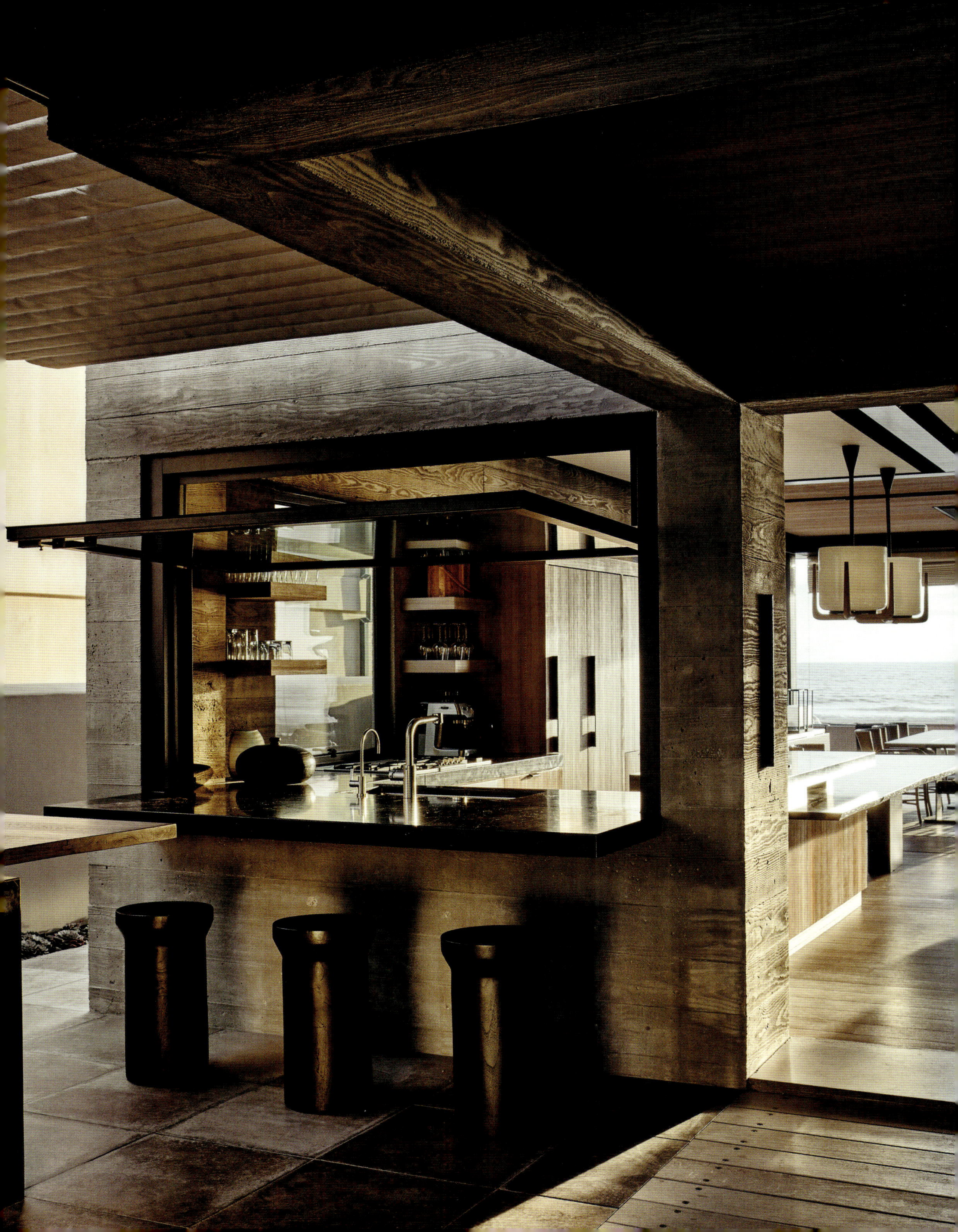

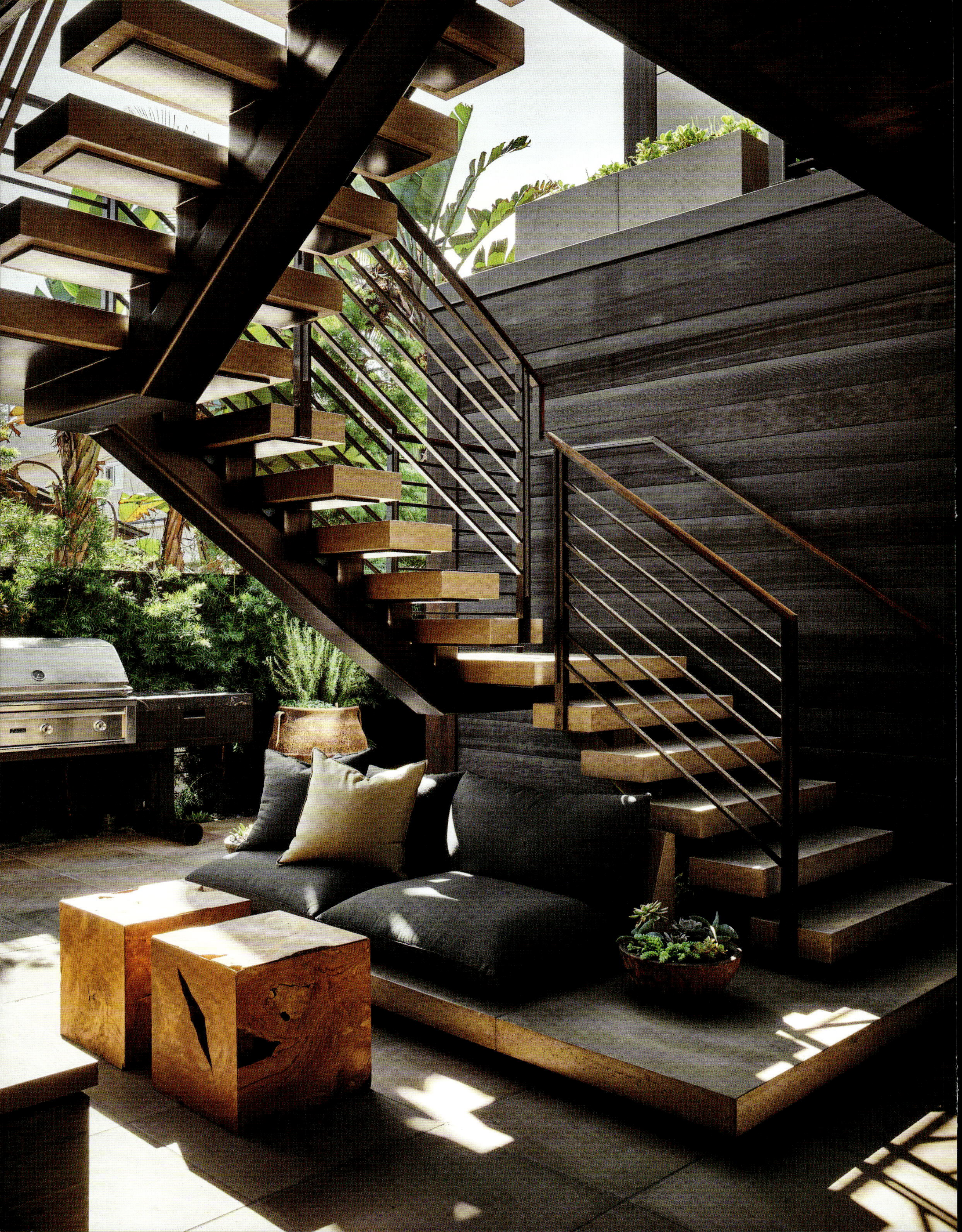

OPPOSITE: David and Suzie Lucas moved some typical indoor functions outdoors, such as an exterior staircase, which echoes the main living area by creating a platform for sofa cushions.

ABOVE: The two homes were conceived as a paired set, each with its own distinct identity. The secondary house is farther from the ocean but also removed from the activity of beach life. Here a darker palette prevails, with serene spaces offering retreat from the everyday bustle of the main house.

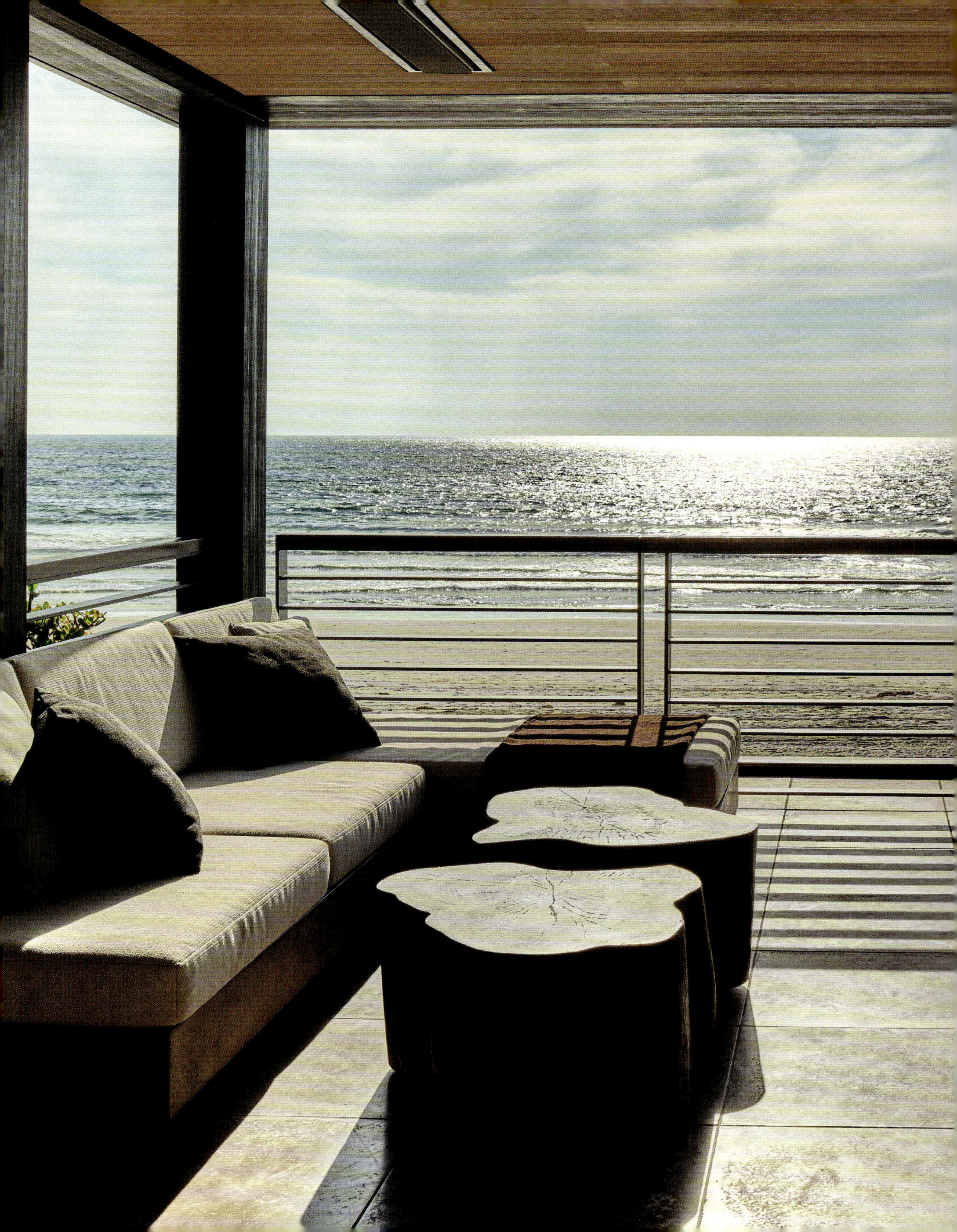

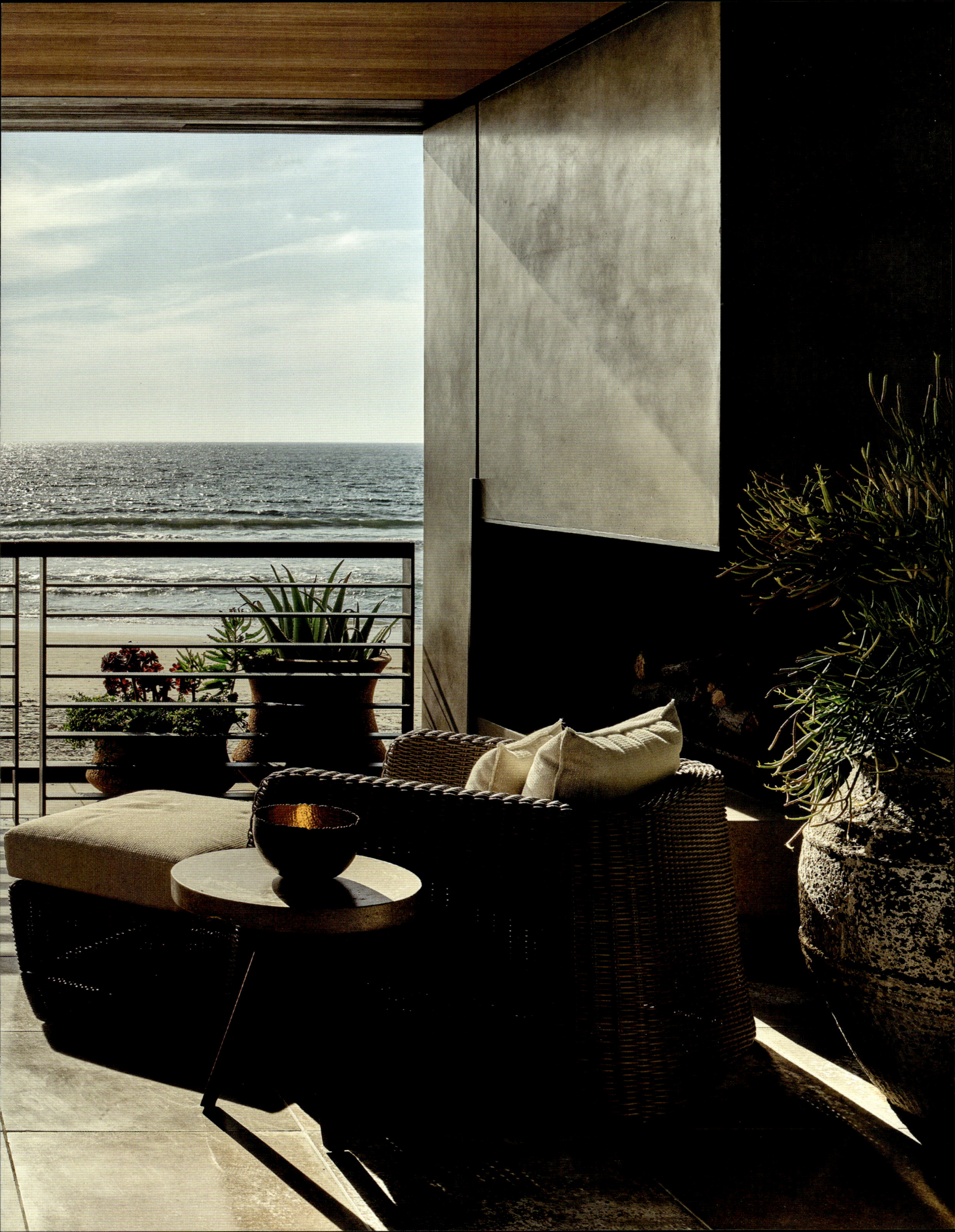

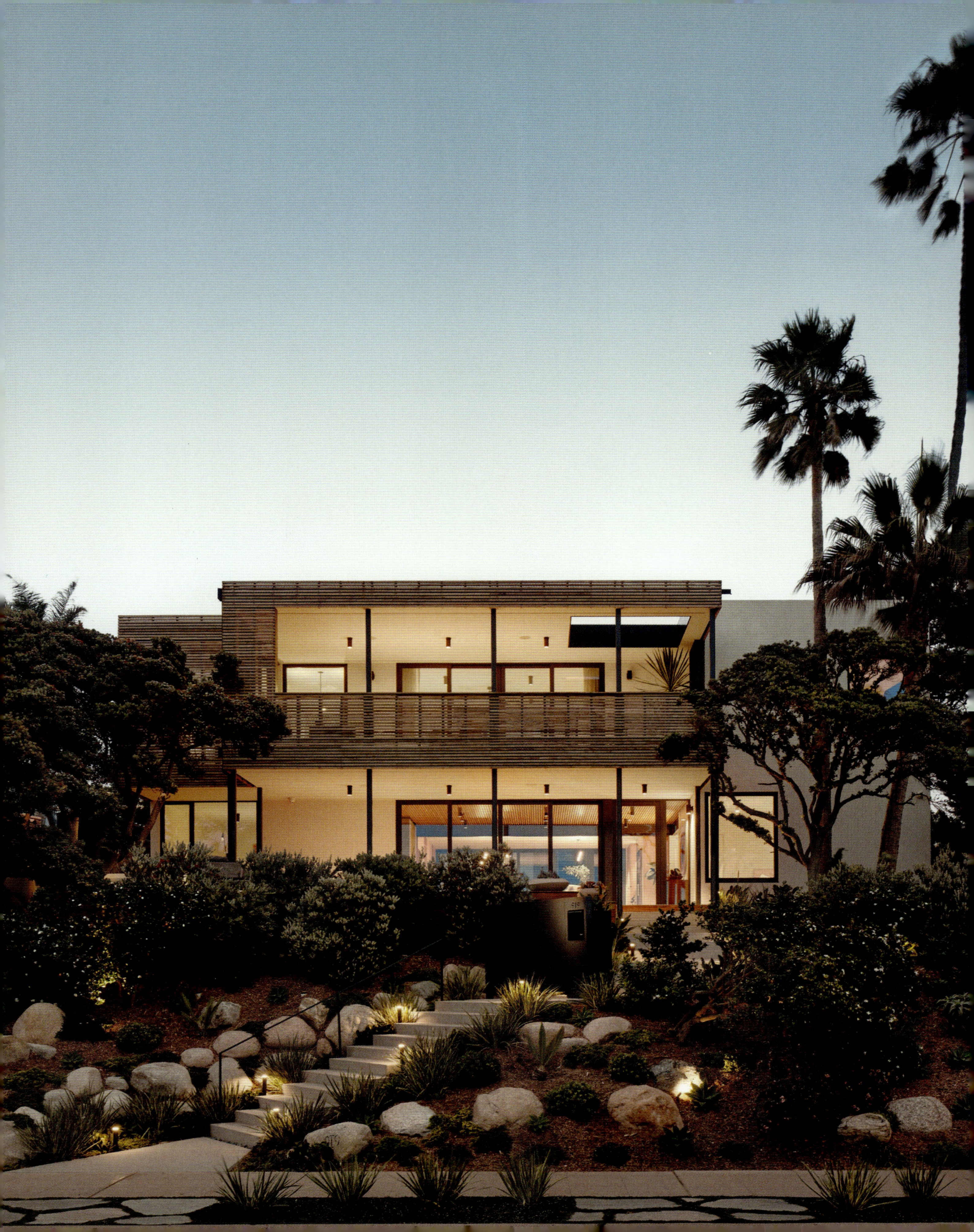

SUNSET CLIFFS

/ SAN DIEGO /

Architect Greg Coleman nicknamed this project the "Good Fortune House" because it seemed that a series of happy accidents brought together like-minded clients and a dream team of professionals with a shared vision and mores. They converged in a spectacular setting and there, at the edge of San Diego's Sunset Cliffs, built a home that manifests not just the ethos of the place but the people who reside there.

The full-time residence was designed for an unusually active family of six; in their case, surfing was a passion and fitness a professional necessity. The property was elevated on a coastal bluff above street level—a boon for privacy—and blessed with a mixture of mature trees that included three New Zealand Christmas trees, coastal evergreens that produce brilliant crimson flowers. Coleman conceived of a two-story residence nestled among the existing vegetation to create a tree house–like experience for the upper level. The main house would be open, to bring natural light into every room. On the street side, it's all about the ocean views; at the rear, a sheltered pool courtyard is flanked on one side by a separate building that houses the gym and guest accommodations.

"San Diego has such an ideal climate that we wanted the house to be wide open," explains Coleman. "We had conversations early on about how you would be able to sit in a Jacuzzi in the back and see all the way through to the ocean. I wanted the house to be thin enough that the cross breeze from the ocean would provide natural ventilation. I'd much rather use the site's natural breezes and sun patterns; I'd be surprised if they ever turn on the air conditioning. But I also wanted to make it so you could close it off to have a protected courtyard. In winter, you still have usable outside spaces; you can sit on the deck facing the pool and enjoy the sunshine."

To fit unobtrusively into the long-established neighborhood and to embrace the ocean while minimizing the road that runs between the house and the view, the rectilinear design makes a quiet yet stylish statement with stucco siding, slender steel columns, and an upper level whose projecting deck and attendant roof are clad in horizontal slat screening made from Accoya, an incredibly durable, moisture-resistant, treated wood. "They were going to be in and out of that house all year long in wet suits," says Coleman, "so we worked with a material palette that was going to stand up to their lifestyle." A consistent aesthetic carries through both structures with polished concrete floors, wood cabinetry, engineered quartz countertops, oak ceilings in the primary bedroom, large windows, and, in the bathrooms, cement tile floors and concrete walls. The patio is a textured cast concrete, the deck is ipe, and the bedroom flooring is wide plank oak. The hand-troweled plaster fireplace with steel details establishes a strong presence in the living room, while nearby white oak custom casework softens the communal space.

For the architect, who was delighted by the opportunity to create a significant legacy project shortly after establishing his own practice, choosing the right builder to construct it was of paramount importance. "I learned over the course of my career that you can have a really great design," Coleman says, "but if you don't get a really great builder on board it won't translate."

Fortunately, Rich Gerace of RGB Group Inc. was working on a house just down the street and immediately hit it off with the owners. He oversaw construction during the pandemic and is still a frequent visitor to the house. "From hiking to jujitsu to archery, there's constant activity," he observes, "so it had to be constructed in such a way that it would hold up. Concrete floors, exposed structural steel beams, hardwood surfaces, and cement tile showers sound harsh, but if done eloquently these materials can be beautiful and fitting for any modern home. This home is probably the most well used that we've ever constructed. Everything in it is purposeful."

The team was filled out by landscape architect Marcie Harris, who designed all landscaping for the property as well as the arrival sequence from the sidewalk via the concrete stair artfully set within the hillside. Harris and Coleman collaborated on the outdoor living areas, such as the back patio and firepit. Inside, while the architect chose the lighting, tiles, and finishes, interior designer Kristin Lomauro-Boom of Kristin Lomauro Interior Design furnished the spaces. "The clients wanted the home to feel relaxed, comfortable, and welcoming, and we needed to play off Greg's detail," Lomauro-Boom recalls. "I showed them natural material, organic fabrics, and lots of texture, and they were thrilled. We focused on a neutral, calming palette so the ocean view would take center stage."

Beyond those ocean views, a main driver of the project was its proximity to surf breaks, which are close by but hard to access. (At times, entering the water necessitates jumping off the cliff.) Coleman designed the second-story office with direct views to several key surf spots. It's the perfect perch from which the owners can revel in their own good fortune every day.

Architect Greg Coleman's design for an oceanfront house in San Diego's Sunset Cliffs neighborhood combines Accoya wood slats and ipe decking with white stucco, painted steel posts, and Reynaers doors and windows. Landscape designer Marcie Harris chose a palette that complemented existing New Zealand Christmas trees. "The wind and salt in the air are hard on the plants. I walked the neighborhood to see what plants were thriving in the microclimate and chose the toughest plants closest to the shore then varied the plants when there was a buffer of a fence and house. All the plants are low water and thrive in the sandy soils that drain well. In the front yard we planted New Zealand Christmas trees, foxtail agave, torch aloe, pittosporum, variegated flax lily, Japanese Garden Juniper 'Nana', and various succulents. In the backyard, we introduced Arbutus 'Marnia' Strawberry Trees, palm trees, asparagus fern, blue flax-lily, Cape rush, 'Myers' asparagus fern, agaves, and aloes."

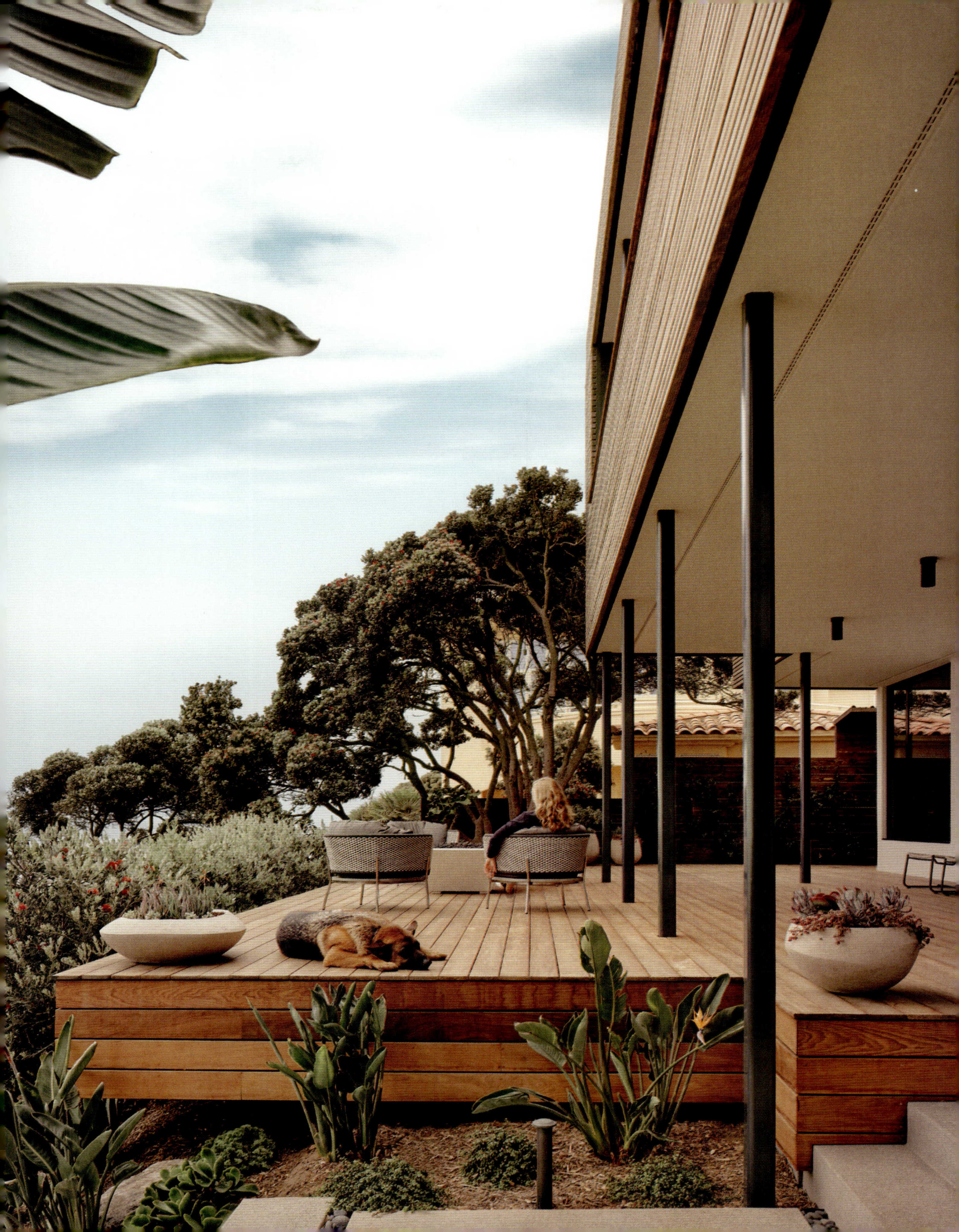

ABOVE: The open kitchen pairs oak veneer cabinetry with countertops of Caesarstone Frozen Terra. The linear pendant is from Sonneman; the sconces are from Schoolhouse. A Subzero refrigerator and a Wolf range are featured. The backsplash is composed of VIA cement tiles. Chairs and stools are from Blu Dot.

OPPOSITE: Slatted ceilings of oak continue the dialogue established on the exterior. The beams are painted steel, and the fireplace is inset into a corner of hand-troweled plaster. A classic Eames lounge chair and an ottoman from DWR are combined with a custom rug from Jaipur Rugs.

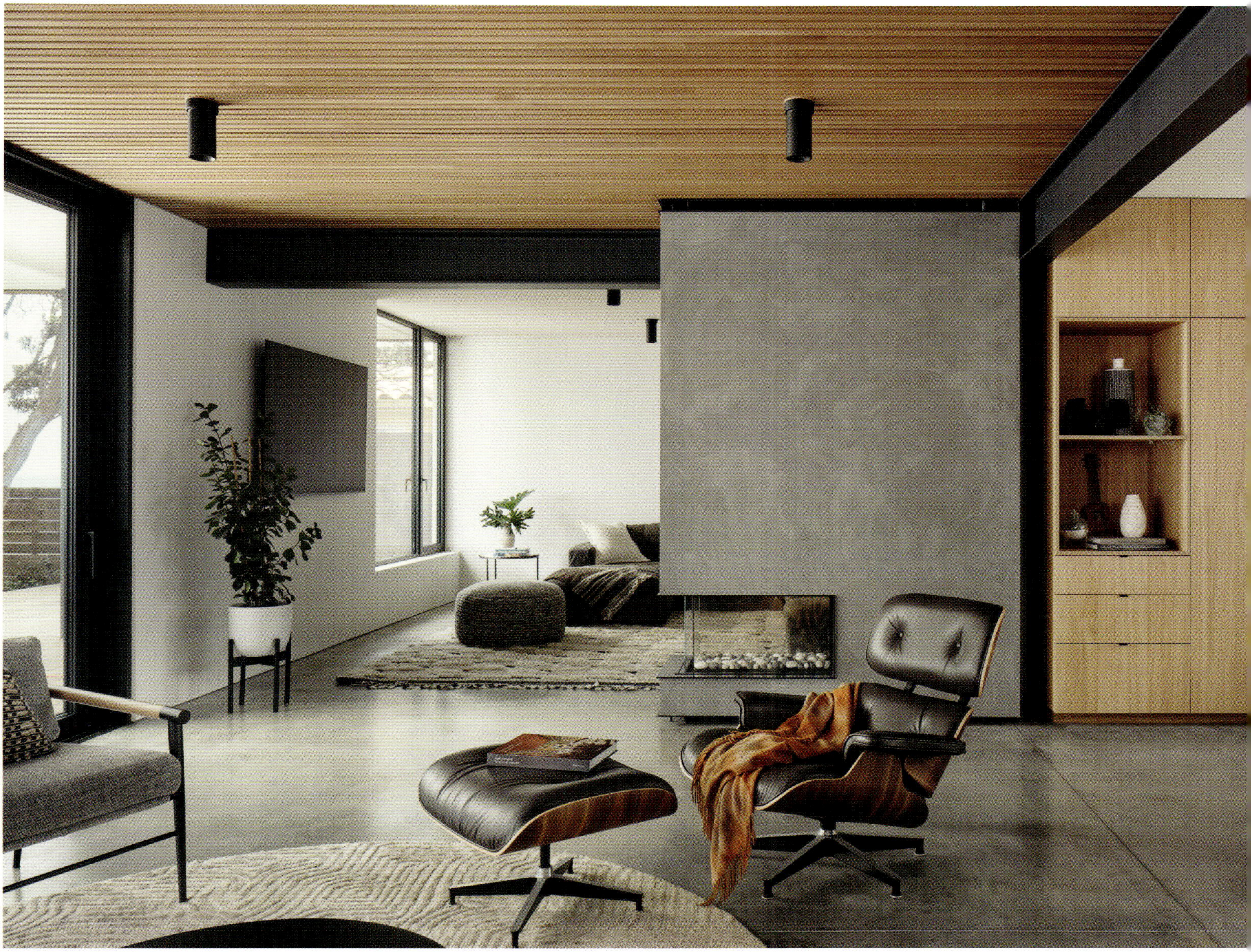

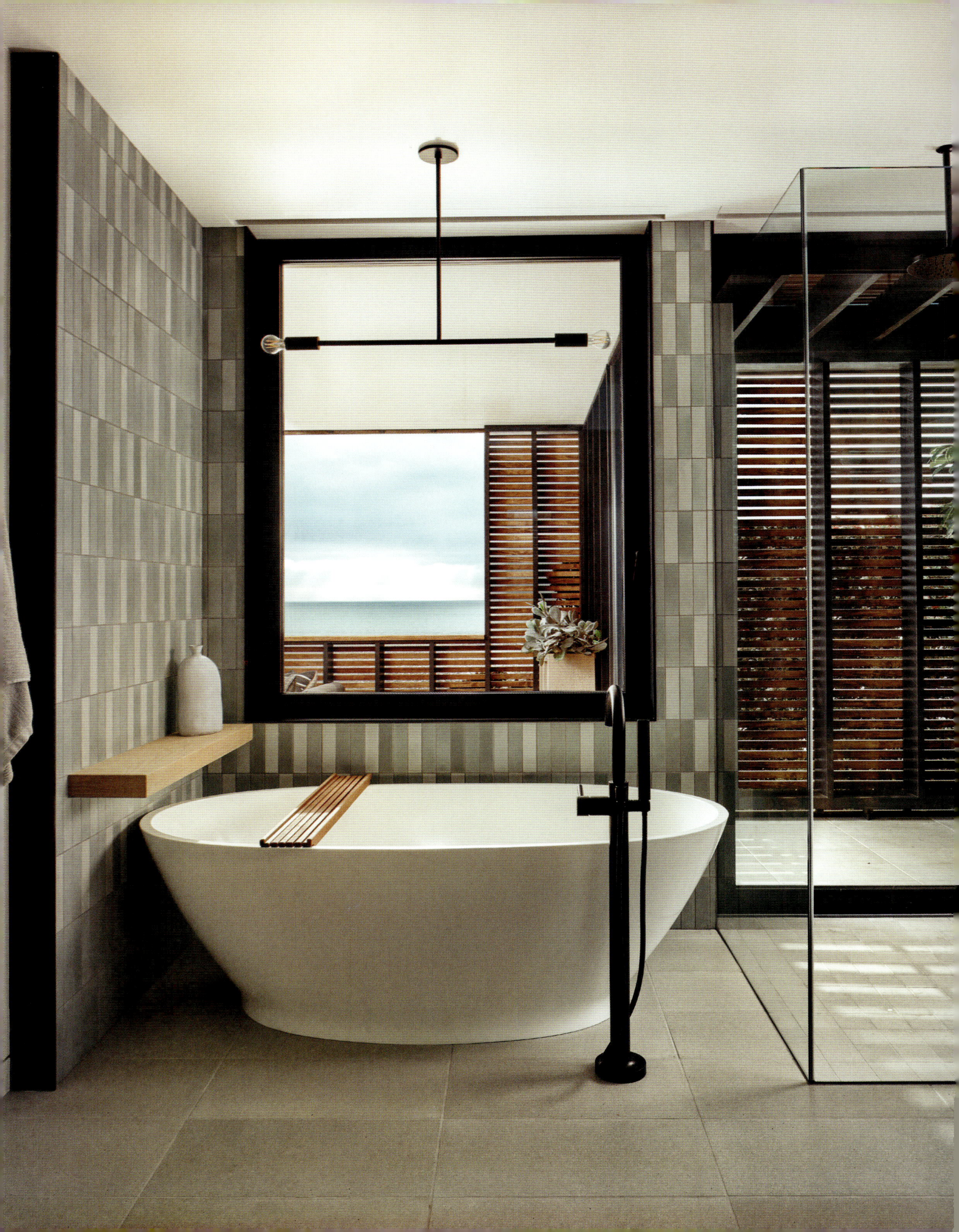

OPPOSITE: Immersed in nature, the primary bathroom with glass shower features MTI's Alissa tub and a single open oak shelf set against Clé concrete tiles. The barbell pendant is by Andrew Neyer; the floor mounted tub filler is Brizo.

ABOVE: In the bedroom, the wall sconce is Serge Mouille, the nightstands and bed are custom by interior designer Kristin Lomauro-Boom, and the rug is custom from Jaipur Rugs.

A second-story deck expands the primary suite while creating a private retreat for the homeowners.

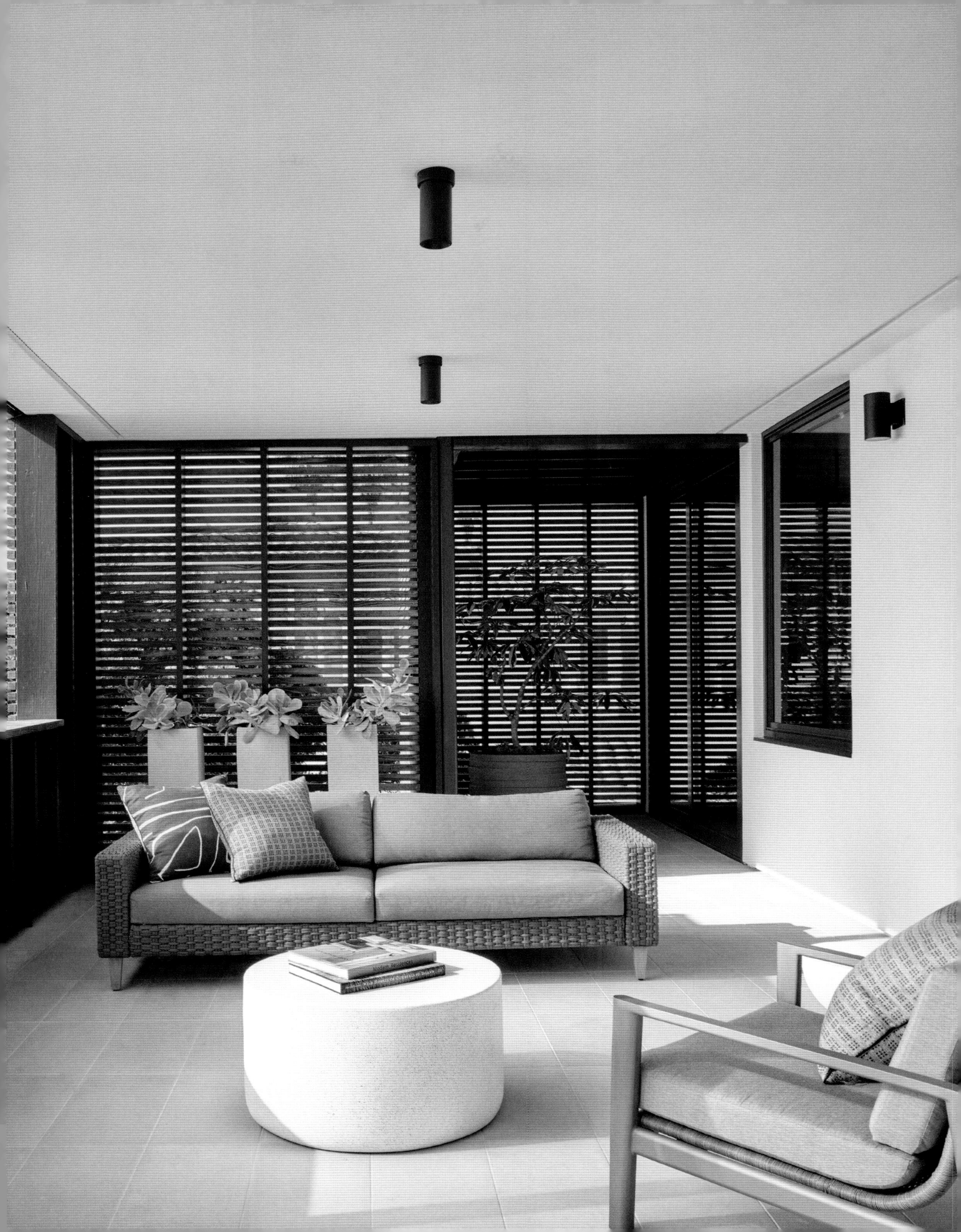

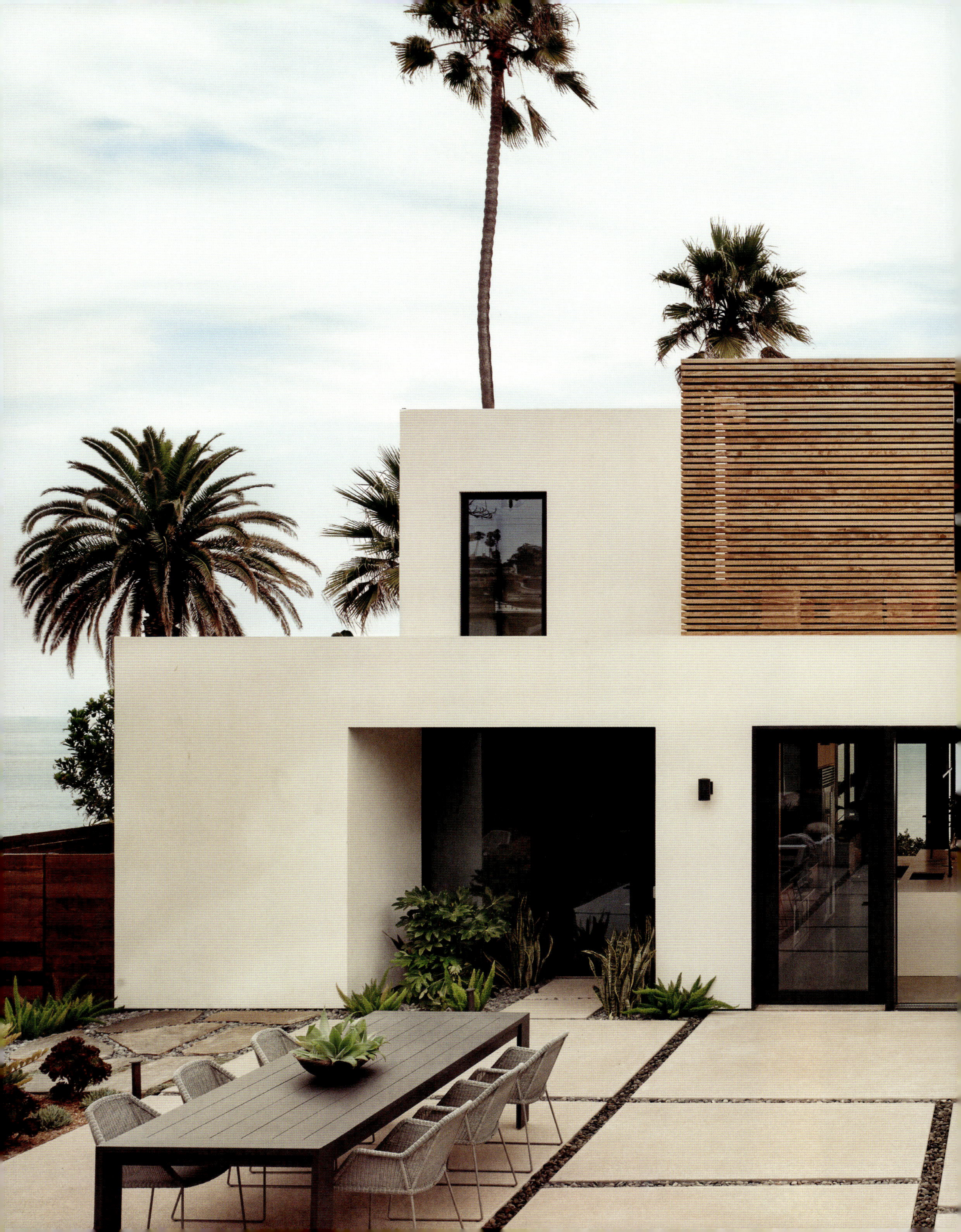

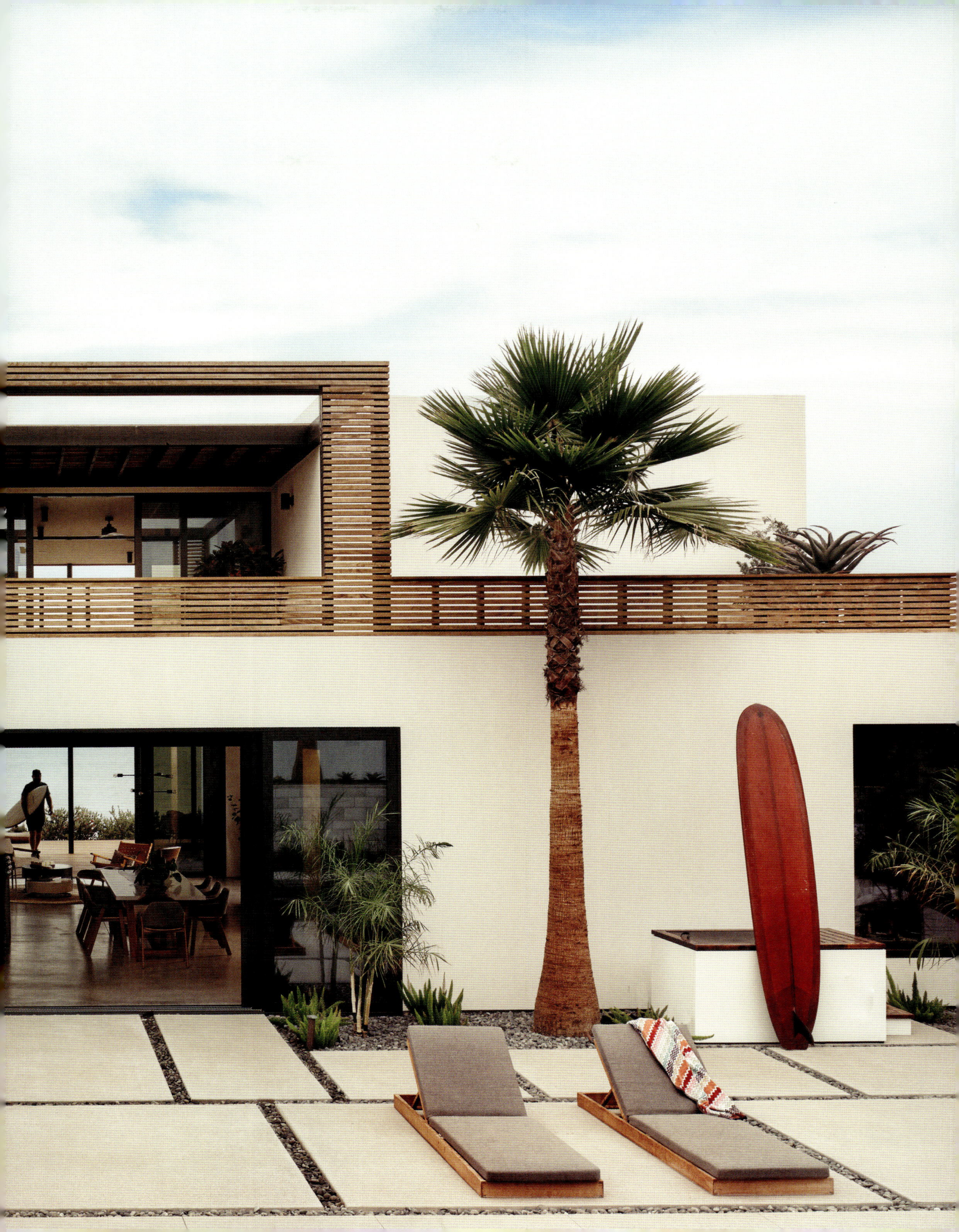

CREDITS

NORTHERN COAST

INFORMED BY NATURE
LOCATION: Sea Ranch
ARCHITECTURE: Butler Armsden Architects
INTERIOR DESIGN: Leverone Design
CONSTRUCTION: Clayton Timbrell & Company
PHOTOGRAPHY: Joe Fletcher

THE COLOR OF SHADOWS
LOCATION: Sea Ranch
ARCHITECTURE: Klopf Architecture
INTERIOR DESIGN: Diana Ruiz
CONSTRUCTION: Empire Contracting
PHOTOGRAPHY: Mariko Reed

LAGOON LIVING
LOCATION: Stinson Beach
ARCHITECTURE: Cass Calder Smith
INTERIOR DESIGN: Cass Calder Smith
CONSTRUCTION: Allen Construction
PHOTOGRAPHY: Paul Dyer

ZEN AT THE BEACH
LOCATION: Stinson Beach
ARCHITECTURE: Michael Mitchell Architects
INTERIOR DESIGN: Skornicka Designs & Construction
LANDSCAPE DESIGN: Skornicka Designs & Construction
CONSTRUCTION: Peter Gubbins
PHOTOGRAPHY: Adam Potts

EAST MEETS WEST
LOCATION: South Bay Area Coast
ARCHITECTURE: Walker Warner Architects
INTERIOR DESIGN: Kristi Will Design
LANDSCAPE DESIGN: Lutsko Associates
CONSTRUCTION: Matarozzi Pelsinger Builders
PHOTOGRAPHY: Matthew Millman

BOHEMIAN SURF HOUSE
LOCATION: Santa Cruz
ARCHITECTURE: Feldman Architecture
INTERIOR DESIGN: Commune Design
LANDSCAPE DESIGN: Ground Studio Landscape Architecture
CONSTRUCTION: True Build Construction
PHOTOGRAPHY: Joe Fletcher, Stephen Kent Johnson

CENTRAL COAST

BIRD'S-EYE VIEW
LOCATION: Carmel
ARCHITECTURE: EYRC
INTERIOR DESIGN: by owner
LANDSCAPE DESIGN: Andrea Cochran Landscape Architecture
CONSTRUCTION: De Mattei Construction
PHOTOGRAPHY: Matthew Millman

BEACH HOUSE + BOARDWALK HOUSE
LOCATION: Carmel
ARCHITECTURE: Luca Pignata
INTERIOR DESIGN: Amber Interiors
LANDSCAPE DESIGN: Joni Janecki Landscape Architecture
CONSTRUCTION: Stocker & Allaire
PHOTOGRAPHY: Adam Potts

GROUNDED IN PLACE
LOCATION: Big Sur
ARCHITECTURE: Studio Schicketanz
INTERIOR DESIGN: Studio Schicketanz
LANDSCAPE DESIGN: Ground Studio Landscape Architecture
CONSTRUCTION: Alderson Construction
PHOTOGRAPHY: Joe Fletcher

PROSPECT + REFUGE
LOCATION: Big Sur
ARCHITECTURE: Field Architecture
INTERIOR DESIGN: Field Architecture
LANDSCAPE DESIGN: Joni Janecki Landscape Architecture
CONSTRUCTION: Alderson Construction
PHOTOGRAPHY: Joe Fletcher

OFF-GRID GUESTHOUSE
LOCATION: Santa Barbara
ARCHITECTURE: Anacapa Architecture
INTERIOR DESIGN: Jessica Helgerson Interior Design
LANDSCAPE DESIGN: Danielle Gaston
CONSTRUCTION: Curtis Homes
PHOTOGRAPHY: Michael Kelly, Erin Feinblatt, Aaron Leitz

SOUTHERN COAST

ATABEI
LOCATION: Pacific Palisades
ARCHITECTURE: Jae Omar Design
INTERIOR DESIGN: Jae Omar Design
CONSTRUCTION: BTC Builders
PHOTOGRAPHY: Tyler Hogan

COASTAL SERENITY
LOCATION: Malibu
ARCHITECTURE: Studio William Hefner
INTERIOR DESIGN: Billy Cotton
CONSTRUCTION: Hanover Builders
PHOTOGRAPHY: Stephen Kent Johnson

BEACH, OCEAN, SKY
LOCATION: Hermosa Beach
ARCHITECTURE: XTEN Architecture
INTERIOR DESIGN: Jorie Clark Design
CONSTRUCTION: Ivan James Development, Inc.
PHOTOGRAPHY: Art Gray

SEASIDE SANCTUARY
LOCATION: La Jolla
ARCHITECTURE: House Design Architects
INTERIOR DESIGN: Lucas Interiors
LANDSCAPE DESIGN: Lucas Interiors
CONSTRUCTION: Hill Construction
PHOTOGRAPHY: Aaron Leitz

BEACH RYOSHA
LOCATION: Del Mar
ARCHITECTURE: CJ Light Architects
INTERIOR DESIGN: Lucas Interiors
CONSTRUCTION: Sweig General Contracting
PHOTOGRAPHER: Douglas Friedman

SUNSET CLIFFS
LOCATION: San Diego
ARCHITECTURE: Greg Coleman Architect
INTERIOR DESIGN: Kristin Lomauro Interior Design
LANDSCAPE DESIGN: Marcie Harris Landscape Architecture
CONSTRUCTION: RGB Group
PHOTOGRAPHY: Casey Dunn

ACKNOWLEDGMENTS

We feel so lucky to live in California—Heather as a lifelong Californian and Chase as a transplant from New England and the Mountain States. We have each raised four kids in Marin County—a magical place to call home. With the San Francisco Bay to the east, the Pacific Ocean to the west, the city to the south, the wine country to the north, and the Sierra Mountains just a few hours away, it is impossibly beautiful and dynamic, blessed with a perfect climate and inhabited by energetic, design-savvy, entrepreneurial people who love the outdoors as much as we do.

As with our book *At Home in the Wine Country*, this project is a love letter to our state and an ode to the people who bring a thoughtful sensitivity to creating architecture and design in irreplaceable habitats. We could not achieve what we do without the scores of architects, designers, builders, artisans, landscape designers and landscape contractors, engineers, art consultants, and more whose work is showcased in our books. We can't thank them enough for their time, their work, and for being willing to share their inspirations and aspirations in creating some of California's best coastal architecture. To the homeowners who sponsor the creation of these spectacular structures, we say thank you for opening your homes.

This book showcases the work of no less than thirteen talented photographers who represent the best of the best and bring the vision and work of each project team to the page in the best possible light. Photographer Adam Potts deserves a special shout-out. Not only did he provide the images for two of the houses we feature in the book, but he allowed us to showcase his ethereally beautiful landscape photography—which so eloquently captures the essence of each coastal region—both within the book and on the endpapers. To top it off, his work appears on both the front and back covers.

As always, our gratitude to our publisher, Gibbs Smith, knows no bounds. Our longtime editor Madge Baird is an icon and an inspiration. We also appreciate the ever-team-spirited contributions of Michelle Branson, Kim Eddy, Michelle Bayuk, and more, all incredibly hardworking, talented, and committed to creating the best books possible. At this point, we've been lucky to work with book designer extraordinaire Rita Sowins on a number of projects. And we are ever grateful to photographer Jocelyn Knight for bringing a keen eye and sense of fun to our portrait shoot at Stinson Beach. To them, and to the Gibbs Smith production design team, thanks for making our work look so good.

Writing a book can be a lonely task, so we are deeply grateful to each other for a fulfilling, productive, and always fun collaborative friendship. Here's to so many coffee meetings, Zoom sessions, client meetings, celebratory work events, and even one blissful writing retreat on the Sonoma County coast. (Sophie and Eric, you are the best!). We couldn't get through the anxiety of deadlines and exhaustion of hours-long meetings without knowing our spouses and children will be offering a cup of coffee or a glass of wine when we come up for air. Art, Charles, and kids—all eight of you—thank you for always being there, listening to us moan about chapters due, cheering us when we meet our deadlines, and rejoicing with us when we hold the first copies of our books in our hands.

Finally, we are grateful for California. Exuberant and spectacularly beautiful across its many regions and microclimates, and unbelievably productive in both agriculture and innovation, our state and its people are also determined and resilient in the face of challenges and inspiring in their environmental leadership. With 840 miles of coastline, ours is a region characterized in large part by that defining moment where the land meets the sea. We love where we live, we're honored to have the opportunity to celebrate it, and, of course, we are always looking forward to the next project.

— *HEATHER SANDY HEBERT AND CHASE REYNOLDS EWALD*

AUTHORS

HEATHER SANDY HEBERT After studying literature at the University of California at Berkeley, interior architecture at the Academy of Art, and business at the University of San Francisco, Heather spent twenty-five years in marketing for an international architecture firm before leaving to pursue her love of storytelling. She now works with creatives—from solo artists to large design firms—helping them tell their stories. Her first book, *The New Architecture of Wine*, was published by Gibbs Smith in 2019, followed by two collaborations with Chase Reynolds Ewald. The mother of four and a lifelong resident of the San Francisco Bay Area, Heather lives in Marin County, just a stone's throw from both her frequent collaborator and the coast.

CHASE REYNOLDS EWALD A longtime writer of the American West, Chase Reynolds Ewald has written close to twenty books, including *Wild Sugar* with artisan baker Lindsey Johnson and *Cabin Style, American Rustic,* and the multi-award-winning *Bison* with Montana photographer Audrey Hall. This is her third book with co-author Heather Sandy Hebert. A graduate of Yale and U.C. Berkeley's Graduate School of Journalism, Chase is a freelance writer, editor, and consultant who helps creatives craft their stories. She lives with her husband and four daughters in northern California, ideally situated between San Francisco Bay and the Pacific Ocean.

Previous books by Heather Sandy Hebert and Chase Reynolds Ewald include *At Home in the Wine Country* and *Design Mixology: The Interiors of Tineke Triggs*.

For Charles, who surfs with sea otters and does so much to protect ocean health, and for my mom, a third-generation Californian—still western at heart!   —CRE

For my dad, whose move from the Midwest to California long ago planted the roots from which I grew; for my mom, whose family has called California home for generations; and for all those who love our coast and work to protect it for the generations to come.   —HSH

First Edition
29 28 27 26 25   5 4 3 2 1
Text © 2025 Chase Reynolds Ewald and Heather Sandy Hebert
Photographs © 2025 as cited on pages 252–53

All rights reserved. No part of this book may be reproduced by any means whatsoever without written permission from the publisher, except brief portions quoted for purpose of review. No part of this book may be used or reproduced in any manner for the purpose of training artificial intelligence technologies or systems.

Published by
Gibbs Smith
570 N Sportsplex Dr
Kaysville, Utah 84037
1.800.835.4993 orders
www.gibbs-smith.com

Book Designer: Rita Sowins / Sowins Design

Printed and bound in China
Printed on FSC®-certified and other controlled material

MIX
Paper | Supporting responsible forestry
FSC® C208677
www.fsc.org

Library of Congress Control Number: 2024941752
ISBN: 978-1-4236-6740-7